AACHEN

The U.S. Army's Battle for
Charlemagne's City in WWII

Robert W. Baumer

STACKPOLE
BOOKS

In memory of my parents,
Edwin H. and Jean F. Baumer,
And my beloved aunt,
Joan Clark

Copyright © 2015 by Robert W. Baumer

Published by
STACKPOLE BOOKS
5067 Ritter Road
Mechanicsburg, PA 17055
www.stackpolebooks.com

Printed in the United States of America

10 9 8 7 6 5 4 3 2 1

First edition

Cover design by Wendy A. Reynolds
Cover photos courtesy of U.S. Army

Library of Congress Cataloging-in-Publication Data

Baumer, Robert W.
  Aachen : the U.S. Army's battle for Charlemagne's city in WWII / Robert W. Baumer.
— First edition.
     pages cm
  Includes bibliographical references and index.
  ISBN 978-0-8117-1482-2
1. Aachen (Germany)—History—Siege, 1944. 2. United States. Army. Corps, XIX.
3. World War, 1939–1945—Campaigns—Germany—Aachen. I. Title. II. Title: U.S.
Army's battle for Charlemagne's city in WWII.
  D757.9.A2B38 2015
  940.54'2135511—dc23
                                                    2014031597

CONTENTS

PREFACE

After Paris was liberated in late August 1944, U.S. intelligence summaries reflected that the end of the war in Europe was within sight. Hitler's armies in the West had been shattered, Paris belonged to the French again, and Allied armies were confidently advancing to the last frontier of the European war. Many American commanders expected their troops would be home for Christmas.

The Third Reich's means to continue the fight would cease when the Ruhr industrial area was destroyed. Berlin would follow. There were four ways for the Allied armies to get there: the plain of Flanders, the Ardennes, the Metz-Kaiserslauten gap, or the Maubeuge-Leige-Aachen axis north of the Ardennes.

On 5 September, Gen. Dwight D. Eisenhower made a fateful decision. He dictated a memorandum to his secretary stating that the American armies would advance rapidly on the Ruhr by pushing through the *Westwall* directly to the north and south of Aachen.

Within days the eyes of all Germans, both military and civilian, were on the fate of the ancient imperial city. Rapidly closing on the border were four U.S. divisions, arguably amongst America's finest. North of Aachen were the 30th Infantry Division, veterans of vicious fighting at Mortain where the main hopes of the German army were first shattered in the West, and the combat commands of "Hell on Wheels," the 2nd Armored Division.

Heading for the Stolberg Corridor south of Aachen was the 1st Infantry Division, experienced from fighting in North Africa, Sicily, and the beaches of Normandy; the "Big Red One" had led the Saint-Lô Breakout from the Normandy hedgerows in late July and was now being escorted to the German border by the 3rd Armored Division, the battering ram that had collapsed the southern anchor of the Falaise Gap and

trapped thousands of German forces attempting to retreat pell-mell back
to the Reich.

This is the continuing story of those American divisions and the
opponents they faced at the *Westwall* of Germany. It lasts five long weeks
during the fight for Aachen, a period that irrevocably changed the
timetable for the end of World War II in Europe.

CHAPTER 1

12 September 1944

"By nightfall, the location of our front line was no longer clear to headquarters. Its disintegration at several points made the situation very serious indeed."

GENERALLEUTNANT FRIEDRICH-AUGUST SCHACK
COMMANDING OFFICER, LXXXI CORPS

At 1130 hours on sunny 12 September 1944, Lt. Richard S. Burroughs's 2nd Platoon of Reconnaissance Company, 33rd Armored Regiment of the U.S. 3rd Armored Division, started out through several tiny Belgian hamlets for the German border. Company E, 36th Armored Infantry Regiment, under the command of Lieutenant A. P. Hall, and a platoon of engineers followed in column. This reconnaissance in force first moved in a northeasterly direction until they reached Botz, then started down a road heading southeast toward the German border town of Roetgen. Along the way, a surprised enemy machine-gun crew surrendered without firing their weapons. A short time later, a frightened bicycle rider disappeared into the woods as the column approached. At 1451 hours, Lieutenant Burroughs's platoon reached the railroad tracks on the western edge of the village, and then the remainder of the armored vehicles came up to wait for the main column of Task Force Lovelady.

By this time the light and medium tanks of the task force were rolling at full speed and without flank protection toward Roetgen, using the same roads the leading reconnaissance in force had just taken. At 1620, the task force commander, Lt. Col. William B. Lovelady, ordered his command group to halt behind the reconnaissance force while roadblocks were set up here and in the southeast section of Roetgen. The only enemy

1

resistance found was near a crossroad east of town; all were made prisoners. A dozen other stragglers, disoriented elements of a German unit left behind to fell trees to block the roads through the woods just outside of town, were also taken prisoner by a battery of the 391st Armored Field Artillery. Less than an hour later the town was declared secure.

Roetgen, 15 kilometers southeast of Aachen and an important road intersection community in ancient Roman times, stood before the tank barriers, pillboxes, and dragon's teeth that formed the outer line of the *Westwall* of Germany. It now had the distinction of being the first town in the Reich to fall into American hands during World War II.

After the reconnaissance forces went forward and set up their defenses closer to the eastern edge of town at the corner of Bundesstrasse and Grune Pleistrasse, Task Force Lovelady started rolling through the village. It was an experience unlike others the soldiers had faced. One participant recalled, "We entered Roetgen minus the applause we were accustomed to in France and Belgium. All the houses had white sheets hanging from their windows, a sign of surrender and giving up. People just stood around watching, curiously."[1] Holding column formation, Lovelady's tanks and armored vehicles moved past these gatherings of confused humanity "half-frightened with the dazed mask of surrender,"[2] and proceeded toward the Dreilagerbach reservoir outside of Roetgen on the headwaters of the Vicht River. Here, Lieutenant Burroughs's 2nd Platoon discovered that the Schleebach Bridge out in front of the column was blown, and this brought the entire task force to a halt. Enemy fire was suddenly coming in from the pillboxes on the opposite side of the demolished bridge, which were occupied by *Oberstleutnant* Friedrich Troster's Reserve Grenadier Battalion 328, attached to the Grenadier Ersatz Regiment 253 of the 353rd Infantry Division.[3] While reconnoitering this area with his scout section shortly afterward, Lieutenant Burroughs was killed by rifle fire from one of these pillboxes.[4]

Unfortunately, the ground near where Burroughs fell offered Troster's men excellent possibilities for its continued defense. Across the blown bridge to the right was a steep, heavily wooded hill where another barely distinguishable pillbox was cleverly carved into its face. The intimidating five rows of dragon's teeth extended westward from here up the slope of yet another hill, and then these belts of pyramid-shaped concrete blocks cut a gash and disappeared into more dense woods. Beneath the bridge itself, the Germans had created a 12-foot-deep crater by dynamiting the stream bottom where the spillway from the reservoir crossed the road. Even if infantry could get by this, the roadway on the opposite side of the demolished bridge presented yet another barrier to Lovelady's armored vehicles. First, the road ran through a gorge clearly covered by the immediately visible pillboxes. A steel gate leaning toward the direction of approach also spanned the road, flanked on the left by another crop of tank-stopping dragon's teeth.[5] And past the first gate, three more steel I-beams, reinforced with thick cable and anchored into place with stout hardwood pegs, visibly stuck up from slots in the road.

Between 1730 and 1800, the squad on point nevertheless moved up toward the blown bridge, the men still unaware of what waited beyond. All too quickly, sniper fire came in from every direction, the worst from a series of deceptive hollow haystacks to the left where fifteen to twenty Germans had hidden and zeroed in on the advancing column of Company E platoons. Lieutenant Hall, commanding the company, was killed by one of these enemy riflemen; his 1st Platoon immediately deployed to the left to avoid more of this harassing fire while the now dead officer's 2nd Platoon dispersed and spread out along the slope in the hill on the other side of the road.

In view of the necessity of pushing forward before darkness fell, Lovelady ordered the men of Company D to advance up the road toward the blown bridge. The fates of war were not to favor these men either. The lead platoon got no more than 50 feet past their line of departure before the soldiers were stopped by both small-arms and machine-gun fire. At this point a frustrated Lovelady ordered the 1st Battery of the 391st Armored Field Artillery to fire down on the roadway with their powerful 105mm guns. Despite these heavy concentrations by the artillerymen on both the road and the pillbox positions, Troster's forces were still able to keep the infantry platoons from advancing. Company D's vehicles were then brought back to Roetgen while the men found protective cover and held in place for the night.[6]

Task Force Lovelady's penetration of the Reich border at Roetgen had been achieved by first passing around the left wing of the 9th Panzer Division, commanded by *Oberst* Gerhard Paul Wilhelm Mueller. On 12 September the 9th Panzer Division was comprised of just three armored infantry companies with about ninety men each and a scant six to nine light machine guns. Mueller, a veteran of the *Afrika Korps* who had subsequently lost an arm on the Eastern Front, also had an engineer company under his command, with another ninety men, and two 105mm batteries with three pieces each. He had absorbed Panzer Brigade 105 into his division on 11 September, but most of the brigade's infantry riflemen had been lost in fights around Limbourg as Task Force Lovelady swept south of Eupen, Belgium, toward the Reich border.[7]

Oberst Mueller was a realist. He was fully aware of the predicament he faced with the arrival of American forces. His first impressions of the *Westwall* evinced that it "did not come up to my expectations. Because we were not prepared for the enemy outside the *Westwall*, although this could have been foreseen months before, and because practically nothing had been prepared for its defense, we did not want to believe how serious the situation actually was."[8]

The *Westwall* was known as the Siegfried Line to American forces. This first ring of defenses actually ran along the entire Reich border. Behind it, in a second line some eight kilometers beyond Roetgen and extending through industrial Stolberg past more rural Würselen, were other pillboxes, virtual concrete forts sited to support each other and to produce closely interlocking fields of fire like that which first rudely greeted U.S. forces. Around Aachen the outer array of antitank obstacles was known as *Vorstellung Aachen*, and the bunkers covering them the Scharnhorst Line. The even deeper, more extensive systems at the second *Westwall* defenses were called the Schill Line (*Limes-Stellung*).

The concrete installations themselves were generally 20 to 25 feet high with a footprint anywhere from 40 to 50 feet wide and 20 to 25 feet deep. Their fields of fire were limited; the path of fire generally could not exceed 50 degrees of traverse. In many locations the pillboxes were partially underground, and overgrowth of grass and shrub often made spotting them extremely difficult. When they were constructed between 1937 and 1940, the pillboxes were generally placed where the terrain afforded the most profitable use of machine and antitank guns; however they were unable to house any weapon larger than a 37mm AT gun, standard for the German army in the late 1930s. Pillboxes were often placed in clusters and linked to each other by communication trenches. Some of the ammunition bunkers that supported the boxes were underground.

The walls and roofs were anywhere from 4 to 8 feet thick, and at some places steel plated to afford additional protection for their occupants. Many of the pillboxes even had living quarters capable of billeting as many as thirty to forty men, with room for roughly seven men per firing embrasure. Pillboxes had inherent weaknesses, however. Assessments of First Army noted:

> The Siegfried Line was constructed before the development of the German military doctrine of "strongpoints," as illustrated by the heavy defenses along the Atlantic and English Channel coasts. It was completed before the Russians had taught the Germans the principle of an all-around "hedgehog" defense. The Siegfried Line was built on the first natural barrier east of the German frontier. Where this natural barrier was weakest, the pillbox concentration was strongest. The basic principle behind the placement of the pillboxes and AT barriers was simple and logical; namely to increase the defensive potential of the terrain along the border. Where tanks and infantry would have a difficult time attacking, the defenses were sketchy. Where a natural corridor existed, there the defenses were the densest.
>
> The basic design of the Siegfried Line called for the employment of mobile field armies operating out of and behind it. The real defense was to be an aggressive counterattacking force basing its offense from the Siegfried Line. The objective of the defenses was not to stop the enemy, but to slow him up and to tire him in the attack and then to hit him with strong counterattacks.[9]

Opposing First Army on the Siegfried Line in the Aachen area was the newly appointed commanding general of LXXXI Corps, *Generalleutnant* Friedrich-August Schack. Some felt he was not the best choice to defend Aachen; he had lost his 272nd Infantry Division during the undignified German retreat across the Seine. He was reported by one observer to be "highly excitable, suffering from stress and was, in fact, on the verge of a nervous breakdown as the Americans approached the Westwall."[10] Schack nevertheless described the situation as he saw it at the time, pointing out some of the fortification's inherent tactical weaknesses even as he was compelled to count on them.

When our exhausted and battle-weary forces finally reached the Westwall they found only antiquated and neglected fortifications. Many of the concrete pillboxes were filled with water, devoid of equipment; others were locked and the keys were missing. In addition, a great deal of the ventilation and signal communication systems was not in working condition. The field of fire was obstructed by vegetation; wire entanglements had been removed; firing slits were clogged with dirt. The type 42 machine guns, with their rapid-cycle rate of fire, could not operate in the available machine gun pillboxes, and therefore had to be used in positions out in the open.[11]

By the time Task Force Lovelady probed the *Westwall* on the night of 12 September, the 9th Panzer Division command post had moved from a farmhouse just over a kilometer northeast of Eynatten to Brand, a southern suburb just outside of Aachen. Surveillance had been conducted the day before near Roetgen by motorcycle platoons, and *Generalleutnant* Schack had even visited Mueller's command post that afternoon. Considering the limited defenses in the southern sector of the 9th Panzer Division, Schack approved a plan whereby the division would retreat by way of Oberforstbach, another Aachen district more to the southeast, behind the *Westwall*. "[We] were withdrawn and moved up into position for the support of the combat group in the municipal forests to the south of Aachen," Mueller recalled.[12]

Three days earlier, on 9 September, the 353rd Infantry Division, commanded by *Generalleutnant* Paul Mahlmann, had been ordered by Schack to prepare for the defense of the *Westwall* in the forest deeper to the south of Aachen where Task Force Lovelady actually attacked. Mahlmann's recollections of the defenses at the time evidenced the German's thin attempts to fortify the positions here.

Units of the Replacement Training Army were employed. South of Aachen were elements of the 526 Ers Ausb Division. Two *infanterie ersatz* (infantry replacement) battalions were committed in the forests. [One was *Oberstleutnant* Friedrich Troster's Reserve Grenadier Battalion 328.] A few flak units, which would be used for antitank defense or as artillery, were also committed. All these units were unready for combat by reason of their organization, equipment and state of training. They had some battle-experienced officers and non-commissioned officers, but also many who had never seen combat. The enlisted men included convalescents and insufficiently trained replacements of all age classes. They had few weapons. Heavy weapons were almost entirely lacking in the infantry replacement battalions. However, the position had to be made defensible with these forces. Division expected to get a few real combat men when the fighting should begin.[13]

Brig. Gen. Doyle O. Hickey, commander of the 3rd Armored Division's Combat Command A (CCA), had also ordered a second task force commanded by 1927 West Point graduate Lt. Col. Leander L. "Chubby" Doan to probe the *Westwall* just south of Oberforstbach and to the east of the Eupen-Eynatten road on 12 September. In this area, hurriedly being reinforced by the 9th Panzer Division, the fortifications ran in a northeast to southwest direction, approximately 1,000 yards inside the Reich border. These defenses, however, were in open, moderately rolling terrain that was also faced with dragon's teeth, and there were indeed pillboxes with favorable fields of fire beyond these tank barriers. But the high ground Task Force Doan occupied later in the day without a fight afforded observation of the entire area; a gentle ridge crisscrossing in an east-west direction looked promising. This terrain allowed for a quick flanking movement to the east and an attack on the fortifications from the south. Lieutenant Colonel Doan remembered, "These factors were to vitally affect the action of the next day."[14]

Yet still unknown was the actual resistance he would face when the morning dawned. The 9th Panzer Division's *Oberst* Mueller later offered this commentary on the cobbled, hastily arrayed defenses then at his disposal opposite Task Force Doan.

Thirty-six stationary (88mm) antitank guns, which for the most part were without sighting mechanisms, were located at Ober Forstbach and were just being emplaced by caterpillar tractors; for each piece there were only three men for service of the guns and only five armored and high explosive shells each. The pillboxes, which were connected with one another by subterranean cables, were neither equipped with telephones nor were there any plans for linking them up, nor experts well acquainted with local conditions, so that not even the command bunkers, for which telephones could have been made available, could establish communication. The division depended on the overburdened public telephone lines by way of the telephone exchange of Aachen.

The two assigned battalions were distributed amongst the local replacement and instruction battalions, neither of which were coherent units welded closely together. On the other hand, we had the advantage that the command remained [under] troop commanders who had a fair knowledge of the region.[15]

A third 3rd Armored Division task force under the command of Lt. Col. Rosewell H. King had also set out on the morning of 12 September 1944. After receiving his orders from the commander of Combat Command B (CCB), Col. Truman E. Boudinot, Task Force King sent a reconnaissance in force through Kettenis, skirting Eupen at Oberstheide before moving via a heavily wooded area through Schoenefeld into the Raerener Woods before Schmidthof. The reconnaissance force was commanded by Capt. Kenneth T. McGeorge and was led by M5 light tanks, followed by medium Shermans and then a company of infantry mounted on half-tracks, with engineers in their own vehicles at the rear of the column.

At approximately 1630, when Task Force Lovelady was crossing the railroad tracks to enter Roetgen, Task Force King encountered a crossroad in the Raerener Woods where teller mines had been cleverly camouflaged, resulting in one tank falling victim to an explosion and an immediate halting of the remainder of the force. The surviving light tanks hurried toward machine-gun positions observed about 100 yards away and mopped them up, and then the engineers worked forward and cleared the remaining mines from the crossroad. The column reformed and continued on its mission eastward to the Reich border.

At 1700 the column finally hit the main road from Raeren to Roetgen, turned southeast, and passed through friendly elements of Task Force Lovelady before abruptly wheeling northward toward Schmidthof. At a bend in the upcoming roadway, Captain McGeorge's lead reconnaissance force found that the column was positioned at the top of a hill before a long, straight stretch of continued gently sloping roadway that was plainly open for what appeared to be the next two miles. Perceiving the excellent fields of fire that enemy troops would have along this road, McGeorge halted his men. Infantry then came forward along the edge of the road while light tanks were sent ahead to draw fire if the enemy chose to attack. Fortunately, no hostile action materialized.

While making reconnaissance on the top of the next hill, however, the point of the column ran into a rope chain of mines that the enemy forces had dragged across the road before retiring to the nearby Koenigsburg hills.[16] From here the dragon's teeth of the *Westwall* also came into view, along with two sets of concrete blocks with wire stretched across the road between them. Fifteen yards north of these obstacles stood a steel swinging gate much like the one Task Force Lovelady faced near the Dreilagerbach reservoir outside of Roetgen. A crater had been blown in the road at the point where the dragon's teeth began, and another gate lay beyond this. Rows of additional concrete obstacles in haphazard but effective patterns and shapes also lined these *Westwall* defenses. Another and larger iron-domed pillbox, some 75 yards northeast of this line, appeared to observers to have the area zeroed in. Even a dirt road that branched into these defenses from another direction was blocked with a rugged iron gate.

Securing the ground beyond this was the immediate mission of the infantrymen, all attached to the 36th Armored Infantry Regiment, so that the engineers of the 2nd Platoon, Company B, 23rd Armored Engineer Battalion, commanded by Lt. Robert M. Eells, could work unhindered on the tank obstacles, thus permitting the rest of the task force through the *Westwall*.[17] It was about dusk when the infantry went straight up the sides of the roadway, trying to maintain some cover. Behind them were two of Eells's leading scouts and the rest of his squad of engineers. Then things went downhill quickly. As these men approached the first obstacles, an enemy pillbox on the right opened up with deadly machine-gun fire, killing both of the scouts and wounding others. Just five engineers survived.

Suddenly American tanks started shooting at the pillbox in support, scoring hits but not knocking it out. The remaining infantry tried to work their way up, but vicious fire was now coming in from both sides of the roadway and darkness had all too quickly set in. "The column was also strung out back to Roetgen," Eells explained. "Orders came to pull back and leaguer."[18] By this time a platoon of three tank destroyers under the command of Lt. Heril L. Brown had put in a roadblock, covering the rear of the task force.[19] The contemplated attack on Schmidthof was canceled. Instead, Task Force King coiled for the night.

Generalleutnant Schack wasted little time and ordered the 9th Panzer Division to immediately reinforce the positions in the area. Remembering this, Schack later said:

> Our thin line of security had disintegrated in several places. To consolidate, we had to fall back a little, increasing the possibilities for concentration and reorganization. The 9th Panzer Division concentrated its units around Eynatten while the 353rd Division manned the Westwall as a security force.
>
> We had no illusions about the condition of the Westwall. But its dragon's teeth and permanent fortifications, visible from a distance, might arouse the enemy's respect and make them cautious. Perhaps their cautious approach would allow our exhausted forces breathing time. These serious questions, and the anxiety resulting, absorbed the attention of every commander at the close of this fateful day. It was clear that perhaps the next day there would be a fight for the Westwall positions.[20]

By this time the first units of the American XIX Corps had arrived just to the south of Maastricht, an important rail and river transportation point 30 kilometers west of Aachen in Holland. On 11 September the 113th Cavalry Group, commanded by Col. William S. Biddle, had made a sweeping 35-mile end run from the Albert Canal to the south, crossing the Meuse River at Liege near Belgium's eastern border. With 1933 West Point graduate Lt. Col. Anthony F. Kleitz's 125th Cavalry Reconnaissance Squadron on the right flank and Lt. Col. Allen D. Hulse's 113th Cavalry Reconnaissance Squadron on the left, the Group continued moving to the north along the east bank of the river on 12 September. The 1st Battalion, 117th Infantry Regiment of Maj. Gen. Leland S. Hobbs's 30th Infantry Division had also crossed the Meuse River at Vise,

20 kilometers northeast of Liege, during the night of 11–12 September. They were moving northward by midday on 12 September.[21] Maastricht was also Hobbs's next objective.

Severely weakened elements of the 275th Infantry Division, under the command of *Generalleutnant* Hans Schmidt, defended the positions around ancient and culture-rich Maastricht. His division was one in name only, as many of its units had been destroyed a week earlier while rushing to escape from the Mons pocket.[22] At the time Schmidt, a stern-faced officer with piercing eyes, reported his total remaining division strength at only two thousand men, of which just four hundred were considered combat worthy. He later explained:

> I succeeded in obtaining officers, non-commissioned officers and men [and] was able to put up some formations with more or less tolerable fighting power. I was supplied with a limited number of heavy infantry weapons and ammunition. As complete formations, one security battalion and one regional defense battalion—the bulk of which consisted of men over 30 years of age with poor training, the remaining portions of an anti-aircraft battalion with two batteries of 20 and 50mm guns, as well as one light anti-aircraft battery manned of labor service men, were subordinated to me. In addition to these, a task force of three companies put up of stragglers and motorized in a makeshift way, arrived in personal carriers under the command of Major Riedel. From remnants of my own division and from stragglers I formed two infantry battalions. On about 10 September I moved into position a battery of four light field howitzers, which was placed at my disposal by a SS formation proceeding to Germany for reorganization. In a makeshift way, the battery was mobile by means of truck and was ready for action on 12 September.[23]

By this time, many of the military and administrative officers had already evacuated Maastricht. Even the town commandant had disappeared. Schmidt, on the other hand, had just received a personal telegram from Hitler ordering that the Maastricht bridgehead be defended to the last cartridge.[24] Schmidt recalled:

In the beginning, the enemy pursued but slowly and with weak forces. Besides, we ascertained that the preceding night [11 September], the enemy had crossed the Meuse near Vise. These enemy forces were estimated to comprise one battalion, but apparently they were stronger and they soon commenced to attack in the direction to Fouron le Comte. With the spearhead of this American force, I had a very disagreeable encounter. I made a trip along the foremost front line. West of Fouron le Comte, we in a hurry took a wrong road, and suddenly from a distance of about 80 meters we were sighted and taken under fire by an enemy patrol of some 10 to 15 men who were about to cross the road from the south. Our situation was rather hopeless. First of all, we succeeded in getting out of our car. When working back along the sunken road we were on, my officer was wounded by a shot into his upper thigh and was later taken prisoner. Also, my driver was shot at and remained lying on the spot. When getting out of my car, I was hit in my left hip. Despite the wound, I did not give up, but with all the energy and force I could command, springing up and crawling on all fours—all the time under fire—I worked back along the road in the direction of the town.

Upon reaching a road bend, I observed another American patrol which apparently was a flank security. I was thus endangered from the front and rear alike. Now I had no other choice, but using every available cover I eventually succeeded by forcing my way back in a northeasterly direction. My attempt to rescue my comrades by a counterattack with our forces I met there failed. The intensified enemy fire inflicted losses and soon tied us down.[25]

Schmidt was correct in assessing that American forces were attacking in strength larger than one battalion on 12 September. After being in contact with his forces all of the previous night, two battalions of the U.S. 30th Division's 119th Infantry Regiment were now also advancing northward toward Maastricht. The regiment's 3rd Battalion, under the command of the experienced and capable Lt. Col. Courtney P. Brown, jumped off at 0800 and reached its first objective at Dalhem shortly afterward. By 1000 hours, the 1st Battalion was going through Longchamp while Brown's forces moved through Bombays toward thinly populated Warsage. At 1125 hours, the leading patrols of the 1st Battalion were near mixed Dutch- and French-speaking Fouron le Comte and were receiving 20mm and rifle fire from Schmidt's forces. A full company finally pushed into the town at 1245 hours, only to find itself delayed when the 275th Division's few light field howitzers delivered some incoming fire from a ridgeline east of the town.[26]

Artillery attached to the 30th Infantry Division crossed over the Meuse late in the afternoon of 12 September behind the 119th Infantry's regimental combat trains and weapon carriers. Schmidt's Regiment 984, under the command of *Oberst* Heinz, had one of its battalions located on both sides of Fouron le Comte by this time. Schmidt, however, had even larger problems to contend with. His officer who was wounded in the ambush earlier that day had with him orders issued that very morning for the 275th Infantry Division's defensive positions. As Schmidt remembered, "Now it was essential to take all countermeasures before the enemy could avail himself of the knowledge gained by capturing this order. Despite my wounding, I remained with the troops to retain the command of the division in this critical situation. But as the day wore on the enemy succeeded in gaining more ground near Fouron le Comte, where he concentrated his main effort. The town was lost."[27]

Later, at 1555 hours Lieutenant Colonel Brown's 3rd Battalion pushed past the right flank of the line established by the 1st Battalion at Fouron le Comte, and advanced to the east of Warsage and eventually some 500 yards inside the Dutch border near Terlinden. "People were ringing church bells when we entered these small towns," remembered Company L lieutenant David F. Knox.[28]

At the same time, heavy fighting was taking place for Eysden, a small trading and shipping center before the war, where losses in the 275th Infantry Division ranks included the killing of the battalion commander defending the area. By nightfall Uheer also fell. Only Battalion Riedel held its position near Schildberg, stalling the envelopment of Schmidt's left wing. His remaining forces began to withdraw to a north-south line along the Gulpen-Cadier road. As Schmidt remembered, "Our intention was to keep the enemy away from Maastricht with the view of holding free the Meuse bridge for the withdrawal of our bridgehead troops." This and other setbacks along the entire LXXXI Corps' front on 12 September prompted *Generalleutnant* Schack to comment, "By nightfall, the location of our front line was no longer clear to headquarters. Its disintegration at several points made the situation very serious indeed."[29]

Meanwhile, in light of this eroding situation, the 12th Infantry Division, commanded by *Oberst* Gerhard Engel, a handsome and highly decorated former army liaison officer to Hitler, was alerted for movement "as soon as possible" to strengthen the defenses at the *Westwall*. This division was battle hardened from combat on the Eastern front in Russia. Heavy losses during defensive battles in the spring and summer of 1944 had resulted in its withdrawal into the West Prussian area around Danzig for rest and refitting and it was now at full strength. On 12 September the division departed Western Prussia with 1.5 times its normal issue of infantry and artillery ammunition.[30] Engel's forces included three infantry regiments with two battalions each totaling approximately 6,600 men, four battalions of artillery with attached infantry that was comprised of another 2,200 soldiers, an engineer battalion with four companies made up of 400 men, and a newly organized antitank battalion with two companies that brought up its strength by another 300 men. With headquarters service personnel and his signal battalion, *Oberst* Engel had 14,800 combatants at his disposal.[31] He remembered:

> On 12 September the division, which was prepared for evacuation, was alerted and evacuated within the shortest time to reach the Western Front as soon as possible. Because of the dangerous situation on the frontiers of the Reich, the drive went at maximum speed. The division drove along the stretch ordered at speed 36, with utter disregard for other traffic. Destination was unknown; the area of Aachen was suspected.[32]

Panic had consumed the city of Aachen by this time. Chaotic conditions at the railroad stations set in during the afternoon of 12 September where, by earlier order of Hitler himself, mandatory evacuation of its civil population was now to occur by train over the next two days. *Generalleutnant* Schack was in the city that afternoon and he saw that "Aachen was in sheer turmoil. Crying women and children wandered bewildered through the city and old women in completely desperate conditions begged for help to get out of the city. They said that the Gauleiter had declared that whoever did not leave the town at once was a traitor. Obviously they were afraid to be dealt with as traitors."[33]

In leaflet form, evacuation orders had been distributed to the civilians of Aachen that morning by the party's respected Joseph Grohe, the *Gauleiter* (Nazi Party District leader) of the wider Cologne-Aachen area. The order read:

German Men and Women

Fellow Countrymen and fellow Countrywomen!

If the enemy approaches the German positions in the West, he should meet our fanatical resistance! His intentions to destroy the Reich and to exterminate our people must be foiled.

He must not be allowed to achieve now that which he could not achieve five years ago, when his highly-equipped armies stood in front of our fortifications. Our children's eyes, which want to see a future, remind us to resist with all means to the last breath. The voices of the many hundreds of thousands who remained on the battlefields for the honor and freedom of our Fatherland, or those who lost their lives to enemy terror bombing, are calling us. The spirits of the heroes of liberty of our glorious history shake us, so that we do not weaken or become cowards during the decisive part of the fight for our existence!

The ruins of our cities and the millions of our fellow countrymen's homes that were destroyed by terror bombing are a silent accusation against anyone who does not do everything for the victory, without which there will be no rebuilding.

Fellow Countrymen and fellow Countrywomen!

We must expect the western front forward areas of our fortifications and also the towns within the fortifications to soon become a battle area. Therefore the Fuhrer [*sic*] ordered the evacuation of the towns and villages in the upcoming battle area for the safety of German life and war-important valuables!

The evacuation proceeds according to plan and without haste. The safeguarding of valuables that are important for the war is being handled by the appropriate authorities; the orderly evacuation of men, women, and children has been taken over by the Party.

The Ortsgruppenleiter [Nazi Party village group leaders] issue the necessary instructions according to the Kreisleiters. The evacuation proceeds to previously designated areas of the Reich, where all preparations for shelter have been arranged. The relocated people will receive the same assistance as those who were bombed out.

Males between the ages of 16 and 60 who are capable of work will for now not be evacuated, but will be deployed at fortifications under construction, as long as they do not belong to the work force who, because of relocation of its factories, move out with them to another part of the Reich.

The fellow countrymen working on the fortifications will be brought back as soon as their work is complete or the situation at the front requires the fortifications to be released to the fighting Wehrmacht.

Fellow Countrymen and fellow Countrywomen!

In the difficult years of war behind us, you had to make extraordinary sacrifices without ever forgetting your duty. It is important that the evacuation now necessary takes place with discipline and mutual helpfulness!

Whoever disturbs measures of the evacuation, or tries to refuse to join the withdrawal, not only puts himself in deadly danger, but has to be considered a traitor against the public community and dealt with accordingly.

And now more than ever:

Long live our Fuhrer [*sic*], our Reich, and our People!

Grohe

Despite Grohe's promises of order and the dire consequences of disobedience, among the first to leave the city was anyone who wore a Nazi Party uniform. Both the Aachen City and Aachen Forest *Kreisleiters*, the official area Nazi Party leaders, fled in the madness. Some lesser party members and Red Cross nurses made an effort to help organize the people, but there were too few to bring order to the chaos.

When Grohe allowed the party leaders to leave the city, the police also followed. By early evening, the entire Aachen police force, including air raid police as well as the fire department, medical service personnel, and all of their vehicles and equipment, were gone. With this, any hopes for an orderly evacuation came to a virtual halt.

Generalleutnant Count Gerhard Graf von Schwerin, the charismatic and much-admired commander of the 116th Panzer Division, also came into Aachen later that day from his command post outside of the city. He, too, was distressed by what he witnessed.

> I found the population to be in a state of panic, without guidance, aimlessly fleeing the city into the night. This view—let it be understood the first view after returning to the homeland from enemy country—made a deep and shocking impression on my officers and me. I took measures to control this panic out of consideration for the troops who would pass through the city. Great numbers of women and children with handcarts and baby carriages [were] walking away on the roads, aimlessly. The unruly movement obstructed mobility of the troops and caused animosity and panic even amongst the soldiers.[34]

There was ample reason for chaos in the city. As the evacuation leaflets fell into the hands of the Aachen citizenry on 12 September, the veteran 1st Infantry Division, commanded by Maj. Gen. Clarence R. Huebner, also pushed to the German border. At 1515 hours, New York native Capt. Victor H. Briggs's Company C of Huebner's 16th Infantry Regiment burst through a gap between the 9th and 116th Panzer Divisions and crossed the last frontier of the European War.[35] During the night the reinforced 1st Battalion of this regiment, under the command of Lt. Col. Edmund F. Driscoll, continued driving forward and pierced the first belt of the *Westwall* in the woods near the Brandenberg Hill, in the sector of Security Battalion 453. A counterattack at 2100 hours with eighty men launched by the Aachen battle commandant failed when these forces marched right into the left flank of Company A and were mowed down by machine-gun fire.[36] The battle commandant, *Oberst* Helmuth von Osterroht, had no choice but to rush more reinforcements into this threatened part of the *Westwall* later that night.[37]

By this time, thousands of confused Aachen citizens still in the city were taking it upon themselves to move into its twenty-two air raid bunkers. However, Huebner's 1st Infantry Division was under orders from Maj. Gen. J. Lawton Collins's VII Corps to bypass Aachen altogether. Instead, after reaching the Corps' initial objective six miles northeast of Aachen at Eschweiler, Huebner's infantry regiments and the combat commands of the 3rd Armored Division were to link up at the road center of Duren with XIX Corps. From here the Americans were to advance to the Rhine River and attack the heart of what remained of Germany's industrial production in the Ruhr. XIX Corps, commanded by Maj. Gen. Charles H. Corlett and positioned to the north and west of Aachen, was to turn east after Maastricht fell and cross the natural obstacles formed by the Wurm River to the north of Aachen, then penetrate the *Westwall* in its zone of operations with forces of the 30th Infantry Division and the 2nd Armored Division before driving farther eastward toward Duren for the linkup with VII Corps.

The ancient imperial city was to be left alone. On 12 September 1944, Aachen—despite the panic inside the city—was of no value to the American army other than as a route for vehicular traffic; its capture was not essential. Fate and the circumstances of total war soon changed this. Aachen, its historical epoch rooted in the takeover of the government by Charlemagne in CE 768, was destined to be surrounded. Air power, artillery, armor, and infantry would eventually subject the garrison to an object lesson in the application of modern warfare before all German troops, arms, materiel, and fortifications were surrendered to the United States Army five weeks later on 21 October 1944.

CHAPTER 2

VII Corps Breaches the *Westwall*

"The only glimmer of hope seemed to be the 12th Infantry Division, due to arrive by train."

MAJ. HEINZ GUNTHER GUDERIAN, *FROM NORMANDY TO THE RUHR WITH THE 116TH PANZER DIVISION*

When *Generalleutnant* von Schwerin took formal command of the Aachen defenses at 0600 on 13 September, one of the first matters he chose to deal with was the plight of the Aachen citizenry; he sent his division staff officers through the city looking for any authorities who "could effect reasonable control of the panicky stream of refugees."[1] They were unable to find anyone, so Schwerin ordered these staff officers to reach out to the people, tell them not to flee, and to instead return to their homes. It was noted at the time that "the population accepted this offer gratefully."

Their circumstances certainly explained why Aacheners were grateful. Arrangements had been made by Grohe for channeling them outside of the city "without friction, provided that the orders of the march and transport leaders were complied with."[2] They had been reminded that disobedience would be dealt with "on the spot." Yellow march order tags were given to mothers and fathers with children under twelve. A blue traveling order was issued to pregnant women and old and sick people. They were told their individual hand baggage could not exceed 30 pounds, but another 60 pounds of luggage was permissible on horse-drawn carriages that would be provided; small carriages and bicycles were permitted for carrying the other 30 pounds. The people could also bring food for three days, one wool blanket, a raincoat, a mess kit, one bottle of beverage, underwear, a wash cloth, a lantern or flashlight, even personal papers. Women were reminded to bring articles for personal hygiene, and milk, bottles, and nipples if they had babies. Everyone was warned to douse any embers that might remain in the fireplaces of their homes; they were told that their water, gas, and electricity would be shut off.

Schwerin's concerns for the people of Aachen prompted him to again leave his command post in the Rahe Chateau in Laurensberg and enter the city early in the afternoon of 13 September. He later chronicled his first stop in one of the city's municipal buildings on his way to see von Osterroht. The fate of the people was still foremost on his mind when he spoke here with Joseph Grohe.

> He had asked me if I was now assuming command of the city. By answering in the affirmative, I again became fully aware of the heavy responsibility I had to assume regarding the leaderless remaining population of Aachen. . . . [I]f the enemy were to advance toward the city from the point of penetration, one would have to assume that he would appear at the southern entrances of the city before my division could get there. There-fore, the time available was so short that it was impossible to evacuate the thousands of people who were still in the city. The majority would fall into enemy hands. In this situation I only had one thought on my mind: what can [I] do to help the unfortunate population if the enemy arrives in the city ahead of [my forces]? From previous fighting in France, I knew that the American Army adhered to the Geneva and Hague conventions, so it seemed possible to ease the fate of the remaining citizens by means of a purely humanitarian appeal to the American com-mander. I acted according to this thought.[3]

After Schwerin determined that a trustworthy postal clerk would remain in the city in the event Aachen was occupied, he wrote a note in English on a piece of paper and handed it to the head postal official, who had vouched for his clerk's reliability to carry out the task. Schwerin then left the office to go to his new command post in the Berliner Hof on the railroad station street to see von Osterroht. The letter had not been put into an envelope, so its contents were undoubtedly read at the time. Schwerin remembered, "The famous lines were worded as follows":

> To the Commanding Officer of the US Forces occupying the town of Aachen: I stopped the stupid evacuation of the civil population and ask you to give her relief. I'm the last commanding officer here.
>
> Gerhard Count von Schwerin,
> 13 September 44 Lt. General[4]

Schwerin then turned his attention to more pressing matters. A Führer order that he had received read: "In the event of enemy penetration of Aachen, every house is to be defended. A withdrawal, such as from the southern edge to the northern edge of the city, will not happen."[5] With this, any lingering thoughts Schwerin had about either surrendering the city or falling back to the second, stronger *Westwall* line meant disobedience. He had ample cause for concern.

At first light that morning, the two companies of the 36th Armored Infantry assigned to Task Force Lovelady renewed their attack north of Roetgen. All three platoons of Company E, now under the command of Georgia native Lt. Verna L. McCord, departed at 0700 from the steep slopes on the hill west of the road facing the dragon's teeth.

McCord moved his 2nd Platoon forward quickly that morning, but a torrent of enemy fire quickly came in from several pillboxes on the other side of the obstacles. One of the squads deployed into a draw, a man at a time, where they were afforded some cover while a second squad rushed through the dragon's teeth and edged around to the pillbox delivering the most fire. McCord ordered another platoon to follow them; the men rushed to a makeshift assembly area and split into columns. One column went left around the pillbox and turned back toward it when its supporting tanks fired rounds of antiphosphorous shells into the front apertures. Then the other column came in from the opposite direction; the tanks rumbled forward, still firing. As McCord remembered, "The sight of this proved too much for the Germans, and they gave up."[6] During this time Company D, now under the command of Capt. Alfred J. Amborst, had moved up to the high ground south of the Dreilagerbach reservoir where nearly twenty other Germans offered little resistance before surrendering. By now it was nearing 1000 hours and the infantry had already squeezed out all noticeable enemy resistance behind the dragon's teeth.

The 1st Platoon of Company B, 23rd Armored Engineering Battalion had also gone forward with the column of McCord's infantry when they pinched the pillbox with the tanks. This platoon, under the command of Lt. George E. Conley, faced the important job of getting the heavier armored vehicles of Task Force Lovelady through the remaining obstacles. As Conley pointed out, "We put the accent on speed, doing only what was necessary to enable the vehicles to keep moving."[7]

Some thirty other men accompanied Conley on this mission, and not far behind were one jeep, a tank dozer, two heavy bridge trucks, and a deuce and a half loaded with TNT, mines, and other explosives. Lieutenant Conley ordered his tank dozer driver to fill the streambed crater that had held up progress the previous night. The streambed proved to be dry, and the dozer filled it without incident. Conley's men dashed forward and wrestled the first I-beam out of the roadway by hand.

When Conley moved his platoon some 300 yards to the next steel gate, he personally mounted the tank dozer and rammed the obstacle a half-dozen times. When it failed to break from its hinges, Lieutenant Conley dismounted, and with the assistance of his hearty staff sergeant, they set three TNT charges around its base, blowing the gate to pieces. His men rushed forward another 50 yards around a slight bend, this time only confronting an unmanned 88mm gun.[8]

The 1st Platoon of the reconnaissance company and the infantry started across the dirt-filled streambed at 1015. Lieutenant McCord's Company E spread out and advanced on the left side of the roadway while Amborst's Company D platoons moved out to the right; the reconnaissance platoon worked up the center of the roadway. Most men had dismounted from their half-tracks and tanks by this time. And with just 50 yards between the groaning armored vehicles and the pillboxes, the German forces they encountered found it wise to quickly surrender. The infantry group continued its advance and passed by two antitank guns, one 75mm and the other 20mm. Both had been abandoned, although large stores of ammunition were still piled up around them. The soldiers quickly removed the sights and moved on, but stopped when the columns came upon some felled trees.

After passing these same unmanned guns, Conley's engineers continued through the woods and picked up some hurriedly laid mines that the Germans had left behind. Artillery was now escorting the task force by keeping a moving screen of smashing explosives some 200 yards ahead of the leading squads. However, as the engineers continued northward out of the woods into the open fields of fern trees southwest of the village of Rott, the Germans fired into both of Lieutenant Conley's flanks. Four enemy 20mm guns and one very loud 88mm opened up on the right, while a sole 88 and a single heavy German tank took aim from the left. The engineers stopped and dug in.

The infantry also encountered problems.[9] After moving out past the felled trees they had been using for cover after the artillery fire started, the squad on point encountered an enemy patrol of six men dismounted from their motorcycles and armed with just a light machine gun. Although this force scattered when they saw the Americans coming their way, both companies were now receiving more incoming fire from Rott. Then two enemy Tiger tanks and another two Panthers appeared. Lieutenant Colonel Lovelady eventually came up and told Lt. Ernest F. Silva to go back to the dragon's teeth, send up as many medium tanks as he could find, and order his tank destroyers forward. Unfortunately, they were of little help. By noontime the opposition had knocked out four of the American tanks, two jeeps, and two half-tracks. It would now be another hour before the infantry and engineers could regroup and the enemy resistance cleared out.

By the time Task Force King resumed its attack at 0800 that morning, the Germans had withdrawn from the Koenigsberg hills.[10] The engineers went right to work with the infantry, first pulling out the Teller mines in front of the swinging steel gate that had held up their advance the night before. Then a tank came forward and nosed out the gate, forcing the hinges to give way from the concrete post on which it hung. At this point the advance elements of the task force started moving, and these men quickly lunged forward to neutralize a more formidable roadblock another 200 yards ahead at the top of the next rise. This roadblock had obviously been built to stop the task force from approaching the village of Schmidtoff, some 500 yards away. The scrubby forest through which the men had just trodden continued to the right of the roadway, but toward Schmidtoff the woods came to an abrupt end and the terrain quickly fell off into a deep draw. The village, which was built on higher ground, was across from this draw. There was also a side road that cut off to the left along the edge of the draw before twisting and then running up to the village. This terrain offered good fields of fire for the Germans, especially toward the roadblock now facing the stalled column.

In front of them was what Lieutenant Eells, leader of the 2nd Platoon of Company B engineers, remembered as "a hell of a big crater, filled with water."[11] As it was elsewhere along the *Westwall*, more I-beam tank obstacles were planted near the steel gate next to the crater. Dragon's teeth also came out of the forest to the right of the gate, as well as to the left of the roadway before it turned and rose into Schmidtoff.

Given this difficult terrain, the remainder of the task force coiled near the railroad line north of Muensterbildchen while Lieutenant Colonel King, Maj. Herbert M. Mills, and Captain McGeorge of the reconnaissance company went forward to study the situation. By now King's Company F was down to sixty men and could not be expected to secure the depressed ground to the left and hold the wooded area on the right while the engineers built a crossing over the crater. Therefore, King decided to ask Colonel Boudinot for reinforcements; Companies H and I of the 36th Armored Infantry were called up from division reserve and ordered forward.

But King was anxious to continue the attack. He reexamined the cards he was dealt, which now included steady rain, and decided to attempt a breakthrough with the hand he held. The available medium tanks were hastily brought up and undermanned Company F was alerted and told to be ready to jump off.

At 1720 artillery forward observers called down a ten-minute preparatory barrage on Schmidtoff and on other suspected enemy positions along the roadway to soften up the advance. The men of Company F departed to the left in platoon column and then down the draw toward the village. The tanks turned west off the roadway at a farmhouse, hoping to edge into a position where they could support the infantry. Almost immediately, however, the tanks came under fire, and two were knocked out. Lieutenant Eells remembered that he "saw one man jump from a tank with his foot blown off, but somehow [he] ran 200 yards to cover, and apparently survived."[12] By this time, heavy mortar fire had completely stopped Company F, forcing them to withdraw and leave exposed the squad of engineers who had gone up to a third roadblock below Schmidtoff.

Capt. Wallace A. Vaughn's Company I, one of the two reserve companies of the 36th Armored Infantry, finally arrived at 1900 hours at the crest of the hill overlooking the enemy positions. It was getting dark and heavier rain was coming down. The men still dismounted their half-tracks, moved off in columns, and worked their way up the roadway before going down the draw. Suddenly, as they got closer to the dragon's teeth, intense small-arms and mortar fire rang out from a house hidden in the woods, stopping the men in place.

At this point the leader of the 2nd Platoon, Lt. W. C. Gordon, went forward with Vaughn and conducted a reconnaissance to look for a place to get though the draw, together paralleling the outlines of the dragon's teeth as they moved carefully in swiftly approaching darkness. Fortunately, the enemy was not manning the roadblocks, nor were they defending the dragon's teeth here. Gordon decided to forego a pillbox to his right after he learned from some civilians in another nearby house that it was not manned. With his men, he pushed to this box, carefully passed it, and then moved into the adjacent wooded area where the exhausted platoon built up a defensive position.

Lieutenant Eells's engineers had attempted to clear the second roadblock so Vaughn's infantry could work their way into Schmidtoff to break up the incoming fire that had now held up Task Force King for more than twenty-four hours. Surprisingly, Eells's men found that they could easily pull the I-beams toward the left of the gate, and in doing so they cleared a narrow passageway. A tank dozer, working under enemy machine-gun and sniper fire, quickly filled the left side of the crater with dirt, but the four tanks that tried failed to make it through. The steady rain had made the ground so muddy that the tanks bogged down and simply could not move.

As a result the attack on Schmidtoff was called off, and Task Force King spent the rest of the night holding its positions. After midnight King discovered that an old wound had been infected; he would be evacuated the following morning, relinquishing command to Major Mills.[13]

The day also ended with Task Force Lovelady stopped short of its objective, but the afternoon had some measured successes.[14] After losing the four tanks and a tank destroyer right after noontime, more German Panthers had appeared. A tank destroyer hit one with a dozen rounds of 76mm fire, forcing its crew to flee as the vehicle burst into flames; tank fire from the edge of the woods destroyed another well-camouflaged Panther in Rott. Artillery helped subdue the remaining opposition and at 1730 Lovelady's tanks, with infantry interspersed between them, moved forward into the village. An abandoned 8.8cm flak gun was found at Konigsbergerstrasse; a 7.5cm antitank gun at Roetgenerstrasse was destroyed; three 2cm guns just to the east were found with their breechblocks removed; and another five were destroyed. Opposition eventually ceased entirely, with the remaining Germans surrendering.

Shortly after this, the advance elements of the task force started out for Mulartshutte, one mile north of Rott. Groups of enemy soldiers were sighted along this route, so Lovelady ordered the artillery to lay down a rolling barrage ahead of the column to scare them away. The attack proceeded slowly, and while the Germans offered little opposition, the bridge across a stream that flowed to the east of Mulartshutte had been demolished, ceasing progress. The engineers constructed a temporary ford that eventually enabled a few tanks to cross and provide advance protection for the column. Infantry then crossed over to secure an area large enough to permit the engineers to rebuild the bridge unmolested. Their work was well underway by 2200. Under the circumstances the task force had no choice but to halt for the night. Lovelady's decision was fortuitous. The engineers kept working on the bridge after midnight, but the light tank that tested the strength of their work caused the entire treadway and trestle bridge that had been erected to collapse.

Task Force Doan met with greater success in its mission on 13 September. Lt. Col. Edward S. Berry's after action report for his 67th Groupment Armored Field Artillery actually described the accomplishments of Task Force Doan at Oberforstbach as "an action characterized by the greatest heroism and self-sacrifice on the part of those engaged."[15] This was not without tremendous difficulties and casualties as Maj. Gen. Maurice Rose's third task force faced its mission during the day and into the dismal night.

Lieutenant Colonel Doan's plan was similar to those of the other task force commanders that day. His tanks were to stay behind the line of departure near his command post in the Eynattener Woods by Langfield before rolling up to support the attack of the 1st Battalion of the 36th Armored Infantry. Under the command of Capt. Louis F. Plummer, these men would first go through the dragon's teeth to secure the high ground beyond the obstacles. The engineers of the 23rd Armored Engineer Battalion commanded by Captain Replogle were to then come up and make a breach in the dragon's teeth before Doan's tanks went through. The time for the general attack was set for 0900, after the infantry first moved out.

Opposing Task Force Doan at Oberforstbach was *Oberst* Mueller's 9th Panzer Division, as well as other units from the instruction and replacement battalions that had come under his command by this time.[16] One of Mueller's antitank units was turned from its position behind the *Westwall* during the day in order to help block the breach Task Force Lovelady made near Roetgen. Still, it was later learned that, in addition to the organic units of the 9th Panzer Division, Task Force Doan was also opposed by sections of the 16th Engineer Battalion, fighting as infantry, the 12th *Luftwaffe* Field Battalion, and the 173rd *Ersatk* (Replacement) Battalion, which had only been in the German army for three or four months. Both of the latter units were in bunkers east of Oberforstbach and were supported by antitank guns of the 7th *Flak* Division. Given his hasty assumption of command of these different units, *Oberst* Mueller had no telephone communications between their commanders and his staff.[17] There were few radios available, and no maps.

Plummer's exact point of penetration had been selected because it was in defile from the pillboxes, except for one lone box to his immediate front about 150 yards beyond the dragon's teeth.[18] There were no signs of activity from this pillbox, or from any others at the time. The attack was actually behind schedule now, as it was past 0900. Plummer had used the delay to call for tank destroyer fire on the pillbox as a precaution. Right after this he moved his men out of the woods and up to a dirt road, eventually coming to a house nearer to their line of departure. At the time, there was still no fire being returned from this pillbox.

A makeshift command post had been set up in this house, and Lieutenant Colonel Doan and Captain Replogle joined Plummer there at about 1100 hours. It was 1230 when the infantry finally proceeded to the right of the house, through the dragon's teeth, and up a rise. But as Plummer's men advanced some 200 yards over its crest, they were suddenly swept by machine-gun fire from a pillbox beyond the first one they had encountered. This fire forced his men to withdraw back to the dragon's teeth, where they took cover. Doan ordered Plummer to shift his men left along the dragon's teeth, and to cross over and attack this second pillbox from the west.

Plummer's men carried out this maneuver, but when they reached a north-south axis that ran between the silent box and another pillbox that was half the distance to the one that had fired at them, rifle shots rang out. Suddenly, even heavier machine-gun fire also came at them, but the direction of the incoming rounds was different. This time the fire had come from the first pillbox, the one that had been quiet, and two badly wounded Germans were now lying outside of it.

A platoon of Company A, 703rd Tank Destroyer Battalion, commanded by Lt. Ralph L. Henderson, was responsible for drawing the enemy soldiers out. Just before Plummer's platoons jumped off, Henderson had noticed a machine-gun nest about 100 yards across the dragon's teeth to his TD's right. The artillery forward observer had directed fire into this position, but the target was missed. Henderson's tank destroyers answered with long lances of direct fire, chasing the enemy machine-gun crew to the left toward the silent pillbox. Four rounds of armor-piercing ammo were then laid directly into the box. A German was killed, one ran, and a third was wounded. "At this point the pillbox was lying low, not returning fire," Henderson remembered.[19]

By this time Plummer had moved a squad toward this box. One of his aid men who spoke German went up to help the wounded enemy soldiers, and when he reached the pillbox he called out for the remaining occupants to give themselves up. Instead, someone yelled back in broken English, "Go to hell. We will fight it out!"[20]

This resolve did not last. Soon afterward the dozen Germans in the pillbox surrendered. For the next two hours, however, others fought on. For a third time, Plummer's men tried to push through the dragon's teeth, without success. Ten tanks had come up and deployed along the obstacles in support by this time. Captain Replogle's engineers even moved up to lay wire and demolitions to blast at the dragon's teeth, all the while under fire from enemy mortars and machine guns. At about 1400, even heavier mortar fire began falling, putting the attack further behind. This prompted Brigadier General Hickey, who had come forward to the command post in the house, to radio Lieutenant Colonel Doan and tell him to come back to discuss the situation. General Rose was now present with Hickey.

Before Doan arrived, a lieutenant told him that there was a makeshift roadway over the dragon's teeth about 300 yards south of Plummer's position. Stone had been filled in and dirt spread between the obstacles, probably either by local farmers to convenience crossing through the dragon's teeth or by German forces to withdraw their equipment. Another officer who had been in the woods confirmed this, telling it directly to Hickey, but he also warned that the roadway looked to be mined. Still, Rose, Hickey, and Doan decided to try to penetrate the *Westwall* in this location.

Doan quickly put a plan in place that called for a Company E platoon of four tanks, commanded by Lt. John R. Hoffman, to investigate the situation and then go through this roadway led by a flail tank. The flail tank—dubbed a "Scorpion"—was a Sherman that was fitted with a whirling chain mechanism and could detonate mines. When the group reached the road, they found that the passage—despite the officer's warning—was not mined. But when the Scorpion mounted the roadway, the loose earth gave way and the tank lurched over to the left. One of the chain flails became tangled in the dragon's teeth, and if the Sherman shifted any farther, the passage would be blocked. The 3rd Armored Division's immediate postwar history described what followed:

> In those long, terrible moments when the flail seemed to spell doom to the entire operation, five men were suddenly very important people. They were Sergeant Sverry "Wiggie" Dahl and his crew from the Scorpion, Gunner Technician Charles Hughes, Technician Milt Jeffery, Private Orrin Madden and Private James L. Ferguson. These men never hesitated. Under intense small arms fire and mortar bursts, all five piled out of their stranded vehicle and proceeded to disentangle the flails from the dragon's teeth.[21]

Despite heavy enemy mortar fire, Lieutenant Hoffman dismounted his tank, hitched it to the flail tank, and tried to pull it out of the roadway. When this failed, another tank hitched up to it and the two finally succeeded in pulling out the endangered Scorpion. "Then they squared off and sailed through," Lieutenant Colonel Doan recalled. "The dragon's teeth had been breached."[22]

But it was not clear sailing for everyone. Company E gunner Clarence Smoyer remembered, "It wasn't easy. There was incoming small-arms fire and there were German tanks lurking around. There was an antitank gun well hidden in a nearby building in the area we were crossing. We never saw that gun until we were right on top of it. The crew must have gotten scared and run off. Then we encountered a pillbox and the platoon surrounded it from three sides and fired away repeatedly."[23]

By 1550 all twenty tanks of the task force were through the gap, probing toward the draw south of Verscheid; they destroyed six enemy armored vehicles in short time. But Lieutenant Colonel Doan suddenly received bad news. First, Lieutenant Henderson's tank destroyers were having trouble getting through the obstacles to support the attack. Second, Doan learned that Captain Plummer had already sustained sixty casualties in his infantry battalion. Plummer had also been badly wounded and command of the infantry had to be turned over to Lt. Col. William R. Orr. Enemy resistance continued to increase, so Doan mounted his tank shortly after 1600 to join the rest of the task force on the other side of the obstacles. He was greeted with "murderous enemy artillery fire."[24]

Doan had just ordered Orr to turn his infantry eastward toward Nutheim, about 2 kilometers from the breach in the dragon's teeth, using the draw to get there. Nutheim afforded command of the roads leading deeper into the Stolberg Corridor; it had to be taken. However, as the tanks of the 2nd Battalion of the 32nd Armored Regiment passed beyond the pillboxes and advanced over a crest covering the draw, they ran into heavier fire from the north and northwest. Other pillboxes, hidden from view but from the direction of Oberforstbach, also delivered 88mm fire. To control his tanks, Doan dismounted his own vehicle to confer with individual tank commanders. Command tanks were being knocked out, including the M4 of Lt. Col. Sydney T. Telford, the 32nd Armored Regiment's 2nd Battalion commander. At one point Doan could see seven of his tanks ablaze. He even witnessed Telford's tank burning, only to learn later that Telford was killed in the melee; Company F's Capt. Abraham S. Kahn died. Company E's Lieutenant Hoffman was wounded, and his radio set was destroyed.

Communications started to break down as the tanks dispersed to get away from the deadly enemy fire. Still, more were hit; at 1715 Doan radioed Hickey for reinforcements, as he had just ten tanks left. Hickey ordered him to return to the command post back in the woods to confer, so a disgusted Doan, not one to leave his forces alone, dismounted his tank and, according to reports, "walked back to the rear."[25]

By this time Hickey had made the decision to use the 1st Division's 1st Battalion of the 26th Infantry Regiment on Task Force Doan's rear left flank. Commanded by Maj. Francis W. Adams from Marion, Arkansas, and assembled in the Aachen-Eynatten woods, these men were ordered to attack at 1830 and take Nutheim from the west. Adams's three rifle companies and his heavy weapons company consisted of just 586 men—36 officers and 550 enlisted—on 13 September. Moreover, there was little time to plan the attack. Capt. Armand R. Levasseur, the battalion S-3, remembered, "From the northeast edge of the woods the line of dragon's teeth could be seen several hundred yards to the front."[26]

> Several of our tanks were burning just short of this barrier. Little could be seen beyond, as the gentle ridge running northeast and southwest masked further observation. A hasty map reconnaissance indicated gentle fields in the open terrain offering little cover from small arms fire. The plan of attack most likely to succeed appeared to be a frontal attack through the barrier for 500 yards, then a change in direction to the southeast. This provided a flanking approach to Nutheim from the rear of the enemy's main defenses. The ridge running northeast and southwest would offer concealment from enemy observation to the north. Little was known of the enemy other than his determined resistance as evidenced earlier in the day.

The attack jumped off on time. Adams first ordered his men to advance in a column of companies across the open field separating the obstacles from the woods. Company A, commanded by North Carolina native Capt. Thomas W. Anderson, led the column approximately 200 yards farther to the north of Lieutenant Henderson's tank destroyer location; they were still held up at the dragon's teeth. The dismounted forward observers of Task Force Doan, as well as each of Adams's company captains, called for armored artillery and mortar support using their SCR 300 radio sets. The 81mm mortars of the battalion's heavy weapons Company D, under the command of Capt. Walter D. Stevens, placed harassing fires on the Germans and were also prepared to fire missions on call.

Immediate trouble waited.[27] As Anderson's men approached the obstacles, heavy machine-gun and sniper fire came in from houses on the left flank of the column while 120mm mortar and artillery shells rained down from the direction of Oberforstbach. The leading platoon broke into a run through the dragon's teeth, temporarily separating Anderson's other two platoons. One remained behind; the other caught up with the lead platoon as they passed the houses from which the Germans were shooting.

Lieutenant Henderson's TDs, fortuitously still held up at the dragon's teeth, now rendered assistance. He remembered:

> There must have been at least 25 to 30 enemy in those buildings. All four TD's laid on the enemy with .50 caliber machineguns, firing about 300 rounds. [I] got permission from the battalion CO to put HE on the houses where the enemy was, and did so. There was no more trouble from the snipers. These snipers, in addition to temporarily holding up the infantry, had been firing on the medics who were trying to evacuate the considerable number of wounded remaining along the dragon's teeth.[28]

As darkness fell, Company B, commanded by Capt. Edgar Simons, plus the platoon that was separated from Company A, moved along the ridge toward Nutheim. Company C, under the command of Capt. Allen B. Ferry, a New Hampshire native commissioned from ROTC in 1941, trailed Simon's men. Both companies had received relatively light casualties when the momentum of the attack carried them through the tank barriers and their covering pillboxes. A barn in the direction of Nutheim burned brightly and served as a guide for them. The sounds of war—tracers and explosions—could be heard as Doan's tanks rolled toward the village to their south. Adams's forces made contact with his armor about 500 yards west of the village an hour later. They suffered surprisingly few casualties during this move, considering the number killed or wounded in Task Force Doan by this time. But they had completely lost contact with Captain Anderson's two Company A platoons.

It turned out that these men had lost their direction during the intense barrage near the dragon's teeth and had proceeded directly north-ward on a roadway beyond the burning barn until they came to a hard-surfaced road near Kroitzheide. Using this road, Captain Anderson turned his men southeastward, thinking this would bring them to the edge of Nutheim.

> Advancing they found telephone wires alongside the road, which were cut. Soon a German soldier on a bicycle came down the road, searching for the break in the wire; he was taken pris-oner. Anderson deduced that the wires must have run to an artillery or mortar position in the town ahead [Schleckheim], so he deployed one squad on either side of the road to work behind the buildings, and one to proceed down the main street itself. The Americans surprised German soldiers eating supper with no posted security. On the left side of the road, they captured an artillery piece and two mortars; and on the right, they captured two 88mm guns.
>
> The prisoners said that they had expected an attack on Nutheim, but had anticipated ample warning of the danger in their location. That statement, and a map check, convinced Captain Anderson that he had overshot his objective, so he decided to go back to the burning barn.
>
> Attempts to destroy the captured ordinance may have alerted surrounding Germans to the American presence in their midst, but in any event Company A came under heavy small arms fire from all sides and withdrew in a running fight, reaching the burning barn at 2100.[29]

Major Adams's command group, which had been with Simon's Company B as they made their way to the barn, picked up Company A radio calls. Captain Levasseur led a small patrol out to guide Anderson's men back to the assembly area. While they safely joined up at around 2300 hours, casualties had mounted for the battalion. The night move had cost Major Adams two officers and eleven enlisted men.

It had also been a long day for Lieutenant Colonel Doan. His task force had renewed its attack at dusk with Lieutenant Colonel Orr's infantry first starting up the draw toward Nutheim to execute the ordered attack frontally. The reinforcement tanks and TDs had delayed their start from the dragon's teeth for an hour while the artillery crews laid fire along their path of advance. But small-arms and antitank fire had been taking a toll on the tanks still trying to work their way toward the village. Lieutenant Hoffman was wounded a second time by an enemy rifleman, this time more seriously as he dismounted his now knocked-out tank. Another had also been hit, and flames from this tank lit up the adjoining countryside as it burned in the dark. By this time Doan was down to only eight of the original twenty tanks he had at the start of the day. After spotting forty enemy infantrymen along the road behind a group of hedgerows, Doan temporarily halted the advance rather than run the risk of further losses from *Panzerfaust* fire in the dark.

The few remaining tanks were dangerously low on ammunition by this time, so the first platoon of reinforcements that Hickey had promised to Doan moved around to protect the right flank of his decimated forces. Armored infantry followed. Then between 2200 and 2300 this combined force reached the western edge of Nutheim, at first mistaking an apple orchard for the predesignated assembly area that was actually in a nearby, more heavily wooded area just to the east. Fortunately no enemy forces occupied the orchard so Doan, still giving instruction and attempting to bolster morale, chose to have the few remaining tanks of his original task force leaguer here.

The night had grown very dark and rainy by this time, but an exhausted Doan still managed to find Major Adams. According to reports he "was relieved to learn that [Adams] had already set up defenses to the west, thus protecting the left flank of his armored force." Others were undoubtedly relieved as well. Another report revealed, "It was Lieutenant Colonel Orr's first day in action. He never expected to see another dawn."[30]

The not-so-relieved LXXXI Corps commander, *Generalleutnant* Schack, took immediate action to reinforce the area. He had erred in his estimation of the Americans' intentions, expecting they would attack directly into Aachen, rather than into the Stolberg Corridor. Task Force Doan's penetration of the *Westwall* 9 kilometers south of the city forced Schack's hand. The 353rd Division moved to Vicht to reinforce the Oberforstbach-Roetgen sector. "It was Corps' intention to improve and reinforce, with all means available, the second line of the Westwall in the southern sector where the main enemy attack was now expected," Schack remembered. "For this reason a regional defense training battalion which was to come from Frankfurt and another regional defense unit were assigned and subordinated to the 353rd Division."[31]

The 353rd Division commander, *Generalleutnant* Mahlman, commented on these changes, later recalling the pathetic state of his division at the time:

> Here ersatz battalions of the 526 Ers Aub Division were employed under the command of an ersatz infantry regimental staff (453), under Oberst Feind. The landesschuetzen ausbildungs (local defense training) battalion was brought up from Frankfurt. When [I] inspected this battalion, [it] was found that a great number of the approximately 800 men were completely unfit for combat, and only partially fit for labor assignments. Twelve men were over 60. [I] ordered thorough medical inspections and sent the least suitable personnel—over 100—back to Frankfurt.
>
> Division in the meantime made plans for the reorganization. After the staffs of Grenadier Regiment 941 and Grenadier Regiment 984 had been taken over by the 275th Division, no combat troops remained to the 353rd Division. Only trains were still available from the infantry, fusiliers and engineers. From Artillery Regiment 353 only a regimental staff [officer] and two battalion staff [members], trains, and a few artillerymen and one howitzer were available.[32]

To add additional forces, the 9th Panzer Division received permission to fall back to the Stolberg-Zweifall sector. During the afternoon, due to the gap that had developed between *Oberst* Mueller's decimated forces and those south of Aachen, half of Assault Brigade 394 reinforced the 9th Panzer Division. Mueller had spent most of his day in Brenig at the command post of Replacement and Instruction Regiment 253 where he mainly worried about this open gap. "The enemy could infiltrate into the wooded area to the northeast of Roetgen, which could not be controlled," Mueller remembered. "The width of the gap and the measure to be taken by the enemy could only be guessed at by the German command."[33]

Mueller also received an engineer replacement unit of about a hundred men from the Cologne area that night. They had already prepared road and bridge demolitions outside of the second line in the *Westwall*, and these men were now moving to Brenig to construct obstacles in the woods nearby. Mueller recalled:

> In the second Westwall line two sectors had been formed. To the right, one under the commander of Panzer Brigade 105, manned by marching elements of the Luftwaffe which had been newly brought up, the fighting qualities of which, however, were very limited . . . another on the left under the commander of Replacement and Instruction Battalion 253.[34]

What Mueller did not know that night was that a Corps order would be handed to him the next morning directing him to give up his division, as "[his] assignment as commander of the 9th Panzer Division was not acceptable to the Higher Command." The successful attacks of American armor and infantry over the past two days undoubtedly influenced this.

Generalleutnant Schwerin's 116th Panzer Division forces had spent the night of 12–13 September conducting security operations ahead of the *Westwall* before pulling out at dawn to assemble in the Würselen area, outside of Aachen. Displacing via Vaals and Vaalsequartier, this first left the division an amazing 10 kilometers behind the positions south of Aachen that it had been entrusted to defend, leaving the thin city forces to contend with the 16th Infantry Regiment's penetration in the area of the Bradenberg Hill at the time.

Lieutenant Colonel Driscoll remembered the fight with elements of Battalion XIX, then under the command of von Osterroht, to keep this real estate that his men got into during the morning:

> [We] first had the hell kicked out of us and casualties were streaming into the command post. Company C was attacked by a company of about 80 men through the thickly-wooded terrain and they first got right into our positions. One BAR man was later found dead beside his gun; his magazine all empty and 12 enemy dead around his position. Two light tanks were moved up and they blasted the Germans with their 37mm gun and machineguns. By noon the attack was repulsed and 12 prisoners were taken.[35]

Meanwhile, General Huebner's 18th Infantry Regiment, under the command of Col. George A. Smith Jr., had attacked the high ground west of the Aachen-Leige road on its way to the Reich border. Two battalions moved abreast that morning: the 1st Battalion, commanded by Lt. Col. Henry G. Learnard, and the 3rd Battalion, commanded by Lt. Col. Elisha O. Peckham. Learnard's men moved through the *Westwall* and took up positions near a forestry fire tower in the Aachen State Forest. From here, a field artillery's forward observer remembered he could see the brushy fields leading right up to the first buildings on the outskirts of Aachen. Peckham's rifle companies took an area directly on the Holland-Belgium-Germany border and set up outposts. Company K, under the command of Capt. William A. Russell, was the first unit to cross into the Reich.[36] By 1115 hours that morning the situation had deteriorated to the point where LXXXI Corps had finally ordered the 116th Panzer Division to clear out the penetration made by General Huebner's infantry in the forest south of the city.

But *Generalleutnant* Schwerin's forces were unable to stop the 16th Infantry's companies when they got there. According to the 116th Panzer Division's historian, "At 2010 hours, Major i.G. Wolf reported to corps, 'Enemy attacked our counterattack. One battalion reinforced by assault guns will be positioned behind the bunkers that are no longer firing. With this the enemy attack through the Aachen city forest widened eastward, up to the Eupen road."[37]

The U.S. forces that the 116th Panzer Division historian described as attacking eastward up the Eupen Road were led by Vermont native Capt. Kimball R. Richmond, the Company I commanding officer in Lt. Col. Charles T. Horner's 16th Infantry Regiment, 3rd Battalion. These men advanced against the 2nd Battalion of Panzer Grenadier Regiment 60. Richmond's riflemen first left Eynatten, riding northward on the decks of several light and medium tanks before deploying in platoon columns to reconnoiter and find suitable routes for their armor to move northeastward. They made first enemy contact with a light machine-gun crew, and when it became apparent there were others in nearby pillboxes, DIVARTY laid down a five-minute artillery barrage.

By this time Richmond's three platoons were deployed abreast, with his light and medium tanks as well as TDs in support. Describing the action, he remembered:

> Yelling and screaming, the company attacked. Everybody in three pillboxes and their surrounding entrenchments surrendered. . . . With their great concentration of firepower from tanks, TDs, antitank guns and small arms, [Company I] had overwhelmed a section of the line, cleaned out the pillboxes that confronted them and had reached unfortified areas in back of the line. They knocked out pillboxes, they rushed a tank with a pole charge and knocked it out, and they suffered some casualties from mortar and artillery fire, but hardly any from the defenders in the line itself. Approaching through woods, it had been possible to come very close to the fortifications before the defenders could place effective fire on the Americans. After getting so close, when all the weapons in the reinforced company opened up, the Germans were unable to withstand the intensity of the assault and the defenses crumbled and fortifications fell.[38]

With a squad on point 300 yards to Captain Richmond's flank, Capt. Robert R. Cuther's Company L advanced to the Eupen road. Here, the Germans counterattacked with small arms and three 88mm guns. Cuther deployed a platoon southward toward another area of dragon's teeth while a second of his platoons pushed up the road, only to be stopped. Two TDs came up to hit the 88mm gun emplacements while a third Company L platoon tried to work its way to the left along the edge of a wooded area to flank the enemy positions. Three German trucks, one antitank gun, and two pillboxes were knocked out. Right after this, Company K, under the command of Capt. Everett L. Booth, also moved eastward up the Eupen Road, following Cuther's men. The attack by Col. Frederick Gibb's 16th Infantry Regiment that day also included Lt. Col. Herbert C. Hicks's 2nd Battalion, which first turned right toward Eynatten before moving northeast along the main road to Brand.

The Maastricht bridgehead was also penetrated on 13 September. M4 Shermans and M5 Stuarts of the 743rd Tank Battalion stood before the city after first light, permitting the 30th Infantry Division's 117th Infantry Regiment, commanded by Col. Walter M. Johnson, to move up to its outskirts during the afternoon. Maastricht fell that night when an attack by two battalions of the 117th from the south flattened the bridgehead while fifteen tanks infiltrated into the city. "The enemy penetrated into Wijk, the eastern part of Maastricht," the 275th Infantry Division's *Generalleutnant* Schmidt noted. "Our forces committed there were fully annihilated, put to rout or taken prisoner. The Meuse bridges had to be blown up in order to cover the rear of the occupational troops in the bridgehead, who withdrew to the north."[39]

Seventh Army's evaluation of the situation during the evening of 13 September was understandably "worded very pessimistically."[40] The 116th Panzer Division's historian now noted, "The only glimmer of hope seemed to be the 12th Infantry Division, due to arrive by train. If the enemy were to attack on the whole [LXXXI] corps front, then the encirclement of Aachen was hardly avoidable."

CHAPTER 3

Penetrating the Schill Line

"Hold the Westwall or go down with the Westwall."

ADOLF HITLER, FÜHRER HEADQUARTERS, 14 SEPTEMBER

After Maastricht fell, a narrow corridor between the Vaart Canal and the Meuse River remained in enemy hands. Since this extended eastward halfway across the XIX Corps' front to the north of Aachen, the area had to be cleared out before Maj. Gen. Ernest N. Harmon's 2nd Armored Division could spearhead the corps' advance beyond the Meuse toward the German border. This mission was given to Lt. Col. William M. Stokes Jr., a peacetime insurance and investment advisor now commanding the North Force of Col. John H. Collier's Combat Command A (CCA).

Task Force Stokes was comprised of the Headquarters Company and the 3rd Battalion of his own 66th Armored Regiment—the oldest armored unit in the Army, the 65th Field Artillery Battalion, a company of the 48th Medical Battalion and two platoons of the 17th Armored Engineer Battalion. To further assist Stokes with his assignment, he was also given the 82nd Reconnaissance Battalion and the 99th Infantry Battalion, the latter a Norwegian-American unit under the command of Maj. Harold D. Hansen. This combined force cleared the critical corridor between 16 and 18 September, causing 918 enemy casualties while suffering just 93 losses.[1]

Major General Hobbs's 30th Infantry Division, nicknamed "Old Hickory" for its Tennessee roots, crossed the German border on 19

September. The main body of Colonel Johnson's 117th Infantry Regiment contacted the *Westwall* across from the small village of Palenberg.[2] Lt. Col. Robert E. Frankland's 1st Battalion, departing earlier that day from a grateful and liberated Dutch citizenry in Heerlen, Holland, reached the vicinity of Scherpenseel, which in contrast looked like a deserted town because just a handful of German citizens remained in their homes. Frankland's Company B, commanded by combat-wise Capt. Robert C. Spiker, was the first unit to cross the Reich border.[3] Here the *Westwall* pillboxes stared out from Scherpenseel along the southeast and northeast sides of the village while more obstacles loomed just across the Wurm River, approximately 1,500 yards to the east.[4] The 1st Battalion of Col. Edwin M. Sutherland's 119th Infantry Regiment consolidated its positions approximately 200 yards east of Groenstraat, Holland. German prisoners captured by American patrols reported that the strongest enemy defenses were in the vicinity of the town of Rimburg and the nearby medieval Rimburg Castle. The main structure was originally built in the twelfth century from scattered Roman-era millstone and had more recently been owned by Gen. Walter von Brauchitsch, chief of the German High Command, until December 1941. The castle, surrounded by a moat, was located between the spring water–fed Wurm River and the Aachen-Geilenkirchen railroad line on the German side of the border. From this commanding location Old Hickory's opposite numbers had perfect observation up and down the Wurm River Valley.[5]

Palenberg and the nearby picturesque village of Ubach were situated on the left wing of the newly arrived 183rd *Volksgrenadier* Division, under the command of *Generalleutnant* Wolfgang Lange. This division, like many other *Volksgrenadier* divisions, was composed of remnants from other staffs at an officer level, including Lange's headquarters staff which came from the former Corps Detachment C.[6] Its activation was completed during the first half of September at the Doellersheim troop training ground in Lower Austria; 51 percent of the division's personnel were from the Lower Danube and Vienna. Many of the enlisted men had been deferred for years; a large percentage were from Alsace-Lorraine, East Upper Silesia, western Prussia, and the Warta district. The 183rd *Volksgrenadier* Division would join elements from the 176th Replacement Training Division, which was comprised of convalescent soldiers of every conceivable age who were equipped with just a few heavy infantry weapons.[7]

In mid-September the 183rd *Volksgrenadier* Division was transported without incident to the Western front where various units took up positions along the 16-kilometer line from Palenberg-Ubach northward to both sides of culturally rich Geilenkirchen. At the same time the 30th Infantry Division arrived on the Reich border, the withdrawing units of *Generalleutnant* Schmidt's 275th Division came under Lange's command here. Elements of the 49th Infantry Division were also added to the *Westwall* south of Rimburg. Lange remembered, "Since the withdrawing divisions were exhausted and our situation and that of the enemy were rather uncertain, the 183rd was obliged to carry out many thorough reconnaissance missions."[8]

General Corlett's XIX Corps plans were to push through the *Westwall* on 20 September, just one day after the 30th Infantry Division arrived on the Reich border, but air support was unavailable because of overcast skies and rainy weather. Since crossing the Meuse River above Liege, a 15-mile zone of operations had evolved across Corlett's front, which extended from the woods west of Geilenkirchen, opposite the 183rd *Volksgrenadier* Division, then southward along the high ground roughly parallel and to the west of the railroad line that ran all the way down into Aachen.[9] This exposure, along with the same shortage of supplies and artillery ammunition that affected Collins's VII Corps, led Corlett to make the decision to postpone striking at the *Westwall* until better weather and elements of the 29th Infantry Division could be brought up from Brest.[10] Corlett not only believed that strength in unit depth was needed to exploit breaching the *Westwall*, but also knew clearer skies were required for air support.

The weather did not cooperate over the next several days, nor did the expected regiment of the 29th Infantry Division arrive from Brest until 29 September. As a result, any assistance to help relieve the pressure brought to bear on the American units south of Aachen when the 12th Infantry Division arrived would now wait until early October.

Oberst Engel's move to reinforce the hard-pressed German units defending the tangled dense woods south of Aachen and in the Stolberg

Corridor had remained undetected because of the same bad weather that plagued the XIX Corps zone. As he remembered:

> The whole division was fortunate enough to reach the operational area. The 1st Battalion of the 27th Infantry Regiment, unloaded at Julich in the morning on 16 September, and the 3rd Battalion, unloaded at Duren, were packed all at once on vehicles.
>
> In the meantime, news reached the division that Kornelimunster, Vicht, Mausbach, Gressenich and the southern part of Stolberg were lost. Enemy reconnaissance forces were said to have entered Atsch. East of Aachen, the Verlautenheide ridge was lost. Quick action was required. There was danger that Aachen could be outflanked from the south and southeast, and the danger of a breakthrough via Julich and Duren to the Rhine.[11]

As it was with the city of Aachen, VII Corps did not intend to attack the mixed-industrial town of Stolberg after breaching the second line of the *Westwall*—the Schill Line. General Rose's plan of operations on 14 September—two days ahead of the 12th Infantry Division's arrival—was for Brigadier General Hickey's CCA to attack toward the west side of Stolberg, and for Colonel Boudinot's CCB to bypass the town to the east. Rose still intended to ignore Stolberg altogether and instead advance directly for the VII Corps objective—Eschweiler—and the eventual linkup with XIX Corps.[12]

Major Mills began his attack at 0900 that morning by first sending Captain Vaughn's Company I through the woods to flank stubborn Schmidthof from the east while Capt. Richard M. Getter's Company H swung down the draw fronting the village and attacked from there. A particularly heavy artillery preparation preceded this attack, helping Getter's men seize the village before noontime with surprisingly little difficulty. Most of the pillboxes that had held up the attack the night before were now empty, and those few that were manned by young boys and old men surrendered.[13]

By 1000 hours it was finally safe to start working on the nearby dragon's teeth. The crater that had held up progress the day before was

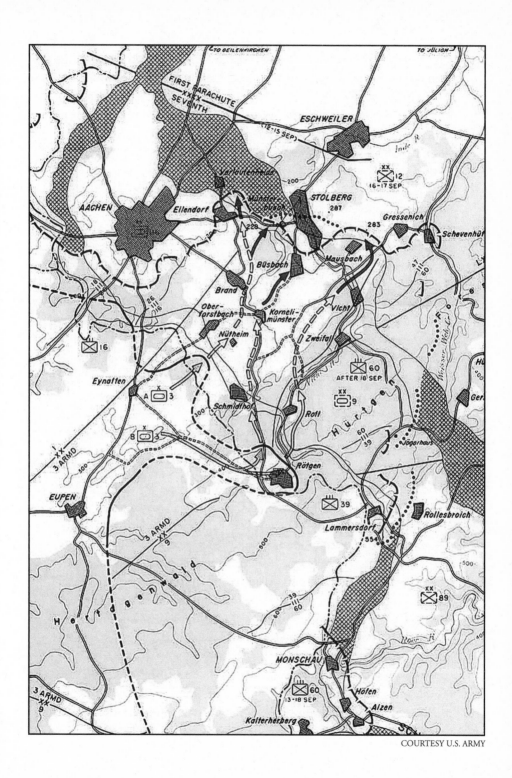

soon being filled; the engineers removed the I-beams and blew the gate crossing the road. But not all went quite as smoothly. They encountered some difficulty filling the crater with dirt since it had already filled with water, so the engineers built a bypass to speed things up. A few of the lead tanks and half-tracks were able to use this makeshift arrangement while the engineers continued working on filling the crater so the full roadway could be opened up.

During this time, Vaughn's Company I was following trails through the woods roughly parallel to the roadway northward. With Schmidthof secured, Vaughn was ordered to reconnoiter the next stream-crossing point, where he found the bridge out just south of Friesenrath, a small historic village 11 kilometers southeast of Aachen. The two platoons with him moved forward to hold the area for the engineers, who soon came up and started their work. At approximately 1500, while the bridge was still under construction, Major Mills sent infantry patrols yet another thousand yards northward to reconnoiter. They had discovered a shallow ford that permitted a platoon of medium tanks from Company F to cross the stream. By this time the main body of the column was slowly uncoiling. Shortly after 1715 hours when, according to reports, "the Corps, Division and Combat Command arrived,"[14] Task Force Mills was well on its way northward, escorted by 105mm field artillery volleys. The armor nevertheless still proceeded cautiously as they started coming abreast of Task Force Lovelady.

Prudence was justified. Minutes later, a large gun was spotted as the column rolled forward; enemy infantry were also seen ducking into a group of nearby hedges. By now it was nearing 1800 and Mills, convinced a considerable number of enemy strongpoints lay farther ahead, ordered his tanks to pull off the road. They soon discovered a blown railroad viaduct close by, its rubble and debris completely blocking the road. This prompted Mills to pull up in his tank to the brow of a hill overlooking Itternberg, and when the tank turned onto a dirt road, two German air corps officers, immaculately dressed, suddenly came out of a farmhouse and surrendered.[15]

Soon after this, a report came in from the commander of Company F indicating that as his tanks had maneuvered into position farther up the roadway they had run into a whole group of dual-purpose 88mm antitank and antiaircraft guns. At about the same time, Captain Vaughn also reported that he had sighted more enemy infantry in and around the hedges off the roadway. After Mills came up and saw this for himself, he ordered Vaughn to deploy his men on both sides of the road and move into the nearby fields to clean them out. In the process, they discovered:

> At least eight of the dual purpose guns, in addition to a towed 105 rife, were located in the hedges and fields of this hill. The weapons were brand new, and about the positions were stacked large quantities of ammunition. The guns were so placed as to cover completely the road on which the column had just moved. If the enemy had so desired he could have wiped out the entire company of tanks and inflicted heavy casualties on the infantry in its halftracks. In short time 75 prisoners were rounded up, and during the next few hours some 25 more were located.[16]

Mills credited the heavy artillery preparation just before he moved into the area with preventing what could have been a disaster for his tanks and infantry. The 67th Groupment, Armored Field Artillery after-action report for 14 September recorded what had actually happened:

> Lieutenant Colonel Berry had established observation well forward in a three-story house and was able to accurately locate CCB's elements on our right and enemy activity in the same area. There was no air cover, but our liaison plane was able to operate unmolested by enemy aircraft or ack-ack. Radio communication had failed frequently due to poor tubes. Used tubes were being reissued for use in our frequency modulated transmitters.[17]

Since it was too late by this time to move farther ahead, Mills made preparations to halt the column for the night. Companies H and I secured the high ground beyond the bridge; Captain Getter reported at 2100 that the area was cleared. Meanwhile, six tanks forded the stream in a shallow spot just to the west of the fallen bridge, and their crews were used to form roadblocks right in Kornelimunster. Infantry patrols even worked ahead in a northeasterly direction toward Breinigerheide, where it was also reported that the area was clear.

Back during the midmorning hours, the advance guard for Task Force Lovelady had been ordered to side-step to the west and strike what at that time was the uncertain enemy strength beyond Schmidthof. Accordingly, Company D's medium tanks, Amborst's infantrymen, and the 1st Platoon of the reconnaissance company started working their way through stone quarries toward Hahn where they found another blown bridge in the middle of the village, but again no enemy resistance.[18]

This reconnaissance platoon then left Hahn, reached the main street through Breinig, and discovered this village was also clear of Germans; they only found three tanks, and Breinig's citizens had rushed to the safety of basements and underground shelters. By 1500 Task Force Lovelady was rolling again and the head of the column caught up with the reconnaissance force. Lovelady then pushed his advance units over the next hill and down into the Vicht valley where they started toward a stream near a gasworks.

Lovelady had planned to cross on the Derichsberg narrow-gauge railway bridge, but it had also been blown up by the Germans. Captain Amborst's Company D infantry was instead sent across the stream to secure the steep wooded slope on the other side, but trouble waited there. Small-arms fire greeted Amborst's men as they started up the slope and into the tree line, so they advanced no more than a hundred yards. After the engineers determined that it would take most of the night to construct a crossing, Lovelady ordered the main elements of the task force to coil back in Breinigerberg. The infantry set up outposts just across the stream, while the engineers waited for more material to be brought up to construct the bridge.[19] Despite the sudden halt, Lovelady had swept over four miles of rolling countryside south of Aachen, and his task force was now close to the Vicht River just to the southwest of Stolberg.

Task Force Doan left Nutheim at about noon with orders to also move four miles northward to the vicinity of Eilendorf, which was midway between Aachen and Stolberg. Except for a brief skirmish at Brand, they encountered little fighting and by 1930 the task force reached Eilendorf where they leaguered for the night.[20]

Major Adams's 1st Battalion of the 26th Infantry Regiment was still consolidating its positions in Nutheim when Doan's tanks rolled out.

During the previous night, engineers had brought up welding torches and cut off the iron rails cemented in the nearby roadblocks. Shortly before dawn, Adams's first vehicles poured through the antitank barriers, bringing up rations and ammunition. Captain Simon's Company B had taken over the key crossroads in the village and these men set up strongpoints to defend against possible counterattacks. Shortly afterward the Germans indeed attacked, and they suffered heavy losses; twenty-two prisoners were also taken.

Captain Anderson's Company A sent reconnaissance patrols southeastward some 1,000 yards into Walheim. It turned out not to be a good way to start the day for these soldiers. As the patrol entered the village, a large volume of small-arms fire forced the men to retire after a brief skirmish. When the full company moved up to subdue this fire, they found an abandoned enemy 88mm gun and three antitank mines on the German's main position; prisoners captured stated that the weapon had been placed with only twelve rounds of ammunition and that they were instructed to destroy the gun if they had no means to take it away. Tanks accompanying the American company made this destruction unnecessary; one armored vehicle rendered the breach block of the 88 useless with a round of its own fiery 75mm armor-piercing ammunition.

During the day most of the heavier fighting fell onto the shoulders of Captain Ferry's Company C, whose mission was to clear the pillboxes bypassed during the previous night. Accounts written shortly after the fighting recalled:

> Most of these pillboxes were not mutually supporting, but those with embrasures permitting crossfire proved hard to attack with hand grenades or anti-tank rockets. Various combinations of fire and movement were [first] tried. One successful method was to position riflemen to shoot into each and every opening to suppress shoulder-fired anti-tank weapons, and to roll up a tank to shoot into the embrasure.[21]

Crossfire from enemy machine guns may have prevented the infantry—even with tank support—from reaching some of the pillbox openings, but Ferry's men now had one significant advantage. This time they were attacking the pillboxes from the German side of the line, and the Americans quickly innovated to capitalize on this. Another report of the day's action noted:

> [Reducing other pillboxes] was accomplished without engineers, but with the aid of a 155 rifle mounted on a M-12 chassis. The infantry discovered the blind spot of the pillboxes, and moved in to assist the approach of the 155. Then a pillbox was fired upon from the rear at a range of 100 yards. The result was to shake the guns loose inside the box and induce the occupants to surrender. Most of the pillboxes were large, holding twelve to fifteen men. Without having broken through [the previous day], allowing approach of the pillboxes from the rear where there were no fields of fire, the assault of the infantry would have been extremely difficult.[22]

Instead, concrete penetrating shells drove about 18 inches into many of the pillboxes. From one box, a white flag was quickly hoisted. In this case, "the concussion was such that guns within the structure were jarred from their position. All 35 prisoners taken had blood running from [their] eyes, ears, nose and mouth."[23]

In the 16th Infantry zone of action on 14 September, Lieutenant Colonel Hicks's 2nd Battalion cut off the Aachen-Brand Road, a main artery into the city. The weather had been miserable all day. Journals indicated that the men "were deployed in mostly thick wooded areas where it was cold, wet and uncomfortable. Jeeps were getting stuck when they got off paved roads. The gasoline situation was becoming quite acute."[24] By this time the expenditure of ammunition also had to be cut.

For Colonel Smith's 18th Infantry Regiment west of Aachen, 14 September was relatively quiet. They encountered very little enemy activity and no artillery fire in Lieutenant Colonel Peckham's 3rd Battalion area. During the night the Company L commander, Ohio native Capt. George D. Folk, sent a patrol out to try to penetrate into Aachen, but these men got into a firefight between Blumenthal and the outskirts of the city and had to withdraw. Two prisoners were taken; the patrol suffered no casualties. Just after midnight, Smith received a request from the

16th Infantry commander, Colonel Gibb, to move Lieutenant Colonel Learnard's 1st Battalion closer to Gibb's own 1st Battalion to support a fire mission the latter unit was putting on as they were establishing defensive positions east of Brand.

On 14 September Brand was in the zone of the 9th Panzer Division. During the day, *Oberst* Mueller reported to the command post of Seventh Army south of Julich. Field Marshall Walter Model, commander in chief of the *Heeresgruppe*, happened to arrive here at about the same time. Instead of being relieved, Mueller was allowed to retain his command of the 9th Panzer Division. He then spent most of the day bringing up a replacement battalion that had arrived in Duren and was comprised of six hundred men before he returned to his division command post, which had been moved to Weisweiler that afternoon.

This new unit had just three machine guns used for training purposes, but twenty other guns with ammunition were later moved up by truck. This gave the battalion roughly six light machine guns for each of its four companies. Mueller remembered what little fighting power this would add to his division:

> No further troops of the 9th Panzer Division were available nor could any be expected owing to the lack of fuel, according to the commander of the 2 Pz Grenadier Regiment, who at the request of the division had reported this on 14 September—with the exception of some tank crews who were awaiting a few newly manufactured tanks at Duren. On the contrary, half of the stationary 88mm anti-tank guns had to be transferred to another sector, which admittedly had not received any guns, but which on the other hand had not been attacked. These had to be withdrawn from the front line prior to the imminent enemy attack in spite of [my] objections. With [the replacement battalion], which naturally had very limited fighting value, the sector commander was to protect the second Westwall line.[25]

By this time, *Oberst* Mueller had received an order issued by *Generalfeldmarschall* von Rundstedt, Supreme Commander West. Just before noon on 14 September, Model had also appeared at LXXXI Corps headquarters. The field marshal had telephoned *General der Infanterie* Hans Krebs in Berlin to describe the situation around Aachen, which he assessed as "dangerous."[26] He then requested more reinforcements, "lest the loss of the city be risked." During an evaluation in the Führer Head-quarters, Hitler said that same morning, "Hold the Westwall or go down with the Westwall." Rundstedt had issued a corresponding order. It is unlikely Mueller was inspired by this directive, and he undoubtedly real-ized its futility.

There was just cause. *Generalleutnant* Schack even remembered this day as one where "the enemy pressure was exerted along the entire south-ern front of LXXXI Corps as far west as Aachen, apparently with the intention of enveloping the city from both sides. The enemy made slight penetrations southwest of Aachen and deeper penetrations south and southeast. The weak forces of the 116th Panzer Division were not able to clear up this breach. In the evening the situation on the left wing was no longer clear."[27]

Colonel Gibb's 16th Infantry Regiment had passed through the deep southern flank of Panzer Grenadier Regiment 60 during the day. The area in Colonel Smith's 18th Infantry Regiment sector had been defended by Panzer Grenadier Regiment 156 and two companies of Infantry Replacement Battalion 453. The 116th Panzer Division histo-rian agreed with Schack about the left wing of the LXXXI Corps zone being troubled, as he stated, "On the evening of 14 September the biggest danger was at the border between the 116th Panzer Division and the 9th Panzer Division, between Eilendorf and Stolberg."[28] However, in defense of his Greyhound Division he offered that the countermeasures of Armored Reconnaissance Battalion 116, which had been pushed back during the day on the Corps' left wing by Huebner's 1st Infantry Divi-sion, "succeeded in at least establishing a new front line during the night along the embankment of the Aachen-Duren railroad." Somber in his assessment of the day's losses, however, he also recorded, "It was only a matter of time before the enemy appeared ahead of the second [*Westwall*] position between Busbach and Verlauntenheide."

Generalleutnant von Schwerin was relieved of his post during the evening of 14 September and command of the 116th Panzer Division was first given to *Oberst* Fritz Voigtsberger before *Oberst* Siegfried von

Waldenburg assumed this duty position on 19 September. For Count Schwerin, this was not the first time the German command had relieved him. While "impressed again and again with his personality"[29] and first welcomed to his reconstituted division with "music and flowers" on 3 May 1944, Schwerin—to his disservice—was often stubbornly loyal to his men. This loyalty had first cost him his command back on 9 August after he tangled with his then-immediate superior, *General der Panzertruppe* Baron von Funck, the commander of XLVII Corps, over a failed attack by Panzer Grenadier Regiment 60 two days earlier.

When he was relieved again on 14 September, Schwerin was ordered to report to Headquarters, Seventh Army. Here, he and *Oberst* von Osterroht were interrogated about the evacuation of the Aachen citizenry. Without mentioning the "famous lines" in the letter he wrote to the U.S. commander, Schwerin explained himself sufficiently for *Generalleutnant* Schack to take responsibility for his actions in his own report to Seventh Army. Still, the letter soon became known to the much-feared Himmler, and an investigation pursuant to court-martial was initiated.

Schwerin could not easily be found to answer any charges; he had literally gone into hiding. Initially protected by his staff, who from the "youngest private to the oldest commander"[30] would not divulge his whereabouts, it took several days and the prodding of *Generalleutnant* Schack himself to finally motivate Schwerin to no longer compromise his men and surrender. This occurred following a face-to-face meeting arranged by Schack on 18 September. Schwerin came out of hiding, and both generals drove off together accompanied by a motorcycle unit of the division, followed by an armored reconnaissance platoon with orders to "stay close to him and report anything unusual and if necessary prevent Count Schwerin from falling into the wrong hands."[31]

Schwerin faced seven interrogation charges the next day, including sabotage of a Führer order, aiding and abetting the enemy, undermining military effectiveness, defeatism, desertion, and unauthorized absence. Eventually all these charges except one—undermining military effectiveness—were dropped. His subsequent trial for this charge before the Reichs War Tribunal was dismissed.[32]

Generalleutnant Schack remembered the morning after Schwerin was relieved from the 116th Panzer Division—15 September—as a time when "major engagements south of Aachen flared up anew."[33] At 0800 Task Force Mills moved out of its bivouac area on the hill southeast of Korne-limunster, and then passed through the village before turning north and advancing unopposed past Busbach. At 1000 the task force reached the high ground south of Bauschenberg and started over a hill that com-manded views of the Vicht River and the picturesque valley to the north-east. At this point heavy artillery fire came in, forcing the head of the column to stay at the crest of the hill while the rest of the task force coiled for three-quarters of a mile behind the lead elements. Jeeps were even abandoned as small-arms fire forced their occupants into ditches. Fortu-nately, causalities were few. Mills remembered, "The enemy artillery con-tinued to fall on the column, but it was apparently unobserved since it hit the crest in front of the task force and continued to pound that area with-out searching in any other position."[34]

Recognizing that his task force would now have to descend a steep, muddy slope off the hill and then cross the river before reaching a more protected wooded area in the hillside on the far side of the valley, Mills determined that the infantry would have to attack. He selected Captain Vaughn's Company I for this assignment; its first objective was to secure the bridge that crossed the river before seizing the commanding ground beyond. While enemy infantry were observed in the hills over the river, Vaughn nevertheless led his men into the valley with Captain Getter's Company H following.

By 1200 Vaughn's leading squads were almost to the bridge, aided in their mission by friendly artillery fire. From observation points in Brock-enberg, the 391st FA batteries laid down three heavy concentrations of M-7 105mm SP howitzer shells. Division artillery joined in the attack, laying rounds on the nose of the hill while VII Corps M-12 155mm SPs also fired other concentrations to the right of the hillside. But when Cap-tain Vaughn's men patrolled up to the bridge at 1230, reports came back indicating it was blown and that it would take considerable work to repair the damage. When Mills reported this to Colonel Boudinot, he was ordered to send reconnaissance out to contact Task Force Lovelady and to eventually follow its columns rather than waiting for engineers to fix the blown bridge.

Lovelady's task force was initially held that morning in Breinigerberg while his engineers determined what to do about the demolished bridge crossing the Vicht River just north of this village. They soon discovered a suitable site near a former streetcar crossing, but rather than rebuilding the blown bridge here, the engineers miraculously completed a nearby 48-foot span with two trestles and a treadway just before 1100 hours. By early afternoon, Lovelady's infantry was pushing up the valley leading toward the smokestacks in the mining settlement of Diepenlinchen. At a crossroad just to the south of this village, these men turned east toward Mausbach where enemy artillery made a direct hit on one tank, slowing up progress. Still, the long, main body of the task force swung in this direction, formed right behind the half-track mounted infantry, rolled by pristine fields of cattle and then into Mausbach shortly after 1500. They found surprisingly little resistance, except for some occasional small-arms and sniper fire.

After the column turned at the main crossroad in the village and moved about a thousand yards northward along the road to Gressenich, an ancient ore mining town, all hell broke loose. Lovelady noted: "The column at this time was almost eight miles long, its tail back across the bridge near Nachitgallschen [*sic*], and it was caught unprepared for the intense enemy attack."[35]

> The enemy was in force on both flanks of the task force. Four or more self-propelled guns were scattered on the ridge on both sides of the column. Heavy fire came from the factory and buildings in Diepenlinchen, while two more self-propelled guns opened up from the rear near Fleuth. The air liaison officer managed to knock out one of these with his tank's fire. Still, [enemy] Panther tanks fired from south of Diepenlinchen. Machine gun and rifle fire of the enemy was also prevalent on both flanks. The fire came as if by a pre-arranged signal, and before the task force could maneuver into cover it had lost seven tanks, one tank destroyer and one ambulance.

These circumstances led Lovelady to direct most of the column back into Mausbach where the task force coiled; some tanks deployed southeastward toward the single crossroad hamlet of Krewinkel where there was more defilade at the edge of the woods. By this time Major Mills's leading elements of tanks and infantry, accompanied by engineers and TDs, had made contact with Task Force Lovelady and bivouacked at Breinigerberg. Lovelady eventually set up his command post in a captured pillbox outside of Mausbach, not knowing at the time that his mission for the next five days would entail overcoming immense difficulties before trying to attack past the cheaply made houses of mining workers now occupied by German infantry in Diepenlinchen. But, Task Force Lovelady had passed the last bunker of the Schill Line to the east of Stolberg; open country lay ahead toward Eschweiler, still the VII Corps objective.

At noontime on 15 September the tanks and infantry of Task Force Doan were before the dragon's teeth on the Schill Line about two kilometers east-southeast of Eilendorf. Doan's patrols had actually started out at first light that morning and moved to the southwest edge of the village to inspect the enemy forces here; several light tanks also got close enough to ten pillboxes to determine that they were manned. They had made contact with a friendly platoon of Captain Merendino's Company B, commanded by Lt. Frank J. Kolb Jr.; his force had just been strengthened with three light tanks, a thinly armored M-10, and a platoon of heavy (.50-caliber) machine guns.

When General Hickey conferred with Doan about whether to attack through the pillboxes, neither officer knew that there was a nearby gap in the dragon's teeth barred only by a few old farm wagons and some loose concrete. This was discovered when Doan sent a platoon of his tanks over to support Lieutenant Kolb's infantry and armor; it was decided to go through the Schill Line here. By early afternoon the tanks had pushed the farm wagons aside and the armored vehicles gingerly started through the gap. Hickey and General Rose were at the edge of a nearby wooded area, near enough to witness the penetration. Not surprisingly, they contacted Doan at 1315 hours and ordered the rest of the task force through.[36]

Meanwhile, the advance guard went northeast beyond the dragon's teeth for about 300 yards and then made their way to a road junction at hillier Am Geisberg. Here the tanks were held up by an enemy armored vehicle and self-propelled gun fire that came in frontally from the direction of the Wurseler Wald, directly across the road junction. This fire was also laid on eight of Doan's tanks and a platoon of armored infantry that were farther back and still trying to make their way through the gap. Concentrated fire directed by observers of the 116th Panzer Division's

3rd Battalion of their Artillery Regiment added to the mayhem.[37] Two American tanks were knocked out when they got inside the dragon's teeth, and two others were hit by antitank fire from a nearby pillbox. Shortly after this a squad of the infantry that had gone through the gap reported sighting three enemy tanks approaching from up the road. German antitank fire soon knocked out two more American tanks.

This prompted Doan to confer with General Hickey, who still insisted that they press forward without interruption. By this time Lieutenant Kolb's Company B platoon had cleaned out several pillboxes, capturing thirty-one prisoners. The other platoons then worked their way up to the crossroad at Am Geisberg, where they swung east, avoiding some ferocious mortar and artillery fire. The company eventually formed a goose-egg position on the road and held there. At 1800 the enemy counterattacked from the Wurseler Wald with one tank and two half-tracks of infantry. At this time Company C, under the command of Captain Briggs, was working its way to a position just to the northwest of the crossroads and to the right of Company B. For a short period the fighting was at close quarters, but the enemy forces eventually withdrew.[38]

Driscoll's Company A followed Briggs's Company C after an artillery barrage was laid down and eventually breached the Schill Line to a depth of approximately 3,000 yards. During this advance, the accompanying platoon of M-4 tanks from the 745th Tank Battalion fired into several pillbox embrasures from about 800 yards, forcing many of the boxes' occupants out into the open and to their deaths. Company A then continued with its penetration, now with the mission of occupying a hillside directly overlooking the outskirts of Stolberg.[39]

This move initially turned out to be problematic. Semi-hilly and heavily brushed terrain slowed the approach. When the company did arrive—aided by using previously captured German tactical maps—it was discovered that the area was dotted with more pillboxes and open emplacements that were manned by enemy troops with machine guns, antitank guns, 120mm mortars, and small arms. Noting that "the enemy was well dug in, in the cellars of surrounding houses, and in the factories in the outlying district of Stolberg with tanks placing fire on our positions,"[40] Driscoll's Company A halted. In this salient position their right flank was open to a large valley and their left flank was exposed to another deep draw covered with slag piles and rubble from earlier Allied bombings.

More of Task Force Doan's tanks had penetrated the dragon's teeth by this time. Three tanks had advanced with the forward elements of Orr's infantry, and another two followed to the rear. Keeping their assault guns and mortars behind the barriers to cover the advance, the armored infantry cleaned out the enemy remaining in the road junction at Am Geisberg and then moved up the roadway. The German antitank guns had also withdrawn, so the advance proceeded another mile without resistance until Orr's three infantry companies reached a road junction near Hamm. Here some fire was still coming into their left flank from the Wurseler Wald, as well as from a factory area to their right.

With darkness now approaching and a major part of his task force still a mile or so to the rear on the other side of the dragon's teeth, Lieutenant Colonel Doan ordered Orr's infantry to button up for the night. A horseshoe-shaped defense was set up across the road junction, facing the enemy. Doan ordered the lead company to fan out on either side of the road, and then he brought up two tanks that he positioned at the rear of his command post; another two emplaced on the edge of the forest. Continued patrol activity seemed to indicate that the Germans had formed in strength again in the Wurseler Wald, but they later discovered that this force was no larger than a company of infantry. After darkness fell Doan moved up more assault guns, mortars, and some tank destroyers, to include a 57mm antitank gun that he emplaced on his left flank in the woods for added protection. Patrolling continued into the night toward Hamm and the high ground west of Schneidmuhle, with a platoon of the 83rd Reconnaissance Battalion also moving out at 2100 hours with the mission of making contact with the 16th Infantry units on the right.

That morning had started with Colonel Gibb's I&R platoon reconnoitering the area northwest of Brand in their five jeeps. They encountered small-arms fire before making contact with Captain Ferry's Company C of the 26th Infantry, but these men were still able to take up a defensive position at a crossroads from which this intermittent fire was coming. Barracks in the area were soon found to be empty, so Hicks's 2nd Battalion was given the mission to take historic Eilendorf, first ravaged back in the Thirty Years' War in the 1600s and ruthlessly pillaged again by Louis XIV later in that century. Now it was the Americans' turn; the 16th Infantry was to seize the high ground here and protect

General Hickey's left flank during his armor's continued drive toward Eschweiler. Hicks assigned Capt. Joseph T. Dawson's Company G with leading the day's advance, assisted by three medium tanks, as well as three light tanks and two TDs. Eilendorf was just two miles from Brand, but Dawson had to take an indirect route that ran for more than three twisting miles, his right flank protected by Doan's then-advancing tanks and infantry. Hicks held the rest of his 2nd Battalion in place, giving his men time to dry out while others worked on some hard-to-start tanks worn down from running continuously the previous day.

Dawson, Texas-bred and the son of a Baptist preacher, started out cautiously when the attack jumped off. Gas had to be hand-carried to his attached tanks and TDs, so they were delayed but expected to catch up. The terrain Company G eventually crossed was flat and open, with little protection, so when the tanks did arrive two of Dawson's platoons mounted their decks and rode for about two miles of the way. As they got closer to Eilendorf, however, machine-gun fire came in from the high ground east of town. This prompted Dawson to order his men to dismount, whereupon they sprinted across 1,500 yards of still-open terrain to a point just south of a railroad line where they took up defensive positions. Fortunately, the company took no casualties during this move.

Bringing the rest of the 2nd Battalion up proved to be problematic for its executive officer, Maj. Edward F. Wozenski, a big man from Terryville, Connecticut. Enemy artillery forward observers had spotted the move, and some shells eventually fell on Company F. By this time Dawson's men had occupied the outer edges of Eilendorf, and after some confusion at a road junction where signs were hidden from view, Wozenski was nevertheless able to get the rest of the battalion closer to the railroad line behind Company G. The location did not inspire confidence. Some men noticed that "the enemy on the forward slope across the tracks could look right down our throats. Why they did not fire is an unsolved mystery."[41] But a later report noted, "The Germans were taken so completely by surprise that they hastily improvised white flags of surrender ranging from babies' diapers and adult's underwear to pieces of sheets."

At 2000 hours Dawson was given a new mission, this time to gain the ground atop the railroad tunnel leading out of Eilendorf and to capture a commanding ridge that would cut off the incoming roads from Verlauntenheide. The order Dawson had been given from Lieutenant

Colonel Hicks was verbal, and when he called his platoon leaders to his command post, he quickly provided background and his own orders.

> The enemy strength and capabilities are unknown, as we do not know what German units are to our front. We do know that there are enemy troops out there in those pillboxes because we saw them running around earlier in the day. We also know that they have some artillery and mortars to back them up, as they lobbed a few in on us.
>
> The friendly situation is a bit clearer. Several thousand yards on our right at the present time is the 1st Battalion, in position in the vicinity of Stolberg. On our right are also elements of the 3rd Armored Division. Company F is in physical contact with the left flank of our 3rd Platoon. When we jump off in the attack we also will have Company E on our right. The mission of the company is to take and hold the high ground northeast of here, clean out the pillboxes in our zone of action, and make contact with the friendly units on our flank.
>
> This is the way we will do it. The 3rd Platoon, with a section of light machineguns and one mortar squad attached, will move from their present positions as soon as possible and proceed up the main road leading northeast from Eilendorf. When you come to the crossroad at the crest of the hill, stop, send out security, and dig in. You will then try to maintain contact with the enemy.
>
> The 1st Platoon will attack along the railroad going east out of town and upon reaching the tunnel will turn left and attack north along the ridge, cleaning out the woods and pillboxes. The objective is to clean the ridge, maintain contact with Company E on the right and with the 3rd Platoon on the left. The 2nd Platoon will move by the most direct route to the vicinity of Knapp and establish contact with the 3rd Platoon on the left and the 1st Platoon on the right, and prepare to defend to the northeast. The remaining mortars will stay in their present positions by the company command post, and will move up when called for. The command post will remain here, and as soon as you are dug in we will run a telephone line to you.
>
> Are there any questions? If not, go back to your platoons and give them the dope I just gave to you.[42]

While Dawson did not know who the defenders in his zone of attack were, it was quite likely either elements of the Armored Reconnaissance Battalion of the 116th Panzer Division or the 9th Panzer Division. It was Armored Reconnaissance Battalion units whose defensive line was pushed back beyond the railroad line during the day when Company G first attacked. The railroad tunnel area was on the border shared with the 9th Panzer Division, their front line defined by the 116th Panzer Division historian as "east and south in an arc to the Ronheide railroad station, then south of Steinebruck—south of Burtscheid to the Aachen-Easchweilwer railroad line. After that, it was almost in line with this up to the tunnel entrance northeast of Eilendorf, and after that it ran to the 9th Panzer Division's sector of the Westwall, except for the deep breach at Mausbach and the second one at the right wing." *Oberst* Voigtsberger also arrayed Machine Gun Battalion 34 near Eilendorf on 15 September, behind Combat Group Berger and elements of Militia Training Battalion II/6.[43]

It was dark by the time Dawson's platoon leaders got back to their positions. Reconnaissance was not necessary; they knew from their earlier observations that day what type of terrain confronted them. The ground was rugged, with large boulders along with a few quarries and some pits. Shrubbery afforded limited protection toward the ridge, situated out of sight in the darkness to the northeast on the top of a long, steep hill.

The line of departure for Dawson's 3rd Platoon was the railroad track near the tunnel. As soon as these men were oriented, they jumped off with two squads forward and one in the rear. The scouts on point were the first to draw fire and the platoon leader, knowing it was too dark to fire back effectively, ordered his men to keep moving. This action cost the platoon three men wounded, but two of their opposite number were killed and four were captured.

As soon as Dawson got word that this platoon was on its first objective, he alerted his 1st Platoon. These men jumped off at 2300 hours, worked their way through a heavily wooded area, and reached their objective after taking some incoming fire from their right flank. The trails in the thick stand of trees proved to be too treacherous to traverse in order to contact Company E per the plan, however. Dawson temporarily suspended the drive, and the men dug in.

At first light on what would be a clear and warm 16 September, Captain Dawson ordered his 2nd Platoon to move out; by 0700 these men were digging into defensive positions between the other two platoons.

Two columns of Germans about a thousand yards away were soon seen
coming in their direction, in close formation. The platoon leader quickly
sensed that these enemy soldiers were simply shuffling into their defensive
positions after a warm breakfast, unaware that Company G now held the
important ridge. He ordered his men to hold their fire until the Germans
got closer. "On the command of 'Fire,'" a later report revealed, "the whole
platoon opened up, caught the Germans with their guard down, and
inflicted many casualties."[44] In daylight now, Dawson could see the tactical importance of the ridge he and his men had just taken. The ridgeline
terrain literally controlled the approaches to Aachen.

The 116th Panzer Division was all too aware of Company G's success, noting in the early morning hours of 16 September, "Strike troop
platoons infiltrated through the remaining near bunkers south of Verlautenheide. Militia and scattered troops deployed in the Westwall are no
longer combat effective. Division Reconnaissance Platoon deployed for
reconnaissance and security toward Verlautenheide."[45]

Dawson also sent a platoon up to Verlautenheide for his own reconnaissance later in the day, but as a friendly tank pulled up to the crest of
the hill overlooking the town and fired six rounds into its western edges,
return fire delivered by *Oberleutnant* Phidias Triantaphylides's 2nd Company of Panzer Grenadier Regiment 156 came in. Since this fire came
dangerously close, the American platoon backed off the hill. Casualties
were starting to mount; this time the platoon suffered two killed and
nine wounded and two others were unaccounted for. To the remaining
men the situation became clearer and very dangerous. They could now
see hundreds of enemy soldiers marching southeast in columns of twos as
far back as their widened eyes allowed.

Anticipating that his 12th Infantry Division's commitment at the
Aachen front could not be achieved with the immediate close employment of its full fighting strength, *Oberst* Engel had decided to have the
first transports arrive and unload in Julich and Duren on the morning of
16 September. This was the 27th Infantry Regiment. Engel ordered "combat transports" for the two battalions he chose to first commit, meaning
each was equipped with heavy weapons (infantry howitzers and antitank
guns) with artillery following as the next transport. As he remembered,

"Thus, at least the commitment of regiments and battalions was sure of not taking place without heavy arms."[46]

Under orders that morning to push back enemy forces wherever they were met, to close the gap between Stolberg and Zweifall, to recapture the *Westwall*, and to reoccupy the pillboxes in these areas, Engel used all of the available transportation vehicles he could muster in order to reach the front. In addition to LXXXI Corps transports, mail cars, workman's buses, and civilian trucks were pressed into service. After a short reconnaissance Engel committed the 1st Battalion of the 27th Infantry Regiment on the road from Julich to Broichweiden to attack toward Verlauntenheide. As he noted, "The plateau of Verlauntenheide was considered to be the key position for the Aachen-Stolberg front arc. This dominating hill had to be in our hands."[47]

This is the very plateau from which Captain Dawson's Company G had looked into Verlautenheide that morning. The vast marching columns of twos represented but one of the enemy forces he would face with other 16th Infantry Regiment 2nd Battalion companies during the encirclement of Aachen. The plateau would become famously known as "Dawson's Ridge" before the fighting ended five weeks later.

With the attack of Boudinot's CCB through Mausbach toward Gressenich and the thrust of Hickey's CCA toward Munsterbusch meeting increased enemy resistance, General Rose decided to commit another task force on the morning of 16 September. Task Force Hogan, commanded by Texan Lt. Col. Samuel M. Hogan, was ordered at 0900 to attack northward and to clear the town of Busbach, located on a knoll of limestone that had been originally mined by ancient Romans. The town was about 2,000 meters from Dorff, and was located on the edge of the Schill Line fortifications. Major Adams's 1st Battalion of the 26th Infantry Regiment had linked up with Task Force Hogan late on 15 September, and would now lead this mission.

Company G of the 83rd Reconnaissance Battalion had also made contact with the Germans at a crossroads just south of Busbach early the same morning. This reconnaissance force was holding the slopes on the southwest side of town. Captain Simons's Company B was given the assignment to go into Busbach itself and clear out any enemy forces holding up in the shadows of the spire marking the St. Hubertus church. Captain Anderson's Company A, supported by two platoons of tanks, was also ordered to clear nearby Brockenberg and to take the high ground in the vicinity of Bauschenberg, a small town with brass producing factories; this move would protect Simon's right flank. These towns were defended by elements of the 9th Panzer Division, reported at the time by its commander to be down to just its reconnaissance platoon, some engineers, and three tanks, altogether perhaps 150 men in the area.[48]

When Captain Simons's men reached the outskirts of Busbach around noon they immediately received plunging machine-gun fire from the St. Hubertus church steeple. In response, they brought forward one of the 155mm SP guns that had proven so effective in reducing the pillboxes back in Nutheim; this time they fired it directly upward, promptly killing the German crew in the spire and neutralizing their gun. Company B then made good progress through the limited resistance left until they reached a roadblock just north of town; small-arms fire from a pillbox slowed their advance. Antitank and machine-gun fire also increased, so the men were simply unable to move any farther. A 155mm SP was again pressed into service to fire at close range; it not only blew up the box, but also broke every window in Busbach with its concussions. Enemy resistance in town ceased later in the day when Captain Ferry's Company C men came forward to mop up.

At about 1500 hours Major Adams ordered Captain Anderson to take up positions on the road just to the south of the dragon's teeth. The movement actually began at dusk with Anderson personally leading, but the uneven terrain combined with growing darkness introduced confusion. Instead of reaching the dragon's teeth, the men discovered that they had stumbled right into the edge of Stolberg; they halted at a railroad overpass when an enemy artillery barrage was laid down. Anderson, meanwhile, joined a patrol to continue reconnoitering even closer to town. Antitank and artillery fire intensified toward midnight; it became even more evident that the Germans were determined to keep the Americans out of Stolberg, so Major Adams radioed Anderson and told him to cancel his unexpected visit and come back.[49]

Anderson's reserve platoon had broken the deadlock by crossing a stream much earlier that night and then moving through 250 yards of open terrain, finally reaching the pillbox cluster near Brockenberg despite being exposed to both horrific grazing and enfiladed fire. Fourteen prisoners were taken from two pillboxes; others were abandoned. Two thousand civilians seeking refuge from the fighting in the area were discovered in a nearby gravel pit.[50]

Task Force Doan spent the rest of 16 September holding in the positions they had taken at Am Geisberg. Every time an advance was attempted, German antitank and gun fire held up movement. Lieutenant Colonel Orr's infantry also found the day's going to be difficult. After waiting for the 16th Infantry Regiment to move up and protect his right flank, Orr moved out at 1600 to take another hill overlooking Stolberg near Schneidmuhle.[51] His Company A, supported by two tanks, advanced just 100 yards before they ran into fire so intense that the men were immediately pinned down. At 1830, Orr's companies returned to their original line of departure and set up an all-around defense for the night. A captured prisoner confessed that more German forces were now engaged in the woods north of his position. These forces had also knocked out two of the three tanks that had accompanied Orr's attack; the third received a round that damaged its track.[52]

The objective on 16 September had been Schneidmuhle, a settlement outside of Stolberg dotted with factories and chemical plants. Three battalions of infantry were to widen the bridgehead within the Schill Line and secure the immediate area. This action was also intended to uncover enemy antitank guns and make it possible for more American tanks to move through the gap opened by Task Force Doan. In the middle of the afternoon, a great deal of vehicular movement was seen in the factory area. Lt. Leonard F. Banowetz, a forward observer for the attached field artillery, answered by calling for a "serenade" with five rounds by everything in the Corps—a time on target arrangement. As Banowetz remembered, "When this barrage was fired, the vehicular movement stopped."

A journalist explained its effect for his paper's readers in Miami:

The smoke was rising everywhere in the heavy wet air of this chill and rainy autumn afternoon. Overhead shells from our 155millimeter guns are whistling every minute or so with a high piercing wail and the hard flat blasts of mortars endlessly fills the air. Shells are falling in an orderly pattern, first on the fringe of woods at the western edge of town, and then across it to the east.

Before us there is a line of little concrete cottages and these homey, pretty little places are catching it from our guns. You might expect vines around the doors. Then you see that their "windows" are machinegun apertures. These are pillboxes with little gabled roofs.

The Germans are struggling like demented men. Three times this morning they counterattacked in a shoulder-to-shoulder line, screaming hoarsely as they came forward and falling in unbroken rows before our tank guns. This is what they used to call a "psychological attack" in Russia. Here it is sheer, utter suicide.[53]

Despite the efforts of the artillery units, 16 September was a difficult day for the infantry overall. On the other side of Stolberg, Major Mills had gone up to Lieutenant Colonel Lovelady's command post in the captured pillbox south of Burghulz that morning. Here, a meeting took place to plan an attack toward Weissenberg with Col. Edgar A. Gans, commander of both of their task forces' infantry. A record of this meeting revealed:

> Colonel Gans was trying to line up his force. He should have had two battalions, less one company, but he could only find four companies. Mills told him of the depleted Company F which he had held in his area and not sent up the night before because Lovelady had not seemed to need them. Mills then ordered the Company F commander to alert his men, and ordered him to see Colonel Gans. Gans should have had F, H and I Companies of the 36th Armored Infantry (formerly with Mills), and D and E Companies (formerly with Lovelady). At 0100 Colonel Gans had been called back to headquarters to receive his orders.[54]

The subsequent attack jumped off at 0832 hours and by 0920 Major Dunn's 3rd Battalion reported that his companies had reached the first phase line just short of a field before a wooded area west of Weissenberg.

Gans ordered Dunn to halt here and wait for Maj. A. L. Robinette's 2nd Battalion, which was running into difficulties at the time because of an enemy self-propelled gun to his front. When Robinette reported that his battalion was still pinned down at 1000 hours, Gans ordered Dunn to cross the field into the woods, despite Dunn's warning that "such an action would be excessively dangerous, but that he would try it."[55] Within minutes, another 88mm self-propelled gun in the woods opened, holding this force down with direct fire.

At 1052, Captain Amborst's Company D reported that the enemy was maneuvering to its right flank, but that Captain Emerson's Company E was working its way around these forces toward a large factory closer to Diepenlinchen. Later, the company reported that its four supporting tanks could not be used for this attack because of the terrain and enemy fire. Captain Getter's Company H reported two hours later that his 3rd Platoon, commanded by Lt. M. E. Hulstedt, was across the field in a corner of the Weissenberg woods, where they were expected to be, but the enemy counterattacked and these men were forced to withdraw. "The company had been called back at each phase line as we advanced," remembered the company Executive Officer, Lt. H. M. Bundrick. "The whole area was subjected to enemy shelling. The men were told to dig in every time we stopped."[56] At this point Lieutenant Colonel Lovelady suggested to Gans that the supporting tanks move up to help Amborst's Company D and Emerson's Company E, which by this time had actually worked its way much closer to Diepenlinchen.

Colonel Gans responded by calling for help from the artillery, and after rounds were laid in, Emerson's men were ordered to continue to the right of the factory area. Captain Amborst's Company D had been forced back into the village, where his men were holding out in eight houses with German outposts no farther than 50 yards away. Shortly afterward, a very long day for the infantry ended when the situation stabilized for the night.

Task Force Lovelady fared no better that day. His tanks started moving northeastward toward Diepenlinchen, but at 1600 hours the task force was hit heavily by German tanks, artillery, antitank guns, mortars, and small-arms fire. Forced back about a mile, the task force leaguered for the night in defensive positions on the high ground back at Burgholz. Lieutenant Silva, the leader of the 3rd Platoon of Company B, 703rd TD Battalion attached to Task Force Lovelady that day, remembered:

> At 1460 the TD section was taken into Mausbach where [we] were having a hard fight. Several of our medium tanks had been knocked out, and the TD's were ordered to set up road blocks to protect our position. One was set up at a crossroad, and another near the church in the center of town. There was considerable small arms fire, but the main difficulty was the deadly shell fire coming from the direction of Diepenlinchen. I climbed the church spire trying to spot this fire, but I could not definitely locate it.
>
> Between 1630 and 1700, amid heavy tank and infantry fighting on the northeastern outskirts of town, my tank destroyers were hit, and both the gunner and the assistant gunner in one of them were killed—even though the vehicle did not burn. An 88mm enemy tank shell instead knocked it out. By this time six of the task force's medium tanks had also been knocked out.[57]

Silva was ordered to hold his destroyers in town until Task Force Lovelady's vehicles had cleared out. This he did, and what remained of his TD platoon was indeed the last to leave.

The arrival through Atsch of the 3rd Battalion of *Oberst* Engel's 27th Infantry Regiment of the 12th Infantry Division was the principal cause for the setbacks experienced by American forces on 16 September. By attacking via Atsch, these forces had reached the Schill Line on both sides of Munsterbusch before moving to the southern part of Stolberg where they linked up with the depleted elements of the 9th Panzer Division. Although deployed later in the day, three battalions of 12th Infantry Division artillery were nevertheless emplaced on a line from Verlautenheide to Stolberg. Reflecting on this day, Engel later remembered its significance for his division:

> The first day of battle for the division on the Western Front had this result: The line Verlautenheide-Munsterbusch-Stolberg was

firmly in the hands of the division, of the 27th Infantry Regiment. In the right sector, the gap could be considered closed. Contact was made with the right neighbor, the 116th Panzer Division, between Eilendorf and Verlautenheide, whereby the threat of an envelopment of Aachen was removed. On this day, [I] realized that the Americans had not noticed the bringing up of a fresh division. Although the targets of the day's attacks were not reached, the first day of battle could be considered a success.

In the meantime, the bulk of the division had been unloaded without any interference in the area of Julich-Duren-Elsdorf. The foggy, overcast weather continued; the absence of any air activity here made the accelerated conveyance of the artillery of the 48th and 89th Grenadier Regiments to the menaced front possible.[58]

With Engel's division now engaged, Seventh Army made several adjustments during the day. His 12th Infantry Division was incorporated into and subordinated to LXXXI Corps. The 353rd Infantry Division was also ordered detached to LXXIV Corps. From Army, Schack received orders to pull out the 116th Panzer Division after the 12th Infantry Division went into action, and to keep its remaining strength in Corps reserve in the vicinity of Eschweiler. These moves were delayed for two reasons. First, the 9th Panzer Division was pulled out and *Oberst* Mueller, despite leading a rigorous defense that day, was finally relieved of his command. "I was transferred to the Fuehrer [*sic*] Reserve," remembered Mueller, "because I had not fulfilled expectations to stop the enemy at the Westwall in spite of all [our] inadequacies, and because of the fact I had predicted [this] daily several times in my blunt reports of the situation."[59] When what was left of Mahlmann's 353rd Division was finally detached to LXXIV Corps on 18 September, he evinced similar bitterness. "Thus an exhausted, improvised unit, insufficiently fed, armed and equipped, awaited the attack of a well-fed American Army, far superior as regards men and materiel."[60]

At 2000 hours on 16 September, LXXXI Corps issued a new set of orders for the continuing defense of the Schill Line. Counting on the Americans to remain on the offensive by massing their forces the next day, *Oberst* Engel's 12th Infantry Division was tasked with defending the positions it had gained and reclaiming the Schill Line in its zone. The weakened 116th Panzer Division, which its historian reported had "a mobility factor of 40 percent, and its battle value the incomprehensibly high level of 'II,'"[61] was to now hold its present main battle line on the right wing of the 12th Infantry Division, and link up with the 1st Battalion of the 27th Regiment deployed near Verlautenheide. Here a mobile reserve was to be established to counterattack the expected American offensive on 17 September.

Summarizing the overall effect of the German accomplishments made on 16 September with the arrival of the 12th Infantry Division and cautiously optimistic about his new orders that night, LXXXI Corps' Schack noted, "The employment of these fresh troops greatly lifted the morale of the population, the battle-weary units, and closed a dangerous gap in the southern Corps' sector."[62]

One order of the day had not been achieved. The Germans had failed to reclaim the Schill Line. Major General Collins's VII Corps also adjusted its plans. "Eschweiler had been the objective for several days," Colonel Boudinot recalled at the time. "On 16 September this dropped from view, and [we] were ordered to clean up the southeast side of Stolberg. The town could now not be bypassed as originally planned because it was too strongly held by the enemy."[63]

CHAPTER 4

Stalemate at Stolberg

"The opposition in the Stolberg area disrupted all of the plans."

BRIGADIER GENERAL HICKEY
COMMANDING, CCA

J ust after midnight on 17 September an enemy patrol of nine men rushed Captain Dawson's Company G position on the ridgeline outside of Verlautenheide. Quick reaction by his men resulted in seven killed before the rest escaped and the night quieted down. Then just after 0530 vicious mortar and artillery fire began anew, covering both Dawson's forces and Company E, whose men were across a gap about 100 yards away in a heavily wooded area. "It was estimated that 4,000 mortars and another 4,000 artillery shells landed in the companies' areas," reports stated at the time. "The barrage lasted until about 0600 hours."[1]

Immediately after this tremendous enemy volley lifted, two companies of about 150 men each from the 1st Battalion of the 27th Infantry Regiment launched a frontal attack with their bayonets fixed. Company G was very vulnerable, as both Dawson's immediate left front and his deeper left flank were open at that moment. But luck was with his men. The heaviest attacks first came against the 1st Platoon, located on the company's right flank, and then into the center platoon before the 3rd Platoon caught the overflow. During the ensuing fight, one 1st Platoon squad ran completely out of ammunition and had to withdraw. Before 1st Infantry Division artillery, 4.2-inch chemical mortars, as well as support from Captain Irvine's heavy weapons company helped in stopping the attack, the Germans had closed to within the length of a football field.

71

Strategically located artillery observation points had given the Germans a significant advantage during this early morning attack. "Their fire was made particularly accurate by excellent observation," an account of the action noted. "From their positions on one hill, which became famous as Crucifix Hill—because of a crucifix which surmounted it—they looked down on the regiment. They observed every move and they poured constant heavy fire on the men below. To move was to invite fire."[2]

A third assault came at about noon, in approximately the same strength as the first attack, following another scathing artillery strike. "They were well disciplined troops and kept coming despite their losses," remembered Captain Dawson. "They got almost as close as they had in the morning and were stopped only after they became completely disorganized. Artillery and mortar fire, plus small arms fire broke up the attack at about 1400."[3] After this, some of the enemy forces remained in foxholes on Dawson's right flank before one of his squads attacked in short rushes, repeatedly throwing hand grenades into the enemy positions; the few remaining Germans in these foxholes were all killed.

Then, at 1800 yet another attack was made on Company G in the same strength and in the same manner as the first two. The attack developed from the small peacetime working suburb of Haaren after yet another smashing artillery volley was called down from Crucifix Hill, known to the Germans as the Haarener Steinkreuz. This time twelve enemy combatants actually reached Dawson's lines before being killed. "Others could be heard yelling to attack, but were kept from doing so by the intense rifle and machinegun fire of the company and from the left flank of Company E," the after-action report noted. "One prisoner of war said they had never run up against such devastating small arms fire."[4] During this action Dawson's 1st Platoon expended an average of six bandoleers of M-1 ammunition per man. At about 2000 hours the enemy forces finally retired after evacuating their wounded and dead, some of whom were officers. The next morning when Lieutenant Colonel Hicks counted the casualties he traded in stopping the day-long attack, two of Dawson's enlisted men had been killed and three Company G officers and fourteen additional enlisted men had been seriously wounded, while fourteen others in Company E had suffered lighter wounds.

At 0515 hours on this same morning of 17 September, other elements of the 27th Infantry Regiment began to fire on Lieutenant

Colonel Orr's 1st Battalion of the 36th Armored Infantry near the road junction at Am Geisberg. The intensity of this fire increased until 0530 and then it became clear that the full attack was imminent. Orr immediately called for defensive fire from his supporting artillery, and three concentrations were laid into the wooded area in which the German forces were assembled. It looked grim. The lines between Orr's Company B and the enemy he was facing were little more than 50 yards apart.

"They came in close waves," Orr recalled. "Even the more hardened of [our] machine gunners became literally sick at the way they had to mow the line of men down."[5] By 0600 the attack was over, but not before a section of tanks had swung around into the gap between the two companies and stopped the enemy advance just short of Orr's command post. When patrols pushed into the woods to determine what remained of the attacking German forces, reports came back indicating that tree bursts from the artillery concentrations had killed a large number of them.

Orr had been ordered the previous night to continue his advance in the direction of Hamm, a center of rail marshalling yards, so his forces finally set out to accomplish this at 0700. But within two hours, they discovered a large number of German infantry troops on Company A's right flank. Small-arms and machine-gun fire pinned these men down; two tanks were also hit. It appeared the Germans were grouping up for another attack. "It was decided that they [Orr's infantry] would jump off again at 1200 following a 15 minute preparation by our artillery," the 67th Groupment Armored Field Artillery after-action report noted. "On very short notice we were able to obtain a 240mm battalion, an 8-inch battalion, an M12 battalion and five 105mm battalions for this preparation. The preparation began with a TOT at 1205."[6]

With his north flank filled with enemy, Orr first sent a patrol through a grove of trees toward Hamm after the artillery ceased at 1220. These men were stopped when fire broke out from a pillbox just outside of a factory building, a spot apparently not hit by the artillery. German soldiers also began firing from houses displaying white flags of surrender. Another of Orr's companies tried to make its way along the road from Munster-busch into Hamm, but structures not marked on their maps proved to again be camouflaged pillboxes loaded with Germans. Under the circumstances, there was no choice but to pull back. The night brought even more evidence that the German forces were growing. "Enemy vehicular traffic moved to the northwest, towards Atsch," Orr recalled. "Tracked vehicles also were heard moving into Schneidmuhle. Patrols sent out into the woods also discovered a new line of enemy about two hundred yards farther northward."[7]

In Munsterbusch, remaining elements of the 485th Home Guard, the 12th Engineer Battalion, the 452nd and 473rd Reserve Battalions, the 6th Lancschutz (Home Guard) Regiment, the 8th *Luftwaffe* Battalion, the 831st Nebel Com—part of the 7th *Flak* Division—as well as the 2105 Panzer Battalion of the 104th Panzer Brigade—all units of the 9th Panzer Division and the 1031st Infantry Regiment—were being joined by the 3rd Battalion of *Oberst* Engel's 27th Infantry Regiment.[8]

Southeast of Stolberg, Task Force Mills also experienced difficulty on 17 September. Colonel Boudinot had ordered Mills to again attack westward by way of Diepenlinchen and Weissenberg, optimistically expecting that his task force could then reach Birkengang, a hamlet on the north edge of Stolberg. From here Mills was to then pivot and secure what would become known as the Donnerberg fortress—Hill 287—located just outside of Stolberg to the northeast. According to Boudinot's plan, Mills would then be able to resume attacking along his original line of advance and link up with CCA.[9]

With Company F tanks in the lead, Task Force Mills pushed northward after uncoiling, and by 0800 most of the column had penetrated the woods southwest of Diepenlinchen. Across the valley approximately 800 yards away, they observed enemy forces digging in on a ridge. The company called for artillery, and after it came down the forty infantrymen left in Company F dismounted their half-tracks and attacked. As they worked their way up the slope fronting the enemy position in a skirmish line, heavy small-arms fire came in from a different direction—the woods to their left. The company commander reported that he could not take his objective without risking heavy losses, so he was ordered to partially pull back while another artillery concentration was called for.

Meanwhile, an enemy Mark VI tank made an unexpected appearance; it had come up through a draw behind another ridge to the northeast. The Americans answered by moving a 76mm SP gun into a nearby wooded area; many doubted it could do the job and they were right. After the gun got off four rounds, three of which merely bounced off the thickly plated Tiger, the German tankers simply turned their turret toward the gun and opened up, putting two rounds right through the front slope plate of the 76mm's chassis, killing one man and wounding two others. The Mark VI then remained in its taunting position; no American tanks were able to challenge it because it would just back off.

A frustrated Mills promptly requested artillery fire on the tank, but all through the day strikes somehow missed this ghostly Mark VI, even when it harassed the Americans and stuck its nose over the brow of the hill into full view. On the ridge where the Germans had taken a stance against the Company F infantry, however, renewed artillery strikes had proven more successful. As soon as this fire lifted, these American soldiers got on the ridge and a platoon of tanks infiltrated at maximum speed up to a defiladed position behind them. But when a section of medium tanks commanded by Lt. John H. Raymond came up in support, a *Panzerfaust* opened fire from a stand of trees to the left and knocked out his lead tank. Mills reluctantly called off the attack, leaving everyone clawing to their positions on the ridge.[10]

Setbacks also struck Task Force Lovelady on that cloudy and rainy 17 September. Major Robinette's 2nd Battalion mission was to attack across a ridgeline to the west from the woods they had occupied the previous day, and then move northwest to the Donnerberg fortress, Hill 287.[11] A German move, undetected, was destined to cause big problems. During the morning two battalions of the newly arrived 48th Grenadier Regiment attacked down separate roads from Gressenich toward Mausbach. A neighboring American unit first broke up the attack, but the enemy advance nevertheless continued in short rushes with their two battalions still abreast. "Apparently the battalion west of the road either reformed and renewed the attack, or was able to continue its advance unmolested. By noontime the Germans were just east of Weissenberg."

Soon afterward they collided with Captain Emerson's Company E, which was near the eastern side of the factory area in Diepenlinchen. They came at the company from both sides and, as one witness explained, "scooped it up. [I] was able to count at least 30 men lined up to march back towards Werth."[12] The Germans had reached nearby Werth earlier in the day and it was now a marshaling area and prisoner-of-war pen.

Another German unit also hit Captain Amborst's Company D very hard that day. Newly arrived forces from the 89th Grenadier Regiment got well around the factory buildings toward the crossroads in the southern part of Diepenlinchen. A large number of soldiers from both companies were captured; Company E had just fourteen active men left after the melee ended; Amborst's Company D had just thirty-two effectives.[13] Those not captured pulled back nearer to the houses southwest of town. Colonel Gans—who had gone forward to help direct the withdrawal of Company E—was captured. Captain Emerson was also missing and presumed taken prisoner.

Amborst's casualties were particularly dreadful. Heavy enemy concentrations of fire had wounded four of his Company D men and killed another in the early going, and then Captain Amborst lost six more killed and another eight wounded before midmorning. He did his best to hold his men together until approximately 1300, but then "he noticed a bush just behind [our] position which the enemy machinegun fire had clipped squarely across at waist-high level, so intense was this fire. Likewise, they laid in lots of artillery."[14]

> The dispersion of the shelling was all to the rear and since the shells hit just behind the men lying on the small ridge, the fragments went behind them and they suffered fewer casualties. Nevertheless, these men were so close to the spot where the shells were falling that geysers of dirt were sprayed over them. A few others in the company had crossed the ridge before the enemy opened up. They were wounded, and as a medic crossed to help them he also became a casualty.
>
> I gave the leader of the 2nd Platoon, Technical Sergeant Hisaw, permission to help out the wounded; he crawled to help them and enemy shrapnel hit him in the leg. A messenger, meanwhile, who was sent back to contact higher headquarters did not return. I then decided to pull the men back, but just as I organized the withdrawal an unusually heavy barrage of 88mm fire hit the area. The fire came in barrages about eight minutes between and the men were lining up to begin the withdrawal during the intervals.

Right after this the situation became even more critical. Hisaw, despite his wounds, had helped the other wounded to withdraw, but many of the men were starting to falter under the strain. At about this time, the Germans moved close enough to lob hand grenades on these soldiers. But better luck was to prevail. Unexpectedly, remnants from one of the platoons that had been out of contact with Amborst for the past hour gathered to the right rear and brought rifle fire into the enemy positions. "Without this, the Germans would have wiped us out," Amborst recalled. "A final difficulty then presented itself when the enemy got enfilade fire with a machinegun on the men lying on the ridge. A few more men broke completely under the strain, but the able men helped the wounded. We withdrew to the line of houses by 1700 where we took a defensive position in the same area we had occupied the night before."[15]

The 12th Infantry Division's *Oberst* Engel regarded 17 September as a success for his forces, although losses had been high for the 89th Grenadier Regiment. "The division expected counterattacks the next day, especially against Stolberg, the hills and dumps of Diepenlinchen and against Mausbach," Engel remembered. "The order for 18 September was—with the approval of the Corps—to hold the line gained, to strengthen the front and to resume the attack as soon as possible, according to what chances of success were inherent in the situation."[16]

> The 27th Infantry Regiment was ordered to continue to capture the pillboxes at Munsterbusch. The hard pressed 89th Grenadier Regiment was to hold the line gained; the 48th Grenadier Regiment with one battalion was to occupy the corner pillar Schevenhuette at night.

Task Force Lovelady remained in essentially the same place on 18 September. His infantry retired to the area just southwest of Diepenlinchen, and simply formed a defensive position. The rain had let up but fog enveloped the area during the early morning hours. It was during this inauspicious period that the fates of war for Captain Ferry's Company C of the 26th Infantry Regiment took a dramatic turn for the worse.

Ferry's men had moved from their position west of Busbach to the southern tip of Stolberg the previous afternoon. Here his men mounted on trucks and traveled to Mausbach where Captain Ferry received a new mission directly from Lt. Col. John C. Welborn, a 1932 West Point graduate and commander of the 33rd Armored Regiment. Company C was to move through Diepenlinchen, envelope the factory area on the edge of Weissenberg, and then seize the area near a pile of sand heaps. Ferry's secondary mission was to rescue as many of Captain Amborst's and Captain Emerson's wounded men as possible and recover any weapons abandoned on their positions. Welborn briefed Captain Ferry on what he knew about the enemy dispositions at the time; Diepenlinchen and Hill 287 north of Weissenberg harbored an unknown number of infantry-defended antitank guns.[17]

Unknown to either American officer, the 1st Battalion of Maj. Gerhard Lemcke's 89th Grenadier Regiment was also assembling in Werth for an attack. Commanded by *Hauptmann* (Captain) Gronbold, the 1st Battalion's mission for 18 September was to "take and hold the Weissenberg cluster along with the hillside and Diepenlinchen and, in the course of the attack Mausbach as well."[18] Certainly *Hauptmann* Gronbold could not have known it was Ferry's Company C he was destined to collide with.

Given that it was rainy on the night of 17 September, Captain Ferry only had time for a cursory map reconnaissance. At 1930 hours the company started forward with a platoon of tanks toward the east side of the factories in Diepenlinchen. A half hour later Ferry's 2nd Platoon suddenly encountered a strong enemy patrol of approximately thirty-five men. These forces quickly opened fire and completely disorganized the Americans. In order to keep the company from being wiped out, Captain Ferry ordered his men to withdraw to the road junction on the southwest edge of town. The company remained here for the rest of the night while Ferry rethought his plan; he determined that a sneak attack was more preferable, without tanks.

At 0430 hours the following morning, in dense fog, Captain Ferry again moved out with his men, this time planning to go around to the left of the factory, skirting Diepenlinchen. The tanks were left in a grove of trees to only cover the advance. Company C's men initially reached the gravel piles, then the foot of the slope immediately below Weissenberg. But here very heavy artillery, mortar, and machine-gun fire greeted them, all zeroed in.[19] Their movement had been discovered.

The Germans had chosen to allow Ferry's men to advance to the piles before firing on them. When the fog lifted, a company of enemy infantrymen came off a bluff some 50 feet high. In order to avoid an engagement with this force, survivors of the melee later recalled that Captain Ferry ordered his 2nd Platoon to withdraw first, followed by what he hoped would be the remainder of the company. At the same time the Germans came off the bluff, however, others came around the east side of the factory and counterattacked using rifle, machine-gun, and 20mm fire.

Some were fortunate. Most of the 2nd Platoon was able to withdraw to the woods southwest of Diepenlinchen where they formed a small perimeter defense. Others were not. Company C had started its mission with 6 officers and 120 enlisted men, but only 20 percent came back. Just 39 men were on hand when the company rejoined Task Force Hogan for a renewed attack against Weissenberg at 1600. Another dozen eventually met up with the company, but before 18 September ended, Company C's roster had shrunk to 2 officers and only 62 enlisted men. The rest were killed, wounded, or captured. Among the missing was Captain Ferry; he had been taken prisoner after enemy fire cut off the point squad he was with on the slag piles.[20]

Major Adams's remaining companies had originally been given the mission of bypassing Diepenlinchen on 18 September. This plan changed at 1130 hours because of Company C's situation. Instead, to keep progress moving northward, General Rose ordered Lieutenant Colonel Welborn to have Task Force Hogan move across the Inde River and then attack directly toward Hill 287, rather than going up through Donnerberg. At the time this task force consisted of only two companies of tanks and the rest of Adams's 1st Battalion. In this new mission Captain Simons's Company B was to protect Hogan's flank by retaking Diepenlinchen and eventually envelop the enemy positions in Weissenberg. This scheme of operations would have Anderson's Company A in support, attacking frontally against the factory area in the latter town.[21]

Hill 287 figured prominently in the Stolberg area, and its capture was essential to deny the Germans the advantage of controlling artillery fire from this vantage point. Occupation of the hill mass was required not just for the successful operations of Boudinot's CCB, but also for Brigadier General Hickey's CCA west of Stolberg. "This was believed necessary since this ground dominated Stolberg itself, and the north to south ridgeline extending south from Munsterbusch in CCA's sector," noted an American officer and an artillery observer. "The high ground to the east and northeast [of Stolberg on Hill 287] was like a balcony from which the enemy can observe the complete show."[22]

The men of Captain Anderson's Company A began their advance toward Diepenlinchen after benefitting from a friendly artillery fire mission. They first worked their way along the edge of the woods to the southwest of town while their supporting tanks crossed the fields on their right. Enemy artillery fire increased as the troops moved up, and when they attacked at 1700 across the field toward the factory at Weissenberg, immediate casualties resulted. Five of Hogan's tanks and fourteen of Anderson's men fell from heavy combinations of enemy machine-gun, small-arms, mortar, 20mm antiaircraft gun, and artillery fire. Captain Simons's Company B had moved into Diepenlinchen against similar stubborn resistance where his men became engaged in house-to-house fighting throughout the afternoon; they were able to capture the slagheap on the northwest edges of the village, but not the factory itself.

> Company B's attack, supported by mortars and artillery, had been more successful, if slow. It was dark before the town was cleared. Forty-nine German prisoners were taken, and the troops from Company C who had been captured in Diepenlinchen were liberated [these were the dozen who returned to the company]. During the day Company D's mortar platoon, commanded by Lieutenant Steven B. Phillips, expended all its ammunition; urgent requests for re-supply had to be submitted up the chain of command. Shortly after dark an enemy counterattack developed from the woods around Weissenberg, apparently seeking to turn Company A's exposed left flank. The battalion's Ammunition and Pioneer Platoon was thrown in to strengthen that flank, and the attack was beaten off.[23]

Sgt. Hans Martens was a platoon leader in 13Co of the 89th Grenadier Regiment's 1st Battalion. The company held full wartime strength on 18 September and his platoon supported the initial attack on

Captain Ferry's Company C with light infantry guns. He reported about this and the continuing action:

> The attack was delayed by dense ground fog. All of a sudden shooting occurred in the slope area left of the battalion command post. In the cover of fog, an American patrol had advanced to the forward area of our marshalling position. US artillery started shelling the area behind the dumps—which was our marshalling area—with deliberate fire making use of phosphorous ammunition. A battery of the 12th Division Artillery Regiment was ordered at once to deliver time-on-target fire in the village of Diepenlinchen, the effect of which was to be exploited by the 1st Battalion of the 89th Grenadier Regiment to take its objective. Everything went well; I don't remember one single shot from the opposite.
>
> In the course of the attack I was ordered by the CO of 1Co to set up my observation post just in front of Diepenlinchen and to cover the right open flank of the battalion against any harm that should come out of a small forest occupied by the enemy of unknown strength, possibly supported by tanks. By now the Americans had recovered from shock and fired from that woodland by means of heavy machineguns.
>
> In the meantime 1Co had taken Diepenlinchen, and our own artillery fire was directed to the south of the village. 2Co led by Lieutenant Rix was ordered to follow up and to attack from Diepenlinchen to the right and to establish contact with the neighboring force. Initially this attack was successful and the company gained some terrain, but it failed in finding the contact. The enemy, recovered now, employed Sherman tanks in growing numbers. My platoon engaged targets at the edge of the small forest west of Diepenlinchen.[24]

Attacks during the day had bogged down repeatedly because the local civilian population had not been evacuated in an orderly fashion; they were running around between the towns. In the excitement the locals often got between the German and American lines, at times forcing the commanders on both sides to hold their fire. Lt. Hans Zeplien, who commanded 14 Co—tank destroyers—recorded in his diary:

> The 1 Co had taken the cluster of buildings, and the 2 Co the slag pile area of Weissenberg and taken numerous prisoners. The 1st RPzB [bazooka] Platoon followed the attacking 1st Battalion along the west side, and the 2nd RPzB Platoon along the east side of the road from Werth to Diepenlinchen. The individual bazooka groups advanced in the rear of the attacking combat companies from cover to cover and at a distance preventing their elimination by the American infantry fire directed at the combat companies.
>
> As soon as the Americans had realized that they were being attacked by forces of a battalion size, they opened concentrated artillery fire. It seemed to me that several batteries were using shrapnel shells when firing into the battalion's sector. Due [to this], losses in that rather open area were extremely high. From the time of taking Weissenberg, the American artillery fire increased, and tanks on their move towards Diepenlinchen took up intervention in combat from distances which were well beyond bazooka reach.
>
> About one hour following the attack I, along with the company headquarters unit and Major Lemcke, the commander of Grenadier Regiment 89, proceeded from Werth towards Weissenberg. When arriving at an area called "Am obersten Busch" and south of that area, we and other soldiers following the attack received shrapnel fire of such intensity that we had to take shelter in a nearby quarry. In spite of this dreadful defense fire, the 1st Battalion managed to take the foremost streets of Diepenlinchen on its first onset, but had to take cover here.[25]

Heavy mortar and small-arms fire had driven Task Force Mills back to Burgholzerhof during the morning. Later reports revealed, "The remnants of Company F were beginning to break under the extended strain; many were shocked and suffering from combat exhaustion."[26] At 1000 hours heavy enemy artillery fell and a large number of German infantry troops were suddenly sighted over the ridge formerly held by the thoroughly exhausted company. When more forces were spotted to the northeast, Mills called for artillery fire, and the German attack fortunately went nowhere. An hour later, Company F made another attempt to take Hammerberg Hill with just six medium tanks. Artillery fire combined with Mills's mortar platoon for flank support on the left while assault guns provided cover on the right, at last permitting the weakened company to take the hill.

The 89th Grenadier Regiment had intended to capture nearby Mausbach and re-man the line north of the Vicht River on 18 September; *Oberst* Engel later assessed the day's progress in CCB's zone of operations:

> At Stolberg, the enemy gained some terrain. The Hammerberg Hill east of Stolberg was lost. Further attacks over the Hammerberg in the direction of Donnerburg were unsuccessful. They were repelled with heavy losses for the enemy. Particularly heavy pressure made itself clear in the center where, from the direction of Mausbach [toward] Diepenlinchen attacks were carried out with many tanks. Diepenlinchen was lost at mid-day; the dumps at Weissenberg could not be held either. In the evening, attacks against [the Donnerberg fortress] north of Weissenberg failed, with heavy losses for the enemy. Weaker attacks from the southern part of Mausbach met with no success either. The loss of the dominating dumps of Weissenberg enforced the withdrawal to the north of Mausbach; only combat outposts were left there.[27]

Captain Dawson's Company G positions on the ridgeline outside of Verlautenheide came under attack again early on 18 September. At 0200 a company-strength force struck; some of these Germans succeeded in getting into Dawson's lines, but they could not penetrate it. The fighting was close and intense. "One machine gunner killed two Germans with his pistol, and they fell across the barrel of his weapon," it was noted in an after-action report. "An enemy platoon was wiped out almost to a man. At about 0300 they withdrew, but the men were 'jumpy' and fired at any noise they heard for the rest of the night. Sniping continued on both sides, then at about 0530 an extremely heavy mortar and artillery barrage fell on Company E."[28]

A half hour later another German platoon made an attempt to charge the slope fronting Dawson's line, this time toward his 1st Platoon. The slope here was virtually a cliff; the soldiers dropped hand grenades on the Germans as they tried to climb up and attack. Supporting 81mm mortar fire, adjusted to fall just some 35 yards beyond the platoon's final protective line, was particularly effective in stopping this attack. Captain Richmond's Company I had filled in the gap between Dawson's men and Company E by this time, adding lateral support to Lieutenant Colonel Hicks's positions during the ongoing morning attack. After fierce fighting, during which Dawson's 2nd Platoon and his machine-gun section expended thirty thousand rounds of ammunition, the attack stopped around noon. The Germans made another attempt at 1400, only to get within 50 yards of Company G's positions before again being repulsed. Company E lost one man killed and ten wounded; Captain Dawson suffered seven wounded, including one of his aid men who had gone out to help a German who was hit, only to have the wounded man's brethren open fire on the American trying to save his life.

At 0800 that same morning, Lieutenant Colonel Driscoll ordered another attack on Munsterbusch, again with the objective of taking the crossroad in the village and the pickle factory at the northeast end of town. This attack jumped off with his Company A on the left, supported by a platoon of medium tanks, while Captain Merendino's Company B moved up on the right with light tanks. As the two companies approached the buildings on the outskirts of town, enemy small-arms and direct tank fire slowed their movement. Driscoll remembered at the time, "The enemy opposing the 1st Battalion was now of a higher quality. Prisoners began to come in from the 105th Panzer Brigade, and two Battle Groups organized as Kampfgruppe Schemm."[29]

A short report written just a few days later by Maj. Heinrich Volker, commander of the 105th Panzer Brigade, revealed the actual state of the troops opposing Driscoll's 1st Battalion at the time. When the brigade withdrew from the *Westwall* on 14 September, 56 officers, 236 NCOs, and 1,705 men made up its combat strength. These men formed a battle group under Volker's command, to include *Kampfgruppe Schemm*, named for its commander *Hauptmann* Gunther Schemm, Training Battalion 473 (3rd Battalion), Local Defense Battalion 6 (2nd Company),

Armored Engineer Battalion 16 commanded by *Oberleutnant* Blohme, Local Defense Fortress Battalion 8 led by *Hauptmann* Baier, Assault Gun Brigade 394 (1st Company), and Antitank Battalion 50. By 18 September, these numbers had been reduced, in Volker's estimation because of "physical decline and exhaustion."[30] Others had been "dispersed and annihilated by enemy and artillery fire" after "nonstop attacks against the bunkers [by American] heavy tank and infantry forces." Losses of his own tanks had been "considerable," in light of previous attacks by U.S. armor. One day earlier the 105th Panzer Brigade had just eight tanks and was expected to be sent back to Julich for refitting.[31]

Volker might not have agreed with Lieutenant Colonel Driscoll that his troops were of "higher quality" as he was even critical of his own men, suggesting that "as soon as the enemy deploys smoke to announce his imminent attack, the first elements leave their positions and hole up in the basements of houses and in the woods." Volker had reason to feel this way; he also noted that "[his] interventions in trying to keep the men in their positions were only momentarily successful since it was impossible to keep the men together. Those men who had been assembled before the large scale operations and had been trained by their own commanders were decimated during the first days to such an extent that it was no longer possible to talk about close units."[32]

Not unexpectedly, by 1600 hours Company A had penetrated Major Volker's forces that remained in place. While one of its platoons got close to the slag piles near the pickle factory, Merendino's Company B ran into difficulties in a nearby cemetery where other tanks and infantry counterattacked. The fighting was at close quarters, hand-to-hand, and Driscoll was eventually forced to pull Captain Merendino's men back to the line initially held by Company A, some 500 yards west of town. This was fortunate. More Germans, not units of the 105th Panzer Brigade, were in the center of Munsterbusch; just one officer and eight men returned from the platoon that had reached the slag piles. At 1730, as the company was consolidating its positions, another German unit attacked from the woods to the north with approximately 140 men and 2 tanks. The company held, assisted by the medium tank platoon with which they had started their mission; however, there was a danger that these men could be cut off by an attack into their right rear by more enemy forces directly to the south in Munsterbusch itself. Fortunately, by late afternoon help was on the way. A company of tanks from CCA arrived, and at dusk they were put in a ring behind Driscoll's infantry.

General Hickey had originally expected the 1st Battalion of the 16th Infantry to take Munsterbusch alone while Task Force Doan and Orr's 1st Battalion of the 36th Armored Infantry attacked northeastward to Schneidmuhle through the breach in the Schill Line at England. Once Lieutenant Colonel Driscoll had taken Munsterbusch and Orr had taken his objective, the two battalions were to join forces. The enemy resistance Driscoll met on 18 September changed this. As Hickey remembered:

> The situation at Munsterbusch was now complicated by two fac-
> tors. One, all three of [Driscoll's] companies were pinned down
> by the enemy. A and C were along the main road west of Mun-
> sterbusch, while his Company B was on the slope southwest of
> town. Two, the chain of command was not rigid. Initially the 1st
> Battalion of the 16th Infantry was never officially attached to
> CCA. Co-operation among the various units existed to a high
> degree, but the actual system of command was not worked out.[33]

With it now clear that the forces at the disposal of both Driscoll and Orr were insufficient to take either Munsterbusch or Schneidmuhle, General Hickey suggested to General Rose that Orr's 1st Battalion be withdrawn from its positions on the far side of the dragon's teeth and recommitted toward Munsterbusch. The 3rd Armored Division's com-mander concurred, and the order was given.

Unknown to any American officer on the night of 18 September, the Germans had cleverly arrayed their defenses in Munsterbusch. Their tanks had been placed in among the taller buildings so that their firing positions and exact locations were difficult to determine. They had fields of fire not just down the main streets, but also down side streets that they could get to by moving their tanks into slightly different positions. Around the paved rectangular road network covered by these tanks, enemy infantry—three companies of the 10th Panzer Brigade and ele-ments of the Home Guard—had built up many strongpoints.[34] These included machine-gun emplacements, clusters of snipers in building win-dows, and other observation points. Cellars in the buildings were even connected by underground passageways. This defense was designed to prevent American infantry from approaching the German tanks and knocking them out with bazooka fire. At the same time, the emplacements of the Home Guard were intended to prevent U.S. forces from getting anywhere near the tanks of the 10th Panzer Brigade.

At first light on that warmer and sunny 19 September, Lieutenant Colonel Orr withdrew his companies from their positions inside of the Schill Line. At the time he had just sixty, seventy, and ninety men in his Companies A to C, respectively. To augment his forces, he was also given the support of Lt. Col. Walter B. Richardson's 3rd Battalion of the 32nd Armored Regiment. But in view of the difficulty of withdrawing under enemy fire to assemble with Richardson's forces south of Buschmuhle, Orr's infantry was unable to join with Driscoll's companies for the renewed Munsterbusch initiative until midafternoon.

The Germans had gone on the offensive much earlier that day. At 0700 they attacked Driscoll's companies, again from the woods to the north and from the western edges of the village. These attacks were repulsed with the aid of DIVARTY, as well as the light and medium tanks supporting his infantry companies; three Mark IV tanks were knocked out during the morning's action. The 1st Battalion casualty reports later showed one officer and twenty-three enlisted men wounded and evacuated during this fight alone.[35] Then at noon, Driscoll met with Lieutenant Colonel Orr. They made plans for the new offensive, with Orr's infantry passing through Driscoll's positions. Orr planned to lead with Richardson's tanks, his infantry following close behind. He would commit two of Richardson's companies just to the south of Driscoll's Company A and Captain Briggs's Company C.

When Orr's battalion moved up, Briggs's Company C was spread out along the road running from Buschmuhle to Munsterbusch facing northward. Driscoll's Company A was farther to the east along the same road, also in positions looking to the north. Merendino's Company B was dug in on the rough ground southeast of Munsterbusch near an enemy pillbox; his troops faced eastward. The attack began at 1500 hours when Richardson's tanks moved out as planned. The armored vehicles moved just 500 yards, and then a German tank hidden in one of the buildings in town opened up, knocking out two of the American tanks. "The enemy had excellent fields of fire from this protective place," Orr remembered.

"It became clear that unless the infantry could get into the buildings first, the attack could not continue."[36]

Led by Capt. Basil I. Mishtowt of Company C and Lt. C. W. Major of Company A, the infantry indeed moved forward in squad groups through the rugged ground west of town. Heavy automatic guns and sniper fire hindered the move, but two of Mishtowt's platoons and one of Major's Company A platoons still managed to dash across the open ground. Two men received direct hits from enemy tank guns before these forces reached the first buildings on the edge of Munsterbusch. This tender foothold permitted Captain Merendino's Company B to move ahead to the right and by 1800 a line had been formed along the buildings bordering Praemienstrasse, the main road in town. Meanwhile, Captain Mishtowt's Company C platoons pushed ahead and reached the pickle factory. The other companies in the attack could not come abreast of these forces, however, so Orr had to pull Mishtowt's company back. His men eventually dug into defensive positions along both sides of Praemienstrasse to the south, tying their right flank in with Merendino's Company B along Amaliastrasse. They set up machine guns to cover the avenues of approach.

Orr's Company B had cut into the flank of the enemy from the south by this time. Strewn along a slope on the road that led out of Munsterbusch to Busbach, these men received enfilade fire during the afternoon from the buildings to their left. "This automatic fire, as well as sniper fire from the buildings, cut the company off for some time," Orr noted later. "The draw down which the enemy was firing behind Company B made contact impossible. They dug in at this position for the night."

"The enemy employed sound tactics, making the attack that much more difficult," Lieutenant Colonel Doan, who was the overall commander of the day's attack, remembered. "Their tanks took concealment by the high walls along the streets, and their infantry prevented [us] from getting at these tanks. When the medium tanks of [Richardson's armor] tried to go in, one was knocked out. The enemy infantry had snipers in the building's windows and men in the basements with submachine guns. By dark most of the town was in the possession of [our] infantry, which had to reduce the strongpoints with house-to-house fighting. About 55 prisoners were taken; the factories on the north edge of town were still in enemy hands, however."[37]

Elements of the 83rd Reconnaissance Battalion had moved into Busbach the previous day and established an observation post in a house on the corner of the main crossroad in the northern part of town. Task Force Miller, commanded by Lt. Col. Clifford L. Miller and comprised of the 2nd Battalion of the 32nd Armored Regiment and Company D of the 23rd Engineering Battalion, had moved up from 3rd Armored Division Reserve to cut off the threat of an enemy attack back through the Schill Line after Orr's companies vacated Busbach to make the attack on Munsterbusch. By this time, the 83rd's outpost had also been vacated. The 36th Armored Infantry Regiment's S-1, Capt. R. W. Russell recalled, "This was to avoid friendly artillery fire several hundred yards farther south. [After this] the enemy filtered through the dragon's teeth."[38]

Task Force Blanchard, another reserve element under the command of Lt. Col. Elwyn W. Blanchard, had also become engaged by this time. One of his medium tank companies, Company D, commanded by Lt. Elton K. McDonald, was ordered up to lend further assistance to Driscoll's 1st Battalion in their continuing attack on Munsterbusch. McDonald moved northeast out of the Brander Wald at approximately 1500 hours on 19 September, and then cut to the open ground near the dragon's teeth. "Only occasional sniper fire was heard by the tankers," he recalled later. "By dark [we] had taken up a position part of the way up the slope towards Munsterbusch near a pillbox where [1/16] was likewise emplaced."[39] Even more help was on the way, this time from Lieutenant Colonel Peckham's 3rd Battalion of Colonel Smith's 18th Infantry Regiment of the 1st Division. A gap still existed on the northeast side of Munsterbusch, and Captain Folk's Company L would fill this opening the next day.

New orders were handed down to Task Force Mills southeast of Stolberg on 19 September. At 0800 Colonel Boudinot ordered Mills to turn to the southwest, move down the valley in this direction, proceed to the Vicht River, and from there turn west. In making this move, Major Mills was to skirt the woods near Burgholzerhof where his tanks had been held up by bazooka fire the day before and then move into Stolberg from the southeast. Task Force Lovelady was to follow.

The morning proved very problematic. When the 3rd Platoon of Company F tanks first started down the small valley to reach the river, the tankmen in the lead vehicle quickly discovered that they had read their maps in error when the original order was given. There was no road on the near side of the Vicht River on which the eight tanks of the platoon could skirt around the woods. Upon this discovery, a Sergeant Watson returned in his tank to meet with Major Mills and discuss the situation. Mills, in turn, elected to personally reconnoiter for an alternate route that would bring the task force into Stolberg, but found that none existed without having to cross the river. Since the only bridge in the area was blown, this was impossible for his tanks.

By this time Mills's infantry had moved out. One platoon from Captain Vaughn's Company I had been attached to the task force the previous night, and these men joined with what remained of Company F's infantry, itself not much more than half a platoon in strength. Meeting little opposition, this small combined force managed to reach the river. Even though the tanks could not cross, the infantry was ordered to ford the river, attack across the woods on the opposite side, and move into Stolberg. Mills, meanwhile, had decided to send his Company F tanks over the ridge near Burgholzerhof where they could pivot and join the infantry forces.

After crossing the Vicht, the infantry drew small-arms fire when they swung west into the adjacent wooded hills; this made further advances impractical without additional support. Sergeant Watson, who was in charge of the light tanks trying to cross the ridge at Burgholzerhof, took it upon himself to conduct another reconnaissance. He soon reported to Mills by radio from a position in partial defile near the outskirts of Stolberg, telling him that there were no visible antitank guns. Soon after this conversation took place, however, the Germans announced their presence with rifle, machine-gun, and bazooka fire, followed by grenades. This had all come from buildings on the edge of the factory town. Still, this did not deter Sergeant Watson. Again he got on the radio to Major Mills, this time informing him that while the ground down the open hill fronting Stolberg was marshy and deploying the tanks here would be difficult, it was still possible for them to get through.

Mills agreed; he ordered the Company F platoon to cross the ridge and join Sergeant Watson. But when the lead tank moved over the crest, "difficult" immediately became the operative word to describe the mission. This armored vehicle drew antitank fire and was knocked out; the rest of the platoon then withdrew behind the ridge into an orchard. Watson, still observing from his advance position on the edge of Stolberg, reported that the enemy was "shooting out his periscopes, firing bazookas and throwing grenades at close range." He was unable to fire back without exposing himself, so Mills decided to lay down a smoke screen to allow the sergeant to withdraw. However, "it became too hot before the artillery could lay down any smoke, so [Watson] pulled out from his forward outpost and ran the gauntlet of enemy fire up over the hill back to safety."[40] Three of his tank commanders had been wounded by enemy small-arms fire by this time, but during his own time at the edge of Stolberg Watson had been able to direct artillery and mortars on his platoon's opposite numbers perched on the buildings in town. It was 1130 hours when he safely returned.

While Task Force Mills was attempting its ill-starred foray into Stolberg earlier that morning, Major Adams's 1st Battalion of the 26th Infantry Regiment had worked its way farther into Diepenlinchen. Accompanied by tanks, Captain Simons's Company B had secured the factory during the early going, and then proceeded through approximately 100 yards of rock piles, crumbled wall, and other obstacles while receiving bazooka, grenade, machine-gun, and mortar fire from the companies of the 89th Grenadier Regiment's 1st Battalion still in the village. Company B had to break off the attack and pull back.

The 89th Grenadier Regiment's Sgt. Hans Martens of 13Co was still in front of Diepenlinchen that morning. He remembered:

> The US [forces] attacked and pushed the 1st Battalion, which had settled in Diepenlinchen, back to its marshalling area of the previous day after hard fighting. The battalion did not tell us of this because we were kept very busy by the enemy. We were approached by a tank mounted by infantry and equipped with a machinegun fastened to the hatch of its turret. Its fire, which was served from a distance of only 75 meters, gave us a great deal of trouble.
>
> Dismounted infantry, deployed in the terrain, also fired at us. Despite a large expenditure of ammunition, the results were not very successful. We had taken cover against the tanks in foxholes,

which due to the rocky underground were only half a meter deep. Shelling continued until [our] counterattack was launched in the late morning. Covered by a smoke screen, the enemy withdrew.[41]

Captain Anderson's Company A also jumped off for Weissenberg again at noon. Two of his platoons, as well as another two tank platoons, deployed into the 400 meters of open but level ground in front of the village only to be deluged with German weapons of every caliber, including 20mm cannon fire. Adams, grimly facing the costly losses his battalion had taken in the past few days, had sent the following message just hours earlier to his commanding officer, Colonel Seitz:

> It is recommended that my battalion be returned to the unit so I can get replacements and re-equip. My unit has suffered heavy battle casualties, and yesterday and today I am beginning to get men suffering from combat fatigue. As of this AM my fighting strength was as follows: A-99, B-91, C-62, D-96. Yesterday I suffered very heavy casualties as follows: 8-KIA, 50 WIA, 57 MIA. I am still attacking today against an objective that is very difficult to take. I shall undoubtedly suffer further heavy casualties. At the present rate I am rapidly losing my combat effectiveness. Yesterday Company C was placed on an independent mission and was caught in a trap. The company commander is MIA; Lieutenant Emory Jones is in command. He has one other officer. The company has 55 MIA's.[42]

This request could not be granted on 19 September; the urgencies of war prevailed. In the new scheme of operations, Lieutenant Jones's undermanned Company C, accompanied by Task Force Hogan's Company G and Company H tanks, was to swing around to the east in an effort to envelope the enemy positions in Diepenlinchen. Simons's Company B would continue through the rock piles toward the eastern part of the stronghold, and Captain Anderson's Company A was to make another frontal attack toward Weissenberg. Lieutenant Colonel Hogan had previously considered this envelopment, but he had rejected it because his personal reconnaissance had convinced him that the ground to the south and southeast of the factory area was boggy and therefore unsuitable for his tanks. Lovelady's task force was to also go to the northwest across the field to the left of Anderson's men and secure the woods bordering the western edge of Diepenlinchen. This would prevent any counterattacks by the Germans from the direction of Weissenberg, which remained the final objective of the day's plans.

When the initial attack began at 1600, Company C quickly lost two of its tanks to heavy artillery, antitank, and mortar fire. Another tank was mired down and then abandoned, only to be destroyed in place when the tankmen and Lieutenant Jones's infantry withdrew. Captain Simons's Company B managed to gain another 200 yards after struggling across the rock piles, but his men could not make any further gains due to the intense fire they received from nearby enemy forces who were protected by a maze of thick walls and supporting pillars. "It was like a trap," Hogan later recalled. "The advance stopped and the troops pulled back at dark. Enemy mortars and artillery from 1600 on plastered the area."[43]

> [Our Company G and H] tanks could not advance because of the terrain; in part they were exposed to fire and elsewhere the piles of stone and slag were too steep. During the attack the tanks moved without infantry up into the open field southwest of Weissenberg, hoping that the mortar and artillery fire would shift to them and away from the infantry. This did not succeed, however, and at 1830 the tanks withdrew to the south of Diepenlinchen. By this time the two companies combined had 20 tanks; Company H having lost six of its fifteen and Company G having lost two of its thirteen.

Lt. Hans Zeplien of 14Co remembered 19 September as a harsh day that inflicted losses on his tank destroyer company in the fight for Diepenlinchen and also wounded the 89th Grenadier's 1st Battalion commanding officer:

> The enemy tank and infantry counterattack [was] partly directed towards the open flank of the 1st Battalion. In the course of that

counterattack they reinforced both of their attacking units. The battalion, now weakened by losses, had to evacuate the foremost streets of Diepenlinchen [in the morning], and withdraw to the Weissenberg slag piles, leaving behind about 30 wounded, including Captain Gronboldt, the commander of the battalion. The wounded had to wait until the next night before they could be taken out of the tunnel at Diepenlinchen by the regiment's engineering platoon who transported them to the village of Werth.

The 14 Co had to register 11 wounded near Diepenlinchen (7 of the 1st Platoon; 4 of the 2nd Platoon) and 14 men were missing. This made the personnel set out of action the past two days amount to 16 men out of 48 in the 1st RPzB Platoon (bazookas), 31 out of 48 of the 2nd RPzB Platoon, and 4 out of the 3rd "AT" Platoon (Type 37, 7.5cm trench guns).

Losses in terms of personnel and equipment were high on the American side as well, as could be realized by the marked slackening of their pressure in the course of 19 September.[44]

Major Adams had held up Anderson's Company A while the action was taking place in Diepenlinchen, waiting until Task Force Lovelady could move up to his left and provide support. Just before 1900, all VII Corps artillery within range delivered a ten-minute preparation in advance of this offensive, concluding with smoke to conceal the movement of the infantry and tanks. Anderson's men became victims of this fire when a number of rounds landed short, causing tree bursts that fell on the rear of the company. All of his men sought cover while a thirty-minute delay was called so forward observers could register again on the enemy targets. Tree bursts still hit the area when the artillery fire renewed, once more sending Anderson's infantry for cover. Adams's concern about more casualties in his message to Colonel Seitz was founded. On 19 September he lost another twenty-two men.[45]

Task Force Lovelady did not fare much better when they attacked. First, Captain Amborst's Company D was hamstrung by a shortage of Browning automatic rifles (BARs), and his men had no radios; they also lacked mortars and did not have a single bazooka available to them. The company got thirty replacements during the day, but a likely grateful

Amborst did not enter the fight. Instead, he took his men nearer to Dorff with the mission of strengthening defenses in that area.

Captain Getter's Company H saw far more action during the day. After the second VII Corps' artillery preparation, two of his platoons attempted to jump off, with one leading and a second following right behind. Lieutenant Hulstedt commanded the latter unit, Getter's 3rd Platoon. Smoke had aided the first platoon, which was led by Sgt. Francis X. Bell in their attack, but Hulstedt's men were quickly pinned down by enemy fire that came in from the direction of tiny Hochwegerhof. Vaughn's Company I faced a similar fate; his men got about a hundred yards into the field fronting their line of departure, and then enemy artillery and mortar fire rained down, forcing the soldiers to retreat back to their start line.[46]

Several enemy tanks were also firing into the wooded area where Getter's platoons had been stopped, so a change in plans came about. His men moved over to the orchard occupied by Task Force Mills. Here Lieutenant Hulstedt was given the mission of cleaning out Hochwegerhof and the hedgerows near a house that was burning. This attack was unsuccessful. They captured an enemy bazooka team, but by nightfall Hulstedt's men were back in a defensive position in the orchard. Sergeant Bell's 2nd Platoon was to their right, stretched out toward the enemy-held woods, looking at the site of Company H's untaken objective that afternoon.[47]

Heavy smoke that had been laid down at 1600 by 81mm mortar fire proved more helpful to Task Force Mills when they first started their attack. While these mortars, joined by assault guns and three tank destroyers from Company B of the 703rd Tank Destroyer Battalion, protected his left flank, Mills's armored vehicles advanced up to the orchard area near another house in Hochwegerhof. Here hotter-than-hell enemy mortar and artillery fire thwarted the attack; one of Company F's light tanks was quickly knocked out by antitank fire. A later report describing the day's continued action noted:

Mills and [Captain] McGeorge roved the area firing on [our] infantry in the orchard and [from the] house where the enemy continued to counterattack by fire. Mills had the tree immediately in front of his tank blown up by a shell, but the attack was repulsed. Heavy explosive, anti-phosphorous and smoke were again fired into the house, but it was hard to get the enemy out. In the meantime, [our] tanks took hits from the enemy bazooka fire. There was little order to the fighting. Tanks and infantry mixed and infiltrated amongst the enemy.[48]

The same report shed more light on the plight of Captain Getter's Company H that afternoon. He held command of both his platoons, as well as Captain Vaughn's twenty men already with Task Force Mills. At 1900 Mills also put his own Company F infantry—all fifteen men— under Getter's command, telling him to organize a defensive position for the night in the orchard. Earlier, Captain McGeorge had brought up an engineer platoon, and he put these men along the high ground facing in this direction. This line was extended farther by McGeorge's reconnaissance platoon. One platoon of Mills's Company A light tanks also remained on the line while the rest pulled back into Niederhof. The remainder of Vaughn's Company I forces could not move over until later that night.

In the center of the attack that day Task Force Lovelady also faltered. After Getter's men moved over to support Mills's initiative, Company E with its six tanks and just one officer, along with another light tank platoon, worked their way across a field toward the woods between Diepenlinchen and Niederhof. Two tanks were lost under a cascade of enemy artillery, mortar, and antitank fire.[49] In light of this, Lovelady's task force returned to the woods from which they had departed.

VII Corps planned more massed artillery strikes at 0700 on the morning of 20 September before the renewed attack jumped off to secure the objectives of the day before. Colonel Boudinot again ordered a general attack to seize Weissenberg and to clear the woods to the west before taking the all-important Donnerberg Fortress—Hill 287. Planning had been completed the night before; one of the participants was Major Adams's S-3, Captain Levasseur. Based on reports from prisoners taken in Diepenlinchen, they expected a counterattack on their left flank. Hogan seized on this and instead developed a plan to have his tanks sally into the woods concealing the German positions beneath Weissenberg. After midnight, this attack indeed went off; Hogan had no losses before German defensive fires started up as he withdrew early in the morning.

Then, at first light Levasseur had a novel idea:

> While shaving, my mind was mulling over the events of the pre-
> vious night, including periodic harassing fires by our tanks and
> artillery on the objective . . . and the dense fog existing at this
> time. I visualized the enemy in entrenched positions sleepless
> and exhausted from our previous day's attacks and frequent
> shelling during the night. I stopped in the middle of my shave
> to suggest to Major Adams and Colonel Hogan that, under the
> circumstances, an attack by our infantry with fixed bayonets but
> without any supporting fires might be more effective by surpris-
> ing the enemy asleep in their trenches. They both considered
> this briefly and agreed it just might work.[50]

Hogan, in fact, requested cancellation for all supporting fires and he
also kept his tanks in place. Aided by the heavy ground fog that limited
their opposite numbers' visibility to no more than 50 feet, Captain
Anderson's Company A jumped off at 0800 and got right into the central
factory area without being detected. The Germans were caught off guard,
many of them indeed asleep, and the main part of the factory fell to
Anderson's men; they took thirty-three prisoners and the company suffered only two casualties. Captain Simons's Company B had attacked
and made good progress through the rock piles; his men seized the east
side of the factory area. However, by this time the Germans had recovered from these surprise attacks, and Simons's last platoon to come up
started receiving hostile artillery fire. This did not stop the advance.
Sending his soldiers forward man by man, Captain Simons soon had the
company infiltrating through the open rock piles toward Weissenberg.
While the Americans remained in the open, they were very fortunate
that the Germans did not fire at them.

This relative calm did not last for long; more hostile artillery fires
eventually opened up. Adams's infantry reached the village by late morning; Lieutenant Jones brought Company C up to join Company B, and
both companies finally occupied the former defensive positions of the
Germans in Weissenberg. Their artillery fire joined with mortars continued to harass the Americans into the afternoon, but a counterattack
never materialized.

Oberst Engel later noted the tactical impact of Major Adams's seizure of Weissenberg on his offensive plans, recalling:

> The terrain in the left sector on both sides of Mausbach was still considered the most favorable direction for [our] attack. There, the observation for heavy arms and artillery, and the terrain for panzers, were thought to be the most appropriate. Here, the original order to reach the first Westwall line could be carried out in the shortest time. The enemy's main communication and supply line—the road Stolberg-Vicht-Zweifall—could be cut.
>
> Therefore, the loss of the dumps at Weissenberg was felt grievously. The dumps dominated the terrain to the north up to Eschweiler and Weissenberg and they enabled a view to be obtained of Mausbach, Hastenrath and the southern parts of the woods of Eschweiler.[51]

Task Force Lovelady also attempted to attack in conjunction with Major Adams's infantry on that cloudy and overcast 20 September. During the early morning, Captain Getter's Company H—with just fifty-four men—first moved along the edge of the enemy-held woods before coming up to the left of Lieutenant Jones's Company C. Resistance was initially weak; Getter's forces encountered just small-arms fire, but as soon as they got away from the woods enemy artillery rained in. This brought about a change in plans. Getter was ordered back to his start line, where his men mounted tanks to ride to Mausbach and collect their half-tracks for another assignment. The rest of Task Force Lovelady remained in the woods in which they had held up the day before.

Captain Vaughn's two Company I platoons had moved across to follow Getter's forces that morning. His men attacked, and by 1100 they had reached some buildings and sand pits 800 yards to the northeast where they encountered dug-in German infantry. Three tanks from Company D of the 33rd Armored Regiment had accompanied Vaughn's men, and these armored vehicles moved up to attack an enemy machine-gun position. The situation, according to a later report, "got too hot to handle,"[52] and Vaughn also had to withdraw. He ordered his thirty men to head back to their vehicles; both Company H and Company I would move over to assist Task Force Mills.

Colonel Boudinot had first ordered Mills to hold his defensive position at Hochwegerhof that morning, while other elements of his task force went over to protect the left flank of Major Adams's 1st Battalion and Lovelady's two depleted infantry companies. Then at noon Mills was called back to Boudinot's bunker command post in the woods east of Diepenlinchen where he received new orders. It was a significant change: at 1430 Task Force Mills was to attack to the northwest, across a ridge, and then directly through the valley leading to the formidable Donnerberg fortress—Hill 287.

This was also a daunting task. Mills had few tanks and infantry available to him. Company F had just six tanks and fifteen men. Mills also had his fifteen Company A light tanks defending in Hochwegerhof. They held off the attack until the six Company I tanks could come up. During the wait a heavy artillery barrage came in from the direction of Hill 287, disrupting the refueling of the tanks and spoiling the pace of reloading their ammunition. Then, just after the friendly fire plan for the attack was worked out, Capt. John Watson and his artillery forward observer became casualties from the enemy fire.

A delayed artillery preparation nevertheless went off at approximately 1530 hours. Concentrations were laid on Duffenter, toward the village of Donnerberg and directly onto Hill 287. Assault guns also spread smoke on the hill mass, while other artillery fire clouded Mills's right flank. Then the attack jumped off, with Companies F and I medium armor leading in lines of five tanks, making a total of three waves, with ten of Company A's light tanks that had moved over from Hochwegerhof following. As the lead tanks crossed the ridge before going down into the valley toward Duffenter, they opened up with their guns on Hill 287. The smoke protection continued doing its job, permitting the tanks to run and fire, combining speed with firepower. Just one tank commander was wounded as the attack advanced through the crossroads outside of Duffenter, then up toward the Donnerberg fortress. "Only the smoke and speed saved the task force," an account of the action noted. "Direct 88mm fire had been coming throughout the afternoon, probably from a Mark VI tank known to be in the area."[53]

Company B of the 703rd Tank Destroyer Battalion, commanded by Lt. G. W. Burkett, had destroyed several other enemy armored vehicles during the attack. The mission of the TDs was to protect the right flank of the task force, which they did by first moving three of their vehicles over to a slope that afforded some defilade ten minutes before the general attack started. A Mark V tank was spotted about 1,200 yards out in front of Hill 287, and the American gunner scored. "The turret of the enemy tank swung around as it was hit," Lieutenant Brown, leader of the 1st Platoon remembered. "Then it shot straight up."[54]

During the general attack, the three destroyers concentrated on the German pillbox positions and their infantry, including soldiers who were laying communication wires. Houses in the valley and in Duffenter were also targets. Aiming above the attacking waves of Task Force Mills, the TD fire was instrumental in helping the tanks reach almost to the top of the hill mass. Then at dusk another Mark V pulled out from behind a pillbox near a church on the back side of the hill and started after the American tanks. This time Brown recalled, "We let the Mark V get halfway from the pillbox to the church, then opened fire on it and knocked it out."

Despite the efforts of the TDs, Task Force Mills met increased resistance after they reached the top of Hill 287. Several tanks were hit by more fire from the backside of the hill before they could take cover. Seven medium tanks were rapidly knocked out, three from Company I and four from Company F. This forced the remainder of the tanks to withdraw back into a defensive position southwest of Duffenter, leaving some of the American wounded behind.

Frantic efforts had been made all afternoon to get more infantry forces up to help out, but none were available. Even a medic half-track failed three times to get up onto the hill and evacuate the wounded. Then just after 1900 the Germans called down artillery fire for forty-five minutes, some of the most intense Task Force Mills had received in the past several days. After darkness fell, small-arms fire opened up from the houses in Duffenter, as well as from the church yard and pillboxes on the hill. Throughout the night, the tankers had to dismount to guard their vehicles. One of Company I's remaining tanks was knocked out by a *Panzerfaust*, and its commander was badly injured.

Lt. Hans Zeplien of 14Co lent perspective to the day's actions in his diary, and also recorded the recollections of another German soldier who saw action against Company A in Hochwegerhof late in the day.

[Unknown to the Americans, due] to high casualties during the previous days, the 2nd Battalion of Grenadier Regiment 89—

so far involved in defensive fighting near Schevenhutte—became employed in the Hochwegerhof-Duffenter sector on 20 September.

Then towards evening [the Americans] set out with an armored group against the farm buildings in Hochwegerhof and took the farm against the violent resistance of the 6th Co/89 of the 2nd Battalion. Unteroffizier [Corporal] Nuebert of 6th Co reported: "Escaped from Hochwegerhof by dawn. Noticed there five halftracks, one heavy machinegun and five tanks of the Sherman type. One group of engineers out of the 12th Engineering Battalion on a mine-laying mission was encountered by that armored combat group, and may have been killed. At the time of my escape, 20 of our soldiers were still in Hochwegerhof; one radio operator, one wachtmeister [sergeant] severely wounded, five members of the air force, six members of 6th Co and seven men from other units. There was one German caterpillar tractor left in the farmyard."[55]

On the other side of Stolberg, the attack around Munsterbusch was also renewed at daylight on 20 September, a day when the 1st Division artillery ammunition situation was so bad that fire missions were refused unless enemy positions could actually be observed. At 0930 Captain Merendino's Company B jumped off with Orr's Company B to secure the road leading from Munsterbusch to Busbach. But the enemy infiltrated throughout their positions while the companies worked through the rows of houses along this roadway. "It was a question of going from building to building," Driscoll remembered. "Rifle squads would go from the bottom to top, with the tanks [Lieutenant Colonel] Blanchard sent up helping some. Civilians found in the cellars were a hindrance in the fighting, but they were left there and later evacuated."[56]

"The enemy had four or more Mark V tanks which kept the streets covered," Orr added. "They fought with great stubbornness."[57]

Finally, the infantry found they had to operate with bazookas and rifle grenades. From behind, tanks would cover the buildings, firing over the heads of the advancing foot soldiers. In squad groups they would move up and take over the buildings, cleaning them out with grenades. Late in the afternoon we got three tanks cornered at a four-way road junction and the infantry moved up with bazookas to knock them out. They caught one in the act of trying to blast its way through the wall of a nearby factory in order to affect an escape. [Driscoll's] men came up on the right to fire with bazookas on the southernmost of the three remaining tanks and blew its turret off. About 100 to 150 prisoners were taken from the buildings south of the railroad spurs which forked around the factory area to the north.

Lieutenant Colonel Blanchard's continuing mission for his 1st Battalion of the 32nd Armored Regiment on 20 September was to open up the Munsterbusch-Busbach road from the north, then pivot southward to attack the pillboxes and dragon's teeth from the rear.[58] This became possible after Orr's and Driscoll's infantry cleared the ground across the stretch where the roadway began. Task Force Miller, meanwhile, was ordered to push north through the pillbox line and regain the main crossroad at Busbach that was evacuated the day before. This attack moved off at 1230, and by 1335 they reached the crossroad. Company D infantry then moved up the main street while Miller's tanks roamed through the backyards of the houses.

Captain Russell, the S-1 for the 36th Armored Infantry Regiment, was an eyewitness to the events that followed. During the afternoon he had been conducting reconnaissance for a new command post so he saw the fight from a good observation point. "The iron gate at the dragon's teeth was not in place and nothing else had been put on the road," he recalled. "No fire came from the enemy as the tanks approached in single column. Lieutenant Colonel Miller sent his tanks through the obstacles after dispatching one tank to the rear of the houses on the road [where I was]. I saw 20 or more Germans beginning to walk from one pillbox close to the road northeastward to a second box. They were apparently unaware of Miller's tanks, now some 100 yards away."[59]

The engineers removed a few mines that were in front of the gap by the dragon's teeth and then the gunner of a tank, as well as Russell's own jeep driver, opened up with their machine guns, pinning the enemy infantry to the ground. Only a few scattered rifle shots answered, so Miller came over to join Captain Russell. After looking the situation over, Miller decided to pin this enemy group down with more fire while attacking the second pillbox. Some of his tanks turned immediately toward this box and fired directly on it with 75mm antiphosphorous ammunition. The shells hit hard. The tankmen then turned their turrets toward the first pillbox and poured fire into the emplacements; again very little return fire came from the Germans. Miller's tanks then attacked a third pillbox, approaching more slowly this time and furnishing a base of fire to support each one as they advanced.

"In the attack, the engineers—acting as infantry—followed closely behind the tanks," Russell noted. "As the tanks moved up to the 20 Germans, those who were still alive surrendered. Shortly thereafter the enemy also came out of the [other two] pillboxes. A total of 81 prisoners were taken."[60] Antitank fire began to come in on Miller's armor as they pushed a little farther north, but none of the twelve medium tanks in the attack were hit. They secured a total of six pillboxes before the force halted; five were on the right side of the road and one was on the left. The 83rd Reconnaissance Battalion made a sweeping circle to the east to mop up, and held about a thousand yards off the Busbach-Munsterbusch road for the night. Other U.S. forces on the move were also slowed. Sniper fire had kept stalling the advance of Driscoll's infantry and Captain Folk's Company L; they also consolidated on line for the night. Driscoll's 1st Battalion had suffered numerous casualties. Earlier that morning, his S-3 had reported to the 16th Infantry Regimental S-3:

> Here is our [rifle company] strength: Company A—4 officers and 98 men; Company B—110; Company C—110. We lost about 300 men in the last five days.[61]

Oberst Engel maintained that "on 21 September the first battle for Aachen died away. The battle could, at least for the sector of the 12th Infantry Division, be considered finished. Neither the envelopment of Aachen, nor the quick breakthrough in the direction of Duren-Julich had succeeded, and the fighting strength of the enemy had decreased."[62]

Engel's assessment was actually quite correct. In addition to losses suffered by Huebner's 1st Division over the past several days, back on 18 September Major General Rose's 3rd Armored Division had just 153 medium tanks out of an authorized strength of 232. The numbers increased slightly by 21 September to 158, but 19 armored vehicles were undergoing repairs in unit shops. Many tanks still in action could not shift into high gear; others desperately needed new engines. Col. Eugene C. Orth, the division's S-4, declared at the time that the number of tanks effectively available for front-line duty was "in the neighborhood of 75-85."[63]

Supply shortages had also become problematic. Sufficient gasoline was available, but there was a dearth of ammunition—particularly 105mm shells. These shells had to come from distant 1st Army dumps since the depots at nearby Liege were not yet fully operational. Orth maintained that the shortage of other necessary ammunition never became critical, as the basic load was 273 rounds of 75mm ammunition per mounted machine gun on the division's armored vehicles. This was available. It was cut into, but Orth could not recall any action where a shortage of ammunition played a decisive role in the fighting.

> In the last analysis, [I] believe that it was the enemy resistance rather than supplies that halted the division. In the general picture, the shortage of tanks and the exhaustion of the troops were obviously important. Nevertheless, it was the stubborn action of the enemy, fighting on his own soil that slowed down and finally halted the attack.[64]

There was also some debate about troop morale at the time. "The strain of the long advance on the armored [personnel], especially the armored infantry, was a factor that was very important, although difficult to measure accurately," Colonel Orth maintained. He and other officers were of the opinion that the infantry "had just about reached the limit of their endurance." Major General Rose, however, believed that the infantry could have continued.

This would have been difficult for the 36th Armored Infantry Regiment.[65] During a late-afternoon meeting an enemy shell fell in front of a pillbox in the woods west of Mausbach, killing Company H's Captain Getter, Captain Vaughn of Company I, the battalion's S-2 and S-3, Lt. Edward Rosenfeld, an artillery liaison officer, and two enlisted men. Major Dunn and a number of others were also wounded.

The tankers and infantry of Task Force Mills also might not have agreed with Rose the next day. Wounded had lain on Hill 287 since the day before, and it was not until 1030 hours that Lt. Paul R. Long led a medic half-track onto the hill to retrieve the injured. The morning was warmer and the weather had cleared after days of rain and fog, so urgent requests for air support were also made at this time. One flight came in, but had to return for fuel after making just one pass at the hill; other flights already had other missions. Another flight, whose targets were first marked by the artillery with red smoke, abandoned its effort because it was determined that friendly vehicles were too close to the drop area. Thus enemy fire, particularly from one dug-in tank still atop Hill 287, continued to harass Task Force Mills throughout the morning and many of the wounded remained where they fell.

Company E had been reconstituted, but it was noted at the time that "one platoon was so fresh that some of the men had done little more than fire their M-1 rifles."[66] Attempts to move onto Hill 287 by this platoon were thwarted by machine-gun fire from houses at Duffenter in the early afternoon. A friendly artillery concentration was followed by a smoke screen at 1400 before the platoon moved out again toward the hill to dig in and outpost the position. During this move, the platoon leader was wounded, and the remaining men got bogged down.

At 1520 Colonel Boudinot radioed Mills with a new mission. In light of the situation on Hill 287, the task force was ordered to move to the northwest along the road joining Donnerburg with Birkengang, then pivot southwest to make contact with Task Force Hogan in Stolberg. During the previous night, Boudinot had ordered Hogan to attack into Stolberg with Major Adams's depleted rifle companies, now just 404 men strong with many of his wounded still not evacuated. Accordingly, Mills withdrew his infantry, where they mounted the decks of their tanks for the attack. Colonel Boudinot had also ordered Lieutenant Colonel Lovelady to come forward with elements of his task force to relieve Mills's infantry. They were greeted rudely. Just as these men arrived a terrific enemy artillery barrage scattered the Americans.

Enemy antitank fire also exacted a toll when Lovelady's armored vehicles reached the road junction south of Duffenter at about 1800. His Company D was down to just five tanks and no officers; Company E had only one officer and six tanks. Two platoons of Company I had also joined in the relief effort; these men were able to retake two pillboxes and capture six prisoners while suffering three casualties. Company H, now commanded by Lieutenant Burdick, reached the crossroad later in the dark, but quickly lost an accompanying tank. Two pillboxes on Hill 287 were joined by enemy artillery and together they rained fire and shells on the company throughout the night, compelling Burdick's force of just sixty-seven men, nineteen of whom were replacements that day, into defensive positions.

Major Mills had started his new attack late that afternoon with just four tanks in his Company F, the three remaining in Company I, and fourteen light tanks from Company A. He opted to take a circuitous path just to the northwest of Birkengang after departing Duffenter, forgoing the direct route suggested by higher headquarters. It proved to be a costly decision. German tank fire came in from the west, hitting the left flank of the moving armor and forcing two of Company A's light tanks to get stuck in some off-road mud. Then as the remainder of the column advanced farther, enemy fire opened up from the rear; it was ineffectual and the armored vehicles kept going. But as they turned southwest toward Stolberg after passing the Birkengang area, more fire came in frontally from bunkers populated with German infantry. These combined enemy actions forced Mills to start coiling his tanks and infantry in a defense huddle. He eventually turned his armored vehicles back toward the factory district in Birkengang where he strung the column along some zinc slag piles for added protection that night.[67]

In order to hold Munsterbusch on 21 September, it was necessary for Lieutenant Colonel Orr to establish a defensive position north and east of the factory area on the brow of a hill that overlooked Stolberg. Orr's Company B and Captain Merendino's Company B of the 16th Infantry Regiment were employed to accomplish this. After an assault with bayonets fixed, they took the hill at 1530 hours with a loss of ten men. They renewed the attack at 1600, this time to reach into the factory area in the northern part of Munsterbusch. Medium tanks supported the attack while the infantry used their bazookas to blast at the walls of the buildings before moving closer to take out the Germans with grenades and rifles. The tanks could not move because of the close quarters, but the infantrymen fought from building to building and knocked out two enemy tanks in the process. Snipers were particularly difficult to deal with; they hampered the attack by staying behind as the enemy forces retreated from one building to the next. Tunnels that ran from cellar to cellar were also problematic. "Every house was contested," one soldier remembered. "Holes had to be blasted, and passageways sealed to prevent the enemy from appearing in the rear of the advancing Americans."[68]

Still, by 1830 all of the factory area was cleared out and two of Orr's companies moved over to claim the slag piles to the north and northeast. Staying here became difficult, however, as fire from the direction of Hamm impeded the worn-down infantry. Orr decided to organize defensive positions where these piles afforded some protection. They took many prisoners; among the 460 civilians that interfered with operations that day were several Germans who had clearly changed out of their uniforms to avoid capture. Captain Merendino's Company B sent out patrols to comb the downward slope of the hill overlooking Stolberg, and with little effort cleaned out the Germans in this area. By nightfall, Lieutenant Colonel Driscoll had taken over the entire sector to the railroad tracks on the outskirts of Stolberg, tying in with Captain Briggs's Company C on the left.

On 21 September First Army finally ordered VII Corps to go on the defense. The Army historian noted:

> On the surface General Collins's order to consolidate looked like sorely needed rest for most of the troops of the VII Corps. Yet the divisions were in the delicate situation of being through the Westwall in some places, being half through in others, and at some points not having penetrated at all. The line was full of extreme zigs and zags. From an offensive standpoint, the penetrations of the Schill Line were too narrow to serve effectively as springboards for further operations to the east.[69]

Orr's 1st Battalion of the 36th Armored Infantry was relieved of its positions and moved to a defensive area near Busbach. Task Force Miller saw resistance vanish in the built-up section of Munsterbusch that they defended; his force moved to the divisional reserve area near Brenig. After knocking out a Tiger tank among the houses south of Munsterbusch, Lieutenant McDonald's Company D of the 32nd Armored Regiment reached a position where his platoons could dominate the Munsterbusch-Busbach Road.

Lieutenant Colonel Peckham's 3rd Battalion of the 18th Infantry Regiment was brought up to the western flank of the American position at Munsterbusch, and Captain Folk's Company L was returned to Peckham's command. His reunited companies relieved the 83rd Reconnaissance Battalion on 21 September. Task Force Blanchard eventually held the line on the northeast side of Munsterbusch where his infantry and armor took up positions overlooking Stolberg.

"When the gap was made through the second line of defenses at England, the plan was revised," Brigadier General Hickey noted as he looked back on the last few days of fighting.[70]

> Two columns were to follow the road from England, northeast to Schneidmuhle. At this point they were to fork. Task Force X [Doan] on the left was to cut north in the woods, then east to the outskirts of Eschweiler, and then north again to the objective— Duerwiss. From the fork, Task Force Y [Blanchard] was to go to Steinfurth, and then take the main road northeast through Eschweiler to Duerwiss. The opposition in the Stolberg area disrupted all of the plans.

Major Adams's 1st Battalion of the 26th Infantry Regiment spent 21 September on the southern outskirts of Stolberg "cleaning out the area house-by-house, kicking in doors, lobbing grenades and fighting at close range amongst the snake-like structures in town." By early the next morning Captain Anderson's Company A was advancing up the main street, Adolf Hitler Strasse, while the other companies held positions along parallel streets. Then at 1500 word came down that the battalion was being immediately relieved and returned to the 1st Division. During the time that his men were attached to the 3rd Armored Division, Adams experienced 27 enlisted men killed; 6 officers and 127 enlisted men wounded and evacuated; 3 other officers and 21 enlisted men with lesser wounds; and an additional officer and 43 enlisted men either injured or otherwise unable to engage in combat due to sickness or capture. On 22 September

Major General Huebner called the 26th Infantry's commanding officer, Colonel Seitz, and told him, "The 1st Battalion did a fine job, and I am proud of them."[71] Three months later, the battalion received a Presidential Unit Citation for its actions in breaching the Siegfried Line wherein it was noted that "over 300 prisoners were taken and twice as many enemy soldiers were killed or seriously wounded."[72]

Task Force Lovelady was relieved by the 2nd Battalion of the 32nd Armored Regiment and other elements of Task Force Orr on 25 September; his men and armored vehicles returned to Brenig for rest and refitting. Task Force Hogan was also relieved after the defensive positions Hogan had been fighting for in Stolberg were strengthened by the 1st Battalion of the 32nd Armored Regiment. Task Force Mills later joined Hogan in assembly areas for rest and badly needed vehicle maintenance after being relieved by the 2nd Battalion of the 36th Armored Infantry Regiment. Colonel Boudinot was also promoted to brigadier general on 25 September.

LXXXI Corps' *Generalleutnant* Schack noted "up to this time every enemy attack to break through south of Aachen on the right wing of Corps had failed. Since nothing of special importance happened during the next few days, 21 September 1944 may justly be considered the final day of the first Battle of Aachen."[73]

During the three weeks of my command we succeeded, in spite of heavy fighting and daily recurring crisis, in filling out the skeleton commands to such an extent that efficient units were organized with surprising rapidity. . . . Everywhere the most astonishing shrewdness and organizational skill manifested itself.

The number of enemy infantry units was only a third greater than ours, but among all the units subordinated to LXXXI Corps only the 12th Division, which arrived toward the end of the battle, could be called [a] normal fully-equipped division. The troops themselves were completely worn out. For the most part the bulk of them, consisting of fragments of combat veteran divisions, had been fighting continuously since the enemy landings [in Normandy]. They could not be allowed to rest because of the units' diminishing strength and the continuous withdrawals. Their socks and boots were in rags. Tired and forlorn, they literally dragged themselves along. Nevertheless they were ready, again and again, as far as their failing strength permitted, to heed the call of duty with eager loyalty. In spite of reserves, the fine relationship between officers and men of all grades held, in unfailing unity, during every action.

The final mission—to hold the Westwall—was accomplished only imperfectly, however, because of the inadequacy of our forces and means of combat. Even at the end of the first Battle of Aachen, the deep pocket in the Stolberg area remained. On the other hand, we succeeded in preventing the decisive break-through planned by the enemy south of Aachen, aimed at the Ruhr industrial area.

Schack was relieved of his command during the night of 20 September. After the war he maintained that his relief was in part because of "conflict with [Nazi] Party agencies," arguing that "up to the very last minute the Party tried to deceive the population regarding the serious-ness of the situation [at Aachen]; that the sad military situation was due to sabotage by the generals." When Aachen was being evacuated, it did indeed lead to serious conflicts between the military command and the Party, particularly with *Generalleutnant* Count von Schwerin of the 116th Panzer Division. Schack, in closing his case later while in Ameri-can captivity, argued, "Added to the paralyzing enemy superiority in the air, a crushing superiority in tanks, artillery and ammunition, there was constant trouble, in matters both great and small, with narrow-minded, spiteful and pompous Party officials."[74]

General der Infanterie Friedrich Köchling was given command of LXXXI Corps on 20 September. A veteran of the Russian front, Köchling had arrived at the corps' command post in Niederzier, 8 kilometers north of Duren, on 18 September. Here he was given a short report by Schack on the tactical situation around Aachen. Undoubtedly consistent with his feelings at the time, Schack also reported on the political complications he was experiencing. That night Köchling went over to the command post of 7th Army, located east of Muenstereifel, for another hasty orienta-tion. Later, snubbing Schack, he offered, "I assumed command in a situ-ation expressed by the General Command as being a 'successful' result."[75] Certainly not in complete harmony with these sentiments, Köchling maintained that "the 12th Division [had] failed to accomplish its mission. It recorded slight unimportant gains and suffered heavy casualties."

The 12th Infantry Division's *Oberst* Engel still maintained that his forces "marred the main aim of the enemy; the envelopment of Aachen was avoided."[76] He later noted that his losses were heaviest during the first two days his division was engaged, 16–17 September. Overall, he cited two hundred men lost during what he called the first Battle of Aachen out of a combat strength of six hundred in the 89th Grenadier Regiment. His 2nd Battalion of the 48th Grenadier Regiment lost another two hundred men, half of its combat strength. Engel's three grenadier regiments totaled approximately six hundred losses, of which 80 percent were fatal.

For the local population, sacrifices were not measured in killed. They were counted by the number who had shown the courage to stay in their homes and assist others. Eilendorf served as one example. "On September 15 1944 Allied troops took our town," wrote the Commissioner for the village.[77]

> True communities of the people were formed in the cellars. Nuns of the Convent, the bakers Kaussen of Rootgenerstreet, Kirchvink and Schmitz did their duty. The same goes for the butcher Schwanon and his brother-in-law. The occupation forces have now arrived, and not one of the population has been mistreated. They took care of the sick and wounded and placed them in their own hospitals. One lone woman and her children sleep in the same cellar with about thirty American soldiers, and not one of them has bothered her.

Limited German attacks were carried out during the remainder of September, although considerable numbers of skirmishes involving smaller unit actions continued in and around both sides of Stolberg. One such action on 24 September resulted in the awarding of the Medal of Honor to the 3rd Battalion of the 18th Infantry Regiment's Company I Staff Sgt. Joseph E. Schafer. Defending an important road intersection in Munsterbusch, Schafer's undermanned platoon was attacked by two German companies that day. When one of his rifle squads was forced out of the intersection and another captured, his few remaining men were left to defend the position alone.

After moving this small force to a nearby house to avoid a two-pronged attack to his flank, Schafer, a Long Island, New York, native, led his men in breaking the first wave of enemy infantry when they came at the house with their flamethrowers and grenades, personally killing or wounding many. When the Germans regrouped for another attack, this time Schafer killed or wounded six more before charging a hedgerow where even more enemy soldiers were following the ones that fell. Here, he killed five others single-handedly, wounded two, and took ten stunned prisoners.

His company commander, Capt. Robert E. Hess, launched a counter-attack to regain the intersection soon after this, where Sergeant Shafer again exhibited exceptional initiative. "Crawling and running in the face of heavy fire, he overtook the enemy and liberated the Americans cap-tured earlier. Schafer, armed only with his rifle, killed between 15 to 20 Germans and wounded just as many."[78] His Medal of Honor, America's highest citation for military achievement, went on to note, "His courage was responsible for stopping the enemy breakthrough that day."

A letter of instruction written by First Army the next day, and then amended on 27 September, defined new boundaries for both VII and XIX Corps. To the north of Aachen, General Corlett's XIX Corps was to protect the right flank of 21 Army Group, which would now make the main Allied effort to envelop the Ruhr from the vicinity of the Arnheim bridgehead. XIX Corps was further instructed to launch a coordinated attack on or about 1 October with the mission of penetrating the *West-wall* north of Aachen, and then gaining contact with General Collins's VII Corps northeast of the ancient imperial city. Corlett's continuing orders were to assist the subsequent advance of VII Corps by seizing and securing Linnich and Julich.[79]

At 0600 hours on 28 September the 246th *Volksgrenadier* Division, comprised of the 352nd, 404th, and 689th Infantry Regiments and commanded by *Oberstleutnant* Maximilian Leyherr, relieved the 116th Panzer Division. The next day Leyherr's forces took on the responsibility for the defense of Aachen.[80]

The 246th *Volksgrenadier* Division had been assembled just a few weeks earlier, but with a full number of men well provided with weapons, vehicles, and horses. However, according to a report by LXXXI Corps, the newly arrived division suffered from "a complete lack of training and welding. Not only were the officers barely acquainted with each other, makeup of the units took place in part during transportation to the deployment area."[81]

> On 9 September, for example, an investigation by Army High Command/General Directorate/Special Staff A of 246th Volks- grenadier Division showed the following overall result: Due to the late arrival of the majority of men, weapons and equipment and the high percentage of young officers with no experience at the front, as well as the inadequate state of training, the division is not ready for deployment at the date ordered (20 September).

Nevertheless, on 29 September First Army issued a new letter of instruction.[82] With a fresh enemy division over the shoulders of the advancing American VII Corps, a noose now needed to be tightened around the city of Aachen.

CHAPTER 5

XIX Corps Crosses the Wurm River

*"I told the men we'd have to get down to the river
somewhere between a fast walk and a dog trot."*

LT. COL. ROBERT E. FRANKLAND

At 1800 hours on 22 September, a four-man patrol from the 1st Platoon of Company B, 117th Infantry Regiment, 30th Infantry Division, reached a haystack at the edge of an open field just east of Scherpenseel. Led by Lt. Robert F. Cushman, these men had been given the mission of determining the width and the depth of the Wurm River and establishing the best place for an assault crossing. Aerial photographs of the area, 15 kilometers north of Aachen, had been studied prior to the mission, and a route to the river had also been carefully selected.

Lieutenant Cushman had Sgt. James A. Billings, Pvt. Glen W. Drake, and Pvt. Brent Youenes with him for this mission. They had agreed on hand signals earlier that afternoon; one snap of the fingers meant go, and two meant halt. Their faces were caked with mud to camouflage them after darkness fell. Each man carried two grenades, a first-aid packet, and one bandolier of ammunition for their M1 rifles. To make the least sound possible, Cushman and Youenes removed the stacking swivels from their rifles; Billings even took off his rifle sling.

Enemy artillery was firing heavily that night, but the patrol used this to their advantage. Whenever Cushman saw the flash of German guns, he snapped once and his men moved out before the concussions were heard. Light rain had already deadened the sounds of their movement and the drowning roar of the artillery fire now also helped them avoid detection by German patrols. At approximately 2200, Cushman led his men away from the haystack, first side-stepping about 200 yards before they dropped down and crawled on their bellies to the brink of a hill. Here they stood up and started moving again, three yards apart along a road through a draw bordering the edge of a wooded area. "Things went well until Sergeant Billings stepped on some broken china that the Germans had strung along the approach," tall, thin Private Youenes remembered. "Then Lieutenant Cushman examined it carefully and we bypassed it."[1]

By now it was nearing midnight, and the men were crawling again. Before too long they came to a barbed-wire fence, the lowest strand about a foot off the ground. Youenes held the wires with his gloved hand and Cushman cut it. Moments later a white flare shot into the air from a nearby pillbox, but the patrol was lucky. No one saw them silhouetted in the sudden light.

While moving in the direction of a house closer to the river soon afterward, a cow made a noise that caused Cushman to whisper, "It sounds like a human being."[2] Private Drake then swore he saw a German guard patrolling the river, and Sergeant Billings thought he saw a lit cigarette in the darkness. The combination of the cow's manlike sounds and the jumpy thinking that they were being watched caused the men to stay still for a full thirty minutes.

When they moved again, the patrol split up; Cushman and Billings went to the right while Drake and Youenes pushed off to the left. Each pair looked ahead and thought that a road was actually the river. Eventually they came abreast, the men now about ten yards away from each other. More ominous noises followed; this time a German opened up with a burp gun, but the echoes of its fire convinced the men that it had come from too far away, and that they were still not likely seen. By now they had reached the road. An enemy machine gunner was firing some tracers to their right, illuminating ghostly outlines of pyramid-shaped slag piles in the distance. An occasional mortar round fell in the area. "Then I began to notice a gurgling, grating sound to our immediate front," Private Youenes recalled. "I said that's a fast running stream and it's going to be shallow. But our river turned out to be some kind of mechanized vehicle which was working up around the pillboxes across the river."[3]

The men moved out again, this time in short rushes, leapfrogging forward until they got to within 20 yards of the Wurm River. Here

Lieutenant Cushman whispered for his men to wait while he personally reconnoitered another 20 yards to the right before coming back and going 10 yards to the north. Then he quietly called for Youenes, and the pair edged up to the bank of the river in the inky blackness of the night. The private thought the river was about 18 to 20 feet deep and told Cushman this before he took Youenes's hand for balance and said he was going to go down the bank to find out how deep the river really was.

Private Youenes later explained:

> Lieutenant Cushman went down into the water with no noises, waded across to the opposite bank and then came back. Two flares again shot up over the pillboxes, but still apparently nobody saw us. When he got back he reached up for my hand to help him up the bank. He was shivering and dripping wet. Then we started back, and didn't give a damn about crawling; we just high-tailed it back as fast as possible. On the way Lieutenant Cushman said he figured the river was between three to four and a half feet deep and averaged 15 feet in width. I told him it was more like 18 feet wide, because he had taken five and half steps when he went across.[4]

The important mission was over at 0230. The plan to use assault boats for crossing the Wurm River was abandoned following the reconnaissance. The route discovered by the patrol was also exactly the same as that used by the 1st Platoon of Morgantown, West Virginia, native captain Spiker's Company B when the 1st Battalion of the 117th Infantry Regiment led the 30th Infantry Division in breaching the Siegfried Line.

"Cushman was a brave son of a gun," remembered Lt. William J. O'Neil, leader of the battalion's Pioneer Platoon. "He came in dripping wet from that patrol and stood at attention in front of Colonel Frankland. The colonel told him 'you've done an outstanding job; you will have saved many lives.'"[5] Cushman also brought back the news that there were no Germans west of the river; rather he had only heard digging on the other side near the railroad tracks some 200 or more yards away. Later that night Cushman told O'Neil that he thought some kind of improvised bridging would work when it came time for the actual attack.

"It turned out everything he suggested as a result of that patrol was sound," Lieutenant O'Neil recalled later.

The overall mission for Major General Corlett's XIX Corps was to rupture the Siegfried Line and envelop Aachen; General Hobbs's 30th Infantry Division would turn southward after the breakthrough. General Huebner's 1st Infantry Division was to contain the city to the west and south, then move northeastward to affect a closure of the roadways and rail lines into Aachen. The encirclement would be completed when the two divisions linked up. The date for the 30th Division's attack was set for 1 October.

The *Westwall* in Corlett's sector was a continuous array of obstacles that extended across XIX Corps' entire front. Unlike the area south of Aachen where the antitank barriers formed the entire outer line of the *Westwall*, dragon's teeth were placed only across the ridgeline just to the north of the city. The Wurm River formed the natural obstacle in the line from this point northward, up to where it joined the Roer River in the northernmost reach of the Corps' sector at Geilenkirchen. Immediately east of the river the railroad line ran northward from Aachen in over 70 percent of the XIX Corps' new sector. Tracks usually followed the river valley; however, to keep the railways as straight as possible numerous cuts and fills had been constructed in the Wurm's wandering streambed.

The pillbox band in the corps' zone was generally three kilometers in depth behind the river-railroad line, with only one noticeable point where the boxes thinned out near the coal deposit–rich junction of the Wurm and Roer River Valleys. While the open land near the junction itself would be a hindrance to cross-country movement by any force, the Germans took few chances. The greatest concentration of pillboxes in the whole XIX Corps' sector occurred on the nose south of the river junction to the east of flat Randerath. Defenses west of the Wurm River from which the Americans would attack consisted mainly of minefields and barbed wire like that encountered by Lieutenant Cushman's patrol. As his men also discovered, the banks of the Wurm were generally abrupt and naturally steep. Any bridging operations would be made more difficult not just by this, but also because bridges would have to be constructed while U.S. soldiers were under direct enemy observation and probable fire.

With the greatest density of pillboxes and other terrain obstacles in the northernmost sector of the line and the next greatest around Geilenkirchen, Corlett eliminated both areas as penetration points. Rather, the Rimburg-Palenberg section of the line, 9 miles north of Aachen and 3 miles southwest of Geilenkirchen, was selected for the breakthrough even before the leading troops of the 30th Infantry Division reached the German border. The road net, pillbox density, and a better opportunity for exploitation of the breakthrough to the north, east, and south without being faced with another terrain obstacle also factored into the decision to attack here.

> Whereas a rupture of the Westwall farther south might bring quicker juncture with the VII Corps, General Hobbs placed greater emphasis upon avoiding urban snares and upon picking a site served by good supply routes. That the enemy's fresh 183rd Volks-Grenadier Division had entered the line from Rimburg north toward Geilenkirchen apparently had no appreciable influence on General Hobbs's selection of an assault site, possibly because the XIX Corps G-2, Colonel [Washington] Platt, deemed troops of this new division only "of a shade higher quality" than those of the 49th and 275th Divisions, which the XIX Corps had manhandled from the Albert Canal to the German border.[6]

Artillery preparation for this assault would begin on 26 September, nearly a full week ahead of D-Day on 1 October. At H-hour minus 120 minutes, IX Tactical Air Command planned to provide nine groups of medium bombers, as well as two groups of fighter bombers, in order to effect a saturation bombing of the breakthrough area, knock out the pillboxes immediately facing the assault regiments, and also eliminate all enemy reserves that could be used for an immediate counterattack. Reinforced 30th Infantry Division artillery also planned to blackout enemy antiaircraft artillery positions fifteen minutes prior to the air attack. Once the infantry got through, Maj. Gen. Ernest Harmon's 2nd Armored Division would follow through the gap, and then drive to the north and east to protect the corps' left flank.[7]

The mission for General Hobbs's 30th Infantry Division was twofold. First, it would make the breakthrough; second, it would swing south toward Aachen to relieve the pressure on VII Corps by linking up with Huebner's 1st Infantry Division. Hobbs's plan was to attack on a narrow front with two regiments abreast: Kansas native Col. Walter M. Johnson's 117th Infantry Regiment on the left and wiry Col. Edwin M. Sutherland's 119th Infantry Regiment on the right. Col. Hammond D. Birks's 120th Infantry Regiment was to initially execute a holding attack against the German defenses in and around Kerkrade, a built-up small mining town with about 25,000 Dutch citizens, and then be prepared to attack eastward or to come through the gap to join in the assault to the south.

The two weeks prior to the new attack date saw little activity along the division front other than routine patrolling, some reconnaissance missions, and an occasional exchange of fire. One thing had been confirmed. The Germans would have good observation over the ground that the assaulting forces would have to cross, some 1800 yards of expansive beet fields that faded into slopes and quarries. Beyond here lay more open fields that sloped downward through scattered draws some 250 yards to the Wurm River. A wooded area bordered the Scherpenseel-Marienberg road, which was the left boundary of the attack zone; the woods also extended to the north-south Marienberg-Rimburg road. The right boundary was the Holland-German border, marked only by barbed wire. Marienberg, last occupied by a hostile force during the Napoleonic Wars, was situated approximately a quarter of a mile southeast of Scherpenseel on the west bank of the river opposite Palenberg, a mixed agricultural and coal-mining village. Wary American recon forces knew every town could be made a strongpoint if the enemy so chose.

The only bridge in the attack zone had already been blown. Moreover, once across the river the attackers would have to advance over approximately 250 more yards of gently rising ground before coming to a high hedge line near the Aachen-Geilenkirchen railroad embankment. Beyond this the infantry might get its first break; some natural protection from enemy fire would be afforded across gently rising, open ground where the well-camouflaged and mutually supporting pillboxes stretched out another 250 yards away. Numerous independent firing trenches dotted the area, and beyond the nine pillboxes in the immediate attack zone for the 117th Infantry Regiment, all clustered around a central crossroad south of Palenberg, other boxes were located to the north and south. A high bluff jutted out from the north edge of Palenberg; more pillboxes were here. Two slag piles on the east edge of the town afforded the German artillery observers 360-degree views over the entire area. In a dispatch to his paper in New York, Drew Middleton described the attack zone as a "countryside where huge slag heaps and tall factory chimneys contrasted queerly with rolling green meadows and heavily wooded hills."[8] Minefields, barbed wire, and antitank ditches also extended across the planned avenue of attack, some 2,400 yards from the initial line of departure east of Scherpenseel to the pillbox area.[9]

Initial corps-level planning for the attack had been based mainly on these terrain and fixed-defense studies with little detailed knowledge of the enemy disposition. Intelligence, in fact, was difficult to secure because of the change in German force strength from day to day in the later part of September.[10] However, just two reinforced rifle companies (later learned from prisoners to be *Leutnant* Hofner's 3Co and *Leutnant* Kartner's 14Co) of Hauptman Buhvogel's 330th Regiment's 1st Battalion of the 183rd *Volksgrenadier* Division were estimated to be in the assault area as Colonel Platt was refining his intelligence assessments toward the end of the month. Army official history noted:

> South from Rimburg, five battalions were operating under the 49th and 275th Divisions. He estimated that the Germans had four battalions of light and medium artillery capable of firing into the 30th Infantry zone, plus a battery of 210mm. guns and one or two larger caliber railroad guns. Observers had detected only an occasional tank in the vicinity. In the matter of reserves, Platt predicted the Germans would have at least one battalion from each of the three regiments of the 183rd Division available for quick counterattacks, while the 116th Panzer Division and contingents of an infantry division recently identified near Aachen might be backing up the line.[11]

The 183rd Division's 330th Regiment 1st Battalion rifle companies in the Palenberg-Rimburg area were indeed supported by Artillery

Regiment 219, comprised of one battalion with at least three antitank
batteries, another battalion with three batteries of 105mm howitzers, and
a third battalion with 155mm artillery pieces. The regiment's reserve battalion, the 2nd Battalion commanded by Hauptman Labs, was located
just behind Palenberg in the village of Beggendorf and could be used as a
counterattacking force. Two regiments comprised *Generalleutnant* Sigfrid
Macholz's 49th Division in the attack zone south of Rimburg: the 148th
and 149th Regiments. This division was estimated to have 5 battalions
with about 450 men in each. *Oberstleutnant* Leyherr's 246th *Volksgrenadier* Division, which Colonel Platt thought might be backing up the
49th and 183rd Divisions, had been ordered to Aachen on 28 September.

The tactical mission for Wolfgang Lange's 183rd *Volksgrenadier* Division, directly opposite the 30th Infantry Division zone of attack, was
defense, and above all to hold the *Westwall*. A German Order of the Day
captured later sheds keen insight into the thinking of its leaders and men
at the time:

> Soldiers! Offensive spirit in defense shall not be relaxed. You
> must show the enemy we are masters of the no man's land. Only
> he [who] is the strongest who can fulfill this requirement. Pris-
> oners must be brought in who can tell us what is going on on
> the other side. I know this inspires many soldiers. Whoever is
> successful will reap the reward. Go to it soldiers: Bring me an
> American! Comrades, act accordingly because we defend our
> holy, beloved Fatherland against an opponent who does not
> belong here and whose greed started this war.
>
> We have many obligations toward our comrades who, in their
> belief in the future, have given the most that a human being can
> sacrifice. That should spur us on to pay our debt to them, to
> hate our enemy, to stop him wherever we can. Some day we
> again will take the offensive; we again will be the hammer and
> the enemy the anvil.[12]

Despite their call to be masters of the no man's land, the grenadiers
would be caught flat-footed as defenders of the German border. The division never anticipated that the Americans were going to attack across the
Wurm River on the boundary of their left wing. As Lange later noted:

The 183rd Division made feverish defense preparations, expecting that any time after September the enemy would continue [his] attacks. Because of the especially lively reconnaissance activity of the enemy at Geilenkirchen, the division anticipated the main part of the effort to be there.[13]

To accomplish the task of penetrating the *Westwall* where *Generalleutnant* Lange least expected it, Colonel Johnson's 117th Infantry plans called for an attack in column of battalions from positions near Scherpenseel, and then eastward to capture Ubach, the D-Day objective. Lieutenant Colonel Frankland's 1st Battalion, leading the assault, would strike south of the village of Marienberg, force a crossing of the Wurm River, and then capture the pillboxes between the railroad line and the western edge of Ubach. After gaining this objective, the battalion would take up a defensive position facing south. Company E of Tennessean Maj. Ben T. Ammons's 2nd Battalion, commanded by Capt. Harold F. Hoppe, would attack on the left of the 1st Battalion during the initial assault and clear the village of Marienberg.

Ammons's remaining companies would then move through the gap made in the pillbox belt by Frankland's forces and swing northward to clear Palenberg. Ammons was also assigned the important task of seizing the high ground studded with pillboxes on the north edge of town, as well as taking possession of the slag piles. Lt. Col. Samuel T. McDowell's 3rd Battalion would render fire support at the start of the attack, follow Ammons's companies through the gap created by Frankland's forces, then thrust eastward toward Ubach. Once the bridgehead was firmly secured, the 1st and 3rd Battalions would strike southward toward Alsdorf.

Company A of South Dakota native Lt. Col. William D. Duncan's 743rd Tank Battalion would follow closely behind Frankland's 1st Battalion to the Wurm River, then cross using a separate improvised bridge constructed of hallow culverts reinforced with logs. A tank dozer would push the bridge into the river, cross over and cut the bank on the east side, then return and if necessary prepare the approaches to permit passage of the assaulting armor; a tank would first pull the bridge to the river on a specially made sled.[14] The 743rd Tank Battalion's continuing mission would be to assist the infantry in assaulting the pillboxes. Company C of the 803rd Tank Destroyer Battalion, commanded by Capt.

Robert Sinclair, would also provide direct support to the infantry. The company would initially assist in the operation from the west side of the river before crossing behind Duncan's tanks to render additional assistance in reducing the pillboxes.

Maj. Antonin Sterba's 105th Engineer Combat Battalion would also support Frankland's breakthrough. Company A, commanded by Capt. James F. Rice, would provide demolition crews and the portable bridges originally conceived by Lieutenant Cushman the night he reconnoitered the Wurm River. In addition, Captain Rice would supply the assault weapons, to include flamethrowers, pole-charges, and satchel charges. His men would also clear mines and other obstacles, as well as physically destroy or fill the pillboxes with dirt after Frankland's companies first had their way with the Germans in them.

The 92nd Chemical Battalion would provide a rolling barrage of 4.2-inch mortars just ahead of the assaulting infantry companies. Capt. Robert Cole would be the forward observer with Company B; these men were responsible for seizing five pillboxes in their sector. Captain Spiker's platoons would follow the rolling barrage, which would move at predetermined distances and time intervals in front of his advancing troops. The mission for the mortars was to keep a wall of high-explosive shells just in front of the moving Americans, forcing any Germans in the assault area to keep their heads down and seek cover until U.S. soldiers were literally on top of them.

Capt. Morris A. Stoffer's Company C would attack to the right of Company B and capture four pillboxes; each company would have two platoons attacking abreast. They would be supported by an assault detachment, a sixteen-man unit carrying the flamethrowers, pole charges, grenades, and bazookas. Lieutenant O'Neil's three squads of seven men each from the Pioneer Platoon would carry the specially constructed ladder boards designed by O'Neil with the help of Staff Sgt. Oliver Pointer of the 105th Combat Engineer Battalion. Pointer supervised the building of these ladders; they were 15–20 feet long and 4 feet wide. They were painted green and would be thrown into the water when the soldiers reached the Wurm. Two would be placed into the banks of the river, forming a V-shaped base. A third, the longer one, would become the actual foot bridge when it was wedged in.

Lt. Stanley W. Cooper's heavy weapons Company D would have its heavy machine gunners split between Companies B and C; one platoon would be on the left flank of Captain Spiker's men and the other on the right flank supporting Stoffer's Company C. Cooper's 81mm mortar platoon would remain in Scherpenseel and participate in the regimental fire plan. Their first mission was to fire along the river line near the left of the battalion sector when the attack jumped off, and then shift to the pillbox area across the railroad track when the assault waves started descending toward the river. Company A, under the command of Capt. John E. Kent, would also remain in Scherpenseel. His men were designated as the reserve company in Lieutenant Colonel Frankland's scheme of operations. If called upon, Kent's men would take over any mission assigned to them.

The plans for Col. Edwin M. Sutherland's 119th Infantry Regiment initially called for Lt. Col. Robert Herlong's 1st Battalion to attack with two companies abreast and first seize Broekhuizen, a tiny village settled in the 1400s, before crossing the Wurm River and securing Rimburg. Company C, commanded by Salt Lake City, Utah, native Lt. Ferdinand Bons, was to attack on the left. Oklahoman Capt. Ross Y. Simmons's Company A would strike to the right. A platoon of Lt. John Lehnerd's Company D heavy machine guns would be assigned to both assault companies. Lehnerd's 81mm mortar platoon would provide general support by firing concentrations on call from a position on the high ground 200 yards south of the east-west Groenstratt-Rimburg road. Herlong's Company B, commanded by Somerset, Kentucky, native Capt. Edward E. McBride Jr., would initially remain in battalion reserve.[15]

Colonel Sutherland, hardened from previous combat in Normandy, later decided to mount the attack with two battalions abreast, instead of sending Herlong's 1st Battalion across the Wurm alone. In order to tie in with the 117th Infantry Regiment assault to the north, Sutherland tasked Lieutenant Colonel Cox's 2nd Battalion, along with a third platoon of the 743rd Tank Battalion's Company C, with attacking to the left of the 1st Battalion toward Rimburg. With this change in plans, Sutherland decided against initially attacking through Rimburg because, as an obvious crossing site, it would be heavily defended from the castle. In this new scheme of operations, Lt. Col. Courtney Brown's 3rd Battalion would be echeloned to the right rear of the 1st Battalion, protecting the southern flank of the regiment.[16]

Maps supplemented by vertical and oblique photos had been important tools in the regimental- and battalion-level planning for the upcoming assault. The oblique photos taken from ground locations revealed details about the pillboxes that verticals taken from the air could not show. Combined with local terrain reconnaissance of the assault area, this permitted the troops to become thoroughly familiar with their zone of operations.

The previous postponement of the attack on 20 September also gave the 30th Infantry Division ample time for special training in order to succeed at its mission. Preparations were actually divided into three phases, the first being the continuing effort to obtain all possible information on the enemy defensive positions. The second phase, training the assault troops, was carried out during the last week of the month even though the battalions were in the line. Using a rotation system, assault companies and all supporting units were given a two-day training period in the rear. This was followed by the third phase, even more detailed orientation and briefing for every man taking part in the operation.

Rotations began for the 119th Infantry Regiment on 24 September when elements of the battalions were relieved to start this intensive training and tactical planning. During the hours of darkness that night, both platoons of tanks and every man with Companies A, C, and D of Lieutenant Colonel Herlong's 1st Battalion, as well as his headquarters company, withdrew from their positions and moved approximately two miles to the rear. Here they received instruction and training on the use of flamethrowers, demolition charges, and bazookas; tactics and techniques of river crossings and assaulting fortified positions were stressed.[17]

Every element of Lieutenant Colonel Brown's 3rd Battalion underwent similar preparations starting on 25 September, and only Capt. Melvin Reisch's Company F of the 2nd Battalion participated in this training; Lieutenant Colonel Cox's other companies remained in the line. Brown, a veteran of very tough fighting with the 1st Division in North Africa, remembered, "This training was of value to the men, mainly because it included work with tanks and they got to know the armored tactics better."[18]

Preparations were comparable for Colonel Johnson's 117th Infantry Regiment. Major Ammons's 2nd Battalion relieved Lieutenant Colonel Frankland's 1st Battalion on the night of 24 September and his men withdrew to positions 3 kilometers west of Scherpenseel early the next morning. The first half of that day was spent familiarizing the men with the detailed plans of the attack, and then more specialized training followed. Some of the men practiced extensively with pole and satchel charges, flamethrowers, and Bangalore torpedoes and made dry runs assaulting pillboxes. Others focused on river crossings. This latter training was repeated again and again in a gully with stagnant water about the width of the Wurm River.

"When the battalion went out to the area, only one man knew how to operate a flamethrower," Lieutenant Colonel Frankland remembered. "All the prior training we had in the states and England was now useless because all of our assault elements had been wiped out in previous battles and there was a complete turnover in battalion personnel. We had to start from scratch. I had learned a lesson. This time instead of training only the assault detachments, we set out to familiarize all personnel with the tools."[19]

"I think the biggest thing we got out of the training period was Colonel Frankland's speech," Lieutenant O'Neil of the Pioneer Platoon remembered. "We had gotten a lot of replacements, and the battalion had been in the line for so long that this was one of the first opportunities for the colonel to speak to the whole battalion at once. The keynote of his speech was speed, speed, and more speed across all the terrain up to the pillboxes. He told us we would be home by Christmas if we cracked this line. But the emphasis on speed was what stuck in the boys' minds."[20]

"I had learned in the hedgerow country [of Normandy] that if you sat still you got mortars and artillery, and so there and here too I said to my men to keep moving fast and they will have less casualties," Frankland added, putting Lieutenant O'Neil's recollections in perspective. "Several of the 1st Battalion officers seconded this thought. I told the men we'd have to get down to the river somewhere between a fast walk and a dog trot. And that's just what they did in battle."[21]

By this time the 1st Battalion was already well acquainted with the attack zone. Lieutenant Colonel Frankland's S-2, Lt. Ernest R. Morgan, and Staff Sgt. Claude L. Flow Jr. had constructed an elaborate sand-based model of the area by boarding up the sides of an existing 5- by 12-foot table in an old German headquarters building that the battalion was using as its command post. A composite description of the sand table arrangement was provided in interviews with battalion officers at the time, and sheds light on its value in the continuing preparation for the operation:

> Cabbage leaves were used for vegetation, inked wooden blocks for houses, and numerous other expedients showed space relationships and strength of pillboxes, wire, the Wurm River, the ridge west of the river, the railroad and other terrain features. Pillboxes were numbered in red and company and platoon responsibilities were clearly drawn on the sand table. Everybody understood and visually saw his mission.
>
> From a planning standpoint Company A had the toughest job. Its commanders and men could not concentrate on certain, specific pillboxes, terrain and points along the Wurm River because they could not be sure they would be operating in the B or C Company sector; so they had to prepare for everything. Night after night while we were waiting in Scherpenseel, Captain John Kent would pull his support platoon out of the line and come back to the battalion CP to pore over the sand table until close to midnight.[22]

The impact was appreciated through the ranks. "The men knew the big and little picture so well that they conversed freely by number about the enemy pillboxes, and frequently showed in their arguments that they knew their flank units and their missions," stated Lt. John M. Maloney, leader of Company A's Weapons Platoon.[23]

After dark on 26 September the 1st Battalion returned to its positions around Scherpenseel and went back into the line. Training continued around the sand table until D-Day. As the day of the attack approached, patrols brought back further information that changed some of the plans. One such patrol on 27 September, led by towering, 225-pound Lt. Donald A. Borton of Company B, obtained additional information about the routes of approach to the river and up to the railroad track.[24] Earlier reconnaissance had revealed that there was an impassable hedge along the side of the railroad line but Borton's patrol discovered a gap where the barbed wire ended, allowing for easier passage. Another change resulted from air reconnaissance missions Lieutenant Colonel Frankland and his S-3, Capt. David Easlick, made in their Grasshopper Piper Cub. The conclusion was drawn that Company B did not have sufficient width of area to maneuver across the open space down to the river; the company's zone was subsequently widened and indicated as such on the sand table.[25]

Major Ammons's 2nd Battalion companies, as well as their tanks and supporting tank destroyers, withdrew from their positions near Grotenrath and entered the training area on 27 September. The battalion used the identical location the 1st Battalion had occupied, jumpstarting their training because the men were able to use the in-place simulated pillbox fortifications, foxholes, and other mocked-up fixed defenses that had helped serve Frankland's companies' training so well.

By this time the artillery preparation for the attack had already started. The mission, which began on 26 September, had four objectives. The first was the destruction of all visible pillboxes in the assault zone and outlying areas. Second was the prevention of any enemy buildup. The third objective was the destruction or neutralization of German artillery, antiaircraft guns, and mortars; the last was marking targets in preparation for the planned air strike. The observable results were mixed. The 105mm howitzers fired by the supporting field batteries lacked the velocity, weight, and accuracy required to destroy the pillboxes. The 155mm self-propelled (SP) guns used by Lt. Col. Bradford Butler's 258th Field Artillery Battalion produced the best results. The battalion succeeded in neutralizing some of the visible pillboxes in the division zone prior to the jump-off, but the overall effect on the enemy troops was again mixed.

Lt. Charles B. Robinson was a forward observer with Company B of the 117th Infantry Regiment; he remembered:

> For nearly a week we managed static OP's and did considerable firing on the pillboxes; the effect was almost negligible. At one time a self-propelled 155mm gun was pulled up at the OP I was on and fired direct at a range of 1500 yards. In 12 rounds fired it

scored 7 hits. The only effect on the pillbox was about four feet of concrete removed and some dirt off the top. The enemy inside was probably shaken up by the impact, but otherwise unhurt.[26]

The 258th Field Artillery Battalion used T-105 concrete penetrating fuses to inflict damage. After very careful prior planning and extensive reconnaissance, the battalion's pieces had been brought into positions under the cover of darkness. Operational security was a priority. In order not to disclose the zone of attack, this mission was extended into a number of sectors outside of the 30th Infantry Division's planned assault zone. From 26 September to 2 October the battalion fired on a total of forty-six pillboxes. Capt. Harley M. Force of the 197th Field Artillery Battalion recalled how using a mixture of the 258th's SP 155mm artillery tubes in conjunction with his batteries of 105mm guns proved helpful:

We fired on pillboxes several times and knocked the camouflage material off, exposing the pillbox for adjustment by heavier artillery. Another effective system we used was to adjust on boxes and stay laid on them while the heavies or mediums fired at them. When the heavier artillery hit a box, the survivors (if any) often ran out of the box in an attempt to get away. We would then fire on them and the effect was usually very gratifying.[27]

Preventing a buildup of enemy forces in the 30th Infantry Division's attack zone, the second objective of the pre-assault missions, proved more problematic. Overcast skies and rain practically every day during the last week of September prohibited the air forces from effectively spotting or interfering with enemy troop movements. In the assault area of the 117th Infantry Regiment, the 3-inch M10 guns of the 803rd Tank Destroyer Battalion nevertheless fired three hundred rounds per day at suspected enemy outpost positions. "We fired at six possible enemy outposts, including the two slag piles on the east edge of Palenberg, the church steeple in Ubach, a smokestack to the right of the slag piles, a cement fort outpost which we could see in the foreground 3,200 yards out, and what turned out to be a shrine on the south edge of Palenberg," remembered Company C's Captain Sinclair.[28] The slag piles were particularly important to his battalion; a catwalk from which enemy artillery fire might be called down could be seen about one-third of the way up. Lieutenant Cooper's Company D rendered additional assistance, firing another three hundred rounds of 81mm mortars into areas along the route of Company B's planned advance. All combined actions of the pre-assault missions still did not prevent the arrival from Düsseldorf of four companies of the 42nd Fortress Machine Gun Battalion when they reinforced the 1st Battalion of the 183rd Division's 330th Regiment on 30 September; three of the new arrival's companies each had sixteen heavy machine guns and the fourth was a bazooka company.[29]

The results of the third objective—destruction or neutralization of enemy artillery, antiaircraft artillery, and mortars—were also mixed. Corps and Division artillery carried out the first two missions jointly, the former placing the emphasis on counter-battery and neutralization of antiaircraft artillery. DIVARTY accepted responsibility for counter-mortar fire. The Germans practiced effective deception by intermingling their mortar and artillery fire to such an extent that it all appeared to be artillery fire. When the sound base failed to pick up the source of fire, the extent of the deception was apparent; however, in the time available it was impossible to locate the mortar positions and substantially neutralize them. The Germans constantly changed their mortar placements and by this practice greatly hindered the counter-mortar mission. Counter-battery strikes were thought to be more successful; however, the same enemy practice of firing their artillery and then displacing to another location made the mission a difficult one.

Aerial observers were assigned the primary task of spotting enemy antiaircraft artillery during the air strikes when the weather permitted. Active positions were promptly taken under fire with notable success and their locations were retained for use during the enemy antiaircraft artillery blackout preceding the saturation bombing on D-Day. Light battalions of DIVARTY found more success in marking the air support targets. Later reports of XIX Corps noted:

> The marking mission was assigned to particular battalions; data was computed and the mission assigned to a battery within the battalion. This battery was then given the requisite smoke for the mission, although violet smoke proved of no value as target

marking agencies because it had a tendency to blend with the predominantly green background of the foliage in late September. White phosphorous, while discernible, was not used to any great extent because of the concern that the enemy would nullify the effort by firing like smoke to cover the targets. Communication between the Division Air Support Party officer, Division Artillery Fire Direction Center and the battalion was continuous during the mission. In most instances direct lines were used, then as the planes approached the area the Air Support Party Officer coaxed the planes over the target area by use of his air-ground radio set. Smoke was fired at his command and an "on the way" was given for retransmission to the pilot. The method of fire was one battery volley, followed up with one round per minute until the target was identified by the air.[30]

During the time of the preparatory artillery strikes the men of the 30th Infantry Division experienced no strong enemy offensives. When they were not in the line, units were sent in trucks to Heerlen where hot showers were available at a coal mine installation. The men received hot meals and were shown movies at a schoolhouse in Scherpenseel. A cigarette shortage developed as D-Day approached, but normal allotments arrived before the men prepared to move into position for their first assault on a fortified line since arriving in Europe. On 30 September the 29th Infantry Division arrived from Brest and relieved General Harmon's 2nd Armored Division in its zone to the north of the 30th Division.

Maj. Ernest F. Jenista's 1st Battalion of Col. Paul A. Disney's 41st Armored Infantry Regiment moved from Jabeek to Waubach, arriving just after 0300 that morning. Here Jenista's tanks and other vehicles coiled to await the crossing of the Wurm River by the 2nd Battalion of the 67th Armored Regiment, commanded by Lt. Col. John D. Wynne. Jenista's battalion was to follow Wynne's and destroy the pillboxes before the Wurm River. Lieutenant Colonel Wynne's armored vehicles would follow directly behind Frankland's infantry, cross the Wurm, and then drive to Ubach before wheeling northward on the Ubach-Noverhof road, protecting the north flank of Jenista's armored infantry after they crossed the river.

On 1 October, plans were completed for the coming operation. All of Jenista's and Wynne's officers joined with officers of the 17th Engineer Battalion's Company C, the 3rd Platoon of the 702nd Tank Destroyer's Company B and the 92nd Field Artillery; they met with Colonel Disney and his regimental staff officers at the 41st Armored's command post. Disney's liaison officer established contact with Frankland's G-3, Captain Easlick, and reconnaissance was made by all of Disney's units along the routes to the air saturation area. All day, very heavy rain covered the entire front. This had changed D-Day to Monday, 2 October, when clearer weather was forecasted.[31]

By this time four 20-foot ladders and eight 15-foot ladders had been hidden by the 117th Infantry's Pioneer Platoon in a haystack along the field between Scherpenseel and Marienberg. "Half of these were for Company B; the other half for the support of Company A and for the 2nd Battalion following along the same route; 250 yards directly south of this haystack, we hid 12 more ladders of the same types, covering them over with mud and straw. These were for Company C initially, and then whichever outfit followed," remembered Lieutenant O'Neil.[32]

Farther southward in the attack zone of the 119th Infantry, patrols from Captain Simmons's Company A had also accomplished an important mission. Every pillbox in the company's zone of attack before the Wurm had been physically located, including those as far eastward in the woods on the near side of the railroad line across the river. "[Our] patrols had actually knocked out two of these pillboxes on the extreme right of the company's sector," Simmons reported in a later interview. "Every platoon in the company ran patrols up into the sector they were to assault."[33]

Some reconnaissance missions were not successful; one seven-man patrol led by Technical Sgt. Wade J. Verweire of Company C on 27 October was supposed to blow up a pillbox across the Wurm just east of Rimburg by the railroad line.[34] It was believed that this box was not occupied, but three German machine gunners fired upon the men when they reached the railroad cut. In an effort to help his trapped men, Capt. Earl C. Bowers was killed. Sergeant Wade, Pfc. Anthony T. Drabecki, and Pfc. John W. Kreigh were among the missing; despite desperate efforts well into the night by survivors of the patrol to find these Americans, they were never found nor were their bodies ever recovered.

October 2 dawned bright and clear; the heavy rains had stopped and
the skies became a brilliant blue. At 0845, combined XIX Corps Artillery,
VII Corps Artillery, and 30th Infantry Division Artillery started delivering the thundering first blows of the assault. The known enemy positions
across the Wurm were sealed off by tremendous concentrations on crossroads and along the avenues of approach to the river. "The whole land-
scape seemed alive with the winking flashes from their muzzles and when
the big 240mm weapons fired, the sound hit one on the chest like the
blow of a fist," remembered war correspondent Drew Middleton.[35] The
62nd Armored FA Battalion fired 360 rounds of 105mm destructive volleys into the left flank of the 117th Infantry's zone of attack.[36] The 118th
FA, in direct support, launched 1,000 rounds, covering the triangle
bounded by Palenberg-Rimburg-Ubach.[37] The 258th FA Battalion fired
the first of what would be 136 rounds at the pillboxes marked in both the
117th and 119th Infantry zones, scoring hits on every one of them.[38] Lt.
Col. Patrick E. Seawright's 197th Field Artillery Battalion reinforced this
fire with their 105mm guns. Through midmorning, Captain Sinclair's
M10s of Company C, 803rd Tank Destroyer Battalion, fired another 300
heavy explosive and antiphosphorous rounds at the slag piles on the east
edge of Palenberg.[39]

At H-120 (0900) the air strike began. During the fifteen minutes
prior to the fly-in, XIX Corps artillery also fired on a total of fifty-one
different enemy antiaircraft installations, while VII Corps artillery concentrated on another forty-nine. DIVARTY participated by firing at antiaircraft positions plotted by the Photo Intelligence Team and the Air OPs
of the division. The effort was greatly restricted because of an ammunition shortage. Instead of firing five to six battalion volleys on each enemy
battery location, it was only possible to put down one or two volleys.[40]
The enemy's artillery fire was consequently not silenced.

Nor was the air strike particularly effective. Of the nine groups of
medium bombers (A-20 Havocs and B-26 Marauders), just four dropped
their bombs on the targeted area after flying in from the southwest. The
other five groups made their approach more from the west, flying in over
the assembled masses of 30th Infantry Division friendly forces. This
caused considerable confusion among the pilots; they were unable to
obtain corrected approaches through ground contact. "Consequently, the
medium bombing was almost a total failure, as all ground observers

agreed," noted a later report.[41] Beggendorf, location of the 330th Infantry Regiment's reserve 2nd Battalion command post, was in the saturation area; it was not hit.[42] There was one important instance where the mediums did do the job, however. "The last bunch that came along, seeing the red smoke and not knowing what else to do, dropped two loads and took the back half of Palenberg off the map," noted Colonel Johnson, the 117th Infantry Regiment's commanding officer.[43]

When the two groups of fighter bombers (distinctive twin-boom P-38 Lightnings and P-47 Thunderbolts) came in, they met with somewhat better success. Their gasoline "jelly bombs" landed in close proximity to their pillbox targets, the pilots aided in some cases by red marking smoke still being laid down by the artillery. Since most of the enemy troops were inside the pillboxes, however, the fighter planes' overall effect was also judged to be "negligible." Later, platoon leaders of Captain Stoffer's Company C agreed. "Fire bombs were seen dropping from three or four planes, but no appreciable damage appeared."[44] In the 119th Infantry zone, the intended burning of the woods and routing of the enemy forces from this stand of trees by numerous jelly bombs failed; the dampness from the heavy rains the day before and the wet, rich green foliage were the two main reasons the bombs' oil failed to ignite in the area.

Immediately following the air bombardment, other supporting weapons began delivering more preplanned fires. In the 119th Infantry zone, Lt. Michael Baran's Company M mortars fired 1,100 rounds, mostly into pillbox locations to keep their occupants inside their boxes.[45] Lieutenant Lehnerd's Company D 81mm mortars fired supporting rounds, even though they lacked good observation from the hillside where they were emplaced west of Groenstratt; it was impossible to see the pillboxes along the west edge of the woods on the right of the 1st Battalion's route of advance.[46] The mortars of the 117th Infantry's Company D fired the first of what would become 1,525 rounds on 2 October, initially at the river line in Frankland's zone and then at pillbox locations and their outlying trenches across the river.

It was now up to the infantry; H-hour was minutes away. Along the line of departure on the right flank of the 1st Battalion of the 117th Infantry, Captain Simmons's Company A and Lieutenant Bons's Company C of the 119th Infantry were abreast. Simmons was on the right; his

1st and 3rd Platoons were the assault elements. Bons's Company C was in the center. To the left, Capt. Buford C. Toler's Company E was arrayed in preparation for their attack on Rimburg; his 1st and 3rd Platoons would lead in the assault with Captain Reisch's Company F following.

Lieutenant Colonel Frankland's companies were also very eager to attack. Captain Spiker's Company B was on the left flank; Borton's 2nd Platoon was the leftmost unit while Lieutenant Cushman's 1st Platoon was on the right. To their south, Captain Stoffer's Company C was in line with Lt. Clarence J. Johnson's 1st Platoon and ready to jump off on the left; Lt. Thomas E. Stanley's 3rd Platoon was on the right. To their front across the wide-open beet fields all of the men could observe the brink of the hill, beneath which the Wurm River would eventually come into view. Farther northward stood Captain Hoppe's Company E; his men were set to attack through Marienberg to the river, protecting the 1st Battalion's left flank.

At precisely 1100 hours, the first rolling barrage was laid down by the 4.2-inch chemical mortars in both regiments' zone of attack. The barrage delivered two rounds of heavy explosive per mortar, and was timed at five-minute intervals to be "rolled" another 100 yards ahead of the infantry. Twelve grids marked each attack zone. When Captain Simmons's Company A left its line of departure, the assaulting platoons received just three rounds. Lt. Raymond C. Filipino, the 92nd Chemical Battalion's forward observer with the 119th Infantry, later stated "the infantry did not push forward fast enough to have it roll. Concentrations were then repeated at the first line."[47]

Lieutenant Bons's Company C received a few incoming artillery shells after his soldiers jumped off. They carried three heavy footbridges, which interfered with their ability to maneuver and, combined with the confusion accompanying the first enemy artillery volleys, slowed their advance over the road at Broekhuizen down to the Wurm River. It was nearly an hour before Lt. Sylvester G. Shetter's 2nd Platoon started to place its bridge in position; the far end of it was underwater. At the time enemy machine-gun fire was already coming in from two pillboxes just west of the railroad line, near where a road crossed the railroad; some of the Germans could be seen firing with their machine guns strapped to their hips. Then another pillbox camouflaged as a house opened with heavy small-arms and automatic-weapon fire on the platoon's left.

Lt. Victor B. Ortega's 3rd Platoon at first fared a bit better; his men got their bridge in with less difficulty and crossed over the river under lighter machine-gun fire. Then as Ortega worked his men up to the open field near the railroad line, fire from another two pillboxes on the platoon became heavier. Sporadic hostile mortar and artillery fire also landed on the troops. Thirteen casualties were suffered and suddenly no further advance was possible by either platoon.[48]

As Bons's men engaged in a firefight in the scattered patches of woods just to the east of the river, the right platoon of Captain Simmons's Company A advanced to the railroad tracks. It was now 1200 hours. Two German companies of the 42nd Fortress Machine Gun Battalion manned the defenses in the immediate area, including the pillboxes and the extensive network of field fortifications in the woods. Friendly artillery and mortar fires proved ineffective; as it started to fall, the enemy took shelter in the pillboxes. When the barrages lifted the Germans would rush out and repel their attackers. "Primarily, it was the quick enemy small arms fire that resulted any time anyone so much as poked his head above the railroad embankment," Simmons later recalled. "Then, too, as the men became pinned down mortar and artillery fire began to take considerable casualties."[49]

A later account detailed just how harsh the conditions had become:

> Throughout the woods the camouflage on the pillboxes and emplacements were superior, thus making it virtually impossible to locate these positions at distances greater than 25 to 50 yards. Both assault companies had been stopped by the final protective fires of the enemy. They were receiving enemy fire not only from their front, but also from the Rimburg Castle on their left flank and from the wood line and anti-tank ditch to their right front.[50]

Captain Toler's Company E met a similar fate. Lieutenant Lehnerd's 81mm mortars had been set up on the crest of the hill overlooking the river, and along with the rolling barrage these combined fires permitted Toler's platoons to first approach Rimburg in the face of little small-arms fire. As they got closer to the river, however, his 1st Platoon suffered considerable casualties. While there did not seem to be too many Germans in Rimburg itself, enemy artillery fire had increased; mortar fire also came in. The company nevertheless moved even closer to the river, availing themselves of what little cover that could be found, but as they advanced they ran into heavier small-arms fire that came in from the Rimburg Castle. While one platoon did manage to work its way down to the river bank, its men had to wait another hour until Toler's support platoon brought foot bridges to them; the assault platoons had dropped them on their way toward Rimburg when the German shelling started.[51]

During the wait, Captain Reisch's Company F had come down to the right of Toler's men. They had expected to use Company E's bridges, which were not in, so Reisch's attached engineers improvised an overpass from doors and fences that they had gathered; the Company F platoons were soon able to start across the river. Their move was greatly facilitated by the presence of a barn across the Wurm, which protected the troops from enemy fire as they crossed. Right after this, Captain Toler's support platoon arrived with the foot bridges and they were able to quickly place them across the river. Using the company's light machine guns and 60mm mortars as a base of protective fire, Toler gradually worked his riflemen across the Wurm; the machine gunners followed while the mortar men stayed back. "All we did was get the men across," Lt. Warne R. Parker recalled. "Then we were pinned down by automatic fire from the wall of the castle."[52]

It would now be hours before the 119th Infantry Regiment's assault could move forward. To their left, Lieutenant Colonel Frankland's attack had made better progress but not without costly setbacks. Captain Hoppe's Company E, meantime, was having its own difficulties reaching the Wurm River. The company did not have the benefit of a rolling barrage when these men jumped off and only one heavy machine-gun section accompanied them in direct support. Hoppe had moved his company out in platoon columns. The 1st Platoon was on the left with his own light weapons platoon and the Company D machine-gun section right behind them. The 2nd platoon was on the right; the 3rd Platoon followed in support.

Minutes after the company left its line of departure, heavy enemy mortar and artillery fire dropped among the haystacks as the men crossed the 400-yard open field on their way toward Marienberg. Then, as the 1st Platoon got closer to the western edge of the village, small-arms fire came in from a row of houses. Captain Hoppe ordered the heavy machine gunners to emplace their weapons, and these men started to work over the buildings from window to window. The main body of the company quickly reached a road parallel to the village, where the sniping fire increased in volume. Hoppe then decided to turn his 2nd and 3rd Platoons sharply southeastward while the 1st Platoon attacked through a wooded area beside the row of houses delivering the fire. These men met the heaviest resistance; one squad forked off to the left to clean out the houses on the north side of Marienberg. Another started to mop up closer to the Marienberg-Palenberg road. But as both squads began to move through the village an enemy shell landed among a bunched-up group of men, killing five, including Sgt. Joseph A. McPartland, one of the squad leaders.[53]

Then, at 1145 while Captain Hoppe was a mere 75 yards away, a church in the center of Marienberg suddenly blew up. He later recalled:

Evidently the initial sniper fire which we received on the outskirts of Marienberg was from a small delaying force which was giving the enemy time to set off their prepared mines and dynamite in the church. The explosion was just like Hollywood, with timbers and bricks hurtling hundreds of feet into the air and the huge square steeple toppling. It must have taken plenty of dynamite because the brick walls were more than seven feet thick. I had used the steeple as an OP, but found it unsatisfactory because the walls were too thick for unrestricted vision through the holes. It's hard to tell whether or not there were many 1st Platoon casualties as a direct result of the explosion, or why the Germans blew it up, except to prevent its use as an OP, or because they thought we already had people in it observing.[54]

Right after the church was reduced to rubble, enemy artillery volleys screamed in more intensely. The 1st Platoon also received renewed small-arms fire from three brick houses on their left. They dug slit trenches right along a hedge just 50 yards north of the ruined church, and many men took cover. Soon afterward, the situation changed dramatically when the platoon leader became a casualty; minutes later the heavy weapons machine gunners arrived. These men quickly ganged up in the cellar of a house just north of the church, where fifteen to twenty American soldiers who were wounded had already been moved to safety.

Lt. Fay M. Parker, the mortar platoon leader from Company D, was with the 1st Platoon observing fire when its leader was wounded. He reacted swiftly, went over to Captain Hoppe and offered, "I know the situation; I'll take the platoon down to the bridge site."[55] After hastily reorganizing the platoon, the stalwart volunteer then led the men down the hill and through the woods lining the road to Palenberg, still directing mortar fire as he approached the banks of the Wurm.

Captain Hoppe by this time had crossed over the Marienberg-Palenberg road to push on his 2nd and 3rd Platoons. He was not disappointed with the outcome. From the top floor of a house on the south side of the roadway, Hoppe directed artillery fire as he watched his men move down to a row of brick houses facing the bridge site. Two pillboxes stood directly across the river, just east of the railroad tracks. Parker ordered light machine-gun fire into the apertures while the riflemen of the platoon tried to find the same openings with their M1s. The heavy machine guns were too far back to reach the pillboxes, so they went to work on the enemy snipers nearer the river as the Americans started to throw in their bridges.

Then came a setback. The planks were not long enough to reach from bank to bank. While German small-arms fire started to rake the area, Sgt. Lewis A. Reeves and Pvt. James W. Harris took matters into their own hands. After jumping into the cold, chest-deep water, both men somehow steadied the planks from tipping and held them in place; Private Harris stayed at his post, even though he was wounded.[56] The 2nd Platoon got across, then crept up toward the pillboxes along the west side of the railroad tracks while the 3rd Platoon crossed the tracks and started working their way around toward the boxes from the rear. Company E was across the Wurm.

At the start of the rolling barrage at 1100 hours, both of Lieutenant Colonel Frankland's 1st Battalion assault companies had also moved out quickly; Captain Cole, the chemical mortars' forward observer with the 117th Infantry noted, "They got used to the bursts and seemed to know when the barrage would lift." For Captain Stoffer's Company C, however, quick movement also brought early casualties. First, his weapons platoon leader was hit by enemy artillery just over their line of departure. Second, both Lieutenants Stanley and Johnson later stated that "they had information that some of the 4.2 mortars slipped in the mud, and the base plates kicked backward in such a way to cause some shorts which fell amongst our troops."[57]

More casualties followed after crossing the beet fields when the assault platoons reached the downward slope just over the brink of the hill. The draw canalized both Company C platoons' advance; German artillery had these men zeroed in. Captain Cole, who had stayed with one of the platoons remembered, "The draw was jammed full of the boys carrying their bridges; the enemy walked up and down the area with their artillery."[58] Six Americans were killed, another fifty-eight were wounded, and twelve others were unable to continue after the resultant melee. Pvt. James A. Smallwood remembered the shells caught his 2nd Platoon squarely. "Almost the entire platoon was wiped out in a few minutes. I looked around me and saw only three or four men who looked as though they hadn't been hit. It was terrible." Stoffer's support platoon was also hit badly. "It was pinned down so hard it couldn't wiggle," Lieutenant Stanley recounted later.

When Stanley reached the river, just five 3rd Platoon men were present as they attempted to get their bridges across the Wurm's banks. Some fire came in from a switching station as well as a large building east of the railroad tracks and from the Rimburg Castle to their right in the 119th Infantry's sector. At the time, Lieutenant Stanley did not know that the assault squads in his platoon had been hit back at the draw, so he waited at the river bank, expecting his men to catch up. A bit later, Stanley worked the men with him across the Wurm and up to a sheltered position on the near side of the railroad track. Lieutenant Johnson did the same with his 1st Platoon. At the track bed, there were just twelve men left with Johnson; Stanley now had fifteen soldiers with him. Here both platoons remained for about forty-five minutes; just two men worked their way across the track into defiladed positions. Heavy small-arms fire was coming in from two pillboxes. Everyone was pinned down. After another forty-five minutes, Stanley finally radioed Captain Stoffer and reported, "I have no assault squad, and I can't assault the pillboxes without an assault squad."[59] It would be another hour before Captain Kent's Company A arrived to take over ravaged Company C's mission.

Casualties may have been heavier for both of Stoffer's assault platoons were it not for the stunning movement down to and across the river by Captain Spiker's Company B. When his assault platoons jumped off from the cow trail along their line of departure, the 118th Field Artillery's M2 howitzers added to the chemical mortars' barrage; its batteries had counted on the men covering about 100 yards every five minutes. Instead they moved faster. "It was fortunate that Lieutenant Walter Hawbaker observed this from his outpost on the third floor of the house he was in, for he had steady communication with the guns firing and kept the preparation rolling ahead of the fast-moving troops," remembered Maj. Raymond W. Milllican, the S-3 of the 118th FA.[60]

First enemy fires nevertheless came in as Lieutenant Borton's 2nd Platoon dashed through the beet and turnip fields aside the Scherpenseel-Marienberg road; this was fire from a pillbox near Marienberg. Only a single casualty resulted before a lone German soldier was observed rushing from this pillbox. He got about 30 yards away, running to the Marienberg-Palenberg road that cut through the beet fields in front of the advance; he had been hit by one of the chemical barrage's exploding mortars. "When we got up to him his whole chest was ripped out and he was plenty dead," Lieutenant O'Neil of the Pioneer Platoon observed.[61] Remembering Lieutenant Colonel Frankland's warnings during planning the attack, O'Neil later recalled, "Its only result was more speed; we took off like big-assed birds."

After Borton's platoon reached the road, they cut south; Lieutenant Cushman's men had been keeping pace, staying abreast of Borton's soldiers, with Lt. Jay Manley's weapons platoon following. Cushman wanted to get the war behind him; he had learned from a telegram ten minutes earlier that he had a new baby boy back in the states. Lt. Whitney O. Refvem's 3rd Platoon was following Borton's men. Each assault platoon occupied a front of about 75 yards as the leading elements reached the brow of the hill less than five minutes after jumping off.

Neither assault platoon had taken any casualties. At the edge of Marienberg, the troops started down a draw and then turned directly for the river. Manley's weapons platoon moved down the left side of the draw along with Refvem's forces and were caught by some of the mortar and artillery fire that had hit Company C as they were racing for the river. Caught now in this better-adjusted hostile enemy fire, both platoons started taking casualties. The assault platoons, ahead of this fire, continued rushing to the Wurm. Cushman's 1st Platoon turned sharply southeastward while Lieutenant Borton's 2nd Platoon wound through a slightly longer path on the left. There was the expected single-strand barbed wire fence in front of them; wire-cutters quickly took care of this. Lieutenant O'Neil later recalled what happened next:

> For some unknown reason everybody stopped at this fence. The men had also started to complain that they were tired from the fast pace and the load of carrying the ladders. Lieutenant Borton yelled "Let's go, guys." I picked up a shovel and smashed it on the fence yelling "Jesus let's get out of here." Borton then ran toward the river, plunged into the water, waded across and slammed one of the bridges firmly on the far bank. Then he put the ladder from bank-to-bank. Then he jumped out of the water, put his hands on his hips and turned around toward his men with the words: "There's your God-damned bridge."[62]

Right after this, Lieutenant O'Neil threw in another bridge and Borton's men then swarmed across the river. Some did not wait for foot room on the bridges; they waded over and got soaked. "Through all this excitement, Borton had complete command of the situation," O'Neil added later. "The last time I saw him he was telling his men to spread out as they advanced up to the railroad tracks."[63] Lieutenant Cushman's 1st Platoon had their bridge in shortly afterward. In this case, they used a 15-foot length but it did not stretch quite far enough to go all the way from bank to bank; consequently the men double-timed across in water almost up to their knees.

At first there was not much opposition between the river and the railroad tracks. Along the track twenty-five to thirty Germans were dug in, but they surrendered as the boot-crunching roar of the assault waves rushed in at top speed. Friendly mortar fire was now shifting to the pillboxes. Company D's 1st Heavy Machine Gun Platoon had already displaced and the squads had set up near their 81mm mortars at the edge of the woods bordering the draw on the southern edge of Marienberg. Lieutenant Manley's weapons platoon by this time had recovered from the enemy artillery and mortar hits they took in the draw while coming down to the river; the gunners were now ready to fire from a rock pile just west of the north-south road which paralleled the river. Only forty-five minutes had gone by since the assaulting platoons of Captain Spiker's Company B crossed their line of departure.[64]

Observers at Colonel Johnson's 117th Infantry Regiment Command Post on the third floor of a building nearer the brink of the hill leading down to the river remembered that he was busily giving instructions to his staff at the time. By 1200 he knew that Company B was across the Wurm. At 1215 he was overheard ordering, "Get a hold of Verify [743rd Tank Battalion]. The assault companies are well across the river."

Then Johnson turned and barked sarcastically at his staff, "They are hollering push from division, as usual."[65]

CHAPTER 6

XIX Corps Breaks through the *Westwall*

"The great success on the American side was the moment of the completely surprising action by the assault on the Westwall across the Wurm near Palenberg on the 2nd of October."

GENERAL DER INFANTERIE FRIEDRICH KÖCHLING
COMMANDING GENERAL LXXXI CORPS

When Lieutenant Colonel Duncan's 743rd Tank Battalion reached the Wurm River with the tank dozer and a tank pulling the sled loaded with the culverts, they were immediately subjected to enemy artillery fire. Everyone was forced to take cover for nearly thirty-five minutes. The original plan had called for the remainder of Duncan's tanks to stay in Scherpenseel until the culverts had been installed. However, as soon as the tank dozer had a chance to start clearing the west bank of the river after the infantry crossed, these tanks were ordered by an anxious Colonel Johnson to start moving out.

Arriving prematurely at the bridging site, their crews found that the tank dozer had pushed just one culvert into the water and it was now stuck in the muddy banks of the Wurm. Two mediums rushed over to pull the dozer out, but they also got stuck in mud that went up over their suspension systems. While the crews valiantly attempted to winch the armor free, German artillery shells, small-arms, and mortar fire killed the effort. As a result the engineers were unable to put the culverts in. Other Americans, also spotted by enemy observers, took cover in hastily constructed slit trenches. No tanks were knocked out, but Company A's Capt. Kenneth R. Cowan was wounded when a shell hit the exposed turret of his tank.[1] Capt. Edward Miller, the Assistant S-3 of the battalion, was also

145

wounded right after he reported to regiment at 1245 hours that the remaining tanks had just made it to the Wurm.

Two suspenseful hours later, Colonel Johnson's CP learned that the engineers were using shovels and picks to try to dig the tank dozer out. At 1510 hours more bad news poured in. Lieutenant Colonel Duncan reported that "the situation is still pretty bad with all that artillery." Johnson told him he had just ordered Captain Rice's Company A of the 105th Engineer Battalion down to help get the tanks across. Rice subsequently reported at 1550, directly by phone to General Hobbs, the very concerned 30th Infantry Division commander, that two tanks remained stuck in the mud but were finally being winched out. Even Gen. William K. Harrison Jr., the assistant division commander, had come down from Johnson's CP to see what could be done; when he got back all he could report was that he had ducked a lot of sniper fire. At 1800 the tanks were still deep in the silt, but the engineers reported that they expected to have them freed up within thirty minutes.[2]

As a result, there was no opportunity to use the well-practiced tank-infantry tactics anticipated by Lieutenant Colonel Frankland as his 1st Battalion companies attempted to accomplish their final missions during the early afternoon hours of 2 October. The infantry would have to go it alone. Men in Captain Spiker's Company B later noted that "the tanks actually caused more harm than good by drawing artillery fire and mortar fire on [our] support and weapons platoons."[3] But at that moment the nine pillboxes capable of delivering fires into the company's positions across the railroad tracks were of even greater concern. Because of the limited visibility through their embrasures, the Germans had placed some of their spotters and gunners in trenches outside of these pillboxes. Many had been driven to cover when the thundering bombs, artillery, and mortar fires announced the start of the American offensive, but there were still machine-gun positions outside of the boxes that were not damaged and with which the company would now have to contend. Complicating matters, the Germans still maintained good observation on their positions from the two large slag piles east of Palenberg; the men could also be seen from houses here as well as from homes in Marienberg.

There was also that upward slope grown over with beets that the men had to contend with before they could reach the pillboxes. A ridge punctuated the terrain they would have to climb, but there were some brief defiladed spots just beyond the tracks where dips in the ground and bomb craters afforded some cover while they attacked. Unknown at the time, shoe mines and other booby traps had also been laid into the slope. Captain Spiker's Company B was assigned to five pillboxes. Lieutenant Cushman's 1st Platoon was tasked with taking Pillboxes 2 and 8 on the right flank of the advance; Borton's 2nd Platoon would reduce Pillboxes 3 and 7 in the center while Lieutenant Refvem's 3rd Platoon came up on the left and captured Pillbox 4. This latter enemy box was actually in Palenberg.

Their planned supporting fires were well positioned. Lieutenant Manley's Weapons Platoon would cover Refvem's men as they attacked Pillbox 4. His light machine guns had been equipped with BAR bipods. These enabled higher shooting trajectories than normal tripod bases afforded, permitting the gunners to deliver longer overhead fire and actually sweep from the Marienberg bridge site all the way through the Company B zone to the south, right into Pillbox 8. Manley's 60mm mortars would add extra firepower and also cover the advance of both Cushman's and Borton's men.

With this support in place, enemy artillery and mortar fire nevertheless combined with small-arms fire when Lieutenant Cushman's 1st Platoon started from the bridge up to the railroad tracks. Shrapnel burst everywhere; to calm himself before jumping off, Pfc. Richard Ballou drew a sketch of the terrain on the back of a postcard. Then shells started landing in the river 8 feet behind his squad. A large hole was blown in the opposite bank. Staying in position was no good. One by one, the men took their loads and jumped off toward the railroad tracks. Shots rang out from the woods to their right but Cushman, in the lead, worked his way up to a hedge bordering the tracks and personally cut away the strands of a barbed-wire fence, encouraging the rest of the platoon to move up. Some men had found concealment by sneaking around a few dead cows that were hit by the earlier friendly artillery fire. This roundabout route delayed the arrival of Cushman's assault squad. Still, the men eventually sprinted forward, hopping away from bullets as they hit the dirt near their feet, and charged up toward the ridge. The support squads then took up positions directly facing the pillboxes on the right side of the company sector. Amazingly, there were very few casualties.

Pvt. Brent Youenes, who had reconnoitered the Wurm with Lieutenant Cushman two weeks before the attack, had volunteered for the flamethrower assignment that waited. Running up to the first pillbox, he quickly squirted two bursts into the front embrasure from just 10 yards away. Pvt. Willis Jenkins rushed forward when the flame cooled, placed a pole charge through the embrasure, and dove to the right as the pillbox exploded. Minutes later Sgt. James Billings and Pvt. Pasquale Vitalone entered the box, and not long afterward the Germans surrendered. "The last five filed out shaking and saying 'Kamerad,'" New York native Vitalone remembered.[4]

By this time Youenes had already started across the road to Pillbox 2. He had transferred the flamethrower to another private, William W. Smith, and as he approached this box Youenes spotted two German helmets outside of a different box—Pillbox 6. This box was in Company C's assault zone, but an enemy machine gunner had opened up on members of Youenes's squad. Sgt. Daniel Preston retaliated by taking quick aim at one of the Germans, killing him, while the second one rushed back into the pillbox. Three other assault squad members, a sergeant and Privates Isadore Polansky and Norman Jandreau, crawled up along the edge of the woods to approach the pillbox from the blind side. Lieutenant Cushman and the support squad covered their advance; Pfc. Hershel D. Jones fired a rifle grenade into the dirt in front of the box, blinding its occupants to the American assault. Polansky crept up to throw grenades in; Jandreau rounded the pillbox with a satchel charge. Cpl. John Curtis and Sgt. Fred Burke, armed with smoke and hand grenades, rushed up to the right side of the box.

Moments later the first grenade was thrown at the pillbox, but it was a rushed mistake and turned out to be yellow signal smoke; the private who threw it quickly reacted by hurling a live grenade into the front embrasure. Polansky, who had been wounded in the thigh while charging the box, still managed to jump up on top of it and quickly throw a grenade down the ventilator. Covered by fire being delivered by Technical Sgt. Waymon R. "Mac" McClurkan, Privates Youenes and Smith then raced over to help with the assault. Warning Polansky to get down from the top of the box, Youenes rushed in while holding the nozzle of the flamethrower and gave the opening a long burst of flaming gas. Private Jandreau, still behind the pillbox, slammed his satchel charge into the open rear door; the charge instantly ripped ragged holes around the edges of the concrete that framed the doorway.

This brought Youenes around to the rear to help Jandreau, with Private Smith two feet behind him still toting the flamethrower. Youenes later recalled:

> I figured that there must be an opening in the center rear, and decided to also give that a burst, which I did when I rounded the pillbox. The only result was a feeble "ph-t, ph-ht-tt" of escaping nitrogen. Just then I saw the blurred head of a German officer come out of the pillbox and he fired three shots, killing Smitty. When Smitty fell he jerked me backward with the flamethrower. As I struggled to get a hold of my rifle, which Smitty had, the officer fired two more shots into Smitty and shortly after that started hightailing it over toward the other box. I tried to get my bloody rifle out of Smitty's hands, but he was clenching it too tight.[5]

Within minutes, the German officer was dead; the first shot had been fired by Lieutenant Cushman, followed by rifle fire from many angry squad members. Private Smith was "sprawled pitifully on the ground, his face in the dirt—helmet on the ground near his head; bulging from each hip pocket was a never-to-be eaten K-ration."[6] The men looked away. Six more Germans filed out of the box, yelled they were surrendering, and were sent to the POW cage; Youenes and Jandreau were left to guard the box in case others were still hiding inside.

Cushman's 1st Platoon now turned back toward Pillbox 2, the first of two the men had been tasked with taking that day; the other two were in different zones. Pvt. Willis Jenkins was the spearhead in taking this box. He ran toward the pillbox with a pole charge, rounded the left side, and thrust it right into the embrasure; the explosion tore a hole about 8 inches in diameter into the opening. However, the private wasted little time and pitched several grenades through it while Corporal Curtis went around to the rear door to throw more grenades into the box. The Germans responded by offering no resistance and surrendering.

By this time most of the 1st Platoon men were swarming around Pillboxes 8 and 9. Lieutenant Manley's supporting machine-gun fires had fortunately kept the enemy away from the embrasures of both boxes, preventing return fire on the attacking Americans. Germans in pits outside of the box had also been driven inside by the work of Manley's mortars; concussions from the earlier artillery fire had already intimidated everyone inside. In a final gesture of persuasion, Lieutenant Cushman's squads lobbed numerous hand grenades into the pillbox, after which the occupants chose to surrender. It was approximately 1300 hours; the 1st Platoon had reduced all opposition in five pillboxes less than two hours after jumping off from the other side of the river.[7]

Lieutenant Borton's 2nd Platoon had also been working on Pillboxes 3 and 7. Technical Sgt. Grady Workman led the assault echelon of sixteen men; Pvt. Victor Kuinis spearheaded the attack with his flamethrower. Two pole charge carriers, Privates Harold Zeglien and Merle Hasenkamp, assisted. The support squad was under the direction of lanky Sgt. George Dail; his men first moved up to the railroad tracks and deployed to provide covering fire while Kuinis, Zeglien, and Hasenkamp led the double-time charge across the beet fields right up to the ridge. No fire was received from either pillbox as the men closed in.

All sixteen soldiers in the assault group first concentrated on Pillbox 3, the left-most box. Private Zeglien led this strike, placing his pole charge in the embrasure. The work of Lieutenant Manley's weapons platoon again became apparent; the pillbox's occupants had "cowed and retired to the living quarters without offering opposition."[8] Following the detonation of Zeglien's pole charge, however, four Germans ran out the rear door and started through the shallow communications trenches outside the box going southward. They did not get far. A yell from Sergeant Dail to surrender resulted in their immediate capitulation.

At this point Lieutenant Borton and Sergeant Workman joined with Dail and switched their attention to Pillbox 7. This time Private Hasenkamp moved over and placed his pole charge at the embrasure; everyone believed the Germans were also huddled in this box. Another soldier worked his way into a position to fire a bazooka round into the doorway of the living quarters, but his first round failed to do any damage. Instead, it provoked return fire and a well-placed machine-gun bullet killed the private.

This brought Captain Spiker rushing up with his operations sergeant, Theodore Lassoff. The same machine gun fired again; it was to the rear of Spiker but he hit the ground anyway. "Sergeant Lassoff, who spoke German, then directed a prisoner to go in and tell the occupants that if they didn't surrender they would be burned to death with a flamethrower," a witness to the action later recalled. "The reply came back that they would come out if they were given cigarettes when they emerged. Captain Spiker complied; however only the German who had done the persuading [was given] one single cigarette."[9]

The last box in the Company B zone was Pillbox 4 and it initially caused a great deal of trouble for Lieutenant Refvem's 3rd Platoon. They were already weakened from casualties taken while coming down the draw to the river, disorganized, and had for a brief time lost communications with the company. Refvem became a casualty when the platoon moved up to the railroad line; he was badly wounded. After Technical Sgt. Howard Wolpert rushed over to provide what help he could, Lieutenant Refvem gave the fierce-looking 6-footer command with instructions to contact Captain Spiker for additional orders. "It only took a few minutes to make the 3rd Platoon once again a smooth-functioning machine," participants recalled later.[10]

Fortunately Pillbox 4 had an embrasure that permitted enemy fire to be delivered just to the north and west. With the pillboxes to the south already reduced, Spiker ordered the sergeant to move his men up to the Palenberg-Rimburg road, then to pivot left and head for the blind side of the box to its rear.

Sergeant Wolpert responded by quickly sending the platoon ahead in a well-dispersed single file to build up a stretched-out line along a hedge about 100 yards behind the pillbox. From here, Staff Sgt. Walter E. Webb first fired a rifle grenade at the southwest corner of the box. No enemy reaction resulted, so Sgt. Albert T. Maudice of Pittsburgh, Pennsylvania, deployed eight riflemen along the hedge where they delivered fire to the side of the box. Pvt. Henry E. Hansen had drawn the assignment to use his flamethrower against the embrasure with Pvt. Andrew Chuckalovchak of Altoona, Pennsylvania, assisting. After Hansen tested his weapon, he moved up and put two blasts of fire in the rear door. Then he hugged the wall and swung around to the front of the box and delivered two more blasts into the embrasure. Circling back, Hansen took a quick look at the back of the pillbox where he saw a German lying in wait in the doorway with a raised pistol. "[I] was in position to burn the German," he later explained while also evincing how he did not hesitate. "One squirt caused the enemy to whirl and one more full in the face caused him to pitch forward into the open door of the pillbox."[11]

Two riflemen then charged the open doorway, where an errant shot first produced a friendly casualty when it ricocheted back on one man moments before two other privates were sent up to guard the opening. Believing the occupants were subdued and would likely surrender, the remaining men proceeded to a reorganization point ordered by Sergeant Wolpert. Private Hansen, however, decided there was no use in carrying his flamethrower back, so before joining the rest of the platoon he and Chuckalovchak went around to the front of the pillbox and sprayed the embrasure until the weapon was empty. Minutes later, smoke and flames were coming out of the rear door. Ammunition started popping inside, and ten Germans ran out and surrendered. With this, Company B had reduced seven pillboxes; two were not even in their assigned area.

By this time Captain Kent's Company A had departed from Scherpenseel to take over the mission of Captain Stoffer's Company C. Using the same route the 743rd Tank Battalion's armored vehicles had taken, Kent's platoons were also subjected to the same artillery fire on their way to the river. Casualties were few, but Technical Sgt. Abby Revier was badly wounded during one concentration; this was a key loss because his platoon leader who was new to the 2nd Platoon leaned heavily on him. Subsequently scared to execute the mission given to him by Captain Kent—to push across the Wurm to the railroad tracks—the rookie platoon leader was immediately relieved. With this, Kent turned to the 3rd Platoon, and when he got to Lieutenant Foote he told him, "I just received word from Lieutenant Colonel Frankland; your platoon will now take Pillboxes 5 and 6."[12]

After swinging his platoon through a wooded area to avoid the harassing artillery fire, Foote took his squad leaders to a high point before the river where they could observe these two pillboxes. They developed a hurried plan; he later recalled, "I wanted to be sure they could tell their men precisely where they were going to go." Returning to the platoon right after this, the Americans then advanced unobserved through the woods to the river. "It took exactly three minutes to run across the open ground from the woods," remembered Sgt. Joseph B. Underwood.[13]

But trouble waited at the Wurm. The entire company had to take advantage of the same bridges Company C had used, which were precisely where the tanks were bogged down. This drew more artillery fire, but as soon as they crossed the river, the U.S. soldiers dashed up to the railroad line in small groups of three or four, hitting the ground only when German small-arms fire became too intense. Eventually they found the remnants of Stoffer's Company C; these men were still hugging the earth, dug in and taking fire from their front and right. Much of this fire was coming from the Rimburg Castle and another large house in the 119th Infantry Regiment sector to the southeast. Despite this stiff resistance, the soldiers managed to work their way into a well-protected position on the west bank of the railroad track within ten minutes. At this point Lieutenant Foote tore across the track alone and took up a position in a little dip with just enough defilade to be under the firing trajectory of the occupants of Pillbox 5.

Since Pillbox 6 had already fallen to Captain Spiker's Company B, this permitted the rest of Foote's platoon to move up with no interference to their left. After the two support squads moved into position on the Palenberg-Rimburg road, these men found themselves just 30 yards from the fallen box. This allowed Sergeant Underwood to place his squad in support of the assault detachment, facing south. These men initially started out from the west side of the road, and then they made their way to the edge of a wooded area located about 20 yards from the box.

Sergeant Underwood had his men train their fires on a German machine-gun nest that was emplaced on higher ground to the east of the pillbox. Other fire was laid into and around the box's embrasure. Lieutenant Foote had joined the assault squad by this time; they had six men, including Pvt. Marvin Sirokin who was the demolitions man carrying the pole charge. Stubbly bearded, powerfully built Pfc. Gus A. Pantazopulos headed up the three-man bazooka team, which included Cpl. Russell Martin and Pvt. Howard King. With the support squads firing at the pillbox and the outlying machine-gun nest, the assault detachment went right into action.

Conveniently, the earlier bombings had left a crater near the front of the pillbox and the bazooka team moved right up to it. Under encouragement from someone who yelled out, "Put it in low Gus and create a disturbance," Pfc. Pantazopulos hurriedly pumped in two rounds; one went into the embrasure facing west and the other glanced off the opening facing southwest toward the river.[14] The first one also tore a hole 3 feet wide in the firing slit; with thick dust filling the air after the second was fired, Private Sirokin shoved his pole charge into the embrasure. It first appeared to quiet the occupants, but one German tossed out a grenade from inside the box that ripped off a piece of Lieutenant Foote's cheek.

Corporal Martin and another private quickly reacted by running up to the pillbox and throwing in a couple of their own grenades. A few seconds later the assault squad and both support squads rushed the box. Pfc. Pantazopulos was one of the first to arrive and he hurled two more hand grenades through one of the embrasures. A few Germans were outside in nearby firing trenches behind the pillbox; one threw his own grenade at the Americans and Private King responded by killing him. Another tried to scramble toward the machine-gun nest east of the pillbox but a charged-up King raced over, closed on him in the trench, and pulled the trigger when his gun was a mere 6 inches from this German's head.

Shortly after this the remaining Germans surrendered. Lieutenant Foote then gave temporary command of the platoon to Technical Sgt. Francis Banner, a fierce-looking warrior, and directed him to lead the men against Pillbox 8, not knowing at the time that Spiker's Company B had already reduced this pillbox. By now the other platoons of Company A had also moved up and Captain Kent soon found that these men were bunched up with the remnants of Company C. This drew the attention of the Germans, and a barrage of their mortars fell among the American troops. An enemy 20mm gun opened up on the men from a pillbox disguised as a brick barn located on the west side of the Palenberg-Rimburg road near the crossroads leading to Ubach. Two more bazooka rounds by Pfc. Pantazopulos helped quiet this threat but his platoon, already having suffered fifteen wounded and one killed since leaving Scherpenseel and taking Pillbox 5, was unable to provide any stronger support. Company C, led by the exceptional initiative of the 1st Platoon's Pfc. Frank C. Brakefield who spearheaded the effort, eventually closed in on the camouflaged barn. Other grenade and rifle fire by Captain Stoffer's men helped force its occupants to finally surrender at 1510 hours.[15]

Major Ammons's Company F had started its mission to clean out the western half of Palenberg by this time. These men had reached the

Wurm just after 1430 hours, and then used the same bridges to cross over the river that Captain Spiker's Company B had taken. There was only slight opposition as they worked their way along the railroad track toward Palenberg, but as the afternoon wore on the men found themselves under more intense rifle and machine-gun fire. This fire was coming from dug-in enemy positions to their front, as well as from homes in the village; a later report noted, "It then became a slow process of creeping around houses and throwing grenades into windows."[16]

While these soldiers were engaged in this nasty house-to-house fighting, Lieutenant Parker's 1st Platoon of Company E was holed up in a row of brick houses closer to the bridge site; the pillboxes nearer Palenberg had firing traverse capability onto the bridge. These two boxes were just east of the railroad track, and the platoon's light machine gunners first sprayed their apertures while the riflemen also took aim at the openings with their M1s. The attached heavy machine guns of Company H were unable to observe the pillboxes; these men instead went to work on the snipers in the surrounding houses within range.

Captain Hoppe then ordered his 2nd Platoon to creep up along the west side of the railroad tracks to the front of the boxes while the men of the 3rd Platoon crossed and started toward their rear. Reducing these fortifications proved to be a different task than that experienced by Lieutenant Colonel Frankland's 1st Battalion companies. As Major Ammons explained later, "The careful training had little relation to the actual way the pillboxes were reduced."[17] Thin, tall Capt. Richard J. Wood, the battalion's S-3, described how it was done:

> We kept small arms fire on the apertures. We did not use flamethrowers at all, but found that bazookas were highly effective at 100-yard ranges. In one of the pillboxes, there were separate rooms for living quarters and where their guns were placed. You had to go outside to get from one to the other. When we fired bazookas on one pillbox the occupants ran out from the gun section to the living quarters and then were apparently too scared to return.
>
> After an unsuccessful attempt was made to bring up two 155mm self-propelled guns to help reduce the pillboxes, Colonel Johnson sent three M10 tank destroyers and they were

of material value. [This had been ordered at 1330 by Colonel Johnson to help Company E on Pillbox 9; the tank destroyers were west of the river at this time.] They were also helpful in silencing the sniper fire from the surrounding houses. Captain Hoppe said every time small-arms fire came from one of the Palenberg houses, one of the tank destroyers would snipe back with their 3-inch gun and blow a hole in the house.

Company F had helped in this effort; they sent a platoon over to assist in reducing the numerous enemy machine-gun positions outside of the boxes. It was during this action when Company F's Pvt. Harold G. Kiner of Enid, Oklahoma, saved two of his fellow soldiers from grenade fire by hurling himself upon one grenade that dropped between him and these men; he smothered the explosion, preventing his fellow soldiers' certain wounding or deaths, but sacrificed his own life during this selfless action. Kiner was posthumously awarded the Medal of Honor.

The Germans actually had a series of withdrawal trenches running from the pillboxes back into Palenberg. Few prisoners were taken when the pillboxes finally fell; it was concluded that others used this escape route. Captain Hoppe put the day's fighting into perspective by later stating, "The opposition from the houses in Marienberg and Palenberg was actually stronger than that from the pillboxes."[18]

By 1600 enemy small-arms fire had been quieted back at the bridge site, so Company G moved rapidly down to the Wurm. After crossing over under heavy enemy mortar and artillery fire, these men cleaned out the rest of Palenberg and then advanced to the factory district east of town. This area was located on built-up ground and was surrounded by a wall that was anywhere from 15 to 25 feet high; this gave the remaining Germans holed up here good observation on the American soldiers' positions, so the men held in place. Later, Company F took up defensive positions beside Company G at the bottom of one of the nearby slag piles, aided by the relentless firing of their supporting tank destroyers "up one side of the pile and down the other."[19]

The 119th Infantry Regiment's attack had not advanced beyond the railroad tracks at the time; the Rimburg Castle had proven to be a tenacious strongpoint and fire from here also threatened Captain Stoffer's

Company C in their positions south of Palenberg. Responding to this, at 1830 Colonel Johnson called the 3rd Battalion's commanding officer, Lieutenant Colonel McDowell, and ordered him to get Company I down to the river and up to the right of Frankland's 1st Battalion to help protect Stoffer's flank.[20] Lt. George Thompson, the Company I commander, had already established a CP in a brick house on the Marienberg-Rimburg road, so he was able to move out without delay. The company, however, suffered five casualties coming over the bridge when well-placed enemy mortar fire came right down into Thompson's column. A heavy machine-gun section from Lieutenant Baran's Company M was also wiped out; one man was killed and four others were wounded. Still, Thompson was eventually able to bring the company up to the pillboxes where they tied in with Stoffer's men.[21]

Despite this, the overall timetable for the day's advance had been set back. CCB of the 2nd Armored Division had been released at 1750 hours from thirty-minute alert for its movement across the Wurm; this alert changed to 0500 the next morning. The exhausted men of the 105th Engineer Battalion were finally able to complete construction of the bridge some 300 yards south of the Marienberg-Palenberg road at 1850; the armored vehicles of Lieutenant Colonel Duncan's 743rd Tank Battalion finally crossed the Wurm here at 2000 hours.[22] Small-arms fire from the slag piles on the northern edge of Palenberg delayed until midnight the opening of a second 45-foot treadway immediately adjacent to the previously blown bridge connecting Marienberg to Palenberg. After mines were cleared from the roadway on the Palenberg side, Captain Sinclair's 1st Platoon, Company A of the 803rd Tank Destroyer Battalion, crossed this bridge and established roadblocks. Duncan's M-10s were eventually able to get into position with Frankland's 1st Battalion and assist in maintaining their perimeter defense, but not until 0300 the next morning.[23]

By this time Lieutenant Colonel Frankland's companies were well dug in with Spiker's Company B at the eastern edge of Palenberg; Kent's Company A was farther south across a big open field and Stoffer's Company C was in the vicinity of the central crossroads connecting Palenberg to Ubach. Major Ammons's 2nd Battalion companies were to their left, except for Lieutenant Thompson's Company I which remained to the right of Company C.

The 119th Infantry Regiment's attack faltered for several reasons on 2 October. Four of Colonel Sutherland's companies had been stopped by the final protective fires of the defending Germans during the early afternoon, not only because of their strong defenses in the Rimburg Castle, but also because the thick woods and steep slopes on the ridge east of the Wurm and south of the castle afforded excellent observation on Sutherland's entire assault area. Moreover, these dense woods provided more than adequate concealment for the already well-camouflaged pillboxes and thus precluded the use of friendly artillery and tank fire to reduce them.

Nor could mortars render close fire support through the afternoon. As Lieutenant Lehnerd, commander of Company D, remembered: "Throughout the operation the chief obstacle to effective heavy weapons support was the lack of observation. Concentrations were fired on call, both on the woods and the high ground east of the woods, but forward observers were unable to judge the effectiveness for lack of observation. By the time [these] observers reached positions from which they could observe the target area, [the rifle companies] were too close to the target for the mortars to be used."[24]

For these and other reasons it also did not go well for the rifle companies of Lieutenant Colonel Herlong's 1st Battalion on 2 October. Captain Simmons tried until dusk to get his Company A across the railroad embankment even as horrific enemy fire continued coming in frontally, as well as from the walls of the Rimburg Castle. To their right, hidden enemy machine gunners delivered grazing fire from the woods' line. This held up Simmons's platoons all afternoon. A few men did get across just before 1500 hours, but they were immediately pinned down and finally had to withdraw with the rest of the company to another wooded area behind their earlier position nearer the Wurm River. Here they spent the night.

Lieutenant Bons's Company C fared a bit better; a squad from Lieutenant Shetter's 2nd Platoon, held up by a pillbox camouflaged as a stucco house during the early afternoon, eventually managed to empty bazooka fire against this box, causing its occupants to surrender. This enabled the rest of the platoon to occupy a small patch of woods south of the Rimburg Castle. These men eventually made contact with Captain Reisch's Company F, which had also been working on this same stucco-camouflaged pillbox when Shetter's men were using their bazookas against it. Bons's 3rd Platoon was unable to move beyond the open field fronting the railroad tracks they were pinned down on all afternoon. Pfc. Francis P. Smith "kept a cool head," organized other men, and prevented a gap in their line from opening. Wounded were evacuated; food and water were brought up but enemy machine-gun fire evidenced no mercy into the afternoon. Lieutenant Ortega was nevertheless able to make contact with the left platoon of Simmons's Company A by nightfall.[25]

Lieutenant Colonel Herlong did not commit his reserve company, Captain McBride's Company B, on 2 October. As McBride later recalled, "He had no room on the left to maneuver or employ [the company] due to the fact that the 2nd Battalion was immediately left of the 1st Battalion."[26]

> After considering the possibility of committing us on the right of Company A, he decided against this course of action because it was his opinion that we would be subjected to and stopped by the same fire which had stopped the other two companies. For these reasons he had decided to hold Company B mobile and to have Companies A and C continue their efforts to advance. At the first indication of any weakening of the enemy defense, Company B would have been committed immediately against that point. The battalion commander was also of the opinion that, when the tanks were able to cross the river and move to positions where they could deliver direct fire on the enemy, both companies would have little difficulty in penetrating the enemy defenses.

Despite direct enemy observation over the assault area, the men of Major Sterba's 105th Engineer Battalion—covered by friendly artillery smoke screens—had been able to construct a 45-foot treadway bridge over the Wurm in the 1st Battalion zone of operations by 1555 that afternoon. Herlong's hoped-for fire support by the two platoons of tanks faded quickly, however, when the lead vehicles crossed over the Wurm an hour later and became mired on the muddy east bank of the river.

Back in the 119th Infantry command post, Colonel Sutherland had been under more pressure from division to "hurry up" throughout the afternoon. At 1315 he wanted to get all of Company B across the river so he could start Lieutenant Colonel Brown's 3rd Battalion down to the right of Herlong's men. He told Herlong this while he was in his command post, a small room on the first floor of a private home in Groenstraat. By 1440 Sutherland was aware that neither of the 1st Battalion companies had been able to cross the railroad tracks. Then he received a report indicating that the tanks were ready to roll across the treadway bridge the engineers had put in, even believing much as Lieutenant Colonel Herlong did that "things will begin to crack when the 'cans' get across."[27] Still optimistic about this, Colonel Sutherland contacted Lieutenant Colonel Brown at 1559 and gave him an alert order to have his 3rd Battalion be ready to move out.

But a little over an hour later more bad news dampened everyone's mood. At 1715 hours Sutherland learned from D-Day Normandy veteran Maj. Vodra Phillips, the S-3 of the 743rd Tank Battalion, that three tanks were now bogged down on the east side of the treadway bridge. Much like it had been for the 117th Infantry Regiment, the 119th Infantry would be unable to use the planned tank-infantry tactics in their zone of action. But the higher ups did not care. Under continued prodding from General Hobbs to move aggressively, at 1728 Colonel Sutherland finally told his commanding officer "[I] am now going to send Brown ahead without tanks."[28] Lieutenant Colonel Brown, also present in the command post at this time, got confirmation of the regimental commander's order to start his offensive just two minutes later.

Deployment of the 3rd Battalion did not completely achieve the desired results, however. Only one of Brown's rifle companies, Clay City, Illinois, native Capt. Leslie E. Stanford's Company L, was able to cross the Wurm. Lt. David P. Knox, the company's Executive Officer, remembered:

> We started out; down the road across a field we went. Everyone was well spread out. The duckboards that had previously been brought down to the edge of the creek were now thrown across. That is, one of them was used; the rest fell in the creek. We crossed the Wurm River. . . . The 2nd Platoon, under Lt. John Tullbane, was leading and [Lt. George A.] Hager's men were on the right. They were just about across the railroad track when one of the men hit a mine. This was the signal; the Germans threw in plenty. The company had to dig in here for the night.[29]

Brown's other rifle companies remained behind the Wurm. His two attached tank platoons were later joined by other tanks from the 803rd Tank Destroyer Battalion's Company B; they were placed in defiladed positions west of the river to help block the possibility of enemy forces approaching up the Kerkrade valley from the south. Company K, commanded by Capt. Harry J. Hopcraft, made contact with Company L at about the time Colonel Sutherland reached Brown and told him to also "get into a good position and try to help Herlong on the left; your two battalions must be tied in."[30]

Given the difficulties the 1st and 3rd Battalions experienced all afternoon, Colonel Sutherland had come to realize that the responsibility for gaining any meaningful bridgehead across the Wurm would have to fall to Lieutenant Colonel Cox's 2nd Battalion. First word of the battalion's progress after Captain Reisch's Company F crossed the river came into Sutherland's command post at 1350. The battalion was getting a lot of small-arms fire from the upper stories of the Rimburg Castle; moreover, their view of the castle itself was obstructed so they had been unable to use their attached tanks to knock out the opposition and subdue the incoming hail of bullets.

"The enemy made a determined stand at the Rimburg Castle," a later report noted. "He also delayed us with extensive mine fields along the road on the west side of the castle and had these mines covered by approximately 10 machine guns in addition to about one platoon of infantry, well dug in along the sides of the road."[31]

By 1420 Lieutenant Colonel Seawright's 258th Field Artillery Battalion was making efforts to get direct fire on the castle, but soon afterward it was reported that his batteries had not even been able to get their guns into a position to do this. Meanwhile, Reisch's 1st Platoon, commanded by Virginia Polytechnic Institute reservist Lt. Thomas J. Bugg, was starting to assault the same pillbox that Company C to their right was attacking at the time—the box disguised as a stucco building. This platoon's work was made easier when a soldier in the 2nd Platoon threw a white phosphorous grenade into the pillbox. The seven Germans in the fortification surrendered.

Captain Toler's Company E lead men were still pinned down not just by enemy artillery volleys, but also by automatic-weapons fire from

the front wall of the castle. The wall stood beside the east-west road
where the ten enemy machine guns and an infantry platoon were positioned; the roadway ran for just 50 yards from the east bank of the
Wurm to the castle gate, and the only cover for the men consisted of a
few trees and bushes. "For a time the old dark castle seemed to be seep-
ing smoke from every one of the slits that forgotten masons had cut for
medieval archers," Drew Middleton later told readers of his New York
paper.[32] German forward artillery observers in the castle presented
another challenge. "Artillery reaction on the 2nd Battalion was heavy and
concentrated," a report noted later. "Here, for a period of forty minutes,
the enemy put over a battery concentration every five seconds."[33]

"The enemy artillery made a vain attempt to stop the company,"
another account noted.[34] Captain Toler, commanding from the front,
had lost contact with the rest of his platoons still down at the bridge
crossing; he sent Pfc. Lazarus C. Montalvo for them. "Moving back, he
was fired on at the bridge and the flat open ground nearer the river. Nevertheless, he brought the platoons up one by one. After the platoons were
in position he returned with instructions for the tanks and to bring back
additional medics. On the way a bursting shell knocked him down and
wounded him in the left arm and right hip. Handicapped and suffering
from the pain, he still managed to limp on and accomplish his mission."

Spurred on by actions such as this, the company gradually worked its
way up to the front of the castle but instead of finding resistance by the
Germans manning the wall, Toler's men discovered most of them had
decided to quickly retreat into the castle itself. The 1st Platoon of Captain Reisch's Company F, commanded by Lt. Franklin H. Masonheimer,
had driven these defenders away; his whole platoon actually got inside
the wall by going through the stone-arched main gate before Toler's
Company E men got there. Inside the U.S. soldiers "cleaned the Germans out, room by room, with grenades and bayonet in a desperate
hand-to-hand struggle which was more like a battle in the time of
Richard the Lion-Hearted than in the day of General Eisenhower."[35]

Unfortunately, bridging operations to support the 2nd Battalion back
at the river were still faltering. Colonel Sutherland learned of this from his
S-3, Major McCown, at 1557 hours. Continued heavy enemy artillery
and small-arms fire had hampered the effort. A little less than an hour

later, the decision was made to feed Lieutenant Colonel Cox's supporting tanks, the 743rd Tank Battalion's Company B, across on the treadway bridge already in place and supporting Herlong's 1st Battalion. Fully realizing the soft footing of the Wurm could still set back even farther the overall timetable of the day's attack if the armored vehicles got bogged down here, Sutherland determined that the infantry "must go ahead."[36] At 1732 hours, he gave Cox this order: "You are to concentrate on getting [a] bridge in at Rimburg and on tying up E and F with the 117th at north edge of woods. Idea is to hold a secure bridgehead for the night."

Cox immediately issued corollary orders to both Captain Reisch and Captain Toler. Reisch, in turn, called his platoon leaders back to a barn on the bank of the river where he had established his command post, and gave them their missions for the night. The company soon had outposts behind the castle. The 2nd Platoon even found and cut wires running from the castle back to the enemy positions in the woods; this line had been used to adjust artillery fire on the Americans. The 1st and 2nd Platoons of Toler's Company E built up their line on the west side of the castle, tying in with Company F. Toler's 2nd Platoon, commanded by Lt. John A. McAuley, was charged with the mission of protecting the bridge site while the engineers concentrated on completing its construction. After discovering a route with good footing around the soft, muddy ground near the 1st Battalion's treadway bridge, Lt. Robert Howell was able to get four of his Company B tanks into supporting positions just off the road fronting the moat of the castle.

At 1819 hours, Colonel Sutherland told Cox, "the success of the entire operation depends on securing the bridgehead and the successful completion of the bridge at Rimburg tonight."[37] The regimental commander most assuredly was comforted when he learned at 2045 hours that the Rimburg Castle was now empty of Germans and completely surrounded by American infantry and tanks. At 2400 hours, the engineers began constructing the treadway bridge to span the blown gap over the Wurm at Rimburg. By 0800 the next morning, Sutherland finally learned that the 60-foot expanse was in.

The Germans were not idle on the night of 2–3 October. In the very early morning hours they launched a counterattack into the 117th Infantry positions near the crossroads south of Palenberg. Two Mark VI tanks, accompanied by approximately twenty enemy infantrymen, first started advancing toward the brow of the hill just to the south of the crossroads. One tank pulled up and stopped 2 feet from a foxhole where squad members under Staff Sergeant Underwood of Company A were dug in. This giant Mark VI fired over the American soldiers into Palenberg, but did not stay in position for long. As one witness to the action noted, "From the rear foxholes, bazooka men and riflemen opened fire, and the tank was hit by a glancing blow and backed up in a hurry."[38]

> The infantry personnel that had come up with our tanks immediately hit the ground and there was a brisk fire fight for a few minutes. After the smoke cleared and the balance of the German infantrymen had withdrawn over the hill, seven of the enemy were left dead within 20 yards of the leading foxhole. One of the seven was a medic armed with a burp gun, whose pockets were full of grenades. The two tanks took up defiladed positions and fired their machineguns on the foxhole crews, but were finally discouraged by more bazooka and rifle grenade fire; they were knocked out.

Sergeant Underwood suffered three men killed and several wounded during this counterattack; later there was only sporadic firing in the Company A area, but some Germans attempted to move over to positions occupied by Captain Stoffer's Company C. As an account of this latter action noted, "The Jerries were picked off as they silhouetted themselves against the skyline."[39] Information later obtained showed that the small counterattack force was the vanguard of a German battalion.

The identity of the attacking unit was unclear. A report from the period identified the 2nd Battalion, Grenadier Regiment 330, with a platoon of Assault Gun Battalion 1183 as being "brought into the area from Beggendorf." This same report said the night attack of this regiment "came to a halt near the chapel south of Palenberg." Curiously, 30th Infantry Division Interrogators Prisoners of War (IPW) Team #42, based on actual POW revelations, reported "2nd Battalion of 330 Regiment moved via Beggendorf to vicinity of Palenberg for planned counterattack which did not come off. Hauptmann (Captain) Labs, CO. During the night of 2–3 October, CO disobeyed an order to attack for reasons he wished not to earn another decoration, but to spare his men."[40]

The 30th Infantry Division IPW Team learned other valuable information on 2 October. Two officers, twenty-one noncommissioned officers, and sixty-three enlisted men from the 330th Regiment's 1st Battalion were interrogated. Organization and strength of the 183rd Division's infantry and artillery units were revealed; commanding officers' names were even given. These POWs also offered that American "tactics in overcoming bunkers [were] well-performed," and that "gaining the heights of Palenberg and then swinging down on the pillboxes was an excellent movement." Perhaps most interesting, prisoners also revealed that they "expected tanks in the first wave, not infantry."[41] Little did they know that General Hobbs's original plan had called for both.

XIX Corps counted the number of German prisoners taken on 2 October at 105; most were either from the 183rd Division or the 176th Division. Six Germans were also captured from the neighboring 49th Infantry Division. A reserve company of this division, along with other sector reserves, had made a counterthrust from the area of Herbach northeastward toward the 119th Infantry positions during the afternoon. German after-action reports recorded this effort as "not successful."

American casualties on 2 October numbered 315; the vast majority (232) were in the 117th Infantry Regiment's rifle companies. With Lieutenant Colonel Frankland's 1st Battalion as the vanguard of the assault, Captain Kent's Company A lost twenty-four men; Spiker's Company B first suffered just two killed and eight wounded in taking seven pillboxes. Overall casualties for his company on 2 October later became three killed and twenty-six wounded. Captain Stoffer's Company C saw the most casualties; six men were killed, fifty-eight had been wounded, and ten were missing. Casualties for the attached machine gunners and mortar men from Lieutenant Cooper's Company D who were with the rifle companies totaled twenty-three. A 1st Battalion history later noted, "Casualties were high October 2. Counting wounded and killed alone, it was the worst day for the battalion in combat."[42]

According to his morning report, as of 2 October Major Ammons's 2nd Battalion of the 117th Infantry Regiment suffered twelve killed and fifty-five wounded with just three men missing at the end of the day; this was adjusted to twenty-nine missing the next day.[43] Captain Hoppe's Company E experienced the most casualties; five men were killed and forty-nine had been wounded. There were sixty-eight killed, wounded, or missing reported among Colonel Sutherland's 119th Infantry Regiment companies on 2 October.

Captain McBride, Company B commander in the 119th, later accurately noted, "At the end of the first day, the enemy was still in command of all critical terrain in [our] area."[44] Cox's 2nd Battalion had established a thin, albeit still strongly defended bridgehead in the northern sector of the 119th Infantry Regiment's assault area in the vicinity of the Rimburg Castle and its neighboring woodlands. Just one company of Lieutenant Colonel Brown's 3rd Battalion was across the Wurm protecting the right flank of the regiment. Colonel Johnson's 117th Infantry Regiment had secured Marienburg and Palenberg, established a fragile bridgehead in Frankland's 1st Battalion zone, and was within a mile of Ubach. For its action on 2 October, the 1st Battalion was later awarded a Distinguished Unit Citation.

General der Infanterie Köchling, commanding LXXXI Corps, noted, "The great success on the American side [was] the moment of the completely surprising action by the assault on the Westwall across the Wurm near Palenberg on the 2nd of October. This surprise [was] based on the wrong appreciation of the situation by the general command, failing air reconnaissance and insufficient ground reconnaissance. On the American side, an excellent camouflage discipline could be ascertained, which did not admit even the slightest motive for the assault intended there."[45]

Generalleutnant Lange agreed. "The [183rd] division was surprised when the Americans attacked at Ubach-Palenberg on 2 October. Although the terrain was somewhat unfavorable for the attacker because the Wurm River had to be crossed, and in spite of the permanent fortifications of the Westwall, our thin defense front was pushed back rather easily."[46]

The U.S. Army official history of the period noted that Köchling had "wrongly assumed that First Army would make a strong bid northeastward through the Stolberg Corridor during the first days of October, with a possible diversion at Geilenkirchen."[47]

Apparently the only commander to question Koechling's [*sic*] opinion was the 183d Division's General Lange; but he also guessed wrong. Cognizant of American armor opposite his division, Lange expected a major attack against his sector. Yet he could not believe that the Americans would try to push armor across the Wurm at the point they actually had chosen because there the eastern slopes of the Wurm valley are higher and afford more commanding positions for antitank guns than do the slopes a few miles to the north at Geilenkirchen. He expected the blow to fall at Geilenkirchen in the very center of his division sector.

Even the one correct German prediction that the offensive would begin during the first days of October was to be discredited before the attack actually began. Noting on 29 September that American air activity had reached such a fortissimo that all daylight troop and supply movements in the LXXXI Corps zone had to be shut down, the Germans attached undue importance to virtual cessation of air attacks during the next two days. In reality, this could be attributed only to unfavorable weather; but when combined with lessening of American artillery fires, the Germans took it to mean that their earlier prediction had been wrong. Although General Koechling [*sic*] himself was not fooled, the fact that he expected the attack on his southern wing southeast of Aachen deprived his opinion of importance. The division commanders immediately concerned, Generals Lange and Macholz, were thoroughly lulled.

A later report citing the overall efforts of General Hobbs's 30th Infantry Division excluded the debate about the German commanders' knowledge of where the attack would come from. Instead, the division's accomplishments on 2 October 1944 were modestly summarized as follows:

On the first day of the attack the assaulting troops made a penetration into the German lines of 1,200 yards, crossing the Wurm River and working their way into the fortresses of the Siegfried Line. This advance amounted to making a river crossing and several successful infantry attacks on a series of fortified positions, in a period of less than 24 hours. It was a good day's work.[48]

CHAPTER 7

XIX Corps Widens the Bridgehead

"It was now evident the enemy, after having succeeded in breaking through the Westwall, intended to continue the attack toward Alsdorf with the aim of encircling Aachen from the north and east."

GENERALLEUTNANT MACHOLZ

While General Hobbs's regiments were breaking through the *Westwall* on 2 October, two battalions of the 29th Infantry Division were making a diversionary attack to the northwest of Geilenkirchen. The mission was twofold. The first objective was to tie down *Generalleutnant* Lange's forces manning the area, and the second was to prevent the Germans from turning south and attacking into the northern flank of the 30th Infantry Division. Colonel Birks's 120th Infantry Regiment made another diversionary attack toward the western edges of Kerkrade, in this case to thwart any buildup by the 49th Infantry Division that could threaten Lieutenant Colonel Brown's tenuous positions on the southern flank of the division.

While sensitive to these feints, *General der Infanterie* Köchling had no reason at all to believe that the Americans were actually going to turn south toward Aachen. There were even questions in the German command as to whether the breakthrough at Palenberg and Rimburg was really "it." Were the attacks only of local significance, or were they the prelude to what Hitler was calling "the big solution," the start of the U.S. XIX Corps' attack to secure a bridgehead across the Rhine?[1]

But there were matters of more immediate concern that demanded Köchling's focus. Even if he was ready to accept that the 30th Division attack was not a feint, reserves were problematic. *Generalleutnant* Macholz's 49th Division had no reserve forces. The 183rd Division's *Generalleutnant* Lange, who had taken the direct hit on 2 October, had the same problem; he possessed only one battalion in reserve—*Hauptmann* Labs's 2nd Battalion. *General der Infanterie* Köchling, therefore, had no choice but to confine both Lange's and Macholz's operations to trying to seal off the American penetration until stronger forces could arrive. Where the Americans would go next would have to wait another day.

The previous night had been uncomfortable for the Germans. When darkness fell, General Hobbs ordered his DIVARTY commander to "hammer through the night" at likely enemy assembly areas and roadways leading into the slim bridgehead held by his forces. Harassing and close-in interdiction fires responded thunderously. XIX Corps' artillery weighed in with even more missions than those fired during the day on 2 October.[2] Lieutenant Colonel Mayer's 118th Field Artillery Battalion alone fired 1,850 rounds from their 105mm pieces starting at 0230. The 62nd Field Artillery fired another 600 rounds in support. "Much of this was used effectively in the salient which the enemy had between the 117th and the 119th Infantry Regiments," the FA's S-3, Major Millican, recalled. "That night many screams were heard from the wooded area between the 117th and the 119th."[3]

However, when first light on 3 October revealed hazy, low clouds as light rain fell, a desperate Köchling felt that he could now move assault guns, armored vehicles, and troops from other sectors to the threatened front because American artillery observers and air reconnaissance efforts would be hampered by lack of visibility. Accordingly, he put plans in place during the morning to reinforce Lange's 183rd Division zone with nearby forces that would come under his command.

The 1st Battalion, Grenadier Regiment 352 of the 246th Division, commanded by *Hauptmann* Kreutner, was detached from its sector in Aachen with orders to move up to the Ubach area. *Generalleutnant* Lange would be provided with two battalions of infantry from the 49th Division: the 2nd Battalions of Grenadier Regiments 148 and 149. To augment his armored elements, Lange would also receive Assault Gun Brigade 902, Assault Gun Battalions 341 and 1183, as well as Assault Tank Battalion 217. These latter forces, scheduled to arrive at the front during the night of 3 October, would report to Lange and be commanded by *Hauptmann* Bracker.[4]

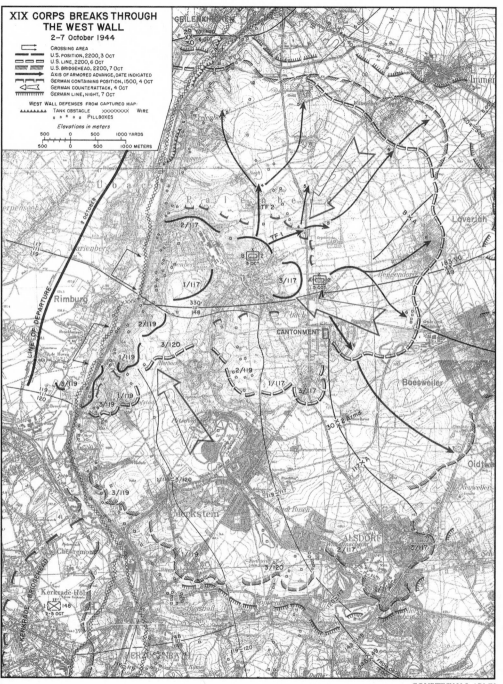

XIX CORPS BREAKS THROUGH
THE WEST WALL
2–7 October 1944

CROSSING AREA
U.S. POSITION, 2200, 3 OCT
U.S. LINE, 2200, 6 OCT
U.S. BRIDGEHEAD, 2200, 7 OCT
AXIS OF ARMORED ADVANCE, DATE INDICATED
GERMAN CONTAINING POSITION, 1500, 4 OCT
GERMAN COUNTERATTACK, 4 OCT
GERMAN LINE, NIGHT, 7 OCT

WEST WALL DEFENSES FROM CAPTURED MAP:
▲▲▲▲▲▲ TANK OBSTACLE   ✕✕✕✕✕✕ WIRE
▫ ▫ ▫ ▫ PILLBOXES

Elevations in meters

500   0   500   1000 YARDS
500   0   500   1000 METERS

COURTESY U.S. ARMY

General Hobbs had also made decisions. During the night of 2–3 October, orders were issued on the American side for the morning's attacks. Colonel Johnson's 117th Infantry Regiment was to secure their original D-Day objective, Ubach, and then cut the Geilenkirchen-Aachen highway and occupy the high ground to the east between Ubach and Beggendorf. This mission, consistent with the planning prior to 2 October, would fall upon Lieutenant Colonel McDowell's 3rd Battalion. Frankland's 1st Battalion was ordered to improve their positions around the pillbox line south of Palenberg and to protect the right flank of McDowell's forces when his companies passed through. Major Ammons's 2nd Battalion was to seize the remaining elusive high ground north of Palenberg, as well as the troublesome slag piles, then finish mopping up the factory area in the eastern section of the village. These attacks would all start at 0700 hours.

The general plan also called for Lieutenant Colonel Wynne's 2nd Battalion of the 67th Armored Regiment and the 1st Battalion of the 41st Armored Infantry to spearhead the 2nd Armored Division crossing of the Wurm on the Marienberg-Palenberg bridge. Wynne's tanks would follow behind McDowell's 3rd Battalion, roll out toward Ubach, and then turn north on the Ubach-Hoverhof road, protecting the flank of their own armored infantry forces as they cleaned up the northern and western ends of the town. General Hobbs was to give priority to the armor of "Hell on Wheels" so that the combat commands could expand the bridgehead, thereby freeing his forces for the southward push toward Alsdorf and the eventual linkup with the 1st Infantry Division.[5]

The 119th Infantry Regiment's mission on 3 October was to attack in the direction of Herbach and Colonel Sutherland had several factors to weigh before determining how he could accomplish this. During the previous night he had concluded that the enemy opposition in the Rimburg woods opposite Lieutenant Colonel Herlong's 1st Battalion was going to make for a tough fight. Nevertheless, he determined Herlong should attack at 0700. Cox's 2nd Battalion was to first finish cleaning up around the Rimburg Castle, and then turn south and assist the 1st Battalion in tackling the stubborn German machine-gun companies holding up their advance. Lieutenant Colonel Brown's 3rd Battalion was to hold the positions his men had gained and continue to protect the right flank of the regiment while the other battalions worked their way to the 119th Infantry's final phase line—the crossroads atop the eastern slopes of the Wurm valley that fronted Herbach.

The attack of the 119th Infantry did not start well. When Captain Simmons's Company A men tried to work their way up to the railroad embankment toward the woods, they made no progress. Simmons remembered, "Colonel Herlong pushed [us] to try to attack the same way that had proved so unsuccessful the previous day, but we were unable to build up any line on the east side of the tracks." Lieutenant Bons's Company C found the early going to be equally difficult. "Both assault platoons jumped off shortly after 0700," he noted. "Fire from the woods to the east continued to give us trouble. We placed artillery [here], and then the 1st Platoon pushed up to the road but got pinned down."[6]

With little hope for reducing the Rimburg woods fortifications with any frontal assault, Colonel Sutherland now realized he had to put other contingency plans developed the previous night into motion. At 0815 hours he alerted hastily organized Task Force Quinn, which he had determined would be commanded by his own executive officer, Lt. Col. Daniel W. Quinn. Quinn's mission was to capitalize on the success of the 117th Infantry's advance of the day before by first moving across the Marienberg-Palenberg bridge, passing through Frankland's 1st Battalion, next turning south to flank the enemy machine-gun positions in the woods, and then pivoting and attacking them from the rear.

Task Force Quinn's infantry component was comprised of Captain McBride's Company B, as well as the reserve company of the 3rd Battalion, Capt. Earl J. Palmer Jr.'s Company I. To add armored firepower, a platoon of eleven tanks from Company B of the 743rd Tank Battalion was also assigned to the task force. To provide even more direct fire support, another two platoons of the 803rd Tank Destroyer Battalion's Company C rounded out Quinn's armored vehicle strength for the attack.[7]

When Lieutenant Colonel Quinn and the company commanders reported to Colonel Sutherland at 0900, details of the operation were disseminated. Task Force Quinn was actually given the mission of cleaning out the entire area across the 119th Infantry Regiment's front. The tanks and TDs were to first advance to the Marienberg bridge up a road running parallel to the Wurm. Since this road was under direct enemy observation, the two infantry companies were to move north using a concealed route just to the west of this roadway. Once at the crossing site, McBride's and Palmer's men were to use the footbridges Frankland's men had crossed the Wurm on the day before, except for one platoon that would wait and accompany the armored vehicles to the other side of the river.

The infantry companies would then join up with the tanks and TDs at Palenberg and make the coordinated attack southward. Captain Palmer's Company I, with the tanks assigned to him, was to strike the upper (eastern) half of the Rimburg woods while McBride's Company B reduced the lower (western) half. The TDs were to first move south of Palenberg and protect the left flank and rear of the task force, but upon the order of either infantry company commander they could be called upon to provide closer support.[8]

Not all went according to plan when Task Force Quinn started out. The infantry companies were first pinned down west of the river by fire from pillboxes just to the south of Palenberg. "Not until tank fire had reduced one, perhaps two of the pillboxes, did the infantry cross the river," remembered the Assistant S-3 of the 119th Infantry Regiment, Captain Smithers. "These pillboxes, previously reduced by the 117th Infantry, had been reoccupied by a considerable number of enemy troops who were only about 200 yards away. [117th Infantry] troops were called over and they herded the Jerries off."[9] Quinn moved his armored vehicles to the Marienberg bridge after this; there were no incidents as the tanks and TDs crossed over into Palenberg.

At 1050 hours, Task Force Quinn, with the infantry companies now joined with the armor, turned south and made its first contact with the Germans in the 117th Infantry sector. In the two hours that followed, the task force captured 135 prisoners from pillboxes near the factory past the crossroads before briskly advancing right into the northern boundary of the 119th Infantry Regiment. When Lieutenant Colonel Quinn reported this quick progress to Colonel Sutherland, the regimental commander cautioned him "not to get too far off the high ground [into the woods], though [your eventual] pressure on the rear of the Germans should pull the 1st Battalion through."[10]

By this time, other actions had given Sutherland reason for this cautious optimism. First, Lieutenant Colonel Cox's 2nd Battalion had secured more area around the Rimburg Castle. Second, Lieutenant Bons's

Company C, having benefited from a loan by Company F of their tanks, was able to capture two pillboxes south of the castle grounds. "Somehow the machinegun fire from the woods on the company's left stopped," Bons recalled later. "Then the borrowed tanks and the 1st Platoon launched another attack against the first of the two pillboxes on the west side of the railroad. Four Jerries ran out and surrendered; two others came out, fought and were killed. We occupied this pillbox and then advanced on the adjoining one. Almost at once another two Jerries ran out and were killed. The second box was captured without any help from the tanks."[11]

Word of this traveled fast. "Members of the 2nd Battalion informed [me at about 1400] that [they] had captured the Rimburg Castle and that Company C had captured the pillboxes," remembered Company B's CO, Captain McBride. "They also stated that [they] and Company C had still been unable to advance beyond the railroad track."[12]

> At this time the tank destroyer [platoon] moved forward and reverted back to regimental control. Two platoons of the task force tanks were also turned over to the 2nd Battalion, since the woods south of the east-west road were too dense for tanks to move through. The task force again resumed the attack and by 1450 had completely cleaned out the area in front of the 2nd Battalion, thus allowing that unit to start moving east up the road.

By this time Company F had received this order to attack into the woods east of the railroad line; Captain Toler's Company E was to attack abreast to the right, but both of his platoons and Company F were to hold their fire until Task Force Quinn had passed to the south. During this movement Quinn's platoons of tanks had been slowly rolling along the open ground just outside the east edge of the woods. However, as the armored vehicles attempted to pick up speed, direct enemy artillery fire came in from Herbach and the vicinity of Merkstein-Hofstadt. Then, as they were moving farther southward, a new directive came down from regiment. The platoon was ordered to stop their vehicles and take up a stationary position along the edge of the woods to protect the left flank of Quinn's infantry.

During this time Captain Palmer's Company I had been advancing through the upper (east) half of the woods and encountering little resistance. On the lower (west) side of the woods, however, McBride's Company B was meeting hardened fire from pillboxes and other emplacements. Pvt. Joseph P. Mehelich, one of the company's medics, was wounded twice, first in his leg and then in his shoulder. He ignored orders to withdraw for treatment, and instead "stumbled and crawled about the area under fire," rendering first aid to six other wounded men.[13] Only then would Private Mehelich seek aid for himself by coming back to McBride's CP in a captured pillbox, but still not until he had first arranged litters to evacuate the others.

Nearby, the fighting went on. Then, at 1512 hours Captain Palmer reported to Quinn that his company was completely through the woods and on their objective. This did not prove to be correct. It was later learned that Palmer was confused and his Company I was north of the Rimburg-Merkstein-Hoffstadt road about 500 yards short of his reported position.[14]

Unaware of this, Colonel Sutherland reached Lieutenant Colonel Quinn and told him to make contact with Herlong's 1st Battalion. A few minutes later, Sutherland radioed Herlong to relay the same order, telling him this time that "he must get up through the woods and contact Quinn's force as soon as he can."[15] Then at 1522, Quinn in turn contacted McBride and requested Company B's location; the Company B commander told him that the leading elements of his company had beaten back the resistance in the pillboxes and were now engaged in cleaning out the enemy positions in front of Captain Simmons's Company A, but the two companies had not yet made contact.

Task Force Quinn was essentially dissolved a few minutes later after Sutherland told Quinn that McBride's Company B and the platoon of tanks would revert "at once" from regimental control back to the 1st Battalion. Herlong got word of this at approximately 1525 hours. Quinn was also directed to release Palmer's Company I back to Lieutenant Colonel Brown's 3rd Battalion, which had spent the day being constantly prodded by Colonel Sutherland to make contact at the south edge of the woods with the now defunct task force.

It had been a very bad day for Brown and his men. They lost a very capable Company L man earlier that morning, Sgt. Richard O. Linehan, who "could have handled the company under any situation by himself."[16] Shrapnel from artillery hit Linehan; the medic "knelt down beside him, but knew by his face and reactions that nothing could be done." They pulled Linehan's raincoat over his head, took his maps and shovel, and sought cover. Artillery and mortar fire came in fast and heavy all day; the company's men escaped from it by sheltering in a small storehouse that was only slightly below ground level. "We threw out the items and kept finding room for one more person," remembered a participant. "It just wasn't safe to move around. The Jerries had plenty of stuff and could observe us, that was certain."[17]

Sutherland's hoped-for results were not achieved; his two forces never got close. Task Force Quinn had only cleared out the woods on a line that intersected to the south with a pillbox just to the east of the Rimburg Castle.[18] Although the 2nd Battalion's executive officer, Major Laney, believed Task Force Quinn's operations were helpful, others were more critical. Captain McBride felt that the task force was prematurely dissolved, even stating later, "It is my opinion that if the task force had not been dissolved, it would have been able to accomplish its mission before the hours of darkness on 3 October."[19] Major Wayne, the 1st Battalion's executive officer, even offered that the task force's fear of enemy antitank weapons made their tanks "timid" and thus positioned in the wrong place to render more effective support for the attack.

> Even if it was unduly dangerous for the tanks to operate in such close proximity to the woods, [they] could have moved south on the west side of the railroad and found suitable crossings in [Lieutenant Colonel Brown's] 3rd Battalion's sector. If they had done this, they would have gotten into position to fire on the pillboxes in the fringes of the woods, probably without even having to doze a crossing of the anti-tank ditch. The main hazard to such a maneuver would have been artillery fire, but artillery fire is not as great a hazard to a moving tank and is a great deal more dangerous to exposed infantry. Actually, the Jerries in the woods either did not have, or did not use anti-tank weapons.[20]

At about 1530 McBride switched his SCR 300 radio back to the 1st Battalion channel to request further orders; Herlong now advised him to hold up where he was until Simmons's Company A and Bons's Company C had passed through. Both of Captain Bons's assault platoons had crossed the railroad by this time and were waiting to receive the order to attack south when Herlong suddenly changed it to attack east. Bons later recalled, "The men went through the woods [after we got the order] without difficulty; no artillery nor small arms fire resistance was met. But on approaching the east edge of the woods, direct fire—the type of which we had never encountered before—was received."[21]

Simmons's Company A had followed Company C by first pushing through the route on which Bons's platoons had advanced, but weakened by losses earlier in the day in his 3rd Platoon, which was practically wiped out, combined with the loss of half of his 1st Platoon, Captain Simmons could offer little help this late in the day.

Captain McBride later offered this perspective in explanation for the failure of these attacks:

> Approximately 45 minutes had elapsed between the time that Company B had been ordered to hold up and the time that Companies A and C attacked. Thus the enemy was given ample time to reorganize his strength and positions.
>
> In the middle and lower half of the woods, [both] companies were able to advance only 20 yards beyond the line held by Company B before they were stopped. On the upper edge of the woods, elements of Company C moved to the rear of Company I. When [we] attempted to move out of the woods to secure better fields of fire the company was immediately subjected to grazing machine gun fire and direct tank fire from the high ground to the east and also from positions in the vicinity of Merkstein-Hofstad. The battalion was also subjected to the most intense artillery fire it had received in the whole attack so far. During one period of 40 minutes an enemy battery concentration landed on the battalion every five seconds.[22]

When Captain Toler's Company E and Company F finally launched their coordinated attack, the Germans also caught both companies with tank and artillery fire as they approached the east edge of the woods. Losses included Company E's executive officer as well as ten other casualties. "Tree bursts from the enemy's artillery were rugged along the edge of the woods," remembered Lieutenant Parker. "Hence, both companies advanced their lines onto the open ground farther to the east."[23]

Company F's Captain Reisch had also become a casualty. An artillery shell killed him while he was in his command post back in the barn nearer the river before the Rimburg Castle was taken; Lt. Edward C. Arn had assumed command, and he never forgot the moments before Reisch was taken down:

> Captain Reisch and I were standing in the huge double doorway of the U-shaped barn studying our map and trying to decide what to do next. We knew that the enemy was in that castle [Rimburg Castle] and in strength. We could even see an imposing Tiger tank drawn up in front of the main entrance. We were also aware that some of our people had reached a group of outlying buildings that, I later learned, comprised a combination of apartments and the castle gatekeeper's quarters. Just a few moments before, Reisch had motioned to me to crawl over to him on the enemy side of the barn's south wing. He pointed to the heavily wooded high ground to the left of the castle. I noted movement in the underbrush at the base of the trees.
>
> Reisch always carried an old, well-oiled, and super clean Springfield, bolt-operated '03 rifle. The piece was even equipped with a special telescope sight mechanism. Reisch was an expert, an excellent shot. A German soldier was crouched in the coloring foliage. He had little idea that he was about to take leave of this mortal earth. The captain calmly balanced his '03 on the rusting spokes of a hay rake's wheel, took aim, and squeezed the trigger. I would guess his target was about two hundred yards away. The unfortunate Kraut never knew what hit him. His body tumbled in the river.[24]

Not long afterward, artillery found Captain Reich and he, too, fell. That night the 1st Platoon had just sixteen men left. Most of the men were lost on the edge of the woods where the determined enemy artillery had stopped the day's attack. Nevertheless, both Arn and Toler made contact and patrols sent out eventually met up with Captain McBride's Company B. Palmer's Company I, although not where he thought he was a few hours earlier, had by this time located on higher ground to McBride's right.

The S-3 of Lieutenant Colonel Brown's 3rd Battalion reported at 1619 that he was "in touch by radio; I Company about 700 yards away."[25] At 1700 all of Brown's units were ordered to consolidate their positions. One platoon from Captain Hopcraft's Company K and another from Stanford's Company L were still holding their positions and protecting the right flank of the regiment; one platoon found refuge in a pillbox with thirty-six bunks in it. "It was a bad situation," remembered an officer. "The mortar and artillery fire were really rough."[26]

That night Colonel Sutherland ordered Lieutenant Colonel Herlong and his 1st Battalion to continue cleaning out the entire woods east of the railroad before proceeding to Herbach.[27] This order came following a call General Hobbs made to Sutherland a little after 1800, during which he told him that his men "had done a bang-up job" and advised they "tuck in for the night."[28]

Hobbs had been quite optimistic overall, perhaps prematurely but nevertheless exuberantly so when he talked with General Corlett a couple of hours earlier. "We have this thing busted up," he told the XIX Corps' commander. "We just intercepted a German document that says we busted up 39 pillboxes; we have broken this thing."[29] When Corlett asked if he could report this to Army, Hobbs ventured: "We are sitting on high ground and looking south; if that isn't busting through, I don't know what it is." A short time later on another call, Hobbs boldly told Corlett, "I don't think it too early to advise our neighbors on the right [referring to the 1st Infantry Division] to start their thing tomorrow. We are headed in that direction; they have to apply pressure south so nothing comes our way." The conversation then closed with an understatement when a somewhat dubious Corlett told Hobbs that "General Harmon says it's sticky around Ubach."

When Lieutenant Colonel McDowell's 3rd Battalion of the 117th Infantry started across the Marienberg bridge earlier that morning toward Ubach, enemy artillery fire was falling only intermittently. The leading companies, Capt. Wayne Culp's Company K and Company L, quickly pushed forward into Palenberg, which was not completely cleared out. At first only small-arms fire proved problematic, but when the leading platoons reached the eastern part of town, determined German artillery and mortar fire started to slow the advance. Small-arms fire was also coming from a pillbox firing northward from the 119th Infantry sector, but astute thinking by the commander of the antitank platoon, Lt. Robert Peters, led to the removal of this threat.

> Our men shot at the pillbox from 300–1,000 yard range, firing from the northeast of the pillbox over a small ridge which barely gave them mask clearance. The first shot from their 57mm anti-tank gun was about a foot high, since they were trying to clear the ridge. The second shot scored on the aperture and the top of the concrete was seen to fall down. One man quickly ran out of the pillbox and was squelched with a round of HE. No further moves were taken, as the fire had ceased coming from that sector.[30]

Still, it was not until nearly 1300 before the battalion got between phase lines 8 and 9, a little less than a quarter of a mile from the western fringes of Ubach. At this time both companies were astride the main road leading into town, with squads on nearby side streets cleaning out resistance in houses; the Germans had boarded the doors, so tanks were first used to blow them open. At 1315, Colonel Johnson learned from Lieutenant Colonel McDowell that the lead companies were still being hit by mortar fire coming from the center of the village. Turning to his staff after the call ended, Johnson quipped with undoubted certainty, "McDowell's got Wild Man Culp up there, with Company K in the lead. This is good, because if you get Culp mad he'll go places."[31] Company K did, as did Company L. Colonel Johnson learned five minutes later that McDowell had one company on each side farther up the "main drag," Company L still to the north and Culp to the south. At this point, how-ever, the fight for Ubach evolved into "a slugfest with house-to-house fighting, the enemy giving ground inch by inch."[32]

Conversations at Colonel Johnson's command post partially revealed why the situation changed so quickly. At 1325 he told his staff, "Power-house ran into the rear of the 3rd Battalion and was stopped cold. Do those tanks need a ribbon along the road to show them where to go?"[33] Powerhouse was the code name for the lead elements of General Har-mon's 2nd Armored Division Combat Command B (CCB), the 2nd Battalion of the 67th Armored Regiment. A few minutes later, the regi-mental commander talked again to Lieutenant Colonel McDowell, telling him, "I want to get the armor to make an end run around the town. There is no reason they have to wait for us. Get to the head of your column and see if you can push them a little."

General Corlett found it necessary, but risky, on 3 October to commit a combat command in a confined bridgehead where an infantry regiment was still struggling to gain enough room for its own operations. However, as the official U.S. Army historian explained, "Corlett was less concerned about likely confusion than about losing the little Wurm River bridgehead altogether. He wanted the weight of the armor on hand before the Germans could mount a sizeable counterattack."[34]

CCB's debut on the Siegfried Line began just before noon. The 1st Battalion of the 41st Armored Infantry Regiment, Major Jenista commanding, moved from its assembly area, where its tanks and half-track personnel carriers coiled to await the crossing of the Wurm by Lieutenant Colonel Wynne's 2nd Battalion of the 67th Armored Regiment. Wynne began moving his tanks over the bridge at 1300, but artillery fire was falling constantly at the time. Each vehicle, as it crossed, also came under fire from an enemy antitank gun located in a pillbox on higher ground to the northeast of the bridge. As observers recalled, "The gun, evidently unable to depress sufficiently to hit the bridge, still put direct fire on the vehicles."[35]

It was about one mile from the bridge to the western fringes of Ubach, and after Lieutenant Colonel Wynne's armor crossed the railroad tracks, he chose to use a more southerly approach route where the artillery and antitank fire were less intense. Buildings lining both sides of this roadway also afforded more protection for his men and vehicles; both were slowed up. Finally, at 1455 hours Wynne's tanks were on the western edges of Ubach. Ten minutes later, however, a clearly frustrated Colonel Johnson was overheard by his staff saying to a division liaison, "What is Powerhouse supposed to be doing? They're messing around a little bit, but mainly sitting there. Somebody has got to move Powerhouse."[36] Johnson learned a short time later that Lieutenant Colonel McDowell had made contact with Wynne and that "they had cooked up a plan; the armored people will be behind him." A frustrated Colonel Johnson added at this time, "It doesn't look like a breakthrough to me."

Johnson was correct. Another account shed additional light on the situation and offered this perspective:

> Units became entangled amid the heavy column of artillery fire delivered on the town by the enemy. Roads and streets were congested with vehicles, and the tempers of commanders ran high. Only after careful coordination between the 3rd Battalion commander and the Armored Task Force commander was the situation disentangled.[37]

There could have been even greater confusion that afternoon. The original plan had called for the armored infantry to clean out the northern and western ends of Ubach. However, by late afternoon just two Company A medium tanks, with eight infantrymen riding on each one, had pushed across the Palenberg bridge. Given the congestion in Ubach, further movement was stopped by the 41st Armored Infantry's commanding officer, Col. Sidney R. Hinds, at 1630 hours. Hinds, who had been in command since the 41st came overseas in 1942, was without question not a happy man. His regiment's motto was, "We stand up straight, we shoot straight, we drive straight, and attempt to live straight." He wanted to get in the fight.

Instead the tanks simply moved off the road and outposted for the night. At 1800, Capt. Henry H. Hastings's Company B was ordered to secure the bridge. His platoons moved across on foot, one at a time, then infiltrated by squads into defensive positions. Company A, commanded by Lt. Russell A. Law, came across next and moved up to make contact with Captain Hoppe's Company E of the 117th Infantry east of the railroad line; Law's men then secured the area westward back to the river. By this time Lieutenant Colonel Wynne's tanks had reached the center of Ubach, where under some presumable truce with the infantry they halted for the night. Even the engineers attached to the assault teams were unable to cross the Wurm until the following morning.[38]

The lack of maneuverable roadway space also impacted the 3rd Battalion's overall mission on 3 October. "We continued to push forward, attempting to flank the resistance we encountered," Lieutenant Colonel McDowell explained later. "But due to the congestion of the route being taken through Ubach because of the presence of tanks from the 2nd Armored Division, [Colonel Johnson] ordered us at 1840 to button up for the night 500 yards short of our objective. The eastern half of Ubach was still in enemy hands."[39]

Companies K and L were nevertheless astride the upper of the two main roads that ran through Ubach, well north and west of the once busy business district. "The Jerries had bolted everything up, and because many of the houses were barred it was hard to take cover from their artillery," noted Spencer, West Virginia, native Lt. Charles O. Hardman, commander of Company L's 1st Platoon.[40] Lieutenant Thompson's Company I had by this time tied into the tail of the 3rd Battalion positions, establishing its defenses around a busted-up schoolhouse and what was left of a church. "We had originally planned to use the tall Ubach church on the western end of town as an OP," remembered Thompson. "But the Germans shelled it heavily and lopped off the steeple and riddled the church."[41]

Lieutenant Colonel Frankland's 1st Battalion of the 117th Infantry Regiment spent 3 October improving their defensive positions around the pillbox line on the crossroads south of Palenberg while McDowell's 3rd Battalion passed to their left toward Ubach. Enemy artillery came in throughout the day; the hardest hit was Captain Kent's Company A. "With friendly and enemy fire whistling over their heads, and while they were subjected to constant shelling, the company devised a bucket brigade system on water and rations," an account of the day's actions noted in explaining how the company coped under the strain.[42] "Men had to stay in their foxholes, so empty canteens were tossed from foxhole to foxhole until they reached the 'rear,' and then they went forward again with boxes of 'K' rations in the same way."

Major Ammons's 2nd Battalion had also continued its attack, with the mission of securing the high ground just to the north of Palenberg that morning. It proved to be a difficult day for these men. "The ridge securing this high ground was very steep and in some places vertical," a report noted.[43] The only approach to the area was through a large draw to the northwest of the high slag piles by the factory district and the Germans held this draw with a strong force covered by pillboxes. Company F was stopped without advancing. Company G fared a bit better; these men were able to clean out the rest of the factory area, in the process capturing a number of enemy positions and a large amount of their equipment and guns. Ammons was released from the mission of taking the high ground later in the day. It was also fortunate that the mortars of Company H had displaced into Palenberg to support his positions in the afternoon, for the first German counterattacks hit early the following morning.

Two counterattacks were made by approximately 240 enemy soldiers of the 219th Engineer Battalion; most of these Germans were attached to *Leutnant* Gutsche's 13Co and *Leutnant* Huber's 1Co. Their mission was to blow up the Marienberg-Palenberg bridge, so they first came through the draw toward Ammons's forces starting at 0700 on 4 October; they were not infantry soldiers, but engineers who had been told to fight to the end with no possible retreat. By early afternoon these attacks were repulsed, in large part because of effective friendly artillery fire placed directly in the draw by the 118th FA. Company F bore the brunt of this attack; the 2nd Platoon played a key role in stopping the enemy forces. Hand-to-hand combat prevailed; because the fighting was so close the platoon leader had to call for Company H's mortar fire on his own positions. American casualties were moderate; the number of Germans killed or wounded was unknown.

The larger German efforts hit Lieutenant Colonel McDowell's 3rd Battalion in crowded Ubach and Colonel Sutherland's 119th Infantry Regiment positions among the tangled debris and pillboxes in the woods south of Rimburg. The counterattacks in Ubach came in three distinct phases. The first two were delivered by elements of the 49th Division's 148th Infantry Regiment. The final counterattack was made by companies of the 1st Battalion, 352nd Regiment of the 246th Division, which had arrived from Aachen.

At about 0400 on 4 October, Staff Sgt. Tolliver Curry of Company L's weapons platoon stuck his head outside the doorway of a house on the northernmost road running through Ubach and saw two Mark IV tanks. One tank pulled up close to the house and its aerial was suddenly sticking into a second-story window while its cannon and machine gun fired westward up the road. When five Germans dismounted and started running into the house, Pfc. Ira Reeder killed two and wounded one other before the other two got away. A private tried to fire a bazooka out of a second-floor window at the tank, but his weapon jammed and all he could do was throw a rifle grenade at the turret as the Mark IV pulled back. The second tank, accompanied by a larger enemy force, had appeared on the other side of the house, and during this time it was raking the structure with machine-gun fire.

"Bullets splattered liberally through the house, particularly on the first floor but most of our personnel were on the second floor," remembered Pfc. Reeder. "But while the tank was firing, some of the machine-gun section men were getting their share of the Germans. Private Antone Montaya took a good toll of enemy running across the open ground north of the house with his BAR; Technical Sergeant George Morris killed two with his carbine. Another machine gunner in the hall was also helpful in stopping the attack."[44]

When dawn broke, the house became an even hotter spot. The Mark IV that had retreated came back and started machine gunning the entire structure this time. Company L's 3rd Platoon, commanded by Lt. Joseph Elinski, was pushed back across the street from the house. Enemy troops that had emerged out of the gloomy rain from a barracks area just to the east of Ubach hit right into the boundary between the men and Captain Culp's Company K. Staff Sgt. Roy Bettes remembered being rudely interrupted by machine-gun fire while eating his breakfast ration. While a BAR team supplied support, Bettes got even by retrieving his M1 and picking off two of the enemy gunners.

Culp estimated that this counterattacking force eventually consisted of seventy-five to one hundred men with six to eight Mark IV's. "Our lines were 50 yards or less apart," he recalled. "There was confusion at times about where the lines were, for enemy and friendly troops were holding alternate houses."[45]

> The enemy riflemen advanced on one occasion with white flags and then, apparently at a pre-arranged signal and spot, suddenly bent over and picked up rifles on the ground and started yelling and firing only 25 yards away from the Company K outposts.

Captain Culp's 2nd Platoon had a particularly difficult time after Lt. Orrin Cooley's 3rd Platoon was cut off. The 2nd Platoon commander and one of his sergeants worked their way back for reinforcements, and then in the face of heavy enemy tank and small-arms fire, Staff Sgt. Henry F. Brand, the ranking noncom, successfully withdrew most of the men. But when others were captured, the Germans regrouped and the house sheltering the weapons platoon soldiers became totally isolated. Other Germans also occupied the next house westward by this time; they were adding their own fire as the tanks continued to blast away with their machine guns and tubes. Then between 0830 and 0900, seven more Mark IVs arrived and tried to cut around the north side of the road and encircle all of Company L.

By probing through the enemy positions until he found a suitable OP to direct friendly artillery fire, Lt. Robert C. Burke, forward observer for Battery C of the 118th Field Artillery Battalion, saved Company L from certain massacre. He had learned that the forward observer at another post had become a casualty. Without hesitation and in the face of certain danger, Burke left his first position and moved through a street subjected to extremely heavy enemy fire, including direct machine-gun fire from a German tank. Arriving at the observation post where his fellow observer had been wounded, he discovered that Germans now occupied it. Running the gauntlet through more raining shells, he carefully darted farther up the street and selected an observation post on the third floor of another building; from here he directed the friendly artillery fire that started turning the hostile attack on Company L into a decisive German defeat. One round of 105mm fire hit square on the turret of an attacking Mark IV, causing wider disruption because at the same time tanks of Major Wynne's 2nd Battalion of the 67th Armored Regiment were rolling along the open ground just to the north of Ubach; a few American tanks actually reentered the town to help out. "The work of the 2nd Armored in coming into position, plus the artillery fire, caused the Germans to withdraw," a later account noted. "The cut-off section of the weapons platoon held out, although isolated."[46]

The Americans barely had time to get organized before the third German counterattack came in from the south edge of Ubach at about 1500. This time Company K's final protective line was quickly breached by several Mark IVs, cutting off twenty men in Lieutenant Cooley's 3rd Platoon from the rest of Culp's company. Only two soldiers from the platoon managed to make it back, but when the company attacked to regain the line seven others who had been held captive in a cellar were freed. The Company L men were not hit as hard during this strike; the cut-off weapons platoon was actually able to break out of the house in which they were trapped and make their way back to the CP. Both companies, however, were down to fewer than a hundred men each.

Lieutenant Thompson suffered a different fate in his Company I's weapons platoon. As German shelling increased through the afternoon, a half dozen rounds dropped in the middle of these men as they were moving up from the schoolhouse on the western fringes of Ubach to support the rest of the 3rd Battalion companies. One squad was wiped out and shell fragments wounded another ten men. The weapons platoon leader, Lt. Shelton S. Turner of Delta County, Texas, was killed.

Lieutenant Colonel Mayer, commander of the 118th Field Artillery, offered his impression of just how devastating the German shelling was at the time. "The Germans must have finally gotten ahold of a copy of our field manual because they were firing 70–100 rounds at once in large battalion volleys. The bulk of the enemy artillery coming in was 105 and 150mm, with some 170mm and 210mm dropping. Unfortunately, the weather was not clear enough because of clouds and haze for us to spot these enemy batteries. [Their] artillery, however, was displaced in a wide arc around us, and they knew by previous observation precisely where to concentrate their fire."[47]

Lieutenant Colonel McDowell later lent this perspective to his battalion's setbacks in the face of these heavy enemy concentrations; his observations were viewed through the lens of adjustments he made to finally thwart the German ground forces:

> Although the 3rd Battalion was originally slated to continue attacking southeastward, the counterattacks, enemy artillery and the continued congestion with the 2nd Armored Division in the area caused a holding up of the plan. These counterattacks had early success because the enemy infantrymen were regularly picking off our bazooka men, thus allowing some Mark IV tanks to roam around at will. We finally stopped this by systematically eliminating the German infantrymen, forcing the tanks to withdraw because they lacked their own infantry personnel.[48]

At approximately 0300 that same morning, enemy artillery started falling on the 119th Infantry Regiment positions in the woods south of Rimburg. An early casualty was the forward observer of the regiment's Cannon Company, Lt. Seymour Shefrin; he was wounded in both legs, his left arm, and on his face. He refused evacuation; first aid was instead given to him before two men helped him over to a nearby knoll. From here Shefrin somehow expected to "adjust fire by sounds of movement and German voices," but his eyesight had been severely diminished by his facial wounds; he still remained on the knoll, forcefully refusing to be taken to the rear.[49]

Two hours later, two companies of the 2nd Battalion, 149th Regiment of the 49th Division with Assault Gun Brigade 902 launched a vigorous counterattack from the eastern edge of the woods aimed at Captain Palmer's Company I. Several Mark IVs first fired into the woods from hull defilade positions before spraying fire from their machine guns as they burst forward into the open in front of their ground forces. Advancing boldly with their tanks now, the German soldiers succeeded in overrunning Company I's defenses, even forcing Palmer's command group out of the pillbox they had been using as a CP; they had to run for it, leaving the position from which Lieutenant Shefrin was blindly "observing" unprotected. "The attack came over to him, and the last thing we heard was his voice over the radio calling for more fire on his position," a later account sadly noted.[50]

The few Company I soldiers who were able withdrew back to the Rimburg Castle. Many others were taken prisoner after a German tank drove up to the pillbox they were in, trained its guns on the embrasure, and ordered surrender. Company B men saw a steady stream of other casualties coming through their lines. Lieutenant Knox of Company L was back in Lieutenant Colonel Brown's 3rd Battalion command post after these attacks and he recalled, "While I was at battalion I heard them frantically calling for Company I. I later learned that they were really broken up; one officer, Captain Palmer, was left. The company had been practically all captured or killed."[51]

Lieutenant Bons's Company C was also driven back approximately 150 yards before Simmons's Company A and Captain McBride's Company B finally stopped this horrific counterattack. Bons's men had bravely attempted to hold their positions; they first allowed the rushing Germans to get within 75 yards of their perimeter foxholes before they started firing back. They could only get a round or two off at a time because the German fire was so intense. There was another very brave incident at the time:

> Pfc. Harmon W. Butler and Pfc. Ray Tucker of Company D, attached to Company C, left their foxholes to man their machineguns in spite of the intense enemy fire. They were alone manning their guns, for the other members were firing rifles to build up a section of fire line against the enemy. Private Samuel A. Breyer had a foxhole between the two machineguns, and by running out under terrific fire he kept them supplied with ammunition. Small arms fire struck the cradles of both guns, damaging them in such a manner that they could only be traversed by dragging their tripods from side to side. They fired 5,500 rounds with the enemy dead piled up as close as 15 yards.[52]

DIVARTY had also been of valuable assistance, but it was the Germans' own artillery fire that finally did them in. American artillery was falling on the rear of their positions, but as Captain McBride remembered, "Their own artillery was getting beautiful tree bursts on the leading elements which were immediately in front of our 1st Battalion positions. At 0940 American planes on armed reconnaissance inflicted more casualties on the enemy, and even knocked out several tanks in Merkstein-Hofstadt."[53] Bons's Company C, right after he reorganized his platoons, retook some of the ground they had lost, including the pillbox near the road where Palmer's Company I had had its CP. "After fire from this pillbox was silenced, we blew the door open with a satchel charge and took three prisoners," Lieutenant Bons remembered.[54]

Unfortunately, the day's stubborn fighting had produced numerous casualties for the 1st Battalion. Captain Simmons lost seven men; McBride's Company B suffered twenty-four losses and Lieutenant Bons experienced another seventeen casualties. Two enlisted men from the 743rd Tank Battalion were killed when a friendly air strike strafed too close to their positions; another three were seriously wounded. Seventeen machine gunners and mortar men from the battalion's heavy weapons

Company D who were with the rifle companies were also lost during the day.[55]

Generalleutnant Lange later claimed to have personally overseen the counterattacks on 4 October from a command post in the gallery of the Boesweiler mine some three miles southeast of Ubach. About these attacks, Lange also offered his impressions of their outcomes:

> Most of the troops of the adjacent divisions took part in the attack. [Lange is presumably referring to the 49th and 246th Divisions, the latter arriving later in Ubach.] It was extremely difficult to get prompt cooperation from all units engaged in the attack. However, in spite of these difficulties the counterattack was carried out. The eventual success was merely a narrowing and sealing off of the penetration. When viewed objectively, more could not have been expected under the circumstances, especially with the proportion of strength. The engineer battalion [in Palenberg] suffered especially heavy losses and did not recover from the blow.[56]

The armor congestion that had helped divert German aggression during the counterattacks McDowell faced in Ubach was partially attributable to Task Force 1 under Colonel Disney. During the day, his armored vehicles rolled by the northwest edge of Ubach to take over the mission for McDowell's 3rd Battalion and cut the Geilenkirchen-Aachen highway 800 yards to the north. Originally scheduled to cross the Rimburg bridge, Disney's task force drew heavy artillery earlier in the morning and had to wheel north to the Marienberg bridge to get across the Wurm. As a result, Major Jenista's 1st Battalion of the 41st Armored Infantry Regiment had to give operational priority to the task force's armor, delaying their crossing while they waited by dispersing into the hills on the west side of the river. One prong of the German counterattack hit Disney's tanks just outside of Ubach, first forcing his armor to fight it out with seven self-propelled guns, which were all destroyed with the loss of just two of his own tanks. By the end of the day, Colonel Disney was just a few yards short of the highway; his task force had still paid a price for this ground. The short advance caused stiff personnel casualties and the loss of eleven medium tanks, but the German infantry they hit suffered far more. They were crushed by the weight of the American armor attack and whittled down to just twenty-five men.[57]

Task Force 2, under Colonel Hinds, had the important mission of anchoring the northern flank of the bridgehead by seizing the high ground near the settlement of Hoverhof, a mile north of Ubach, that afternoon. Major Jenista had used the time his armored infantry was waiting on the west side of the Wurm by making a personal reconnaissance into Ubach with his S-1, Lt. Kenneth W. Woods. This paid dividends. His assault, mop-up, and support teams moved to the village without attack or casualties after they finally got the go-ahead to cross the Marienberg bridge at 1200. However, enemy artillery that participants stated was of "greater intensity than any of the men had seen before" greeted their arrival in Ubach just over an hour later. The infantry had to take cover in houses.

The yeoman's work by Major Jenista in helping his men avoid casualties up to this point took an ironic turn shortly afterward. The attack toward Haverhof was scheduled to go off at 1500, but it had to be delayed when Jenista himself was struck by shell fragments while he was helping his jeep driver change a tire. He was evacuated; Lieutenant Woods went back to the rear command post in Marienberg and brought up Capt. R. A. Williamson, the battalion's executive officer, to assume command.

The fortunes of war dealt another blow after the assault forces finally jumped off at 1600. Williamson, with a group of other officers, was in an orchard just to the north of Ubach watching the progress of the attack when a concentration of shells hit. He was severely wounded; two company commanders became casualties, the driver of the jeep when Major Jenista got hit was also wounded this time, and the radio operator of an accompanying tank was killed. The battalion surgeon, although he had also been struck and wounded by shell fragments, managed to give aid to the others and direct their evacuation. Only Lieutenant Woods and a motorcyclist escaped injury.[58]

For a second time that day, Woods returned to the rear, this time only to Palenberg, to bring up a new commanding officer. Captain Hastings, who led Company B, came up to Ubach, where the pair found Colonel Hinds and Lieutenant Colonel Wynne. At the time, no word had come back on how the assault was going, so Hastings went forward to see for himself. He came back encouraged.

When the advance began, forward artillery observers riding in tanks called for fire to drive the enemy out of the trenches and pits around the pillboxes along the Ubach-Hoverhof road. Wynne's armor followed closely, moving 100 to 150 yards behind the friendly shells with Hastings's infantry trailing, followed by TDs to provide flank protection. Lt. Michael Levitsky of 1st Platoon, Company A, commanded an assault team—comprised of tanks, infantry men, engineers, heavy machine guns, and a tank dozer—which had moved up the road to a point just east of a hill close to the village when heavy enemy artillery fire suddenly came in. There were several pillboxes nearby and, suspecting the occupants included German forward observers who were calling down his men's location, Levitsky ordered everyone off the road. He then wisely decided to bypass this hill altogether.

This move enabled his team to work their way even closer to Hoverhof, where the men turned abruptly to the west to attack three pillboxes which they quickly captured. Then they reversed direction and overtook three more 300 yards to the east, above Haverhof. The hill on which the pillboxes were situated overlooked the village so Lieutenant Levitsky's men, having accomplished their mission, stopped there. A second assault team, commanded by Lt. Andrew P. Smith, had also advanced north of the village; these men turned west and captured seven additional pillboxes before they occupied a second hill looking into Haverhof. The mop-up team, commanded by Lt. Joseph T. Harper, captured many of the enemy personnel that the assault teams had not killed or wounded. Most of these Germans had hidden in the pillboxes' sleeping quarters.

In just one hour and fifteen minutes, Captain Hastings experienced his first assault as an acting battalion commander with fifteen pillboxes seized and not a single friendly casualty. He captured five German officers and seventy-five other enemy combatants. His men had also progressed 1,000 yards farther north than planned. It was also Hastings's last drive. At 1830 Maj. John W. Finnell, who had been the executive officer before he was wounded and then the Assistant S-3, came forward to take overall command of the armored infantry.

By this time Lieutenant Colonel Herlong's forces had renewed their attack in the Rimburg woods, but with little success. "We were supposed to meet tanks that would support us where the road from Rimburg

crosses the railroad tracks," remembered Company A's Captain Simmons. "But no tanks appeared. Between 0900 and 1000 three TD's did
show up, and they agreed to help us. They got into position in the field
to the west of where the road crossed the railroad and covered the pillbox
just north of the tracks with fire."[59]

Simmons had no more than a platoon and a half with which to
attack, however. The company was still able to take this first pillbox, but
only because the Germans retired to another box behind it when the
TDs opened fire. Company A simply did not have enough strength to
strike at this second pillbox; the enemy soldiers capitalized on this, counterattacked, and took back the first box. The cost to Simmons was high.
"After this engagement, during which we took additional casualties, we
only had 22 fighting men left," he explained later.[60] Flanking fire had
also raked the company from the high ground in front of Lieutenant
Bons's Company C during the enemy counterattack; this was because
Bons had instructed his platoon leaders not to move forward until Company A had advanced farther. Instead, Company C built up a line along
the road that ran through the high ground they were on and held here
for the night; his men dubbed this location Shrapnel Hill. Captain
McBride's Company B tied in along the road to the left; Herlong suspended operations at 1830.

With stiff resistance and little gain being made inside the Rimburg
woods, Colonel Sutherland made the decision to move Lieutenant
Colonel Cox's 2nd Battalion up toward Ubach. From here, Companies E
and F would turn south and first reduce several pillboxes along a stretch of
gently sloping ground just outside of the woods. Sutherland hoped that
this would finally help out Herlong's rapidly depleting forces and also
accelerate the drive to Herbach. This movement got off to a bad start,
however. At the intersection of the Rimburg-Ubach road Captain Toler
was wounded; command of Company E shifted to Lieutenant Parker.

With Ubach still under counterattack and confused congestion at
the time, both companies ran into heavy artillery fire as they got closer to
the village—"really big stuff that came in like an express train," according
to later accounts.[61] Further casualties were few, fortunately, but instead of
attacking southward that afternoon, Parker's and Lieutenant Arn's men

dug in just to the south of the main road in Ubach. Tanks and TDs joined them here for what would now be an attack the next morning.

But all was not quiet during the night. Lieutenant Parker sent out four- to five-man patrols to see how close they could get to the pillboxes; one patrol led by Pfc. Lane E. Gluba actually returned with fourteen prisoners, but he could not identify on Parker's overprinted photomap the pillbox from which his patrol had taken them. Parker then decided to send another patrol into the vicinity where Gluba thought the box was, and after they jumped off, these men, commanded by Sgt. Robert R. Allen, spotted Germans heading toward it. Racing to see who could get there first, Allen's patrol won, but in doing so they also created some anxiety for Lieutenant Colonel Cox. Word of their success had not been sent back, so Cox got what little sleep he could—assuming through the night that the entire patrol had been captured.

Lieutenant Colonel Brown's 3rd Battalion never made contact with Herlong's 1st Battalion companies in the Rimburg woods on 4 October. "Battalion was convinced that our company could not move," recalled Company L's Lieutenant Knox. "Lieutenant Colonel Brown convinced regiment of the same thing, although Captain Stanford continually sent out patrols to see if they were near us." Brown later ordered one of Captain Hopcraft's Company K platoons to move back to the Rimburg Castle to help with the reorganization of Captain Palmer's badly battered Company I, leaving a second platoon to the right of Stanford's Company L. A third Company K platoon went back to the regimental CP, now also in the Rimburg Castle, to be a security force on the bridge for Colonel Sutherland and his staff.

The German command decided to bring more units into the area of the XIX Corps' penetration before 4 October ended. *General der Infanterie* Köchling ordered three units from the sector of *Oberst* Engel's 12th Infantry Division southeast of Aachen to the Ubach area: a *Landesschuetzen* battalion, an assault gun brigade, and a howitzer battalion. From the 246th Division in Aachen, he ordered up an antitank company equipped with six 75mm guns and a tank company, somewhat curiously named as such since its weapons were actually touchy remote-controlled robotic assault guns. Köchling also decided to restore the boundary between

Generalleutnant Lange's 183rd Division and Macholz's 49th Division, removing the single command he had entrusted to Lange because the anticipated additional forces would be unmanageable under him alone.

Uncertain that these units would be able to assemble and move quickly enough before the day was over, Köchling took further steps to gain an even greater concentration of troops to stop the Americans. This time he decided to relieve the entire 404th Grenadier Regiment from the 246th Division in Aachen, and at the same time free up Lange's 343rd Grenadier Regiment opposite the 29th Division northwest of Geilenkirchen so this unit would also be available for the fight around Ubach. With ten batteries of 105mm howitzers and seven batteries of 150mm howitzers currently at his disposal, Köchling nevertheless determined that he needed additional artillery support. By 6 October he hoped to have another twenty-seven 150mm guns and thirty-two 88mm antiaircraft weapons to assist in throwing the Americans back into the chilly waters of the Wurm River, bringing the total number of artillery pieces at LXXXI Corps' disposal to nearly 120.

General der Infanterie Köchling had not made these decisions independently. With the severity of the situation raising alarm, he had visitors at his command post in Niederzier that day. Commander in Chief West Model and *General der Panzertruppe* Brandenberger, commander of 7th Army, gained the impression that Köchling's expected force strength was still insufficient. To remedy this, Brandenberger lined up additional ground forces for transfer; two were from noncommissioned officer training schools in Dueren and Juelich, another an infantry unit from the 275th Division then fighting southeast of Aachen in the Huertgen Forest under LXXXV Corps, and the last a fortress machine-gun battalion. To augment Köchling's artillery strength even more, Brandenberger also promised an additional artillery brigade with two batteries of 150mm howitzers and one battalion of very heavy howitzers.

The morning sky revealed signs of clearing weather for 5 October. It also undoubtedly brought discomfort to Köchling for it meant that American artillery and air reconnaissance would likely interfere with the troop movements he had planned. This proved true. VII Corps artillery delivered heavy fire on the *Landesschuetzen* battalion, delaying their arrival after they detached from the 12th Infantry Division. The NCO trainees from Dueren and Juelich promised by Brandenberger were tardy, not arriving until after first light in the area of Lange's 343rd Regiment, thus preventing this unit from disengaging and moving south to reinforce the area north of Ubach. The 404th Regiment of the 246th Division did reach the front, but not until after noon. Like the day after the Americans first broke through the *Westwall*, Köchling lost the chance to deliver an early ground strike on 5 October; he would again be forced to commit his units piecemeal, depending on the direction of the American attacks.

This direction was now more evident to the Germans. The 49th Division's *Generalleutnant* Macholz later revealed why:

> From entries on a map, captured in the counterattacks on 4 October, it was now evident that the enemy, after having succeeded in breaking through the Westwall, intended to continue the attack toward Alsdorf with the aim of encircling Aachen from the north and east, while covering his left flank toward the west. This meant the division's front would be rolled up from the north. [We were,] therefore, greatly concerned about the future.[62]

CHAPTER 8

South toward Alsdorf

"Alsdorf was a ghost town when we came in.
It was so damn quiet it scared you."

CAPT. JOHN KENT, COMPANY A, 117TH INFANTRY REGIMENT

The 117th Infantry Regiment's new objective on 5 October was indeed to seize Alsdorf, which would cut off one of the two main highways running northeast out of Aachen. Colonel Johnson's initial plan called for Lieutenant Colonel Frankland's 1st Battalion to relieve McDowell's men in Ubach and then attack south, but during the night he revised this to have the battalions attack abreast. When morning dawned, Captain Spiker's Company B started working its way through Ubach to take up positions to the right of the 3rd Battalion on a grassy ridge just outside the village; Captain Kent's Company A had already assembled there. Ubach still proved to be difficult to get through, even in the early hours of the new day. Spiker was delayed; his men had to leapfrog in small groups from house to house to avoid renewed enemy artillery fire. Kent's men had avoided these volleys by moving through an orchard just to the south. After starting out, Stoffer's Company C was held up near battle-torn Palenberg, and both shelling and congestion also slowed these men up as they tried to reach the assembly area. Consequently, Frankland's companies were not ready for the attack.[1]

Instead, hasty changes by Colonel Johnson now had Lieutenant Colonel McDowell's 3rd Battalion launching a coordinated strike from Ubach with just Companies E and F of Cox's 2nd Battalion. The first objective was the small village of zu Ubach, just to the southeast of

199

Ubach. Lieutenant Thompson's Company I and Company L had been selected for the lead and these men attacked astride the main road while Wild Man Culp's Company K was held in reserve. Five tanks accompanied Thompson's platoons; the tanks drove on the road surface and the infantrymen moved on the right side of the roadway. Lt. Richard C. Timpe's 1st Platoon led the assault but the Germans that the battalion had met the day before in Ubach, the 2nd Battalion of the 149th Regiment, spotted these men as soon as they reached the far edge of the village. After letting the American platoon advance, mortar, small-arms, and machine-gun fire came in from the barracks building just to the southeast, forcing the soldiers to dive for the banks of the road, seeking cover. "Much of the machinegun fire was coming from the second story windows and was whistling 50-feet over our heads," Timpe remembered. "But there was also enough close to the ground to keep our heads down."[2]

"The Germans had all the road exits from Ubach well-blocked," a later report added. "Nobody seemed to be able to bypass the enemy's direct fire weapons."[3] When the tanks tried to move up to assist the infantry, all five were hit. Three erupted in flames; another was hit in the rear engine compartment and the fifth directly in the driver's compartment. Three men were killed and four were wounded.[4] One TD from the 803rd Tank Destroyer Battalion in Ubach tried to help, but as Lt. James Cushing, the commander of this unit, recalled, "The 2nd Armored Division was still in the area and the roads were clogged. So we tried to sneak the TD around to the east and deliver some flanking fire on the enemy weapons, but they were dug in and too well protected. It was also hit and burned."[5]

Neither Company I nor Company L was able to reduce or outflank the Germans as the morning wore on. McDowell later noted that his battalion moved a mere 800 yards on 5 October. Enemy artillery fire increased throughout the afternoon, leaving Lieutenant Thompson to later remark, "Timpe's platoon was pinned down practically all day; it was more or less isolated. The worst problem was trying to keep an OP long enough to direct friendly artillery fire on the enemy strongpoints. Every time an observer mounted the second story of a house, the Germans would shell it with artillery."[6]

Lieutenant Colonel Cox's 2nd Battalion did better that morning. He elected to have Company E lead the assault; Lieutenant Parker chose his

2nd and 3rd Platoons for this assignment, and these men were to the right of Lieutenant Arn's Company F when they jumped off. Seven tanks and four TDs accompanied the assault force; the TDs were given the mission of protecting the battalion's left flank so the tanks could work directly with Parker's infantry.

Their line of departure was just to the south of the main drag through Ubach. Lieutenant Parker's plan called for the pillboxes they were attacking to be approached in an order laid out by code on his photomap; he would accompany the 2nd Platoon, but Sgt. Harold L. Holycross of Perryville, Indiana, would provide its direct command and control. A number of these pillboxes were on higher ground before the terrain sloped downward into a steep draw about a half kilometer away. Two other pillboxes were scattered farther back between the high ground and the draw. Parker felt it was essential to capture the latter two in order to prevent any counterattacks; he was certain the Germans in these pillboxes would have the drop on his men. In all, there were about a dozen pillboxes that had to be reduced. But Lieutenant Parker had a more immediate problem with which to contend first.

"When we got ready to attack, there wasn't a flamethrower or pole charge in the company," he remembered.[7] Instead, his men improvised and used the tanks. When they emerged from their dug-in positions at 0700 to start the assault, Sergeant Holycross had one tank lay antiphosphorous ammunition on the first pillbox. He then directed another tank to put heavy explosive against it at the same time, close enough to have the fire ricochet and hit his opposite numbers in the box's adjoining trenches. They achieved the desired result. The heavy explosive fire scared the Germans and they dashed inside the concrete shelter; the antiphosphorous fire actually penetrated the box's embrasure. Holycross and four of his men had rushed forward underneath the trajectory of this deadly fire and when they got within 100 yards of the box, he ordered the fire lifted. Pfc. John Perez threw a grenade into the aperture as he closed in. When the smoked cleared, a white flag was lazily waving from the doorway. "We just held the bag as they surrendered," one of the Americans wryly noted.[8]

During this time Lieutenant McAuley's 3rd Platoon had been working on another nearby pillbox. Parker had already radioed him and suggested he use the same methods that had reduced the first box; they worked and the Germans surrendered, with the assaulting squad not suffering a single casualty. As luck would have it, the pillbox just to the south of this one proved to be the box captured the night before, so Parker moved over and used this as a command post to deliver further orders. He put McAuley's 3rd Platoon on the defense, and then told Sergeant Holycross it was now his men's honor to attack the next group of pillboxes.

Enemy artillery fire had found his squads by this time, so Sergeant Holycross made the decision to leave two of them behind. Jumping off with a single squad of four men, he first directed the tanks to fire not just on the next pillbox, but on all four pillboxes farther to the south. Advancing under the loud, friendly fire as they had done before, the squad reached the first box and the Germans here "poked a white flag out the door and meekly surrendered."[9] By this time the confident American tank gunners had their fire roaming from box to box; one pillbox turned out to be empty, but between forty and fifty prisoners were taken from the others. Holycross later pointed out, "In each case the white flag was displayed after the tank fire ceased, as the Jerries in the pillboxes were apparently afraid even to open the door to show their readiness to surrender until this fire was lifted."[10]

Sergeant Holycross's attention now shifted to the pillboxes down the slope before the steep draw, from which he feared a counterattack might start. This time when he requested supporting fire, the tanks became timid because of the risk of *Panzerfaust* fire; accounts even said they "almost refused to go on unless the draw was cleared."[11] Lieutenant Colonel Cox responded by ordering Company G, his reserve company in that day's operations, to come up and clean out the draw.

Lieutenant Colonel McDowell's 3rd Battalion of the 117th Infantry Regiment was attacking to Company E's left at the time. Sketchy reports had also been coming in saying that the 120th Infantry Regiment had already reached Herbach, the day's objective for the 119th. This proved to be false, but for Lieutenant Parker it meant that he couldn't call on any artillery fire to help his men with what was left of their mission because of the proximity of friendly forces.

There was a hutment area just to the northeast of Herbach, so Parker instead ordered McAuley's 3rd Platoon to move over there and clean it out. These men did so with little difficulty, even though there were just thirteen men left in the platoon by this time. Sergeant Holycross, meanwhile, had built up their flank with his own men. Now, with the boxes reduced by the 3rd Platoon, this permitted him to use their men for flank protection and he led the attack on two more pillboxes. Stronger enemy fire was coming in from a wooded area to Holycross's front. Lieutenant Parker's answer was to call for the company's weapons platoon to fire their machine guns into the woods. Searching and traverse fire found the Germans and silenced this threat; Holycross and his men were then able to reduce the next two pillboxes.

Company E had now captured more pillboxes than it had strength to defend, so Lieutenant Colonel Cox ordered Lieutenant Arn's Company F to take over. "They were doing such a good job in capturing the pillboxes that Colonel Cox did not want to change over," remembered Arn. "But at 0900 Company F was given the mission of occupying the pillboxes Company E had captured."[12]

> In doing this, the only opposition consisted of artillery fire from the southeast. This, however, was extremely heavy and forced the advance elements to move by rushes from one foxhole to another. The foxholes were those previously dug by Company E. In the late afternoon the 3rd Platoon was given the mission of cleaning out the woods. After a small patrol had been sent out and reported finding no Jerries, Staff Sergeant [Roger B.] Todd and a complete squad were sent out to outpost it.

Loaded with grenades, M-1s, BARs, and machine guns, the remainder of Company F had few problems securing the pillboxes. In all, Parker's Company E captured eleven pillboxes; Sergeant Holycross's group was responsible for taking eight of these, even though the supporting tanks were low on HE and out of AP ammunition when he was going after the two pillboxes back in the draw. The company suffered only one casualty during the day's attack. Company E had pushed all the way down the ridge to a point just to the east of Herbach. Only one pillbox remained on the tip of the high ground fronting the village. Lieutenant Parker wanted to take it, but without tank support he had to let this pillbox wait until the next day.

The 3rd Battalion of Colonel Birks's 120th Infantry Regiment, commanded by Lt. Col. Paul W. McCollum, had been attached to the 119th

Infantry Regiment at 1530 hours on 5 October; this was the unit that was reported to have already reached Herbach. But McCollum's mission was to first cross the Wurm at Rimburg, and then attack south to fill the gap between Cox's 2nd Battalion and Herlong's 1st Battalion, the latter still heavily engaged in the dank Rimburg woods. McCollum's forces did make it to the line held by Lieutenant Parker beneath Herbach, where they consolidated for the night. Absent was Lieutenant Colonel McCollum. The North Carolina native had been killed by artillery fire while returning to his CP after inspecting one of his company positions; his executive officer, Maj. Howard W. Greer, was now in command.[13]

Without armored support, it indeed was another very rough day in the Rimburg woods for Lieutenant Colonel Herlong's 1st Battalion. Captain McBride remembered, "The attacked jumped off at 0700 with Company C on our left. When we advanced about ten yards, intense fire from two mutually supporting pillboxes 50 yards to our front forced the company to return to its original position."[14]

Lieutenant Bons's Company C was also unable to make any immediate progress. After both companies made several more futile attempts to gain ground, Herlong pulled them back approximately 75 yards and then called for artillery and mortar fire on the enemy positions. This fire was delivered on a time schedule, and the moment it was lifted both companies rushed forward but were again stopped by hostile fire. Friendly artillery was again called for while the heavy weapons men also lobbed their 81mm mortars at the Germans this time. But the rifle companies made no progress. "This procedure was repeated several more times without success," Captain McBride recalled later. "It became apparent that when the artillery began falling the Germans would move into their pillboxes and dugouts. Then as soon as the artillery lifted they would rush back and man their positions."[15]

McBride was obviously not satisfied with this predicament. He was also convinced that Company C was not being aggressive enough, so he decided he would have one of his own rifle platoons assault the high ground that Bons's men were supposed to take. The Company B captain only had about twenty soldiers apiece in each platoon at his disposal, so this was a daunting challenge. Captain McBride's plan boldly called for both platoons to move forward while rapidly employing marching fire as they dashed toward the pillboxes. He wanted the element of surprise and speed. There were just two light machine guns left with the weapons platoon; he decided to have both gunners fire from a hip position and accompany the platoon on the left; their mission was to take the higher ground in front of Company C. The heavy machine gunners would fire on the flanks of both platoons as they advanced, and then swing their fire at the pillbox embrasures when the riflemen closed in. To strengthen the attack, McBride also determined that he needed flamethrowers to accompany each platoon. There was one problem—he had no one in his own ranks to carry the flamethrowers; no one knew how to use them.

Captain McBride requested the two flamethrowers he needed from Lieutenant Colonel Herlong to solve this problem; Herlong quickly agreed to find these men. McBride then briefed his platoon leaders and reinforced the plan of attack he had developed. He reiterated that rapid, simultaneous movement forward with maximum fire on enemy positions was essential to the success of the plan. Timing would be everything. The flamethrowers were to be as far forward as possible so they could blast the pillbox embrasures early in the assault.

At 1130 an engineer platoon leader with two men arrived at McBride's command post. There was a new problem, however. When the Company B captain explained the plan, the platoon leader told him General Hobbs had decreed that engineers could no longer be used to operate flamethrowers since they had suffered too many casualties and had to be saved to construct bridges and do other work. McBride answered by withdrawing four of his own riflemen; the engineers gave them hasty instructions on how to operate a flamethrower.

Shortly afterward, Captain McBride's two platoon leaders came back to his location and reported their men were briefed and ready. When the newly trained flamethrowers appeared a few minutes later, McBride gave the order to attack.

The sudden fury coupled with the psychological effect caused by flames licking at his positions startled the enemy, and before he could regain his balance the assault troops were overrunning his position. The effect of the flamethrowers was increased when one German who had been set on fire ran screaming through the area before he was finally burned to death. Satchel charges placed against the rear doors of the pillboxes and hand grenades dropped down their ventilators encouraged the rest of the Germans occupying the pillboxes to surrender.[16]

Company B even managed to attack another 200 yards southward before they were stopped. During this advance, McBride's left platoon, which had initially overrun the high ground in front of Company C, turned south and moved back into their own company area to help mop up. Throughout the remainder of the afternoon, however, neither company was able to advance any farther. Replacements were badly needed, so Herlong ordered both companies to dig in at 1700 hours. Later that evening, he received seventy-four new men. Twenty-two went to Captain Simmons's Company A, bringing his strength to fifty-five men. Captain McBride got another twenty-two; he would have seventy-five soldiers for the next day's attack.[17] Company C added eighteen men, bringing their fighting strength to eighty, and twelve others replaced the lost machine gunners and mortar men in the heavy weapons company. At normal strength a company had almost two hundred men; none came up to half of a full roster, but the war went on. Lieutenant Colonel Herlong received instructions from Colonel Sutherland to resume the attack at 0700 the next morning and to clean out the remainder of the woods. There were still several hundred yards left before these men could step onto the Rimburg-Merkstein-Hofstadt road, head farther south, and finally be freed from the surly bonds of the Rimburg woods.

The 2nd Armored Division's CCB achieved mixed results in its efforts to build up the beachhead to the east and north on 5 October. Colonel Disney's Task Force 1 was stopped short of its objective—Beggendorf—after crossing the Geilenkirchen-Aachen highway; a gain of only a few hundred yards was made. During the afternoon, the 404th Regiment of the 246th Division arrived in the area and by nightfall these new forces sealed off the German line from Muthagen to the western outskirts of Beggendorf.[18]

Task Force 2 under Colonel Hinds made more progress toward Geilenkirchen that day; Frelenberg and Zweibruggen were the objectives. The 41st Armored Infantry Regiment's Lieutenant Smith was able to quickly move his assault team over to Zweibruggen before turning south and taking thirteen pillboxes that were still in enemy hands east of the Wurm. "Tactics that were successful the previous day were used again," a report detailing the day's actions noted. "The team had no difficulty, as the enemy seemed thoroughly cowed by the attack of the day before."[19] Lieutenant Levitsky's assault team had also made quick work of the Frelenberg phase of the attack, mopping up eight pillboxes before 0900 and taking the crossroads in town shortly thereafter.

During the latter part of the morning, Captain Hastings's Company B moved to the village and set up a defensive line to prevent reoccupation of the captured boxes. This enabled Levitsky's infantrymen, engineers, and tanks to sweep the area as far south as Zweibruggen. They encountered a minefield on the road immediately north of this village, and they cleared it before they made contact with Lieutenant Smith's forces. It was only noontime at this point, so Major Finnell decided to capitalize on the rapid advance and keep the drive moving. The 2nd Battalion of the 41st Armored Infantry Regiment displaced his 1st Battalion in Frelenberg, enabling a thrust toward the high ground north of the Frelenberg-Breil road. Lieutenant Levitsky's assault team, with Lieutenant Harper's mop-up men assisting, attacked at 1600, secured this line by nightfall, and dug in. Lieutenant Colonel Wynne's 2nd Battalion of the 67th Armored Regiment had reported that Breil was cleared by this time, but enemy fire still came into Finnell's newly won positions through the night.

The Americans had taken 25 pillboxes during the day. The armored infantry suffered just 9 casualties; 5 German officers and 150 of their enlisted personnel were made prisoners. The entire 67th Armored Regiment was heavily engaged on 5 October. Observed direct and indirect artillery fire had hit Lt. Col. Clifton B. Batchelder's 1st Battalion when they crossed the Marienberg bridge and moved up to Frelenberg; six tanks were lost and although personnel casualties were small, one officer—Company H's CO, Lt. Philips T. Bixby—was wounded in the leg.[20]

Very interesting intelligence about the German mindset on 4 October later emerged. A member of the G-2 section of XIX Corps was inside a captured pillbox in Palenberg trying to determine the extent of its damage when, to his surprise, he heard the deep gonging of the box's telephone. He picked it up and heard the occupants of two other enemy-held pillboxes openly discussing their present conditions. It turned out that several pillboxes were wired together such that they could all communicate simultaneously; Pvt. Siegfried F. Brand of the 117th Infantry's Headquarters Company and T/5 Earnest A. Pokel of IPW Team 42 of the 30th Infantry Division were quickly tasked with writing up the subsequent conversations.

Late-night exchanges between the pillboxes first revealed the German passwords "Gold" and "Silver." "Gold" was the challenge word. A fellow soldier identified himself as a German comrade by responding with "Silver"; failure to answer the challenge could result in being shot. One pillbox reported it was out of rations; another identified six casualties—Hagen, Wallentag, Hoeflen, Schmidt, and Fredlen, plus the caller himself with a face wound. One reported two men by name missing, one of whom took a heavy machine gun with him; yet another pillbox reported four more casualties and that a dead man had been brought to their bunker. Finally *Leutnant* Hofner, commander of 3Co of the 330th Regiment's 1st Battalion, called from his bunker and told *Unteroffizier* Janovsky in another pillbox "if you see any tanks coming from Frelenberg, call me immediately and ring four times."[21]

At 0910 Janovsky rang and reported—"Sir, we sighted two tanks on the road Marienburg-Frelenberg." The line fell silent until 1030, but then a nervously excited Janovsky called Hofner again and stated, "Sir, we have sighted 80 tanks coming over the bridge." Hofner, seeking clarification, replied, "Did you say eight tanks?" Janovsky replied back, "No sir, eighty. They came over the bridge in close column." Hofner's reaction: "Himmel Donnerwetter [God dammit]!! I'll request artillery barrage immediately."

Then, at 1200 Janovsky reported to Hofner: "Sir, the Americans shoot smoke shells along the whole line. I believe they prepare to attack." Another bunker confirmed this and then at 1230 a jittery voice stated, "Sir, the Americans also shoot incendiary shells and move towards the coal mine." Ten minutes later, Jankovsky called Hofner and yelled, "We receive enemy fire! Three of my men are badly hurt. Two are shell shocked and one passed out. My strength is now two or three men. We hold the bunker as long as possible and then . . . ? There is no way of retreat any more." Hofner's response: "We'll see if we can evacuate your wounded man after dark. Stay inside from now on. Heil!"

By 1555 Hofner was in a different bunker; he had vacated his because it was being overrun. Over the open line he asked, "Is there any news?" Someone answered: "They are firing at us with machine guns now." A few minutes later conversation from one bunker to another was overheard, this time saying, "I can't get connected with the CP [Hofner's pillbox] anymore. How about you?" The answer: "Hell, we can't get in touch with them either. That son of a bitch beat it, without notifying us. Ten tanks are now approaching the power station. What the hell are we going to do?"

Combat Command A (CCA) was ordered to cross the Wurm and add even more armored weight to the bridgehead on 5 October. Two columns were formed; the left column was commanded by the 66th Armored Regiment's CO, Colonel Stokes; the right column was under the command of his 1st Battalion's Lieutenant Colonel Parker.

At 0930 the 3rd Battalion of the 29th Infantry Division's 116th Regiment arrived at the assembly area for attachment to Stokes's left column, and then at 1000 hours these forces were placed on thirty-minute alert for movement. At noon the column rolled out, but as it approached Marienberg, heavy enemy artillery rounds started coming in. This fire continued as the column crossed the bridge and moved through Palenberg, eventually causing Stokes's forces to stop short of Beggendorf for the night. Lieutenant Colonel Parker's right column, following Stokes, had the mission of securing the high ground near the village of Oidtweiler, located less than a thousand yards southeast of Baesweiler; establishing security here would cut off the main roadway to Alsdorf, an extension of the Aachen-Settrich highway and one of the supply routes into Aachen. While Parker advanced farther than Stokes's left column, he was unable to reach his objective, instead coiling past ancient Roman roads about one mile to the west of Baesweiler for the night. Enemy resistance was heavy all day long, but both columns suffered just eight casualties, with two killed in action. Stokes lost two tanks while Lieutenant Colonel Parker's force captured thirty-five Germans during their advance.[22]

With constant pressure by the 2nd Armored and 30th Infantry Divisions in clear evidence, concern in the German command grew throughout the afternoon on 5 October. While the 404th Regiment of the 246th Division held the line from Muthagen to the western edges of Beggendorf, preventing CCB's advance in the direction of Geilenkirchen was dependent upon the arrival of the German NCOs from Juelich and Dueren. Heavy American artillery had thwarted this move, and it was only accomplished by way of infiltration. Delayed until later that night, this new force finally connected to the 404th Regiment and was deployed in a northwesterly direction up to the *Westwall* about one kilometer north of Frelenberg. During the night, German attempts to regain this village failed.

LXXXI Corps noted:

> On 5 October, the enemy continued his attacks to expand the penetration area. In an easterly direction, he advanced to the western outskirts of the village of Beggendorf; however he was not able to capture it. The attack to the north and northeast along the road Ubach-Geilenkirchen and to the northeast of it, after repeated unsuccessful attempts, led to a breakthrough with tanks and infantry in the direction of Breil and pushed our troops back to the line—southern outskirts-Breil-southern outskirts-Waurichen.[23]

Clearly, the German High Command still expected XIX Corps to continue their attack to the east. It would take another day before more reinforcements arrived to address the American penetrations to the south and the line Merkstein-Herbach-Hofstadt defended. It would be too late. As the Army official historian noted:

> The Americans were now getting set to exploit their bridgehead; the Germans would have to go to extraordinary measures to assemble sufficient strength to push them back to the Wurm. Although Field Marshall Model could not have known it at the time, any counterattack he might devise at this point would be directed more toward preventing a link between XIX and VII Corps northeast of Aachen than eliminating the XIX Corps'

bridgehead. Successes on 6 October clearly indicated that the fight for a Westwall bridgehead was nearing an end.[24]

But it did not appear as evident to the U.S. soldiers attacking through the Rimburg woods when first light started peeking through shell-smashed trees that morning. Lieutenant Colonel Herlong's 1st Battalion of the 119th Infantry Regiment began its attack at 0700. Captain McBride's Company B was to the right of Lieutenant Bons's Company C at the start, and both companies initially advanced slowly—too slowly. McBride, like he had the day before, again made aggressive command decisions and soon got his men moving. By midmorning Company B had reduced the last pillbox in its zone and cleared out the entire woods right down to the Rimburg-Merkstein-Hofstadt road.

Bons's Company C had again not managed to advance on line with Company B, so Herlong ordered Captain Simmons's Company A to move down and protect the flank and rear of McBride's platoons. This took a while, but by late morning Simmons's men were in these positions, at which time McBride's men crossed the road and began advancing south. By 1210 they had reduced four additional pillboxes and cleaned out 900 more yards of woods. Captain McBride reported his new location to Lieutenant Colonel Herlong by 300 radio and the battalion commander told him to hold in place until they had put in telephone wires; he had further instructions, and wanted to assure operational security before giving them to McBride. A wire team had followed Company B all morning, so the line was available in less than five minutes.

Herlong took McBride somewhat by surprise when he informed him that the regiment had now given the battalion the mission of capturing Merkstein-Hofstadt and setting up defensive positions to the south of the village. He also told him that the engineers had cut a roadway through the railroad embankment where the Germans had previously blown an overpass and then followed with word that a platoon from the 743rd Tank Battalion had come through and would now support the attack. This was undoubtedly very good news to Captain McBride. It would be the first time in days that the armor was able to help out. Herlong also told McBride that his men and the platoon of tanks would be on the right, while Bons's Company C attacked to the left. McBride responded by telling the battalion commander that he would be ready in ten minutes, but he was uncertain of Company C's location; McBride's patience had grown increasingly thin with his neighbor. It turned out that Bons's men were still 500 yards to the rear of Company B; twenty minutes later these men arrived at Captain McBride's location. Herlong had come down from his command post by this time; the company captains joined him and the platoon leader from the 743rd Tank Battalion to receive the attack order. Bons and McBride exchanged harsh words; Herlong helped sort this out, but he remained focused on the mission. Company B would clear out the remaining portion of the woods; Bons would still attack to the left. Once the woods were cleared, Company C would be responsible for cleaning out the eastern half of Merkstein-Hofstadt while McBride's men reduced the west side of the hard coal mining town. The tanks were to initially operate on the right of Company B, and then assist the companies as the situation dictated when they reached Merkstein-Hofstadt. Captain Simmons's Company A would follow Company B and protect the right flank of the battalion.

When the attack jumped off, Captain McBride and his platoons again displayed exceptional initiative. By 1400, they had cleaned out the woods in their zone with the assistance of the tanks that first fired into its western fringes and had taken twenty prisoners. Company C was still back in the woods, so McBride, unhappy with Bons, ordered his left platoon to join with the tanks and again take over Company C's mission. After conferring with Captain Simmons, McBride directed his left platoon to be responsible for this task; Company A would now provide close support. By 1630, McBride's platoons had cleared out the upper part of Merkstein-Hofstadt to either side of the north-south roadway that ran through it and had taken fifteen more prisoners. At 1715, Bons's Company C finally arrived and assisted in securing the factory area to the south of the crossroad through town. An hour and a half later, the battalion consolidated its positions; they established defenses to the east and south. They had accomplished their mission.

"This was the last day of heavy fighting for the 1st Battalion in the Siegfried Line operation," Lieutenant Colonel Herlong noted a few days later.[25] The battalion journal also noted it was a day for which they could be proud. "Battalion praised by corps and division on their stubborn and aggressive fighting," it stated.[26] In part, this was because reducing the Rimburg woods and capturing Merkstein-Hofstadt had finally relieved the pressure on the left flank of Lieutenant Colonel Brown's 3rd Battalion; his forces would now be able to launch an attack against the pillboxes to the southeast. But it was still a day where losses were particularly hard-felt in the 1st Battalion. McBride lost Technical Sgt. Adrian F. Vetter and Lt. Kenneth R. Knowe. Both had been killed. Lieutenant Bons was also slightly injured, but he had continued on through the day. Captain McBride aptly summarized:

> In the five days of attacks the 1st Battalion had made an open river crossing and captured 19 pillboxes, one enemy town, one enemy factory, 245 enemy soldiers and an undetermined quantity of their equipment. The battalion paid a high price for these accomplishments; the rifle companies sustained a total of 354 casualties.[27]

At daylight on 6 October, elements of two battalions of the 49th Infantry Division's 148th Regiment launched a determined counterattack against Lieutenant Colonel Cox's 2nd Battalion from the ridge on the east edge of Herbach. Following a very heavy artillery strike, two fearsome looking Mark VI Tiger tanks emerged down a draw and fired on Company E's forward outpost. Charged-up German infantry attacked and captured every man in this position, except for one sergeant who hid in some underbrush. The Mark VIs then turned their turrets and fired at the pillbox that was the joint command post of Lieutenant Parker's 1st and 3rd Platoons. Like their opposite numbers when they were attacked, the Americans who were in the outlying trenches raced inside the pillbox. The Germans used the same tactics that the Americans had and poured in rapid and heavy small-arms fire while they rushed forward with smoke charges, quickly closing the apertures of the box to return fire. Taking advantage of the holes the Americans had put in the pillbox when they captured it the day before, the Germans threw hand grenades through these openings. Lieutenant Parker's entire 1st and 3rd Platoons, to a man, had no choice but to surrender.

The Mark VIs confidently resumed their hunt, this time moving into the woods that had been captured the previous day on the battalion's left flank. To the right, three more enemy tanks suddenly appeared. Again, methods the Americans had used on the Germans were turned against them. Two more pillboxes fell; all the friendly troops in these boxes surrendered. Parker's weapons platoon personnel were the only ones who put up a real fight. It was costly. Seven men were wounded and one soldier was killed before the Germans took their pillbox back.[28]

A similar fate befell Lieutenant Arn's Company F. At about 0530 that morning a two-man patrol from Staff Sergeant Todd's squad reported that they had heard tank movement to the southeast of the woods. Then at dawn, fire from these tanks—Mark Vs—was directed at the pillbox occupied by the 1st Platoon. Lt. Henry F. Bayard, commanding the 3rd Platoon, witnessed what followed and remembered, "The next thing I saw were Jerries approaching the pillbox, followed by [Lieutenant Mason-heimer's] 1st Platoon running into the woods with their hands up. They did have men in the trenches adjoining the pillbox. The hostile infantry-men rushed the position so rapidly after the tank fire lifted that the pla-toon was caught off balance and surrendered."[29]

Lieutenant Colonel Cox had been frantically calling for tank support since the counterattacks began, but none was available because the armored vehicles were being resupplied with ammunition. The German tank strike raged on. Fortunately, one very quick-thinking runner in the 2nd Platoon, Private Sewell, left his pillbox before the Germans attacked and raced several hundred yards back to the box that Lieutenant Arn and Lieutenant Bayard were in. Subsequently, the lieutenants called in artillery and mortar fire; it was Arn who was later credited with doing a "great job" in directing this fire. From a trench outside the box, his 300 radio operated satisfactorily; he had range. He stayed here, calling adjust-ments, despite hostile return artillery fire by the Germans, and began to turn the situation around.

Another alert private added more momentum to the fight when he noticed a smoke screen at the northeast edge of the woods. Fortunately, by this time the American tanks had reappeared with their ammunition loads; communication between the tankers and the infantry suffered from the confusion at that moment, but not for long. Lieutenant Arn again displayed exceptional leadership. This time he exposed himself to enemy fire, left his trench, got right on top of the pillbox from which he was commanding, and directed the tankers with hand motions; radio contact had failed. One M-4, commanded by Lt. Walter D. Macht, fol-lowed Arn's signal to place fire on the northeast edge of the woods by taking the initiative to move forward. Fifteen rounds were laid in; one Mark V turned and ran.

But German infantry reaction was quick; this time they placed a machine gun on top of a recaptured pillbox and aimed it at Lieutenant Arn's box. There was just one 60mm mortar left in his weapons platoon and Sgt. Karl L. Jilig, following Arn's hasty order to start setting it up, discovered that the tube had been hit by a shell fragment and was defective. Again, quick thinking proved fortuitous. The 117th Infantry was 200 yards away on the left at the time, so a mortar man—Pfc. Conley—made a hasty round trip and returned with a borrowed mortar and some ammunition. Sergeant Jilig went right to work with it, placing a round directly on top of the pillbox housing the enemy machine gun and then laying smoke and fire on the side where the aperture was located, rendering the box useless as Germans fell to their deaths.

Others fought on. Some of these infantrymen had worked their way around to the south of Lieutenant Arn's command pillbox by this time. Arn had just twenty-five men with him and when he saw the counterattack coming he ordered everyone to grab their weapons and take up positions in the adjoining trenches. Incredibly, the men were slow to open fire when the enemy skirmish line approached. Arn's personal reaction had been to empty three rounds of his carbine toward the Germans, but then the weapon jammed. The Company F commander yelled for someone to give him an M-1, but as Lieutenant Bayard noted later, "No one volunteered because [his] words galvanized the men into action and every weapon opened up on the advancing enemy. One of the most effective defenders was Private Floyd J. Mikula, who placed his machine-gun in a Jerry-dug position and kept firing as long as there was a German standing."[30]

This single spirited defense was not the only reason the counterattack was stopped. It was sunny on 6 October, permitting air support for the first time in days. Eight P-38s responded to calls initiated by Lieutenant Colonel Cox and laid their bombs on a coal pile just south of the woods where more enemy forces were assembling to strengthen the counterattack. The work of Lieutenant Macht's tank platoon was also critical; they eventually knocked out three Mark Vs, their charred hulls later found smoking at the edge of the woods. Company H's 81mm mortars delivered approximately 1,200 rounds, which were accurate and effective. Friendly artillery fire also made a difference. "Lieutenant Arn was in the best position to adjust both the mortar and artillery fire, which he did," remembered Sgt. Raymond O. Beaudoin, Company F's communications sergeant.[31]

"Lieutenant Colonel Cox was a mountain of strength throughout the counterattack," others agreed. "His calm voice on the radio under the most critical of circumstances was of inestimable value to all subordinate commanders."[32]

Lieutenant Parker did not have good communication that morning; his 300 radio was out of commission. Still, his Company E benefited from the support of Captain Hopcraft's Company K, which had come down from the Rimburg Castle in the afternoon to retake the four pill-boxes lost that morning. The Germans ran when the company attacked. Parker was able to prevent other pillboxes from being captured because he, like Lieutenant Arn, had ordered his remaining soldiers to man the outside of the boxes. "This meant that when the hostile infantry advanced, they were mowed down by rifle fire from the trenches," Parker stated later. "Artillery also knocked out two Tiger tanks and forced three others to withdraw. With their tank support gone, the enemy infantry-men soon pulled back."[33] Major Laney, the executive officer of the 2nd Battalion, maintained that the credit for repulsing the counterattack also belonged to the accuracy of the air strikes.

It had nevertheless been a very costly day for Lieutenant Colonel Cox. After their hostile ground forces withdrew, the Germans plastered the crest of the hill fronting Herbach with artillery. Many Americans in the pillbox trenches became casualties from this fire, as well as from 75mm direct enemy fire delivered from positions in the town. Company E had started the day with 165 soldiers; it ended with just 35 fighting men left. Lieutenant Parker was barely able to form one platoon, which he put under the command of Sergeant Holycross. When the counterat-tacks were over, Lieutenant Arn's Company F was down to twenty-three enlisted men and just two officers. Lieutenant Masonheimer's 1st Pla-toon had been almost at full strength before they were all captured; Lieu-tenant Bug's 2nd Platoon started with thirty-two men, the 3rd Platoon with thirty-eight, and the weapons platoon with twenty-eight. Company G had assisted in repulsing the counterattacks; many of these men accompanied the tanks when they attacked. With all of the pillboxes lost during the day recaptured by 1910 hours, Cox ordered what remained of his battalion to dig in for the night. Herbach was flanked on two sides by this time. Major Greer's 3rd Battalion of the 120th Infantry Regiment had endured a counterattack by approximately 100 Germans at 0745 that morning, but by 1600 his companies had worked their way on line to the right of the 2nd Battalion.

For Lieutenant Colonel Brown's 3rd Battalion of the 119th Infantry Regiment, the day involved adjustments, some movement, and ducking artillery fire. Captain Palmer's reconstituted Company I took over Company K's duties to watch over the Rimburg bridge and help guard the regimental command post in the castle. Stanford's Company L had maintained contact through the day with Herlong's 1st Battalion, and as they progressed out of the Rimburg woods the company was able to move ahead ever so slowly. Two pillboxes in the woods south of the castle were captured and fifteen prisoners were taken. The company suffered several casualties during the attack, including Lieutenant Hager, who was wounded in the shoulder. It was enemy artillery that many remembered as particularly frightening, however. "It was suicide to walk around," recalled another officer. "Any moving that was necessary was done on the run from one covered spot to the next covered spot."[34]

During the time Lieutenant Colonel Cox's 2nd Battalion was experiencing their troubles with the pillboxes near Herbach, Colonel Stokes's left column of CCA struck to the northeast, with their first mission securing a crossroads in Blanstein. The leading company in his assault wave took heavy concentrations of antitank fire on their south flank as they approached the town, so they called for friendly artillery fire. While these enemy guns were being neutralized, Stokes dispatched a separate task force toward the northeast consisting of Company D of the 66th Armored Regiment, Company K of the 29th Division's 116th Infantry Regiment, and a platoon of tanks from the 702nd Tank Battalion. Their mission was to finally secure Beggendorf, and they accomplished this before noon.

Linking up with General Huebner's 1st Infantry Division was now uppermost in the minds of the American commanders. During the morning, General Hodges made it clear to General Corlett that his plan to use CCA to expand the bridgehead eastward and secure crossings over the Roer River had to be put on hold. Instead, Hodges wanted the operations of General Harmon's 2nd Armored Division mainly confined to holding the *Westwall* bridgehead and assisting with the linkup. In the early afternoon Corlett followed Hodges's decision with his own order to have CCB hold in place along the northeastern and eastern fringes of the bridgehead, while also ordering CCA to attack to the southeast in support of the 117th Infantry Regiment.

This changed Colonel Stokes's plans for the afternoon of 6 October.[35] After the 14th Armored Field Artillery Battalion reduced the enemy antitank fire in Blanstein, he turned his right column toward Oidtweiler. This village was located just to the south of Boesweiler and to the northeast of Alsdorf. Led by the armored vehicles of Company I and accompanied by the infantry support of the 116th Infantry's Company L, this task force met German resistance throughout their attack, including more antitank guns and artillery fire. Confronting an antitank ditch outside of Oidtweiler as the afternoon wore on, Company L first flushed some twenty Germans from their cover before a tank bulldozer filled the sunken area with dirt so the armored vehicles could cross. Staff Sgt. Richard Hickman was particularly helpful during this action; he dismounted the bulldozer several times while under direct enemy fire so he could guide the driver to the spots where the dirt was most needed.

Late in the day, Company I secured the high ground outside the village. They destroyed two antitank guns and killed thirty German infantrymen, and also took thirty prisoners. Stokes ordered his columns to establish 360-degree security with the Aachen-Settrich highway as their front line that night. Undoubtedly, the presence of CCA brought more discomfort to the German command. Losing Oidtweiler would not only sever the main highway running northeast out of Aachen, but also position CCA for an eventual drive toward the Roer River town of Linnich.

CCA's right column had advanced quite close to the left flank of Colonel Johnson's 117th Infantry Regiment as his forces continued their drive toward zu Ubach on 6 October. It started out slowly for Lieutenant Colonel Frankland's 1st Battalion, however. Jumping off from Ubach at 0800 and then moving across an open field that sloped upward, Captain Kent's Company A first attacked toward the four pillboxes lost at that

Aachen citizens leaving the city before the evacuation was halted.

U.S. soldiers examine pillboxes built into hillsides.

Twenty-Sixth Infantry troops readying for the attack on Nutheim.

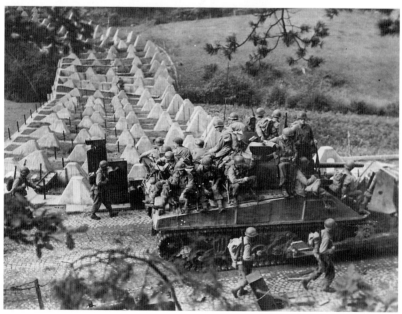

More American forces cross through the dragon's teeth.

Tank recovery vehicle fording a stream.
NATIONAL ARCHIVES

U.S. reconnaissance
troops examine a
captured German
Panzerfaust.
NATIONAL ARCHIVES

A bunker with double steel doors built in a hill of solid rock found in Stolberg. NATIONAL ARCHIVES

This pillbox dome shows damage from artillery hits. NATIONAL ARCHIVES

Americans practice using a flamethrower. NATIONAL ARCHIVES

Mortars set up and fire.

An American armored vehicle enters Palenberg.

M-10s in the streets. NATIONAL ARCHIVES

POWs in Ubach.
WARREN WATSON, A 30TH ID
HISTORY WEBMASTER; ORIGINAL
FROM THE NATIONAL ARCHIVES

"Flames licking"
from a flamethrower.
NATIONAL ARCHIVES

Master bedroom in Rimburg Castle.
NATIONAL ARCHIVES

Chandelier used to hang
GI laundry in captured
Rimburg Castle.
NATIONAL ARCHIVES

American armored vehicles on the defense. NATIONAL ARCHIVES

Aerial view of bombed-out Aachen. NATIONAL ARCHIVES

Engineers
prepare V-13.

Some of the
damage caused to
railway station at
Aachen during
Allied attack.

Germans surrendering. NATIONAL ARCHIVES

Twenty-Sixth Infantry heavy machine-gun crew. McCORMICK RESEARCH CENTER

An American soldier
observes the effects
of grenade fire.
NATIONAL ARCHIVES

Damage inside St. Joseph's
Church. NATIONAL ARCHIVES

A tank bulldozes an opening through Rothe Erde railroad station.
McCORMICK RESEARCH CENTER

A tank comes through Rothe Erde railroad station to support infantry forces.
McCORMICK RESEARCH CENTER

155mm SP gun.

U.S. forces battle down an Aachen street.

A pillbox hidden inside of what looks like a German house near Ottenfeld. NATIONAL ARCHIVES

U.S. infantry moves through streets of North Bardenberg. NATIONAL ARCHIVES

After heavy fighting, a Würselen street is empty as the
119th Infantry closes the gap. NATIONAL ARCHIVES

American tank fires down an Aachen street.

Aachen state theater.

American soldiers fire
down Monheims Allee.
McCORMICK RESEARCH CENTER

Gaunt skeletons of Aachen ruins. McCORMICK RESEARCH CENTER

German graves in Aachen. NATIONAL ARCHIVES

Oberst Gerhard Wilck and staff during surrender.
McCORMICK RESEARCH CENTER

Surrender of Germans at Aachen. Nazi half-track armored vehicles filled
with soldiers ready to quit, and bearing white surrender flags,
are taken into custody. McCORMICK RESEARCH CENTER

time by Cox's 2nd Battalion of the 119th Infantry. Captain Spiker's Company B moved on the left, but both companies' advances were slowed up just 1,000 yards from their line of departure by heavy concentrations of artillery fire. The attack quickly bogged down and then stopped.

Lieutenant Colonel McDowell's 3rd Battalion was supposed to attack to the left of Frankland's companies, but the German barracks east of Ubach were still giving him problems. Support from the 2nd Armored Division's tanks finally helped reduce this threat when McDowell's Company L launched a coordinated attack early that morning. One participant remembered the joint effort as "fighting up a storm and firing into the barracks,"[36] but the plan developed by McDowell with the armored commander had not gone off exactly as he wanted it to. "The original plan was to have the 2nd Armored Division come down east of the barracks while [we] enveloped from the west," McDowell stated later. "As it actually worked out, they cleaned out the north side and then cut north without making a complete encirclement."[37]

While the men of Company L were mopping up the barracks area, the fighter-bombers of IX Tactical Air Command were dropping their loads to the south. Close-support missions were flown during the morning; an early one missed zu Ubach, but after later missions in the afternoon hit the village both Company L and Lieutenant Thompson's Company I were able to finally push off again at 1630. Lt. Floyd M. Jenkins's Company B of the 743rd Tank Battalion went along with these men; the infantry double-timed across the open ground to avoid enemy artillery and mortar fire. Fewer dug-in tanks and antitank guns opposed the advance due to the air strikes and friendly artillery fire, so four of Jenkins's M-4s worked cross country while a fifth went right down the road into zu Ubach. Between the tanks and the rapid move of McDowell's men, the Germans were caught by surprise and their flanks were surrounded when the companies arrived at the hamlet.

By this time Frankland's 1st Battalion had also arrived in the area. Captain Spiker's Company B came in from the northwest, captured the east side of zu Ubach, and set up defenses. Kent's Company A had come through a patch of woods just to the west of the village; his men dug in on its southern edge. The big catch went to Company L. These men took about fifty prisoners, captured the opposing German battalion's command post, destroyed their working telephone system, and in the process seized their maps. The maps indicated that the Germans had expected the attack to come in from the northeast. With the American attack coming mainly from the north and northwest, they had arranged their defenses in zu Ubach along a road facing in the wrong direction.

When the defeated commander of the 7CO of the 149th Infantry Regiment was questioned about this after he reached the POW cage, his interrogators noted:

> Both of his flanks were pushed in by our tanks, causing him to lose contact with the adjacent unit. Asked why he did not withdraw in the tactically logical easterly direction, he replied that pressure was strongest from the north and west, thus forcing them to the south. PW claimed that their defensive strategy was "sabotaged" by our surprise attack from the north.[38]

CCB had its defensive arc running from north of Frelenberg eastward along the spur railroad below Geilenkirchen, then southeastward through Waurichen and almost to Beggendorf when 6 October dawned. The mission for Major Finnell's 1st Battalion of the 41st Armored Infantry Regiment that day was to cross the railroad and take the high ground just to the north that commanded Geilenkirchen. Two teams jumped off at 0830 and immediately ran into trouble. There were thirty to forty foxholes containing one to three enemy soldiers each just south of the railroad line, and every other hole contained either emplaced automatic weapons or "tank-busters." One squad under Lieutenant Levitsky took a pillbox in the early going and attempted to advance, but the fire from the German foxholes became so intense that his men were driven back. Tanks and infantry under Lieutenant Smith were also stopped.

Taking advantage of a lull in the antitank fire about midmorning, Smith moved his team to the northeast and reached the hamlet of Jacobshauschen where his Company A infantrymen climbed up to the second story of a building and started delivering rifle fire on the enemy holes. At the same time, Smith's armored component, the 3rd Platoon of Company F from the 67th Armored Regiment, deployed and fired their machine guns at the Germans. His forward observer from the 92nd Field Artillery Battalion also called in artillery fire. Even a tank dozer joined in the assault, covering the holes with the Germans still in them until the dozer's commander was wounded. The ground south of the railroad was cleared by 1300, but Smith was also wounded in the process. Major Finnell held the men here to await the advance of Lieutenant Colonel Wynne's 2nd Battalion of the 67th Armored Regiment to his right, while his own armored infantry's 2nd Battalion came up on the left. Thirty prisoners had been taken thus far, with between fifty to sixty Germans killed.

When Wynne's armor and the 2nd Battalion failed to arrive in force because of hostile artillery, an anxious Finnell decided to renew that attack at 1700. It was a mistake. Even though taking the high ground overlooking Geilenkirchen may have led to its early capture, the tanks were unable to cross the railroad because of its high cuts and fills. Enemy antitank fire coming in from a wooded area north of Briel and from another cut in the railroad line also made bypassing the area impractical. The Germans by this time had also accurately ranged on the railroad with their mortars and artillery; it was impossible for any of the armored infantrymen to get across the tracks so they pulled back to the ground taken earlier in the afternoon and dug in. Three American officers and fifteen enlisted men were casualties that day.

Colonel Hinds had been in personal contact with his battalion commanders throughout the day. In accordance with General Corlett's order to confine operations mainly to holding the *Westwall* bridgehead, as 6 October wound down his 41st Armored Infantry Regiment concentrated on defending the general line held by Finnell's 1st Battalion southward to Ubach and westward all the way to the banks of the Wurm River. For the next two days, the regiment continued to improve these positions, fend off minor counterattacks, lose some ground, and then take it back. Troops were shifted, but most were digging in, placing trip wires, booby traps, and mines in front of their positions. The Americans had taken sixty-four pillboxes; the engineers either destroyed them or troops used them as shelter. Total prisoners captured since crossing the Wurm on 4 October totaled 556 by 9 October.

The entire 67th Armored Regiment encountered heavy resistance on 6 October. "In several instances the enemy remained in pillboxes after they had been taken," a report noted. "From these vantage points they had directed artillery fire on our troops."[39] Lieutenant Colonel Wynne's 2nd Battalion did manage to attack to the northeast and his armor, reinforced by Company E of the 41st Armored Infantry and one section of the 702nd Tank Destroyer Battalion, first provided some fire support to Finnell's infantry as they attempted to cross the railroad line and then make contact with the unit on their right. The 1st Battalion moved its line 1,500 yards. Any attempts to advance by the 3rd Battalion were strongly opposed by heavy enemy artillery and antitank guns. "The enemy had good observation on our movements and positions," one participant remembered. "Their OP's were located on high points such as smoke stacks, towers and slag piles."[40] Over the next two days, the Germans withdrew toward Immendorf, one American platoon reached Beggendorf to assist with its defense, and the 1st Battalion established outposts in Waurichen. The Americans mined the roads fronting Immendorf and laid some concertina wire in the vicinity. Listening posts were established and "active defense" was noted in every day's operations reports.[41]

When Beggendorf and Waurichen fell on 6 October, *Generalleutnant* Macholz of the 49th Division noted that it "tore a gap that was extremely dangerous"[42] between the inner wings of his 148th Infantry Regiment and the adjacent unit of *Generalleutnant* Lange's 183rd Division; this was the 404th Infantry Regiment of the 246th Division that had come up from Aachen the night before. Lange received Machine Gun Battalion 54 on 6 October to fill this gap. In an attempt to strengthen the line opposite Colonel Stokes's right column of CCA in the vicinity of Oidtweiler, the 2nd Battalion of Grenadier Regiment 48 was arrayed to the left of Machine Gun Battalion 54; the grenadiers took up positions spread along the Settrich-Kloshaus-Alsdorf line. They were destined to tangle with the 117th Infantry Regiment as Colonel Johnson moved his forces farther southward from zu Ubach the next day. From here westward right up to the *Westwall* east of Kerkrade were elements of the 2nd Battalion of Grenadier Regiment 149, both the 1st and 2nd Battalions of Grenadier Regiment 148, and the 1st Battalion of Grenadier Regiment 689.[43]

The 1st Battalion of Grenadier Regiment 149 had been pushed back from the *Westwall* when Colonel Birks's 120th Infantry Regiment 1st and 2nd Battalions seized Krekrade. Assembled as a reserve force in the area of Bierstrauss—just southwest of Alsdorf—on 5 October, the 1st Battalion of Grenadier Regiment 149 was destined on 7 October to find itself wedged between the southward drives of Major Greer's 3rd Battalion of the 120th Infantry Regiment and Lieutenant Colonel Herlong's 1st Battalion of the 119th Infantry Regiment. The XIX Corps advance this day would also threaten the flank of the 246th Division responsible for Aachen. LXXXI Corps' reports would later reflect that on 7 October "the enemy's intention could still not be clearly identified."[44] The Americans, however, would remember it as a day of exploitation against a beaten and disorganized enemy.

The weather was again clear, but even warmer. Colonel Sutherland's 119th Infantry Regiment's mission was to pivot toward Herzogenrath; Herlong's 1st Battalion was to first finish clearing out Merkstein-Hofstadt. Major Greer's 3rd Battalion of the 120th Infantry Regiment, again under Colonel Sutherland's control for the day's operations, was to mop up in Herbach and then move through Merkstein to their objective, the road that ran into Aachen just north of Noppenberg. Lieutenant Colonel Cox's 2nd Battalion, with Captain Hopcraft's Company K attached to augment its strength, was to first secure Adolphschacht. This small hamlet was just northeast of the coal-mining town of Merkstein, between Floes and zu Merkstein; Cox's continuing mission was to occupy the high ground to the east of Merkstein and prevent any enemy infiltration into the village from this direction. Brown's 3rd Battalion had the mission of holding the pivot for the day's operations and cleaning out the pillbox line on the right in the 119th Infantry Regiment's avenue of advance.

Lieutenant Colonel Herlong's 1st Battalion started out slowly at 0752, reached the road intersection northeast of Merkstein Wildnis at 1155, and then stood before the northern edge of Merkstein at 1230. Major Greer's forces, on Herlong's right, cleared out Herbach and by 0910 were 600 yards south of the town. At 1033 Greer moved on to Merkstein Plitschard; this was the first time his men did any fighting in a German town. They set fire to any house occupied by enemy resisters; six burned to the ground. But by 1100, heavy enemy fire from a slag pile to the south held up his Company L. A little over an hour later, the company was able to bypass this area and arrive at zu Merkstein; the Germans on the slag pile surrendered to Lieutenant Colonel Cox's Company G without a fight and eighty prisoners were taken. By this time Greer's 3rd Battalion of the 120th Infantry Regiment was close to Merkstein and at 1312 his lead company reached its northern edge. The 1st Battalion entered Merkstein without heavy fighting, but in doing so Lieutenant Colonel Herlong remembered, "We flushed a lot of PW's into the zone of the 3rd Battalion, 120th."[45]

Cox's 2nd Battalion was first held up by fire from enemy positions in Adolphschacht, but by 0900 Captain Hopcraft's Company K was able to move on the battalion's right flank, capture seventy prisoners, and stop this hostile fire. This enabled the rest of Cox's forces to take the town. Despite having trouble disposing of 200 to 300 civilians, the 2nd Battalion was able to reach the high ground east of Merkstein by 1200 hours. At this time, Hopcraft's Company K detached from Cox's control, moved to the west of Merkstein, and rejoined the 3rd Battalion.

Colonel Sutherland had requested an air strike between Merkstein and Herzogenrath before Greer's and Cox's forces moved farther south, but this did not hold up Lieutenant Colonel Brown. "After Merkstein-Hofstadt was captured, fire from the left flank of the 3rd Battalion was eliminated," he later noted. "With the help of a platoon of tanks and two TD's, a successful attack was launched on 7 October against the pillboxes to the southeast that had been holding [us] up since the beginning of the operation. Tank fire drove the enemy infantry into the pillboxes and when our infantry came up they filed out and surrendered."[46]

One of Brown's officers added his own perspective to the day's operations. "The morning of the 7th the situation began to look better. The 1st Battalion was moving and we were first to establish contact with them," remembered Company L's Lieutenant Knox. "The 1st Platoon sent a patrol out, contact was made and Captain Stanford then took the company to the 1st Battalion."[47] However, Herlong's forces had moved out in a "big hurry," leaving one Company L platoon behind. "A squad leader was left, pinned down with his squad," Knox continued. "He brought his troubles to me; he had been able to withdraw his men and he pointed out the exact position of the Germans. I told Colonel Brown the situation."

By this time Company K was back under the 3rd Battalion's control. Brown explained to Knox that Captain Palmer's reconstituted Company I would attack to their left. The Company L squad previously left behind quickly took twelve prisoners, and then Captain Stanford moved the rest of the company up. "Things really began to break loose after that," Knox recalled.[48]

Before nightfall the company had helped clear about 20 pill-boxes. The officers and SS men had all left. Those that were there were not interested in fighting. They told us how they had been locked in the pillboxes by the SS troopers. It was a great haul, the most this company ever gathered up in one day. Every-one got a pistol, a new map case, a watch, a new knife or what-ever he wanted. We set up that night in a pillbox that had once been an aid station. Prisoners continued to come in all night.

Following the midafternoon air strike between Merkstein and Her-zogenrath, Major Greer's 3rd Battalion of the 120th Infantry Regiment moved steadily forward across open ground until it reached the road leading into Aachen opposite Noppenberg; this town was just east of Bierstraf, which was on the northeast outskirts of Herzogenrath. Greer's companies occupied a line approximately 1,500 yards wide, anchored to the east just above Zopp. During the day, his forces had captured 406 prisoners, including a battalion commander and his staff in Merkstein.[49] Brown's 3rd Battalion secured the right flank when Merkstein-Worm was occupied at 1600. His left flank was next to the railroad line leading into Herzogenrath; booby-trapped mines connected by primer cords filled the streets here. Herlong's 1st Battalion companies were between Brown's and Greer's forces on a line centered south of Ritzerfeld; the road from here led into Herzogenrath before intersecting with one of the two main roadways into Aachen. Lieutenant Colonel Herlong's right flank was on the other side of the railroad track opposite Lieutenant Colonel Brown's 3rd Battalion. Colonel Sutherland's front line had been extended from the former 120th Infantry Regiment's position near Kerkrade—where the feint attack ordered by General Hobbs had been directed back on 2 October—southeastward to within 500 yards of the western outskirts of Alsdorf. The Germans' effort to check the 119th Infantry Regiment's penetration had definitely collapsed.

In Colonel Johnson's 117th Infantry Regiment zone of operations on 7 October, two battalions attacked abreast from zu Ubach for Alsdorf. "The 3rd Battalion really opened up with a power drive," noted one account.[50] A 1st Battalion history mentioned the attack that day "provided a welcome relief from the slow slugging previously encountered in the Siegfried operation."[51] A little over 5,000 yards from zu Ubach to the southeast, Alsdorf fell before noon.

The 3rd Platoon of Company A, 743rd Tank Battalion, led this attack ahead of Lieutenant Colonel McDowell's 3rd Battalion companies. Rolling out at 0700, Company I's CO, Lieutenant Thompson, pointed out, "The tanks were a tremendous morale factor when they started to work cross-country and spray the German foxholes with machine gun fire."[52] Advancing right behind these armored vehicles, Thompson's men and the soldiers of Company L were able to stay close; Lieutenant Tempe's 1st Platoon spearheaded the drive for Company I with Lt. Gale Dougherty's 2nd Platoon of Company L to his left. These officers had a bet on who would reach Alsdorf first. It was later judged to be a tie; so fast was their advance across the open farmlands that German soldiers were caught sleeping in houses here during the race toward the town.

"The Germans were dug in the beet fields northwest of Alsdorf," one of Lieutenant Tempe's men remembered. "They kept their heads down when the tanks were firing, and then surrendered in large numbers when our infantrymen came up behind the tanks."[53] Many were nabbed before they could offer any resistance. Lieutenant Colonel Duncan, commander of the 743rd Tank Battalion, later noted that overall resistance was generally "light" for Company A, and two enemy armored cars were knocked out nearer to Alsdorf. The tanks were on their objective at 1030.

The American infantrymen encountered some hostile artillery fire around the railroad track that cut across the main road just outside of Alsdorf, and then scattered small-arms fire greeted them when they got to the edge of town just before noon. Lieutenant Tempe later recalled that they also met a little bazooka and antitank fire, but not long afterward Company I's Sgt. Leroy Gurley found twelve German artillery observers in a cellar and captured them along with fifteen radio sets. Others were taken prisoner while they were still digging defenses. A battalion commander's jeep, complete with maps and a working radio, was also seized. Major Ammons's 2nd Battalion had moved down from their positions in Ubach to join the attack that day. His men followed the 3rd Battalion, mopping up and protecting the regiment's exposed left flank as the assault companies kept striking toward Alsdorf.

Company A's 1st and 2nd Platoons of tanks spearheaded the attack in Lieutenant Colonel Frankland's 1st Battalion area. Captain Spiker's Company B moved to the right of the main road to Alsdorf while Captain Kent's Company A advanced across the open fields just to the west. Lieutenant Foote, still commanding Kent's 3rd Platoon, remembered the tank/infantry actions that day as "the best co-ordination my platoon has ever seen."[54]

The tanks moved about 200 to 300 yards ahead of the infantry to the right of the road. Company A first made contact with German forces manning defensive positions in a large farmhouse known as Neu Merberen; they were taken prisoner before the men moved rapidly to the village just west of Alsdorf-Wilhelmschact. The company had taken one hundred prisoners thus far; most had simply come out of their foxholes and surrendered when the tanks got close. Wilhelmschact fell quickly and the Americans then moved into Alsdorf through its western fringes. "Alsdorf was a ghost town when we came in," remembered Captain Kent. "It was so damn quiet it scared you."

> There were evidences that the place was full of civilians, but not one was to be seen. All activity seemed to have stopped abruptly only a few minutes before. Not a sound was to be heard, nor a movement seen. Actually, residents of Alsdorf were surprised at the arrival of the GI's, did not know what to do, and fled into the depths of their houses in terror. Advance units arrived at about 1000, well ahead of schedule and sweated out an air strike due at 1030. Orange signal panels were quickly spread over the top of the attached tanks and oncoming planes spotted them in time to keep from bombing the captured town.

This air strike had actually proved very beneficial. Fifteen P-47s came in and bombed and strafed a retreating German column around a slag pile on the western edge of Alsdorf. After this, both Kent's Company A and Captain Spiker's Company B moved to the southeast edge of town. Captain Stoeffer's Company C had also arrived by this time; it was noted his company was "entrenched on the extreme right flank of the town, facing Aachen."

By nightfall, Colonel Johnson's 117th Infantry Regiment was well established in the village. Major Ammons's 2nd Battalion had taken up defensive positions in Wilhelmschact, and Lieutenant Colonel McDowell's 3rd Battalion was straddled across the road that led into Würselen, then Aachen, through Birk; his right flank was at the intersection of the road that came into Alsdorf from Schaufenberg. "But, the situation did not look good," noted one account. "The left flank was wide open to counterattack from the east, and the regiment attacking on the right [Greer's 3rd Battalion, 120th Infantry Regiment] had lagged far behind. The 117th Infantry's positions stuck out like a 'bump on a log.'"[55]

Colonel Johnson's forces nevertheless held positions across one of the two main supply routes into Aachen. This had not gone unnoticed by the German command. Reports covering 7 October revealed the following:

> A further push in the direction of Mariagrube was prevented. In the evening, however, a gap of two kilometers had opened up at the southeastern outskirts of Alsdorf which had to be closed. As a consequence, an attack was planned with the newly brought in Mobile Regiment von Fritschen, attached II Battalion, Grenadier Regiment 689 (246th Division), Engineer Battalion 246, and Panzer Brigade 108 with attached elements of heavy Panzer Battalion 506 (four Tigers) for 8 October. At 2200 the briefing for this operation was held by the commanding general [*General der Infanterie* Köchling] at the command post of the 49th Infantry Division.[56]

Two Shermans, one Stuart, and an attached M10 tank destroyer were lost to antitank mines when CCA's left column attempted to enter Boesweiler on the morning of 7 October. Led by Col. Ira P. Swift, who had just taken command of CCA from Colonel Stokes, this column first waited for Company A of the 17th Engineer Battalion to sweep the minefield, and then forces under Lt. Col. Lindsay Herkness's 2nd Battalion of the 66th Armored Regiment took the town, demolishing four pillboxes in the process. Over a hundred prisoners were rounded up before a small task force under Herkness comprised of Company E tanks and Company L of the 116th Infantry Regiment was assigned the mission of attacking southeastward toward Oidtweiler to assist Lieutenant Colonel

Parker's 1st Battalion in taking this town. This attack started off inauspiciously in early afternoon when the task force ran into direct antitank fire and lost their lead tank.

Lieutenant Colonel Parker's 1st Battalion had launched their drive into Oidtweiler from the south by this time; his two assault companies were also met by well-placed heavy enemy artillery fire as they rolled toward the western edge of the village. Aided with friendly fire delivered by the armored vehicles of Herkness's task force, Parker's tanks were eventually able to knock out two German SP guns and occupy sections of Oidtweiler east of the roadway leading into Aachen. Two of his tanks were lost and numerous prisoners were taken before all CCA offensive operations were terminated at 1800.[57]

They established defensive positions before nightfall and into the evening. A semicircle of armored vehicles and infantry ringed the eastern edges of Boesweiler with the easternmost positions across the highway leading into Aachen; the right side of this line extended to the roadway running down to Oidtweiler. Lieutenant Colonel Parker's line covered the ground to the west of the roadway, then southward across the road before opening up approximately 500 yards on his right flank into more open ground directly west of Neuweiler. A north-south gap of equal distance still existed across the boundary between CCA and the 117th Infantry Regiment's left flank on the northeast outskirts of Alsdorf.

The *Westwall* bridgehead was now almost 6 miles long and more than 4.5 miles deep. Reaching the 30th Infantry Division's final objective, the east-west road through Würselen that was also the boundary of General Huebner's 1st Infantry Division and their objective in the linkup, now appeared to General Hobbs to be a relatively easy task. Just 4,000 yards separated the two divisions. The operations of 7 October had reinforced his exuberance, so much so that Hobbs had confidently told General Corlett by telephone during the night that the battle for the *Westwall* was over. "We have a hole in this thing big enough to drive two divisions through," Hobbs proclaimed. "I entertain no doubts that this line is cracked wide open."[58] His confidence even carried into the next day; early that morning he told Corlett, "The job is finished as far as this division is concerned." By noon on 8 October, General Hobbs most assuredly came to the conclusion that his confidence was misplaced and premature.

A low-hanging thick mist covered the battlefield that morning. Regiment von Fritzschen had come 100 miles from Luxemberg, traveling
through the night to reach Mariadorf after being delayed the previous
day by U.S. air attacks and fuel refilling problems. Their mission was to
recapture Alsdorf at all costs and block the road into Aachen. The German command planned to have Regiment von Fritzschen's two organic
battalions with its eleven attached tanks, twenty-two assault guns, and
engineer and infantry battalions attack at dawn; however these forces did
not arrive until after dawn, thereby losing the opportunity to advance on
Alsdorf under the morning's weather cover.

Instead, the Americans attacked first at 0700; Colonel Johnson's
117th Infantry Regiment's objective for the day was Mariadorf and inter-
dicting the Aachen-Juelich highway, the second artery for enemy supplies
to reach the 246th Division in Aachen. The 1st and 3rd Battalions were
selected for this assignment; Lieutenant Colonel McDowell chose to use
Lieutenant Thompson's Company I and Company L. Captain Kent's
Company A joined with Spiker's Company B in Lieutenant Colonel
Frankland's zone of operations, which ran from the southeast edge of Alsdorf, then across an open field to a sunken railroad track several hundred
yards in front of Mariadorf, and finally to the 1st Battalion's objective—
the western half of the village.

At jump-off, McDowell's companies attacked to the left, their mission to take the small shop- and farmhouse-lined eastern side of Mariadorf; their right flank boundary was the railroad line running into the
village from the small hamlet of Kol Kellersberg. The early going was
slow. The rifle companies first experienced some problems cleaning out
the southern part of Alsdorf, and then they ran head on into more stubborn resistance as they started across the open field and made their way
toward the railroad tracks.

Thompson's Company I, leading the charge, first trailed and then
got out ahead of its supporting armored vehicles when enemy antitank
fire flared up. Then, heavy incoming machine-gun fire from the front of
a slag pile beside a coal mine pinned them down. The tanks, attached to
the 3rd Platoon of the 743rd Tank Battalion, experienced trouble getting
at the Germans with their mounted machine guns; one tank crew instead
hurled grenades into their foxholes. Three of the platoon's tanks were

soon knocked out, but their crews dismounted and continued fighting on the ground as infantrymen. Tank A-16 was the only tank operational so the unwounded crewmen from the other tanks soon mounted this armored vehicle and joined in the fight. By this time, Thompson's men were also fighting at close grips and at bayonet point in front of A-16. To their left, Company L's mortars were captured; the Germans were setting them up to fire back on the Americans. A hastily ordered counterattack proved fortuitous. The mortars were retaken at great cost to their opposite numbers. Close by, a Company I sergeant had been captured, but as he was being searched at rifle-point, one of his squad members fired his M1 and caught the German guard squarely between the eyes.

Frankland's 1st Battalion was experiencing similar problems. Captain Kent's Company A had been given the assignment of first clearing out the quaint stucco settlement houses originally built for coal mine workers in Kol Kellersberg, immediately southwest of Alsdorf, while Spiker's Company B attacked across the open field. During the early going their movement was less challenged than that faced by McDowell's companies and the men were able to reach the sunken railroad track fronting Mariadorf by midmorning. Kent's Company A had been held up in Kol Kellerberg; Captain Spiker's platoons still raced forward. But after they crossed the railroad track, all hell broke loose when a forceful German counterattack struck from the direction of Mariadorf; three supporting tanks were knocked out and casualties ran high in Captain Spiker's 1st and 2nd Platoons. "Lieutenant Burton's platoon was sliced off and he and his platoon sergeant and 25 others were captured or killed," remembered Lieutenant Colonel Frankland. "The support platoon then built up with a section of heavy machineguns in the little village of Blumenrath and started to paste the enemy with small arms and some 60mm mortar fire."[59]

Another thrust of enemy tanks and their infantry also circled up through the southern edge of Schauffenberg as McDowell's 3rd Battalion forces were fighting along the railroad tracks. Retaking Alsdorf was this force's objective and it was destined to threaten the battalion's outpost. It was about 1020 when this attack started, and Lieutenant Thompson would later say, "If we had been held up initially in our advance, we would have caught this force before it slipped behind us."[60]

Once they got through, I contacted Colonel McDowell at his OP and asked him if Company I should pull back to cover Alsdorf. "Hell no," he replied. "You go ahead and secure Mariadorf; I can take care of the situation here."

McDowell later remembered the situation as "the toughest [his] battalion had encountered since the beaches."[61] His OP was in a three-story school building on the southeast edge of town where, while commanding from the upper floor, he could barely see the company of enemy infantry riding on four Mark IV tanks as they closed in through the mist.

The attack quickly swept into the edge of Alsdorf.[62] With Lieutenant Colonel McDowell were two other officers, commander of Company M—Lieutenant Baran—and Lt. Samuel Kessler, Liaison Officer. Both departed the third floor of the building for the lower level to disperse the meager supply of firepower personnel on hand to the windows. Baran then returned to the top floor as the German attack started encircling the building. The defenders were just four strong: McDowell, his radio operator, Pvt. Roy C. Wheeler, and Lieutenant Baran. Some enemy soldiers had already managed to get behind the building; one Mark IV was also to the rear of the OP, ranging up and down the main roadway. One of its rounds had even set the battalion antitank gun's prime mover on fire.

Manning the lower floors of the school building were men from the battalion wire team, including Sgt. Melvin E. Morris, Pfc. Levi H. van der Kolk, as well as Privates Marta C. Spires, Howard W. Willingham, and Gerhart H. Housell. Also in place were Pvt. Tad Tragasz, a battalion runner; Privates Elmer Chlan and Robert F. Cooper, both members of the battalion Pioneer Section; and Pfc. Webster E. Phillips, a battalion intelligence scout. Lieutenant Kessler oversaw all of these men.

The all-around defense produced remarkable results. While the one Mark IV continued cruising deliberately to the rear as the others rolled toward his OP, Lieutenant Colonel McDowell, with just his M1, personally killed four of the German grenadiers and wounded at least three others. Lieutenant Baran was responsible for five more and Private Wheeler accounted for two casualties. Combined with the fire delivered by the men on the first floor, as well as tanks from the 743rd Tank Battalion that knocked out three of the Mark IVs, the attack was stopped by noon. Lieutenant Colonel Duncan noted:

Sergeant Donald L. Mason in A-16 observed the enemy vehicles, armor and infantry and called for and adjusted artillery fire. Sergeant Mason also notified the tanks of the 1st and 2nd Platoons and the command vehicle in Alsdorf by radio. This tank notified the 117th Regiment of the counterattack. It was the tanks from the 1st and 2nd Platoons that took the German tanks under fire and destroyed the three.[63]

After what was later recorded as "a field-day of pot-shooting," McDowell conservatively estimated that twenty Germans had been killed or wounded near the OP. Machine-gun fire delivered from sections of the heavy weapons company with Thompson's Company I and other well-placed artillery rounds called in by the forward observer of the 118th Field Artillery mowed down more in the field outside of Alsdorf.

"The tankers knocked out the three vehicles to our front," McDowell explained later. "But a fourth and another from somewhere wandered up and down the streets of Alsdorf all day."[64] Interestingly, one of these Mark IVs was dubbed "The Reluctant Dragon" by Regimental Headquarters, which was just 150 yards behind the school building that day. This tank, after eluding TD fire and traps by bazooka teams from Major Ammons's 2nd Battalion all afternoon, escaped later that night. The other had been finally chased out of town when the leader of the anti-tank platoon slipped up behind it and fired a round of bazooka ammo into its back end, damaging but not stopping the panzer from running.

Other battles raged on in the open ground southeast of Alsdorf and just north of Kol Kellersberg all that afternoon. Lieutenant Colonel Frankland's 1st Battalion managed to stop another drive the Germans made at Alsdorf in the early afternoon; this was brought to a halt by Captain Kent's 3rd Platoon. After this, Captain Spiker's assault platoons tried again to move forward from the railroad track, but as they approached Mariadorf they were stopped by very heavy artillery and small-arms fire. Many casualties were sustained; those who could went back to the depression near the railroad track where they set up a defense with just one supporting tank. Kent's 3rd Platoon, after spending the rest of their afternoon tangling with Germans in the heavy woods on the battalion's right flank, joined Spiker's depleted numbers at the rail line later in the day.

Lieutenant Thompson's Company I had also struggled to get into Mariadorf that afternoon. Trouble began right at the railroad tracks where the Germans had stationed machine guns on an overpass; Lieutenant Tempe's 1st Platoon was practically wiped out by this fire. Just six men returned that night, but those remaining fought on.

> Believing, apparently, that the Americans were about whipped, a German officer rose to his full height and with a sweeping gesture in true Ft. Benning "Follow Me" tradition, waved his men onward in an open skirmish line. Company I held its fire for a few moments and then opened with every weapon, eliminating almost all of the "field manual" Germans.[65]

This attack having failed, the Germans tried to bring up tanks on Thompson's left flank. Luck was with the company this time. Lt. Dewey J. Sandell had been able a few minutes earlier to direct fire on a barn at the edge of Mariadorf, causing it to collapse. This distracted the enemy panzers. Although Thompson's men had been leveling ineffective bazooka and rifle grenade fire at these armored vehicles, he still remembered, "The tanks withdrew temporarily either in fear of the bazookas, or because the building suddenly caved in."[66]

Sandell vainly attempted to adjust more fire right after this, but as he recalled later, "There was so much confusion over the 536 that nobody quite knew what or where the artillery was going to land. The first concentration dropped behind our positions. I called the artillery observer to raise it 800 yards and it was still short, so I had to raise it 800 again, then adjusted it to start chasing around after some tanks but I switched left and right so fast that the observer got pretty disgusted with me. But the artillery made the tanks retreat."[67]

Later in the day, more German infantry wearing uniforms of captured Americans attempted to take the place of their tanks. Sneaking in on Company I's left flank again, Thompson took a few casualties before his alert men spotted the ruse; the enemy soldiers gave themselves away because they were carrying their standard yellow ammunition boxes. They were quickly mowed down by angry American rifle fire. Dusk fortunately set in shortly afterward, prompting Lieutenant Colonel McDowell to pull the battalion away from the much too close enemy heavy weapons to better defensive positions north of the railroad tracks. Half a squad at a time cautiously withdrew under friendly rolling artillery barrages; it was impossible to recover any of the wounded until well after dark. Just thirty-three men from Company I made it back that night.

Colonel Sutherland's 119th Infantry Regiment continued to pierce the thin front held by the German 148th Infantry Regiment above North Bardenburg on 8 October. Lieutenant Colonel Brown's 3rd Battalion was first given the mission of clearing out the regimental right flank along the railroad line running into Hergozenrath; the battalion's Ammunition and Pioneer Platoon swept the roads for mines before Brown's companies jumped off and by 0805 all the pillboxes were emptied. Herlong's 1st Battalion mopped up the town itself and was halfway to Kamerhof by 0900 before encountering trouble. Numerous enemy-laid mines here became difficult to bypass, stalling his companies until Brown was ordered by Sutherland to move over and provide assistance. They removed the mines within two hours, permitting the 1st Battalion to continue down to the southern edge of Kamerhof; by noon, Herlong's men were fighting in the edge of the woods just to the east of North Bardenburg.

During the afternoon Colonel Sutherland decided to move Brown's companies over to the right of the 1st Battalion to take the small hamlet of Pley; they accomplished this despite increasing artillery fire, and Brown's forces were eventually able to get nearer to Huhnernest. By this time Herlong's companies were out of the woods and on the fringes of North Bardenburg, receiving mortar, machine-gun, and rifle fire. With enemy resistance now becoming more apparent, Sutherland ordered defensive positions put in place and contact established between the two battalions. They had done this by 1800, but as one 3rd Battalion officer recalled later, "The Germans were now really throwing in their artillery. All the troops took cover in what buildings they could find. At one point there were the larger part of three companies in one barn."[68]

The southern division boundary had nevertheless almost been reached and the 119th Infantry expected to send patrols out to contact General Huebner's 1st Infantry Division. "Everyone in the [30th] Division thought a meeting would be made within two days at the most," remembered Lieutenant Colonel Cox.[69] But Cox also noted a problem when he added, "The 119th and 120th Infantry Regiments were supposed to make contact near Bardenburg, but a gap existed between the two regiments."

This gap was destined to be thoroughly exploited by the Germans in the days ahead. It was also recorded in their 49th Infantry Regiment's after-action report on 8 October: "In spite of the many tanks committed by the [Americans], he was prevented from crossing the big road."[70] Even though the long-anticipated attack to close the gap separating Aachen and its major supply line from the southeast had already commenced this very day in the 1st Infantry Division zone, it was now becoming more evident to the Americans that the linkup with the Big Red One would not happen too quickly.

CHAPTER 9

Verlautenheide, Crucifix Hill, and the Ravelsberg Fall

Guess the only way to do it is to send up some engineers, eh Captain?
No, I wouldn't ask a man to commit suicide.
I told you I'd do it myself.

CAPT. BOBBIE E. BROWN, COMPANY C, 18TH INFANTRY REGIMENT

The events at Alsdorf on 7 October convinced the American commanders that it was time to force the issue in Aachen. When the 30th Infantry Division's General Hobbs urged that VII Corps launch its part of the encirclement maneuver, General Hodges quickly agreed. Fortunately, the broad outlines for the endeavor were determined before First Army approached the German border back in mid-September. Thus General Huebner, in his small, brick, three-story forward command post in the little town of Hauset, had been afforded the time he needed to refine his scheme of operations, and as such he was able to order the attack that very night.

Huebner's plan actually called for a multiphase strike. The first task in the initial phase, assigned to Colonel Smith's 18th Infantry Regiment, would focus on encircling the city by capturing Verlautenheide; the village's topography permitted excellent fields of fire for the Germans to the northeast, over toward the regiment's second objective, commanding and pillbox-studded Hill 239, christened "Crucifix Hill" by the Americans. A quick rise on the western part of the hill, surmounted at almost 800 feet by a huge 60-foot stone cross, gave Hill 239 its dramatic name; with

237

360-degree visibility for miles, the Germans had been using the cross as an artillery outpost. The next phase of Huebner's bold plan was to seize Ravelsberg Hill.

The Ravelsberg, a wooded mass arrayed with more pillboxes along its rolling heights, was located another 1,500 yards to the northwest of Crucifix Hill. Observation from atop the 231-meter-high Ravelsberg overlooked the Aachen-Würselen Road, the main supply route into Aachen, and the Aachen Weiden Road, another avenue of approach into the city from Jurlich. The Ravelsberg also commanded views over the railroad line that ran into the city from Würselen; from atop the hill the gritty factory district in the northeast section of the Aachen, with its foundry, rolling mills, and pillboxes, could also be seen on a clear day. Thus, the Ravelsberg position was important for several reasons. If the Germans retained it, *Oberstleutnant* Maximilian Leyherr's 246th Division would enjoy a secure resupply route into Aachen. Observation from the hill also enabled the Germans to direct artillery fire into the flank and rear of the positions held by the 16th Infantry on the ridge outside of Verlautenhide where the men here were actually protecting the entire 1st Division from a counterattack. Moreover, as long as the defenders retained control of the Raveslberg, they would be able to prevent any American thrust into Aachen during daylight hours.

Huebner's final phase portended another challenge if it became necessary. Once Ravelsberg Hill succumbed to the 18th Infantry, *Oberstleutnant* Leyherr would be given a twenty-four-hour ultimatum demanding surrender. If he failed to agree unconditionally, Colonel Seitz's 26th Infantry Regiment would follow a targeted artillery and tactical airstrike and launch an immediate ground attack into the city.

As the first major urban center in Germany threatened with capture by Allied troops, Aachen was now symbolic for far more than its military value. Hitler, who could not afford the propaganda defeat that would be handed to his regime if Aachen fell to the Americans, had repeatedly ordered the city to be defended to the last man and bullet. The veteran Big Red One, now being given the honor to demonstrate to the world that the demise of the Third Reich was inevitable, eagerly looked forward to demoralizing Hitler and all of Germany with Aachen's surrender.

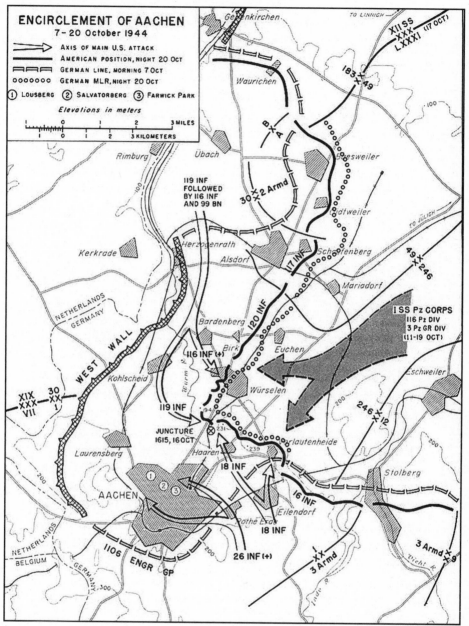

ENCIRCLEMENT OF AACHEN
7–20 October 1944

AXIS OF MAIN U.S. ATTACK
AMERICAN POSITION, NIGHT 20 OCT
GERMAN LINE, MORNING 7 OCT
GERMAN MLR, NIGHT 20 OCT
① LOUSBERG ② SALVATORBERG ③ FARWICK PARK

Elevations in meters

0   1   2   3 MILES
0   1   2   3 KILOMETERS

COURTESY U.S. ARMY

Capt. Robert Botsford of the 1st Division G-2 Section put the situation at the time in this perspective:

> During the month of October, the eyes of all Germany were on Aachen. The enemy had to solve a problem that was far more than a purely local operation. On the political side, the enemy had to decide whether to minimize the importance of Aachen and prepare the homefront for its loss, or to face the fact that it was the ancient imperial German city, the testing ground for the Wermacht's determination not to yield a foot—or at least a conspicuous foot—of sacred German soil.[1]

By this time most of Aachen's prewar population of 165,000 had fled, and as the Americans were planning their attack it was estimated that not over 15,000 to 20,000 civilians remained in the city. Capt. Edward W. McGregor, the S-3 of the 18th Infantry's 1st Battalion, cautiously noted, "The 246th Division [defending Aachen] now included a conglomeration of naval personnel, physical misfits, deferred defense workers and new recruits. The static defense units were a bit better. Owing to the poor quality of the personnel and the limited training they experienced, the combat efficiency and morale of these units were quite low. However, they were defending well-prepared fortifications and many of their leaders were skilled Wehrmacht officers. These defenses were constantly being improved and backed up with more and more artillery as each day went by."[2]

Colonel Smith's plan called for the night attack ordered by General Huebner to be led by Lieutenant Colonel Williamson's 2nd Battalion. His companies would first filter behind the positions being held by the 16th Infantry on the ridge outside of Verlautenheide before seizing the main village. They would then establish blocking positions to the north and farther east to prevent any counterattacks. Once they accomplished this, Lieutenant Colonel Learnard's 1st Battalion would move up and then swing to the northwest to take Crucifix Hill. Lieutenant Colonel Peckham's 3rd Battalion would also launch an attack to seize barren-ridged Hill 192, just northwest of Haaren, thus diverting attention from the regiment's main effort against Crucifix Hill.

The mood of the officers and men in the attacking combat teams was best described at the time by Captain McGregor:

The men faced the Aachen offensive with mixed feelings. In as much as the division had achieved a series of outstanding successes along the historic path from Normandy to Aachen and the gates of Germany, they were battle veterans with a sense of destiny—a feeling that they were always selected for important tasks because they had always accomplished their mission. Thus, esprit de corps was excellent.

On the other hand, there were causes for personal misgivings concerning the forthcoming operations. The rapid dash across France and Belgium and the apparent destruction of the German Army in the west had raised hopes of final victory and a sudden end to the war. These hopes had been shattered by the abrupt increase of resistance on German soil. The Siegfried defenses, although manned by troops with low morale and poor combat efficiency, were proving difficult to reduce and it was apparent the enemy intended to defend his homeland by waging a fierce war of attrition against the invader. Casualties were mounting, and morale, while good on the whole, was a factor that varied with the comparative success or failure of each day's operation.[3]

The steps taken by the 1st Battalion in preparing for the upcoming attack reflected the wisdom gained by two long years of combat experience. Nearly all of the current senior officers had first waded ashore together in North Africa, and they honored Big Red One's motto: "No mission too difficult, no sacrifice too great—duty first!" The Aachen fight would be no exception. After being relieved by Lt. Col. Hershel E. Linn's 237th Engineering Battalion back on 2 October, McGregor and the S-3 of the 2nd Battalion—Maine-raised Capt. Robert E. Murphy, who served as a heavy weapons company commander from November of 1942 until the Saint-Lô breakthrough—as well as the 3rd Battalion's former rifle company commander Henry R. Sawyer, met at the regimental command post to start planning for the upcoming battles. Later that night, McGregor, himself a former rifle company captain, returned to his post to discuss the plan with his boss, Lieutenant Colonel Learnard, a thin, intense, pipe-smoking commander who parted his thick hair in the middle and kept a German shepherd close by for company. Joining them were the battalion's 32nd Field Artillery liaison officer, Harvard-educated Capt.

Malcolm Marshall. The trio huddled together well into the night, studying maps, aerial photographs, and overlays of the German positions on Crucifix Hill and the surrounding area; before bedding down, they made plans for a detailed reconnaissance of the attack zone the following day.

McGregor and Learnard, who often sported a walking stick, joined with their heavy weapons company commander, Capt. Robert E. Bowers, to visually reconnoiter Verlautenheide and Crucifix Hill that morning. They could see that the ridge between the village and the hill was crowned with bunkers, especially on its southern slope facing Eilendorf. Large pillboxes studded the crest of distant Crucifix Hill; with their binoculars they could see that the firing ports of the boxes were overlooking their intended avenue of attack. Together they counted as many as forty separate pillboxes on the hill. There was no way to tell if the slopes were mined, but belts of barbed-wire entanglements protecting communication trenches that ran from pillbox to pillbox were slightly visible. Learnard whispered that it was quite evident the Germans had excellent visibility from the hill, and fearsome looking fields of fire. McGregor waved his finger toward Verlautenheide and then westward to Crucifix Hill, underscoring the fact that there was little to no cover from the village edge to the trenches at the foot of the hill. Marshall, with his eye for calling in positions for artillery strikes, surmised that the best approach to first reach Verlautenheide appeared to be along a road that curved out of the northeast end of Eilendorf and snaked its way up to the village; this route provided some protection from direct fire for about half the distance between the villages.

There were other drawbacks. Little information was known about the enemy dispositions, but their probable strength had been estimated; intelligence reports had indicated that Replacement Battalion 453 occupied Verlautenheide, and that a reinforced reserve company of Grenadier Regiment 352, composed of hand-picked men—the supposed best in the regiment and recently rushed up from Weiden—was manning the fortifications on Crucifix Hill. When McGregor returned with Learnard and Marshall to their battalion command post later that afternoon, they met with all their officers, and again used their maps, aerial photographs, and overlays to facilitate a detailed briefing with the knowledge gained from that day's reconnaissance mission.

SKETCH MAP — Showing
Terrain And Road Network
of "CRUCIFIX HILL" And Vicinity.
Attacked By Co 'C' 18th Infantry.
7-9 October, 1944 ~

VERLAUTENHEIDE

QUINX

HAAREN

COURTESY McCORMICK RESEARCH CENTER

The next day brought further preparation; this time all of the rifle company commanders participated. The approach to Verlautenheide recommended by Captain Marshall was agreed upon. Later, Lieutenant Colonel Learnard closed the follow-up briefing back in the CP by directing each company commander to continue reconnoitering the following day, this time with all of their platoon leaders, noncoms, and individual squad leaders. This was appreciated through the ranks. After viewing the terrain and plans for the attack, one noncom expressed the value of Learnard's thoroughness in preparing them for the upcoming fight:

> Every bit of enemy activity was noted and recorded; every pillbox closely watched; every likely approach studied; every discernible fold in the ground was tucked away in our memories. Not deeming it sufficient to permit each man to rely on the evidence of his own eyes, we later critiqued the operation until we were certain that we were getting the best and fullest and most reliable information possible. The importance of the mission was drilled into us. No stone was left unturned to ensure that this operation would be a complete success with the fewest possible casualties.[4]

A pilot from the Ninth Air Force reported to Lieutenant Colonel Learnard the next morning. The pilot's role as air liaison officer was to direct fighter bombers to targets requested by the 1st Battalion during the attack. Again, Learnard and McGregor returned to Eilendorf, not just with the air liaison officer, but also with platoon leaders from the supporting tank and tank destroyer companies, as well as the Regimental antitank company. McGregor then made plans to return in the morning for one last reconnaissance, this time with just the company commander who would lead the assault on Crucifix Hill.

Capt. Bobbie E. Brown, commander of Company C, had been selected for this task. At forty-one, he was closer in age to Colonel Smith than he was to any other company commander in the regiment; the average age was twenty-six. Brown was a rough-looking six-footer who had lied about his age to enlist in the Army; he was fifteen at the time, but claimed he was eighteen. The army took him. Born into a large family in Dublin, Georgia, his father died when he was just two years old; after living with relatives the army became home to Brown in 1922, and it did not take long for him to make quite a reputation for himself. He was a skilled boxer and had scored thirty-eight victories in competitions during the inter-war years. He was also a Mustang, a sergeant who received a battlefield commission to lieutenant during the 1st Division's fighting in Sicily. By this time, Brown was a gambler and a drinker, and was scarred all over from knife and gun fights. The battalion commander who promoted him to captain after the Normandy invasion also remembered, "Bobbie had an intense desire to kill Germans and was shrewd in figuring out ways to do it. He was an expert at ambushing, patrolling, and scouting techniques. He had a sense of timing that was unusual. He was a scrapper, and when it came to soldiering he was right there. He was absolutely fearless."[5]

On 7 October, McGregor and Brown made one final reconnaissance of Crucifix Hill. Brown carefully studied the ditches at the foot of the hill, estimating that they were about 75 yards short of the first belt of pillboxes and about a dozen yards wide. The pillboxes themselves looked daunting; they were generally covered with brush and branches, except for their turrets that Brown could see poking out in the direction from which he would be attacking. Several questions arose. What was on the reverse slope? How well was it fortified? Were more enemy reserves here? They discussed all these factors at length, but both McGregor and Brown knew answers were not possible without actually reconnoitering the backside of Crucifix Hill, which could not be done; it would have to wait until the day of the attack.

Lieutenant Colonel Williamson's 2nd Battalion patrols had also been conducting daylight reconnaissance during this period. While the enemy unit in Verlautenheide had been identified as multiple-company strength, there had been no way to determine the Germans' actual dispositions; this concerned Williamson. His primary fear was that they could bring up reinforcements from behind the village without being detected. Another concern was the avenue of advance into Verlautenheide; it was initially downhill and observers had determined that the area would be subjected to small-arms, mortar, and artillery fire if their move was detected. Williamson's men would then have to reduce several large pillboxes that guarded the ridge leading into Verlautenheide; of even greater concern was what the German reaction would be. Would artillery fire get called in from positions on Crucifix Hill? Would fire arrive from the northeast edge of Aachen? Would his men be facing frontal fire from Verlautenheide while deafening shells roared in from their rear?

For a week now, Lieutenant Colonel Peckham's 3rd Battalion had been holed up in Eilendorf, right under the nose of the Germans atop Crucifix Hill. Constant shelling and mortar fire had made their stay unpleasant; only limited reconnaissance by Captain Sawyer and others had been possible toward Hill 192. It had been determined that the Germans occupied the nearby factories in Haaren and would have excellent observation on their moves when they commenced their diversionary strike. But by now other measures had been put in place to keep the Germans off balance.

At the start of Williamson's attack toward Verlautenheide, Colonel Gibb's 16th Infantry Cannon Company and every mortar unit in his regiment would put on a show to further distract the Germans. Other moves by the 26th Infantry's 2nd and 3rd Battalions were planned to add more confusion when Crucifix Hill was attacked; Lt. Col. Derrill M. Daniel would move a company supported by tanks and TDs toward Rothe Erde, right on the edge of Aachen proper.[6] His other 2nd Battalion companies would make a move up the Brand Road leading into the city. These maneuvers would hopefully convince the Germans that the core of Aachen might be under attack, but strategically the goal was to bring Daniel's companies in contact with Lt. Col. John T. Corley's 3rd Battalion men.[7] They were dug in around the higher ground community of Beverau in preparation for the real fight when the 18th Infantry drew the noose around the city, and if the order came down from General Huebner to actually step into Aachen.

At 2215 hours, just ahead of midnight on 7 October, Lieutenant Colonel Williamson's 2nd Battalion of the 18th Infantry moved to Brand, where his men detrucked and continued on foot to their assembly area behind the 16th Infantry. The opening blow of the southern encirclement of Aachen began at 0300 when eleven friendly light, medium, and heavy battalions laid preplotted artillery into Verlautenheide. Mortars and other fire poured in from the 16th Infantry positions. An hour later, the infantrymen jumped off with Company E, commanded by

Capt. Hershel T. Coffman, attacking to the left and Capt. Alfred E. Koenig's Company F assaulting to the right. Surprisingly, there was little German activity in response to the American advance until a sergeant in Company F yelled too loudly at a struggling soldier. The startled defenders then filled the night sky with parachute flares, and once Koenig's command group was spotted, an enemy machine gunner opened up on them, quickly sending these men in three directions to avoid being hit.

Now absent his radioman, Captain Koenig lost all communication with his platoons and battalion.[8] Yet quick thinking produced results. He knew where his men were supposed to be heading, so he dashed to the left, organized stray soldiers as he came upon them, and then slid to a sudden stop when he heard the hushed voices of a German patrol. Koenig quickly got the drop on them, and every man was mowed down. This revealed his position to others, but the American captain was still a step ahead of them; he saw a second group of Germans first, and cut them down. By this time most of his missing men had reached the edge of Verlautenheide where they were already engaged in street brawls and hand-to-hand fighting. It only took until first light to get control of the immediate situation, and Koenig's men were prepared for counterattacks.

It was the Americans' good fortune to have a blanket of fog hanging over the area as the other companies of the 2nd Battalion moved up. Visibility improved after early morning light burned through, but by this time Captain Coffman's Company E was inside another section of Verlautenheide. It was not as easy a move for Capt. Gordon A. Jeffrey's Company G; the Germans had artillery zeroed in on his positions, but his men were able to move up after taking just a few casualties; by midmorning they were engaged in house-to-house fighting on the west side of the village.

But strengthened enemy artillery, *Panzerfausts*, mines, and poor road conditions took a devastating toll on the Shermans of Company B, 745th Tank Battalion as these men tried to come up toward midmorning to support the attack. One tank got stuck in mud before leaving Eilendorf; another was knocked out by artillery fire as it neared the railroad overpass just north of the village. A third Sherman hit a mine, blocking the road over to Verlautenheide. Soon afterward, a German scored a direct hit on another stalled tank with his *Panzerfaust*, leaving just one operational Sherman that pulled off the road into an orchard to wait out the time it would take for engineers to come up and clear the mines off the road.

A similar fate crippled a second platoon of tanks as they moved up. One Sherman fell out with mechanical problems; another hit a mine. The three remaining tanks had to stop well south of Verlautenheide. Tank commander and suburban Chicago native Sgt. Earl R. Jacobsen remembered this all too well, later saying, "We experienced the worst artillery fire I have ever seen. The tanks had scarcely an opportunity to return fire. They couldn't move."[9]

Better luck enabled tank destroyers under the command of Lt. Emmett R. Duffy to lead in reducing the pillboxes outside of Verlautenheide when they got there at midmorning; his TDs fired fourteen rapid rounds at their embrasures while squads from Captain Coffman's Company E charged the back of the boxes with satchel and pole charges. Good news began to make its way to Colonel Smith's command post as the morning wore on; at noon Williamson reported that Verlautenheide was under control, with just a few stragglers still on the loose. Two of Lieutenant Duffy's TDs were in place near Company E's CP in a square guarding the northern approaches into the village; two others were farther to the south at the Company F command post; Koenig's men were watching the Quinx road center.

Earlier that morning, Colonel Smith had ordered Lieutenant Colonel Learnard to move his men out of their cellars in Eilendorf and to prepare to move up to Verlautenheide without delay. Learnard had protested, hoping Smith would wait until the "all clear" had been received from Williamson, but the anxious regimental commander insisted that they start moving. Learnard complied, but he first sent Captain McGregor up to the village to confer with Williamson's S-3, Captain Murphy, so he could learn for himself just what the situation was.

When McGregor arrived at the 2nd Battalion command post 500 yards south of the village and found Murphy, the noise from crashing mortars and artillery was horrendous. The men could barely hear each other, but Murphy nevertheless yelled in his Maine accent, "We don't really have things under control in town, Mac. Why don't you pass your companies through and at least get up on the ridge. We'll stay and clean up here."[10]

McGregor's return to Eilendorf with this information prompted Lieutenant Colonel Learnard to make the decision to move his command group up before asking his men to do the same; this was the kind of leadership that earned their respect. Within a half hour, the lead officers were running through a steady gauntlet of enemy artillery fire; miraculously they made it to the 2nd Battalion command post without taking any casualties. After Learnard contacted a relieved Colonel Smith to report their arrival, he arranged for a heavy smoke screen to be placed on either side of the approach into Verlautenheide so his rifle companies could move up under this protective cover. Ominously, an exploding enemy shell cut the line to regiment moments afterward.

Then Learnard made another decision; he personally led the command group during their move up to the extreme western edge of Verlautenheide so they could set up their forward command post and get ready for the attack on Crucifix Hill. But when they got close they found this section of the village was still sheltering some Germans. This time the officers literally fought their way through several houses, sending some running, and killing those who tried to fight back so they could finally lay claim to their new post.

It was now 1000 hours; Learnard radioed Maj. Robert E. Green, his executive officer, and told him to start infiltrating the companies forward, one at a time. The called-for smoke was laid in, but by now the wind had picked up and the intended cover simply blew away. The Germans smelled blood. As the 1st Battalion companies made their way past the discouraging line of Shermans that had been stopped earlier, hostile artillery started hammering away. "Casualties were high in all companies," one officer remembered later. "This was despite our extreme caution, despite the use we made of all possible cover and concealment, despite the perfect dispersion. In spots where Jerry could not directly observe us, he had previously registered his supporting fires. We had to move in single file; it was a slow tortuous move."[11]

Company A, commanded by Capt. Herbert A. Scott-Smith Jr., was hit the hardest; he lost nearly a platoon of men. Captain Brown managed to get nearly all of his soldiers into a small shaded cemetery near a church on the edge of Verlautenheide, but Learnard wanted them in the cellars of the houses nearer to the CP. It was here that Brown's pensive men shifted to, and together they huddled over their situation maps, hurriedly studying the pillbox locations on Crucifix Hill one last time. The company's executive officer, Michigan native Lt. Clement Van Wagoner, was giving pep talks to the mostly very young soldiers, leaving Brown free to think through any last-minute adjustments. What he did next was what he knew best; he would not endanger his men without knowing as much as he could about what waited outside of the cellars. He made the decision to personally reconnoiter out toward Crucifix Hill.

> I had my artillery and 81mm mortar observers get on a housetop where they could observe the objective area. I had also placed the heavy machineguns on other nearby housetops so they could have a good field of fire. I then put out my covering force and had all the platoon leaders join their platoons to await my return from my ground reconnaissance.[12]

Captain Brown took his SCR-536 radio and raced off westward by himself. For a short time he wasn't spotted, but hostile rifle fire came in as he got closer to the hill. Then enemy machine gunners found him. Brown reacted:

> I hit the ground and crawled in the direction of the small arms fire and again several more bursts from machineguns came in my direction. I then withdrew to the cemetery where I had placed my covering force. One of them opened fire, and three enemy put their hands up and surrendered. I took the prisoners back to my command post, where I discovered the Ranger Platoon also had 22 others in a cellar.[13]

It was at this point that Brown assembled all of his platoon leaders and reviewed the final attack plan. His 1st Platoon would move along the trail leading up the right side of Crucifix Hill, reducing each pillbox that got in the way; the 2nd Platoon would attack on the left slope with the same mission. The attached Ranger Platoon was being used as a security force to protect against any counterattacks; they were given just one box to reduce. Brown ordered his 60mm mortars to first go into a position just outside of the village, and then move up with the attached heavy machine guns from Company D upon his command; it would come by radio. The 81mm mortar spotters and forward artillery observers were to accompany the two assault platoons so they could call down fire and adjustments.

Brown then made sure everyone was certain of the communication protocols and knew their passwords. He checked to be certain his platoon leaders would always have someone on their SCR-536s; he told them one of his radiomen would be carrying an extra SCR-300 belonging to the Ranger Platoon so he could maintain contact with everyone, and also have two ways to talk to Lieutenant Van Wagoner. "I then checked to see that everyone knew the signals to lift fires, and to call for fires. Final watches were set, and the time was 1140 hours when we did this. All the platoon leaders were then directed to return to their men and give them these instructions."[14]

Of this final briefing, one soldier remembered: "Half in jest, but with butterflies in our stomachs we christened the coming operation either 'Operation Massacre' or 'Operation Decimation.' It was now thoroughly obvious to us that the job ahead was to be a rough one."[15]

By this time Captain Brown was back in the battalion CP with Lieutenant Van Wagoner and his communications sergeant. Lieutenant Colonel Learnard came up to him while he was going over some final details and handed him the written order from regiment. It simply told him what he already knew he had to do. "You will neutralize and destroy all enemy activity on Crucifix Hill. You will then organize and prepare a permanent defense on the hill and be ready to repulse any and all counterattacks."[16]

The time of the attack was set for 1330 hours. Completely satisfied with Brown's preparations, Learnard looked him straight in the eye, saluted him, and simply said, "Good luck, Bobbie."[17]

Whatever thoughts he now had Brown kept to himself, yet he had to have some concerns going through his mind. He was relying heavily on air support when the attack began, but when the tanks were stopped that morning, the air liaison officer, who was in one of the VHF-radio-equipped Shermans, never made it up to the CP. Two prearranged flights of P-47s would still fly their missions, but there would be no further air support as Company C's attack evolved. He had little time left to ponder this. By now the opening rounds of the scheduled artillery barrage were pounding Crucifix Hill. The loud Pratt & Whitney "Double Wasp" piston engines of the fighter planes roared overhead; the rounds delivered from their .50-caliber machine guns toward Crucifix Hill were deafening. This was it. Bomb doors opened; 2,500-pound payloads dropped, too close it seemed—roughly 200 yards away, but behind the fast moving men, not to their front.

Then, more things started to go wrong.

An enemy forward observer on the southern slope of Crucifix Hill brought down a tremendous barrage of artillery fire on Brown's men; it was believed the batteries delivering the rounds were positioned in Aachen. Numerous American casualties resulted before anyone could even get close to their assigned pillboxes. The Ranger Platoon also took fire from two boxes on a ridge closer to the hill. Through all of this, Brown and his command group still raced forward and then he, his radio operator, and a runner were able to jump over an embankment and dive into a muddy ditch that provided some cover. A call came in on the SCR-300 moments later: Shell fragments had wounded Lt. Joseph W. Cambron, the Kentucky native and leader of the Ranger Platoon. Seconds later another call arrived on the 536: Van Wagoner reported that both of the assault teams were completely pinned down at the base of the hill; no one was moving.

Brown's platoons had been able to get over to Crucifix Hill because the Germans had concentrated their fires on the Ranger Platoon. "Although they were pinned down," Brown would lecture later, "they were taught that as long as any member of an assaulting force could maneuver, you were not pinned down."[18] But at that moment Brown was frustrated because they were not moving, so he decided he would have do something about this.

As if reading his mind, his radio operator yelled, "Jesus, the air force and the artillery didn't do a goddamned thing to those pillboxes, did they! What the hell happens now?"[19]

Brown, having absorbed the totality of the situation, responded with, "I guess I'll just have to take them myself."

The startled radio operator then uttered an incredulous "Sir!" as if to question Brown's sanity, but the determined captain, never taking his eyes off the gun barrels peeking out of the apertures of a camouflaged pillbox, responded flatly with, "What we'll need are a couple of pole charges. And throw in some satchel charges, too."

Brown's runner nodded, and then said, "Guess the only way to do this is to send up some engineers, eh Captain?"

"No, I wouldn't ask a man to commit suicide. I said I would do it myself."

Lt. Charles Marvain, the 2nd Platoon leader, had managed to work his way forward with a couple of his men by this time, so someone threw a satchel charge loaded with sixty quarter-pound blocks of TNT on the end of a three-second fuse over the bank to Captain Brown.

> I picked the charge up and crawled to the pillbox in front of me, and then I ran up to the aperture. At the time an enemy rifleman opened the back door and started out. However, when he saw me, he dashed back inside. I jumped at the door and tried to slam it shut, expecting to trap them all inside; however the excited German had left his rifle in the doorway. I instead opened the door, pulled the fuse on my charge, tossed it inside the bunker, slammed the door and jumped back over the embankment as the pillbox and its occupants were blown up.[20]

Brown then hightailed it back to the ditch his men were in just in time to receive another call on the SCR-300, and this time Van Wagoner was on the channel; Lieutenant Cambron had been hit a second time, yet the Ranger Platoon had been able to take their assigned pillbox. "But my assault platoons were still pinned down, and receiving more artillery and mortar fire," Brown explained later. "My runners and I picked up more pole and satchel charges so we could move over to another pillbox. Then we fired a yellow smoke grenade from the south side of the pillbox we wanted in order to signal the 155mm guns in Eilendorf to lift their fires so we could make the assault."

But "we" really meant Brown had gone alone again. Armed with two of the explosive charges, he took a wide, circuitous path up a 100-foot rise, crawling much of the way under the trajectory of continuous enemy fire coming out of the box. As he worked his way closer, machine-gun rounds started spraying the ground around him. Dirt flew up, slapping him in the face; bullets ricocheted off nearby rocks, but the fragments missed him. He could not get to the rear door this time, so before the Germans could even try to emerge from the box, Captain Brown rose up and charged the front aperture, pulled his charge's fuse, threw it in, and then dove into a nearby crater. Seconds later the pillbox exploded. Certain the Germans were reeling from the concussions inside the box, Brown dashed for the aperture yet again, this time casually lobbing a TNT-loaded satchel charge in; from the bottom of the hill his men could see more explosions, then smoke and flames rising into the air, much of it from the pillbox's vents.

At some point Brown received a wound in one of his knees, but he ignored it. When he got back to the base of the hill, he was told Lieutenant Cambron had been hit again, this time while he was attempting to aid a wounded sergeant, and had been killed.[21] Cambron's communications sergeant took command, but all he could do was keep his men under cover; withering small-arms fire was still coming in from what seemed like every direction around the platoon.

By now one of the squad leaders from Brown's own 2nd Platoon had also been hit, but the sergeant who took over bravely told him his men were nevertheless prepared to launch an immediate attack. Captain Brown needed no urging, but he was pleased his men were starting to get their own courage up. "The squad had a flamethrower, so I assigned them to a third pillbox, which they went after, and with the help of a good rifleman to keep the aperture on another closed, a fourth pillbox was soon neutralized. This relieved the pressure on both assault platoons."[22]

And while this was happening, Brown had charged up Crucifix Hill yet again, by himself, to go after one of the largest pillboxes on the summit. By now the 60-foot massive stone cross, in place since 1890, had come down, probably as a result of either the air strike or accurate American artillerymen getting even with the Germans for using it as an outpost to direct fire at them.[23] An 88mm gun was on the nearby pillbox's dome toward which Brown was charging, short barreled with a turret that revolved a full 360 degrees. On both sides of this weapon were .30-caliber machine guns, and above them were a pair of 20mm guns. Rifle or machine-gun muzzles poked out of every lower aperture; approximately forty-five Germans and three of their officers manned this box. There was also a steel door in the rear of the pillbox that faced another thick slab of concrete located right behind it—what Captain Brown determined was most likely the entrance to an underground bunker that held supplies for the defenders in the main box.

There he waited until a German soldier came out and started making his way down into the bunker. When he emerged, his arms loaded with shells, Brown quietly snuck up on him just as he was heading through the back door to deliver this load to his comrades. With perfect timing, Brown waited until the stocky German put his ammo down to close the door, then he lunged at him, dropped a lit satchel charge at the man's feet, slammed the door in his shocked face, and ran like hell as a tremendous explosion lit up the summit of Crucifix Hill.

Captain Brown had chosen not to head back down the hill at the moment. As he explained to his artillery liaison, Captain Marshall, later that night:

> I decided I better hop over the other side of the hill and see what Jerry had. Didn't want to be caught with a counterattack coming up the other side, and no idea what was there. So, I ran over the top and just then a machine gunner gave me a burp. So I hit the dirt. Lucky to be in this little hallow. Stuck my head up. Got a blast. Wiggled over to the right after a time. Stuck my helmet up on my hand. Got another blast. Couldn't go right or left now. Knew we'd have to get our holes dug, so there was nothing to do but come straight back over. Jumped and ran like hell, and that gunner only nicked my arm.[24]

Brown was actually wounded twice this time, once on his elbow and before that on his chin; he dismissed the latter wound as "just a scratch." After he went down the hill to rejoin his men, Brown remembered, "I saw that three more pillboxes had been reduced from actions of the assault platoons, so I sent a runner back to give Lieutenant Van Wagoner an oral order to move up all the remaining detachments and the support platoon to one of the fortifications, then for him to proceed to the battalion command post to let the battalion commander know the situation."

Lieutenant Colonel Learnard was incredulous when he got the word. It was inconceivable to him that all this could have already happened; it had only been forty minutes since the attack commenced.

But those closer to Captain Brown knew better. The same sergeant who had questioned his sanity before Brown went after the first pillbox this time exclaimed, "You did it, Sir! That finished 'em for good. The hill is ours!"[25]

Brown's modest reply was simply, "Good, it was the only job they expected us to do."

Just after 1410 hours, Brown and his small command group trekked up Crucifix Hill to survey the damage to the German fortifications. Lieutenant Snyder, commanding the 1st Platoon, had been wounded earlier, but he led his men in checking other pillboxes. Brown ran into the 2nd Platoon's Lieutenant Marvain as he was coming off the hill a bit later; the lieutenant told Brown he wanted to show him something. Together they went down toward a pillbox on the lower slope of the hill that overlooked the small cemetery that Brown had used for cover when he did his reconnaissance before the attack; it was no longer manned. Nine Germans lay dead around its perimeter.

When a smiling Brown turned away, he caught a hand signal from Lieutenant Snyder out of the corner of his eye; all the pillboxes in his area were also cleared. Brown ordered his support platoon to move up right after this, and then he radioed Lieutenant Marshall and asked him to line up artillery fire for the back side of the hill; Brown knew the Germans would counterattack, likely that very night. He then concentrated on his wounded men; they needed to be evacuated to the battalion aid station in Verlautenheide. To solve this problem, Captain Brown went over to the POW cage, ordered the German prisoners to attention before him, and then told them to remove their bunks from the pillboxes they had been defending so they could use them as stretchers.

Other problems were not as easy to solve. Brown's flank was badly exposed because Scott-Smith's Company A, attacking through a ditch that led in from Haaren while Brown was on Crucifix Hill, only managed to advance 300 yards before being stopped. Attempts to move again were halted by all kinds of enemy fire; casualties mounted, putting Lieutenant Colonel Learnard in a position where he had to adjust his plans. He weighed employing direct artillery fire to get Scott-Smith out of the bind his men were in, but at the time he was uncertain of where Company C's positions on the hill were. Learnard decided instead to put Capt. Jesse R. Miller's Company B into the gap between Verlautenheide and Crucifix Hill, giving Brown the support he would need to hold the hill while at the same time forming a solid line back to the village where Miller would link up to the 2nd Battalion's left flank. This combined defensive wall of American fighting power was now necessary to also prevent counterattacks from the ridge to the east of Verlautenheide.

While Lieutenant Colonel Learnard was satisfied with the day's progress, he still had to concern himself with the fact that the battalion had not cleared the entire zone of enemy-held pillboxes on Crucifix Hill, and that an unknown number of Germans were still housed in pillboxes between Miller's and Scott-Smith's positions. Remembering the tentative mood at the CP at the time, Captain McGregor explained, "The battalion was jutting out to the west like a sore finger with a cancerous growth. The pillboxes were in defilade from our tanks that had finally moved up to Verlautenheide. Rain was starting to fall again, night was coming, and visibility was limited."[26]

> Defensive preparations then proceeded rapidly. Close-in barrages as well as concentrations on both sides of the ridge were planned by Captain Marshall. The battalion's anti-tank guns and the attached regimental anti-tank platoon were brought up; additional heavy machineguns from Company D were displaced forward while the 81mm mortar platoon was sent into Eilendorf where their fires could be coordinated with the supporting field artillery. Re-supply of ammunition was completed by nightfall and the dead and remaining wounded were evacuated to Eilendorf. New field phone lines were laid, and the circuit leading to the regimental command post soon came back to life.

Long before the 1st Battalion began organizing for its defense that dismal night, Lieutenant Colonel Peckham's 3rd Battalion had jumped off from Eilendorf for the diversionary attack on Hill 192 beside Haaren. Capt. Robert E. Hess's Company I and Capt. William A. Russell's Company K led the attack. The hill fell quickly; it took less than two hours and there were few casualties. Captain Folk's Company L was then tasked with cleaning out the north end of Rothe Erde where seesaw fighting soon developed in a large rubber factory: an American platoon held one half of the building, the Germans the other. Early that evening orders came down from regiment directing Lieutenant Colonel Peckham to take Haaren the next morning.

During the afternoon, while Brown's men were on Crucifix Hill, Colonel Seitz's 26th Infantry Regiment also made their planned diversionary strikes; Company F got its limited drive started from a slag pile, first crossing muddy terrain pocked with bomb craters, and then the men reached the desired section of railroad line next to Triererstrasse, a main road into Aachen.[27] But the real noise was made by the 1st Engineer Combat Battalion, commanded by Lt. Col. Bill Gara, a clear-thinking, industrious officer with a wicked sense of humor.

His men had found two abandoned streetcars on the same railroad tracks, which were elevated some three hundred yards above the city of Aachen at this location.[28] They had also previously discovered a captured ammunition dump with German teller mines and other explosives. Gara came up with the brilliant scheme to load one of the streetcars with a couple tons of these explosives, including roughly six rockets, fifty 88mm shells, two boxes of 20mm ammo, another two boxes of 37mm shells, and some hand and rifle grenades for good measure; it was well booby trapped and had a five-minute time fuse. The engineers planned to get the bomb rolling down the line toward Aachen; Gara added a personal touch and had a big sign tagged onto it reading "V-13," trumping the German V-1s and V-2s that had been flying over Aachen in the past few days.

He had even invited members of General Huebner's staff to join him at an observation post to watch the big show. It opened when the engineers gave the streetcar a shove with a tank dozer, carefully calculated in thrust so the car would be set in motion and gain enough speed to reach its destination—the edge of Aachen—before the time fuse set off the rolling bomb. Daniel's 2nd Battalion men had been told that the engineers were going to try to pull this off, but as the streetcar passed their positions there was sweat on the brows of the brass in the observation post; was it going fast enough?

Sure enough, it was. At first, anyway. Halfway between Daniel's line and the city's edge it blew up; the motor had not been disconnected and had acted like a brake, causing the show to stop short of its intended audience. But Daniel recalled that there was a tremendous explosion for his men to witness, and that it had caused the Germans to expose their positions when they fired rifles at the streetcar. It certainly took the attention away from Crucifix Hill, if for only those few shining moments.

Lieutenant Colonel Corley's 3rd Battalion diversion coincided with Lieutenant Colonel Williamson's dash up to Verlautenheide in the early morning hours. His men had passed several darkened homes on their way to Beverau, necessitating that they circle back and clean out the houses one by one when they were attacked from the rear. "It was time consuming, but it illustrated to the battalion commanders just what lay ahead in painstakingly and thoroughly clearing each house, and each room in the houses," the after-action report noted later.[29] This report also revealed that prisoners taken that day had told their interrogators reinforcements and supplies were still coming into Aachen on the roadway between Crucifix Hill and the Ravelsberg.

Back in the 1st Battalion CP in Verlautenheide, Lieutenant Colonel Learnard's staff had transitioned to planning the next morning's attack on the still-active pillboxes in front of Scott-Smith's Company A. But the line from regiment lit up just as everyone was gaining comfort with the new strategy; it was Colonel Smith. General Huebner wanted the Ravelsberg plan put into place immediately. The 2nd Battalion, which had just reported a heavy German buildup to the east of Verlautenheide, would extend its lines to Crucifix Hill and become responsible for its defense, Smith told Learnard. Remembering his reaction, Captain McGregor later wrote, "This did not set too well with the battalion commander."[30]

By now the tempo of artillery and mortar fire along the entire Crucifix-Verlautenheide ridge was increasing hourly, the typical German pattern before an imminent large-scale counterattack. Ravelsberg Hill had never been mentioned to Learnard in any discussions during the advanced planning to take Crucifix Hill. With such short notice and very little intelligence about the German dispositions on the Ravelsberg, any planning would now have to be done with a simple map reconnaissance. Learnard discussed these disquieting facts with Colonel Smith; it won him over. Smith told him to clean up to Scott-Smith's front, but first brace for the impending counterattack on Crucifix Hill and still get a plan for the Ravelsberg.

Outside the CP, the German shelling was now growing louder and louder and "falling like rain" at one-minute intervals. Captain McGregor remembered, "The ridge literally shook with the impact of crunching shells. In the inky blackness of the rain-swept night, the men cursed and dug, prayed and waited. The silence between each succeeding round was deadly as the weary men strained their ears and other senses for tell-tale signs of an unwelcome visitor."[31]

Shortly after 0400 hours, the German shelling suddenly stopped. Then whooping Germans appeared on the northern and western slopes, hoping to take back Crucifix Hill by storm. "Three waves of infantrymen and assault engineers came over," remembered Captain Brown. "I ordered my men to hold their fire until the Germans were almost on top of us. Then, as the enemy was silhouetted by our artillery flares and illuminating shells, they opened up with murderous grazing fires that piled the onrushing Germans up in front of their foxholes."[32] His heavy machine gunners, commanded by Company D's Lt. Thomas Yarbor, added to the mayhem, swinging their guns with free traverse and blazing away the entire time.

It was too much for their opposite numbers. "The Germans then withdrew as suddenly as they had attacked, leaving behind 40 dead within rock throwing distance," Captain Brown told everyone later. "Over one hundred others could be seen lying in the path of our fires." Captain McGregor recalled, "Crucifix Hill was an erupting volcano. The effect on the Germans was deadly. Their bodies were stacked like cord wood in front of Company C's positions." "Huns dropped like flies," said Lieutenant Yarbor. "We counted not more than 75 yards from our machinegun positions about 50 dead."[33] Prisoners later identified the bodies as soldiers in companies of Pioneer Battalion 12 and Fusilier Regiment 27, both attached to the supposed saviors of Aachen, the 12th Infantry Division.[34]

Later that morning, two self-propelled 155mm guns emplaced north of Eilendorf ravaged the Germans still holding out in front of Captain Scott-Smith's Company A. "This completed one of the most difficult and important missions ever assigned to the 1st Battalion," Brown wrote later. "We lost one officer, Captain Cambron, and five enlisted men. Two other officers were wounded; 33 enlisted men were as well. No one was captured by the enemy."[35]

"As was expressed by witnesses to the action," Captain McGregor noted, "the success of Company C in accomplishing this extremely difficult mission was largely due to the effort of one man, Captain Bobbie Brown. His incredible action had inspired his men with an unbounded fighting spirit. For his brave deeds, Captain Brown was awarded the Medal of Honor."[36] The award presentation took place in the White House after the war, where President Harry Truman had said he would have given anything to trade places with Brown. "He was worth a regiment to me," added an equally admiring General Huebner.[37]

Lieutenant Colonel Williamson's 2nd Battalion was not as fortunate on 9 October. When their artillery pummeled Crucifix Hill, the Germans also laid an intense bombardment across Verlautenheide, hitting both Captain Koenig's Company F and the battalion command post just west of the Quinx crossroads. At the time Brown was counterattacked, the enemy deployed another battalion-sized force against Williamson's positions; these were two companies of the 12th Engineering Battalion and one company of Regiment 27. At 0420 hours, a platoon from Captain Jeffrey's Company G was almost overrun; shortly afterward the attackers closed to within 40 yards of Captain Koenig's company perimeter. Then, the Germans gained control of the railroad junction and the street just across from the battalion CP.

The Americans reacted swiftly; Koenig rushed a squad toward the building holding the command group where these men set up a firing line. But the Germans were quick, too. A fire was ignited in a nearby barn to add more to the shock of the attack; Captain Jeffrey had a platoon sheltering in a potato cellar here. Flames were engulfing the structure; cries from within could be heard. Fast-thinking Sgt. Walter L. Reed saved the day for these men by emptying his Thompson submachine gun into the Germans barring escape, and his men were able to rush out and avoid being totally overcome by smoke. Then, there was a lull in the action, but not for long.

Forty-five minutes later, the regrouped Germans started firing *Panzerfausts* around the streets; a group even crossed over and got right outside of the battalion CP. Koenig's firing line held them off, but only briefly.

By now faint, first light had started to filter in; a desperate Williamson called for tank support and at dawn five Shermans and four

of Lieutenant Duffy's TDs answered by lining up on the same side of the
street as the CP. Williamson radioed words to the effect of "shoot at
everything," and moments later the tanks and TDs were blasting buildings, anything moving on the streets, and every German they could see
with their 75mm and 76mm machine guns. Duffy later explained: "If
any more Company F doughboys were on the other side of the street,
they were probably in cellars and pinned down. One destroyer literally
sprayed the buildings. During the engagement an enemy shell fragment
ripped the radiator off this vehicle and another was hit shortly after-
wards, leaving us with three damaged TD's. All remained in action."[38]

As did the infantry. A platoon from Captain Koenig's Company E
and another squad from Jeffrey's ranks joined in the fight, finally forcing
the Germans to pull back. The line was restored by 0830 hours; three
Americans had been killed, many had been wounded, and twelve were
missing. Seventy-five Germans and two of their officers were made prisoners, and an unknown number had been killed or wounded.[39]
Williamson's emphasis had certainly not been on their wounded. He
ordered half-tracks to keep dashing back and forth between Verlautenheide and Eilendorf during breaks in the still-constant German artillery
strikes so the bloodied Americans could be carried to aid. He also
ordered a search of every house in Verlautenheide, and to shoot any
German straggler who chose not to immediately surrender. Williamson
learned later that another attack by the 246th Fusilier Battalion on the
ridge where the 16th Infantry was protecting his flank had thankfully
come to nothing.[40]

Enemy artillery and mortars also hit both Hess's Company I and
Captain Russell's Company K at daybreak on Hill 192. The shelling
lasted for about an hour, then it was lifted so the Germans could infiltrate forward to counterattack. Sgt. William A. Nickell, a tank destroyer
commander, first answered by leveling machine-gun fire at the leading
squad, and then Company M's heavy mortars were lobbed in; the rifle
companies and the Germans were too close to risk friendly artillery fire.
Although many of the attackers had already fallen, Hess ordered his men
to employ their final protective fires, waiting until those still advancing
got even closer. When they did, close-range M-1 rounds felled most of
those left; a few tried to cut and run. They didn't get far.

During this time, Captain Folk's Company L was still fighting in Rothe Erde, but by late morning the northern sections of the village were cleared out. The platoon struggling in the rubber factory finally overcame their opposition and Folk's command group celebrated by climbing up to the top of the building where they could see right into the center of Aachen. A thousand rounds of hostile artillery had fallen on Peckham's 3rd Battalion during the morning; combined with the fierce attacks that had come across his entire front, Colonel Smith, on orders from General Huebner at noon, postponed Peckham's assault on Haaren and Learnard's move over to the Ravelsberg.

In Omnia Paratus, "In All Things Prepared," became the 18th Infantry Regiment's motto after President Abraham Lincoln authorized its formation in 1861. Today would be no exception. Lieutenant Colonel Learnard, now freed from a simple map reconnaissance of the Ravelsberg, spent that afternoon with Captains McGregor and Miller visually inspecting its layout from atop Crucifix Hill. What they saw concerned them. Unlike the barren hill they were on, the Ravelsburg was covered with trees and shrubs, concealing any German preparations, pillbox locations, or troop dispositions from view, even with binoculars. They would have to cross the "big road," the artery carrying supplies and funneling reinforcements to the Germans in Aachen, to get there; traffic was visible, even at that time of the day. The stretch across the road to the foot of Ravelsberg Hill was wide open. Weighing all of this, everyone agreed that the only viable approach was along a bare ridgeline they could make out across the roadway, then through an orchard that led to the southern slope of the hill mass.

By early afternoon Williamson finally had the situation under control in Verlautenheide. Now General Huebner wanted the attack on the Ravelsberg to go off without delay; he specifically directed Colonel Smith to leave most of Learnard's 1st Battalion near Crucifix Hill; Huebner did not want the Ravelsberg strike to exceed two reinforced rifle companies. Colonel Smith chose to assign Captain Hess's Company I to the operation; Captain Miller's Company B would still be representing the 1st Battalion, with Learnard providing command and control. But the Raveslberg assault continued to be an enigma; because it would take the remaining afternoon hours to get Hess's men up from Hill 192, the attack would now have to wait until nightfall.

Miller, who had known McGregor since the regiment's time in North Africa, was briefed right away. He was told the new news first; the attack would be unsupported by artillery, or any noise for that matter. His men would be in the lead. It was to be a surprise attack, with no communication wires laid. Radio silence would be maintained until he actually started making contact with the Germans. He would have heavy machine guns and mortars attached to augment his strength, but other than Hess's men, that was it. It was late afternoon; darkness would fall soon. Hess finally showed up with his company at 1830; with just a minimal briefing, he lined his men up behind Miller's and the column started out in complete darkness along an unimproved dirt road that snaked around the western slope of Crucifix Hill.

Loaded down with their rifles, bandoleers of ammunition, grenades, mortar plates, tubes, ammo cases, and light machine guns, the men soon reached the flatter ground that would funnel them down to the Aachen road. It was a single-file move later described as "so difficult each man could reach out and touch the back of the man in front of him without seeing him."

> With Captain Miller walking slowly as the first man in the column, he could see practically nothing as he slowly made his way down the western slope of Crucifix Hill. He was relying solely on his compass and his memory of the terrain features. What he would find en route to Ravelsberg Hill was anybody's guess.
>
> The first recognizable terrain feature he encountered was the Aachen-Haaren Road. No sooner had Captain Miller reached this point at 1955 hours than he heard a group of men approaching from the northeast. He passed word back to halt and get down. The column proved to be German infantry marching toward Aachen. Lying on the roadside, he could have reached out and grabbed any one individual by the boots, but his instructions were to reach the Ravelsberg without a fight, so he elected to remain silent.[41]

After the enemy column moved past, Captain Miller carefully began infiltrating his line of men across the road. It could have been costly. His

3rd Platoon started over at the same time another enemy column led by two Germans on a horse-drawn cart came toward them, halted for no apparent reason, and then let the platoon cross in front of them without firing a shot. Why, no one knew. More traffic appeared behind this group, both vehicular and marching troops, so it was nearly two hours before the assault companies, nearly three hundred men strong, reached the other side of the roadway, still undetected.

Captain Hess now joined Miller at the head of the reformed single-file line before the anxious Americans quietly started moving through the orchard toward the base of the Ravelsberg; they came so close to a line of pillboxes that they heard Germans milling about. One soldier even remembered, "Three enemy could actually be seen sitting on top of a pillbox, smoking and talking. Six to eight more were spotted parallel to the column."[42]

Two long and suspenseful hours later, both companies reached the foot of Ravelsberg Hill without contacting any more Germans; one of Miller's platoons had cleverly repurposed their communication wires as a hand-to-hand guide trailing back hundreds of feet so the men could more easily follow one another. It was near midnight, very black and moonless, but the formidable hill seemed eerily unoccupied; it was too quiet. The company captains ordered an all-around perimeter defense set up; the men then systematically investigated all the pillboxes in their company sectors. "This careful search was rewarded when, in one pill-box, they found a regimental commander and the reconnaissance party of a German unit," Captain McGregor learned later. "They had been asleep and were surprised to find themselves being made prisoners."[43]

Several more boxes were cleared before first light and by 0800 all of the fortifications had been emptied of slumbering enemy soldiers without a single shot being fired. A detail of four Germans approached with the morning meals for their comrades; instead they joined them as prisoners of war and the Americans chose to forego their cold rations and eat the hot meals meant for their opposite numbers instead. Later that morning eight Germans left a nearby chateau and unwittingly turned their vehicles off a roadway under observation by Hess's men. They stopped in full view, got out and started marching toward the bunker that had formerly been occupied by the captured German regimental commander and his party for what was likely their usual morning meeting. Instead, an American rifleman greeted them with a Browning automatic; he opened up and killed two who were officers, and another two who turned out to be recent replacements. A lieutenant colonel and two sergeants were taken prisoner. The other two managed to escape.

The previous night had been agonizing for Lieutenant Colonel Learnard. Captain Miller had only made a brief report by radio when the long line of Americans got across the big road and were approaching the Ravelsberg. Colonel Smith had even come over to Learnard's CP in Verlautenheide in the middle of the night seeking more updates; there were none. Finally, at first light Learnard ordered Captain Brown to send a patrol over to the Ravelsberg to investigate; when these men returned with the good news that Miller and Hess had been successful in getting their men on the hill, "the weary battalion commander uttered a string of unprintable words. He then joyfully informed an equally weary regimental commander of the success of the mission."[44]

Later that morning, Haaren fell to Captain Folk's Company L. On the Ravelsberg, Captain Hess shifted his men into a position where they would have direct observation over the big road; he was also able to effectively tie in a platoon with Captain Brown's extended line, which by now ran off Crucifix Hill and down to his side of the roadway. Captain Scott-Smith's Company A shifted their positions over to the western slope of the hill on Brown's immediate left. The 18th Infantry now stood shoulder to shoulder over the ground they had been ordered to seize after paying for it with much bloodshed, effectively closing the jaw along the northern flank of the 1st Division salient outside of Aachen.

The noose was tightening. The city was now much closer to being completely cut off and surrounded.

CHAPTER 10

Ultimatum and the First Attacks on Aachen

We coined a slogan—"Knock 'em all down!"

LT. COL. DERRILL M. DANIEL
CO, 2ND BATTALION, 26TH INFANTRY REGIMENT

Although there had been no actual linkup between the 1st and 30th Infantry Divisions, the still-open gap between these forces was under observed fire by both XIX and VII Corps. This and other factors led First Army to proceed with the plan to determine whether the German garrison was willing to surrender. Following a call from General Huebner to the 26th Infantry's Colonel Seitz in the early morning hours of 10 October, Pfc. Kenneth Kading of LaGrange, Illinois, joined with an interpreter, Lt. William Boehme of New York City, and the regiment's S-2, Lt. Cedric A. Lafley of Enosburg Falls, Vermont, who was now carrying the actual surrender ultimatum.

At 1020 hours, the trio departed from the Company F command post into a chilling autumn rain and proceeded down Triererstrasse toward a railroad underpass on the southeastern side of the city. Young, tall Kading, "gulping with nervous excitement," carried the white flag, which was actually a bed sheet.[1] No shots were exchanged. Instead, three soldiers of the 6th Company, 352nd Regiment, emerged from behind one of Aachen's old buildings, waved, and said "Come here" in German. They led the Americans to a pile of scattered wreckage strewn around the underpass and Boehme overheard the German soldiers talking among themselves about what to do with them. They apparently made a decision; a few tense minutes later the Americans were told to give them their handkerchiefs. They were blindfolded, and this time led farther up the street to a bunker.

Here, the surrender party's blindfolds were removed so they could face an officer who told them to state their business. Boehme, in German, told him that his detail wished to give an ultimatum to the military commander of Aachen; the German officer, a lieutenant, obliged and ordered all three blindfolded again. They were then led to what they believed was the German battalion's command post.

This time they were shuffled down a stairway into a basement before their blindfolds were removed; they were presented to two more lieutenants—one named Keller identified himself as the battalion adjutant, and again demanded that the Americans state their business. Lieutenant Lafley stepped forward and handed Keller the surrender ultimatum; the German officer, without reading it, signed and stamped the attached receipt and handed it back to Lafley. Boehme then told Keller in a deliberative tone that their orders obliged them to be certain that the document was delivered to the Aachen commander. Keller got out of his chair, appeared insulted, and said his commander was not available and that he, as adjutant, had suitable authority to accept the ultimatum.

After the two exchanged steely stares, Keller sat back down. As he finally read the ultimatum, Boehme gazed at his Iron Cross, another war decoration, a combat badge, and a Russian campaign ribbon. The room was silent.

> The city of Aachen is now completely surrounded by American forces who are sufficiently equipped with both air power and artillery to destroy the city, if necessary. We shall take the city either by receiving its immediate ultimate surrender or by attacking and destroying it.
>
> While unconditional surrender will require the surrender of all armed bodies, the cessation of all hostile acts of every character, the removal of mines and prepared demolitions, it is not intended to molest the civil population or needlessly sacrifice human lives. But if the city is not promptly and completely surrendered unconditionally, the American Army Ground and Air

Forces will proceed ruthlessly with an air and artillery bombardment to reduce it to submission.

In other words, there is no middle course. You will either unconditionally surrender the city with everything now in it, thus avoiding needless loss of German blood and property, or you may refuse and await its complete destruction. The choice and responsibility are yours.

Your answer must be delivered within 24 hours at the location specified by the bearer of this paper.[2]

Keller, expressionless, made no comment when he finished reading; instead he just stood up. Boehme told him that accepting the terms meant sending a representative under a flag of truce to the railway station; his forces would then pass through the line in groups of fifty after weapons had been surrendered. Their business concluded, cigarettes were then exchanged, an odd but old soldierly tradition in such circumstances. The three German guides who first brought the Americans to the command post were quickly summoned, and Keller made out a pass permitting the party to return to their own lines. Boehme overheard him cryptically state, "They are evidently unit commanders,"[3] prompting Keller to dismiss them with a quick salute. Lafley, Boehme, and Kading returned it, and their blindfolds were put on again before they were led up the stairs and out of the building. On the way back, their German escorts stopped briefly beside some of their comrades, took a nip apiece from a bottle of liquor that was being passed around, but did not offer the same to the Americans who had just shared their cigarettes with them.

Their blindfolds were removed when they got back to the railroad underpass. At 1157 hours the trio finally walked back into the Company F command post, which was crowded with war correspondents full of questions. One later wrote, "They looked neither elated nor depressed as they told newsman what had happened."[4]

Unknown to the Americans, Keller had taken immediate steps to inform *Oberstleutnant* Leyherr, the Aachen battle commander, of the ultimatum. Stamped 1050 hours on 10 October, his message read: "The battalion is enclosing two documents from the Commander of the American

Army, which were delivered to this CP by two officers and one sergeant
[*sic*] as plenipotentiaries."[5]

Leyherr, the son-in-law of former Hitler chief of staff *Generaloberst*
Franz Hadler, responded in his own hand on the back of Keller's message
a little less than an hour later: "Any new plenipotentiary is to be told
through an officer that a capitulation is out of the question. This statement is to be given verbally only."

Undoubtedly disconcerting to the defiant Leyherr, the U.S. Army
had taken every possible step to ensure that the terms of the ultimatum
would get the widest possible exposure. Two public address systems
broadcasted the terms to his front-line troops. The Luxembourg radio
channels were used to communicate the conditions of surrender directly
to the Aachen people; German stations answered by unofficially reporting that the ultimatum had been rejected. American propaganda shells
were fired into the city; over two hundred 105mm rounds encasing thousands of copies gave the details. Thousands more were dropped from
Allied aircraft. All read:

TO THE GERMAN TROOPS AND PEOPLE OF AACHEN!

Aachen is encircled. American troops surround the city. The
German command cannot relieve you.

The time has come for an honorable surrender. We Americans do not wage war on innocent civilians. Already many Aacheners are living peacefully in areas we occupy. But if the military
and party leaders insist on further sacrifice we have no course
but to destroy your city which has already suffered so much.

There is no time to lose. On our airfields bombers are waiting
for the final order to take off. Our artillery surrounding the city
is ready to fire. Our troops are alerted for the final advance.

Act quickly. Go now to those responsible and make them
stop useless bloodshed and destruction. The time has come for
your civilian leaders, for you to speak boldly. Tomorrow—may
be too late.

There is only one choice—honorable and immediate surrender, or complete destruction.

The American Commander[6]

Two prisoners were taken from the 1043rd Battalion by the 1106th Engineer Group that afternoon; they said that they had heard the terms of the ultimatum from the public address systems and had decided to give up at once. The commander of a company holding an isolated sector in northwest Aachen notified the Americans that "he was not sure what the remainder of the garrison was going to do, but he was ready to quit," a correspondent reported back to his stateside paper.[7]

But there was little hope that the warnings would be heeded in larger numbers. Some white flags started appearing in parts of the city that still housed nervous civilians, but detachments of German soldiers called them traitors and forced these Aachen citizens to take them down. "Indications were clear that the ultimatum would be refused, and that the offer to remove the civilians would also be turned down," Headquarters 26th Infantry activity reports noted that day.[8] A war correspondent was even more sanguine in a dispatch sent to New York. "It is expected the Germans will be ordered to fight to the last in the ruins of Aachen. Goebbels will try to make Aachen the rallying cry, similar to Dunkirk for the British, and Pearl Harbor for the United States. The siege is likely to be long and bloody, paralleling Stalingrad."[9]

Hitler apparently agreed, as a change in command for Aachen was ordered that very day for the expected grueling fight ahead. *Oberst* Gerhard Wilck, a twenty-eight-year veteran of the German army, many of those years spent commanding infantry units, would take charge. Wilck was a fighter, a Prussian; many thought Leyherr's relief was to spare his family from the legacy of having lost the first major German city in the war if Aachen fell. LXXXI Corps' *General der Infanterie* Köchling was more direct in affirming this rumor. "Purely political reasons were decisive for this," he explained about Leyherr's relief after the war. "But Colonel Wilck surely was the firmer and more determined personality."[10] Wilck, who certainly knew he was being handed "the dirty end of the stick," was sworn in on the afternoon of 12 October by his old friend, *General der Panzertruppen* Brandenberger "in the name of the Fuehrer [*sic*] as commandant of the fortress Aachen, and told to hold the city to the last man."[11] A later account written by author Samuel W. Mitcham describes this meeting in stark terms:

It was a formal declaration that he would not surrender Aachen; if he violated this oath, the Fuehrer [*sic*] was empowered to

execute his family. Both officers knew Wilck dearly loved his
wife and children; both knew that Aachen would be defended to
the utmost. After he affixed his signature, Wilck noticed that
Brandenberger had tears in his eyes.[12]

Wilck would need more than Brandenberger's empathy and his firm
style of command to defend Aachen. In General Huebner's most recent
intelligence estimate, his G-2, Lt. Col. Robert F. Evans, had identified the
German battalions that were penned up in the city: two battalions of the
689th Regiment; nine hundred to a thousand men of the 352nd Regiment, including two platoons of 120mm mortars, each with just four
guns; about five hundred soldiers from the DIENDL Battle Group, made
up of "odds and ends from other units"; another five hundred in the XIX
German Air Force Battalion, a *Luftwaffe* unit converted to infantry soldiers; the 1043rd Battalion, now less two prisoners of war; and the 246th
Field Artillery Battalion.[13] All had been suffering from heavy attrition.
Captured soldiers from the recently formed DIENDL Battle Group were
unable to remember what company they were in when they were interrogated. It was estimated that the units in Aachen had been cobbled
together from as many as fifty-two different companies, but their total
strength was no more than four thousand to five thousand men.

Armored support was even weaker; Wilck would inherit as few as
five Mark IV tanks. His inner-city defenses beyond this included six
horse-drawn 105mm howitzers, another six 75mm pieces, and only a
half dozen 150mm guns. He would have other artillery support, but only
from outside of Aachen if communications remained intact.

With the 18th Infantry overlooking the roadway into Aachen, the
Germans could do little to get reinforcements into the city. Adjustments
were necessary, really the only option at this point. *Oberst* Engel was
ordered to move his 12th Infantry Division's boundary westward beyond
Verlautenheide and closer to the big road. But even he was realistic. "The
envelopment of Aachen was taking its course. If no stronger forces could
be brought up to break through the ring of encirclement, Aachen would
be lost."[14]

Supreme Command West had anticipated this. Back on 7 October,
the 116th Panzer Division was ordered back to the Aachen front from its
position near the Arnheim bridgehead; another hysterical Führer order
was the basis for this.[15] The 3rd Panzer Grenadier Division had also been

given orders by this time to move to Jurlich from Metz in northeast France. Both divisions would come under the command of 1 SS Panzer Corps with the mission to "rectify the situation around Aachen by eliminating the entire penetration north of the city."[16] Within days, VII Corps would identify four new battalions of the 3rd Panzer Grenadier Division and the entire 116th Panzer Division in the sector opposite to the 18th Infantry Regiment along the wide expanse of Colonel Smith's positions on the hills and ridges north of Aachen.

Two battalions of the 1st Engineer Assault Regiment had already hit Lieutenant Colonel Williamson's lines in Verlautenheide that very morning. The first attack came at 0200, hours before the surrender ultimatum was delivered in Aachen. Hostile artillery fire escorted two enemy companies as they departed from a draw to lunge for the northern approaches into the village. The fist of this attack was in squad strength; the Germans quickly got into the courtyard that bordered most of the houses where Company E's men were trying to get some sleep. Machine guns and mortars joined with long lances of TD fire thwarted the attack. These volleys were directed into the draw in order to stop any renewed enemy effort with greater muscle. It worked. Coffman later said, "They never really made a full attack; instead they withdrew leaving just a few snipers in the houses."[17]

The Germans came closer to overrunning Captain Koenig's Company F command post that morning.[18] Another artillery strike preceded this effort at 0400; the Germans hit hard between Koenig's right flank and the left flank of Jeffrey's Company G and closed to within 40 yards of Koenig's CP. This was as far as they got. The attack was over by 0830, but both companies had to spend the rest of the day simply getting reorganized. Hostile artillery never let up, making evacuation of the wounded to Eilendorf very risky; the Americans at least had the satisfaction of seeing German medics spending most of the day removing their dead and wounded. Three U.S. soldiers had been killed; twelve others were unaccounted for and presumed captured. The casualties of the 1st Engineer Assault Regiment were uncertain, but the 2nd Battalion took two of their officers and seventy-five enlisted men as prisoners.

Captain Brown's Company C kept busy by strengthening their defenses along the ridge leading down to the big road; Brown even ordered roadblocks on the roadway itself. His men were not attacked.

Peckham's 3rd Battalion also had a productive day. Captain Folk's Company L men were able to mop up the northern outskirts of Haaren with little trouble and they even extended their flank toward Verlautenheide. Captain Russell also sent a reinforced platoon of his Company K with tank destroyers down to the rail line on the southern edge of Haaren, where they captured six officers and eighty-three enlisted men. These gains proved disheartening to *Oberst* Engel; his 12th Infantry Division reported that Lieutenant Colonel Peckham's real estate grab "was particularly unpleasant—the fact that the enemy gained more ground in Haaren and crossed the railroad bend to the south."[19] This was justified; if Brown's roadblocks didn't stop resupply efforts for Aachen, Peckham's companies now could.

Colonel Seitz's 26th Infantry Regiment used the rest of 10 October to prepare for the anticipated strike on Aachen itself. The general plan called for a two-pronged attack with Lieutenant Colonel Corley's 3rd Battalion first working through the dense factory district between Aachen and Haaren. Farwick Park was then Corley's first objective; St. Elizabeth's Church dominated one edge of the park; a strip of older homes bordered the southwest side of the hill along Monheims Allee and odd-shaped houses squared off the northwest blocks.

Farwick Park had been gouged out over the years; it had once been filled with Aacheners who during more pleasant times enjoyed its tennis courts, gardens, walks, spas, and even an artificial lake. Two prominent buildings stood above the scrubby underbrush on the forward slope of the hill: the luxurious five-story Palast Hotel Quellenhof, which would become the command post for *Oberst* Wilck when he entered Aachen, and the Kurhaus, designed by famous Aachen architect Jakob Couven and built in the late 1800s for spa guests; in better days patrons reveled in its medicinal 70-degree waters. The park and its gardens overlooked the magnificent Aachen Cathedral, Charlemagne's final resting place. The Americans would come to call the park Observatory Hill because of a four-story tower on the very top of the hill mass; it housed hostile artillery observers.

Corley's second objective was to reduce prominent Salvatorberg, where Charlemagne's son Ludwig had first built a chapel for the dead before a Benedictine monastery was founded in CE 996; now there was an air raid shelter built into the slope of the hill for Aachen's overflowing twentieth-century citizenry to survive the upcoming American offensive.

Corley's last objective was to wrestle control of the 264-meter-high Lousberg, which overlooked the city center to the south and Soers to the north. A quarry on the hill was first cut in Neolithic times, thousands of years before the Romans came to Aachen. Local superstition had it that the Lousberg was created by the devil himself from huge amounts of sand he brought from the North Sea after he was tricked into believing he would receive the soul of the first living creature when the great Aachen Cathedral was finished. According to lore, the first soul belonged to a wolf, so the devil erected Lousberg in disgust. But it was now Lieutenant Colonel Corley's turn to establish his battalion's own curse on the Germans populating the Lousberg.

Lieutenant Colonel Daniel would have the honor of commanding his 2nd Battalion's attack into the center of the ancient imperial city; his flank would be approximately 200 yards south of Corley's, roughly equivalent to a large Aachen street block. His men would move in an east-to-west direction along bomb-pocked, debris-filled roads and blasted-out buildings, through the core of the ancient city, all the way to its western edge; his soldiers would experience urban warfare for the first time, tactics for which were not even in Army field manuals. Two battalions of the 1106th Engineer Combat Group would hold the perimeter on the southern side of the city while Daniel's companies crossed its front and planted their own legacy into Aachen's already deep historical roots.

The planned air and artillery strikes would first pound the perimeter and targeted centers of Aachen over a two-day period, commencing when the ultimatum expired. The city had already been reduced to rubble in many locations by earlier Allied strikes so no wide area bombardment was planned before the new attack; a steady use of dive bombers on preselected targets, irregularly spaced, would be made instead. Artillery fires would follow and be used to inflict as many casualties as possible, soften up enemy defenses, and cover the opening performance of American forces during the upcoming Aachen drama. Targets had been carefully selected.[20] Corley's forces would benefit from these strikes—intended to kill German soldiers and diminish their overall fighting ability as a unit—

when a gas works, a soap factory, a machine factory, a wagon factory, an electrical machinery shop, an iron factory, a car factory, a boiler factory, and even a winery in the factory area were bombed and blasted. The quarry atop Lousberg was in the air drop zone, as was the observation tower in Farwick Park; brickyards, bus stations, railroad stations, post offices, and even streets into the city on its southern and western perimeters would also be hit to block reinforcements from entering Aachen. Hospitals and other known medical facilities were not to be targeted.

The 2nd Battalion's Lieutenant Colonel Daniel explained how his men would then choreograph their opening act:

> The general plan was to use artillery and mortar fire across our immediate front to isolate the area, thus preventing the Germans from entering (or for that matter from leaving), and then to use direct fire from tanks, tank destroyers, anti-tank and machineguns to pin down the defenders and chase them into cellars, and then move in with bayonets and hand grenades to destroy or capture them.
>
> We continually pressed the necessity for keeping up a continuous stream of fire with all available weapons. We coined a slogan, "Knock 'em all down," which became the battle cry because the soldiers came to realize that the defenders could hardly deliver accurate fire with buildings falling about their ears. We had practiced this knocking down technique with marked success by making platoon raids on houses known to be occupied by the enemy.[21]

During his planning, Daniel anticipated several problems and found creative solutions for them. First, he required large amounts of ammunition. Coordination and control between units fighting in the streets would be problematic. This would be exacerbated by the stubborn fact that his front would be some 2,000 yards in dense, populated urban terrain, nearly twice the frontage prescribed by Army doctrine at the time. He had to decide what to do with civilians, as well as figure out how to effectively use the tanks and TDs in claustrophobic city streets without risk of loss to enemy antitank weapons. The Army Field Manual provided little assistance; Daniel had to use creativity.

We established a battalion ammunition dump, stocked with all types of ammunition for all of our weapons in the battalion and attached units. It was planned to keep this dump moving so that all units would always have an ample supply immediately at hand. Second, we worked out a "measles system" whereby all street intersections and important buildings were numbered and the number circled on a map so that it would be easy to report exact locations accurately and quickly. In addition, constant positive liaison and contact between units was stressed.[22]

Pragmatism governed how to handle the Aachen citizenry:

If they were not evacuated as we overran the abodes, the chances for German soldiers to masquerade as civilians behind our lines would be great. We decided, therefore, that the way to clean out an enemy city was to clear everyone, civilians and soldiers, from each building before passing to the next. We planned to search every room, every closet, every cellar, even manholes in the streets, to be absolutely certain that no German was left behind our front lines. We knew this would be a slow process, but the only alternative was to be subjected to sniping from our rear.

To tackle the problems for his tanks and TDs during the upcoming street fighting, Daniel and his staff planned to initially place them on side streets so their turrets and machine guns could poke around corners, firing all their weaponry to escort the infantry forward. Then, as soon as another street was cleared, his foot soldiers would protect the tanks by first destroying any German antitank emplacements or guns on a perpendicular street. Up would come the tanks and TDs and they would repeat the process, block by block; these combined tactics would essentially have the infantry protecting the armor from *Panzerfausts* while their fellow soldiers in their thick-plated vehicles rudely engaged any strongpoints that tried to hold them up.

All of Daniel's rifle companies would be used in the assault. Lt. Beasoe B. Walker's Company G would be on the left and Company E, commanded by Oklahoman Capt. Ozell L. Smoot, owned the center; Capt. Rowland A. Weeks's Company F would attack to the right. Each company was organized as a small task force; two tanks and a pair of TDs would accompany each of the rifle companies. Capt. Gilbert H. Fuller of Ludlow, Vermont, would split his heavy weapons Company D; the two 50mm machine-gun platoons would join the flank companies, and an 81mm mortar section would be attached to each company with embedded observers maintaining the necessary coordination with the company commanders for targeting Germans. Three squads of engineers equipped with flamethrowers and dynamite charges were also assigned to the companies.

On 11 October the skies cleared; the slanting rain and dreary clouds of the day before gave way to midmorning sunshine, but another front was forecasted to bring more showers later in the afternoon. No word about the ultimatum filtered into the company CPs. Heavy mortar and intermittent artillery fire hit Corley's 3rd Battalion before daybreak. Allied planes dropped more leaflets over the city an hour after first light, giving *Oberst* Wilck's forces another chance to give up. A few did. At about 1000 hours, twenty Germans came through Lieutenant Colonel Corley's outpost perimeter along the Aachen-Haaren rail line and surrendered to the first Americans they saw. Others attempted to do the same; a spokesman for the deserters said many more had followed them, but were driven back by officers who threatened to shoot anyone else who tried to cross the tracks. In some cases, they did. Americans witnessed German officers actually firing on their own soldiers who surrendered to Weeks's Company F, but most of the enemy soldiers made it to the POW cage.

The promised assault on the city started with a working over by fighter bombers at noon, within an hour after the expiration of the ultimatum. DIVARTY first marked targets with red smoke, then P-47 Thunderbolts made one run each on Aachen. The P-47s, with their supercharged 2,000-horsepower Pratt & Whitney R-2800 engines roared in, bled off their 325 knots of airspeed, and then dove like stones and dropped either two 1,000-pound bombs, or fired ten rockets, depending on their targets. One flight dove in and laid a pattern of explosives on Farwick Park. To the men on the ground, it looked like the fighters started at one end of a street and bombed it one building at a time; then after a short interval another would come in and start on the next street. "It was so quiet in those strange lulls," wrote correspondent Don Whitehead. "You could hear the birds singing and the wind singing through the trees. There was not even the sound of a rifle shot. At our feet a black cat with white stockings lay in the straw and purred."[23]

Twin-boom P-38s, powered by twin Allison in-line 1,150-horse-power engines came in next and strafed the city; in front of their pilots' sight lines in the canopies at the leading edge of the plane between their contoured fuselages, four .50-caliber machine guns and a 20mm cannon delivered fires during long slanting runs on their objectives. Some of the fighters also dropped 2,000-pound payloads of deadly bombs from barely visible bays beneath their wings. "When their bombs were dropped they climbed back steeply, circled and then came back down again and strafed the enemy," remembered Whitehead. "They were not even challenged, and I did not see a single burst of ack-ack thrown against them from inside or outside Aachen."[24]

Before their missions were over, some 300 fighter bombers unloaded 62 tons of bombs. Observers indicated that all had hit their targets as marked. Twelve battalions of VII Corps and 1st Division artillery then poured 4,800 rounds, nearly 170 short tons of explosive, into the city starting at 1555 hours. Most of the barrages were directed into the center of Aachen, as well as its southeastern and eastern edges to wreak havoc and more destruction ahead of the infantry strike.

But there were unintended consequences, as the men on the ground were to soon discover. The fire and damage from the bombing and artillery created dust, haze, smoke, and frightening psychological damage to ordinary Aacheners, yet it also heaped rubble into piles that would be used by the U.S. soldiers' opposite numbers to defend their positions. Lieutenant Colonel Corley even sent patrols out after the artillery shelling stopped to assess its effect in the factory district; his men determined that the German defenses "had not been too greatly impaired."[25]

Regiment also warned Corley at the time not to push more aggressive patrolling because his battalion could be needed to help beat back a large-scale enemy thrust that had started up across the 18th Infantry's entire front lines.

The 12th Infantry Division's mission that day was to probe the regiment's newly won positions on the Ravelsberg, recapture Crucifix Hill, throw the Americans out of Verlautenheide, retake the bunkers north of Quinx, and finally sweep into the northern section of Haaren and reinforce the few Germans that were still holding out in houses here. The attacks were conducted by the 1st Assault Engineer Regiment, the 27 Fusilier Regiment, and the newly activated Sturm Pioneer Regiment 1.

Every unit eventually failed in achieving its mission; *Oberst* Engel explained why:

> In a dashing attack, the Haarener Steinkreus [Crucifix Hill] and the pillboxes located on the heights were recaptured, but things looked all the worse with the left battalion of the Sturm Pioneer Regiment 1 [with] respect [to] the attack diverted at Haaren-Verlautenheide. This battalion failed. Over-hasty organization, poor cooperation between officers and men, and the fact that they lacked their own heavy weapons all made themselves seriously felt. The gap to the houses in Haaren was closed, but the battalion itself lost it again, and by evening was back in its initial positions and no longer fit for combat.
>
> The 27 Fuesiliers [*sic*]held out heroically against fierce American counterattacks carried forward with a vast expenditure of ammunition in Verlautenheide . . . the Haarener Steinkraus itself; i.e., the summit, was recaptured by the Americans during the evening.[26]

Nor were Engel's efforts any more successful against the Americans holding onto the Ravelsberg. Just before dark, two enemy tanks, accompanied by twenty grenadiers, attacked Captain Miller's and Captain Hess's positions from the southern edge of Würselen, but the tanks made a hasty departure when artillery fire came down on them; four of the grenadiers were killed in the melee, another was captured, with the rest retreating in a rush under the protective cover of their armored vehicles' machine guns. "They were stopped cold, with no ground lost," the 1st Battalion's after-action report noted.[27]

Lieutenant Colonel Peckham also earned his pay that afternoon. Earlier in the morning, he had moved the other two Company K platoons into Haaren; along with Captain Folk's Company L, the attack by the 27 Fusilier Regiment was cut off. Their men in two pillboxes just outside of Haaren were the first to cave and surrender; after Russell's men hustled down to the railroad tracks, they took more prisoners, set up roadblocks, and removed mines from the roadways. They also stopped two enemy motorcycle crews escorting three horse-drawn wagons with rations into Aachen. The entire roadway from Haaren up to Verlautenheide was reopened by dark; antitank guns and tanks were moved up to offer more protection. Peckham moved his CP into Haaren. The two companies promised to him by a liaison officer from Lieutenant Colonel Corley's 3rd Battalion who had come over to the new CP to coordinate the move learned they were not needed. At 2100 hours Corley instead ordered renewed patrolling into the factory district.

By this time a grim *Oberst* Wilck had passed by the red brocade wall hangings and the grand gilt frescos on the pillars supporting the entryway into the Palast Hotel Quellenhof lobby and settled into his command post on a lower level. Before his arrival he had attempted to convince *Generalfeldmarschall* Model to simply surrender Aachen, or at the very least to allow him to fight his way out of the city; Model vigorously turned down both requests. Now his adjutant, a veteran from earlier fighting in North Africa, told him about his opponent in Aachen; the 1st Division was going to be a "tough nut" as they are "probably the best division in the American army," he said.[28] Wilck would begin to see this for himself the very next day.

Two flight groups of P-47s and one group of P-38s dropped another 5,000 shells and 99 tons of steel bombs, hammering Aachen again on the cloudy morning of 12 October. Then, at 1100 hours, Corley's 3rd Battalion opened the 26th Infantry's preliminary assault by heading for the foundry and rolling mills in the factory district.[29] Capt. Lucien L. Corwell of Marshall, Kentucky, commander of Company K, led the battalion down Julicherstrasse with his platoons in columns. Lt. Walter F. Nechey's Company M followed, with his heavy machine gunners prepared to set up and fire as the rifle companies needed them. Corley's command group was right behind these men. Capt. Seth S. Botts, a University of Kentucky ROTC graduate, with his Company I tanks and TDs, made up the rear guard.

Corwell had planned to take his Company K down a side street to attack the foundry, but as soon as the men began to make their turn here two enemy machine guns hidden behind wire barricades suddenly opened fire; a tank was called forward, and twelve rounds of 75mm fire from the Sherman knocked down both emplacements. Captain Corwell and his soldiers started down the street only to find themselves confronted by sturdy foundry walls, reinforced with sheets of steel normally used to make German tank parts; direct cannon fire was now useless. Corwell had no choice but to deploy his men into the punishing enemy fire, where they first had to clear paths through barricades and obstacles before they could even storm the buildings in the foundry.

By this time Lieutenant Colonel Corley had made the decision to shift Botts's Company I and Lieutenant Nechey's heavy weapons company to the right of Company K; he assigned these men to nearby streets and other buildings so that the battalion could eventually link up at the local railroad station. Through the afternoon, the German defenders launched numerous counterattacks, most directed at Corwell's men in the foundry. Vigorous hand-to-hand fighting and loud, rapid small-arms fire answered these savage assaults as the skirmishes raged on. When an entrance to a building was finally forced and the ground floor secured, the Germans had to be pried out of the cellars with hand grenades and mortars. Tunnels between buildings were discovered; these also had to be cleared. Many desperate Germans found temporary refuge in the patchwork of stinking sewer pipes that connected to the different buildings. In the prolonged bloody fighting, the Americans prevailed; few Germans wanted to become prisoners. Most of the defenders chose to hold their posts to the end. Corwell's riflemen or Nechey's machine gunners shot the ones who tried to run.

At 1345 hours Companies K and I made contact near the railroad station; a little over an hour later Lieutenant Colonel Corley reported to the regiment's S-3, Maj. Henry N. Clisson, and told him that the factory area had been cleared. Total prisoners taken reached 125; American casualties were amazingly low with just one man killed and eleven wounded, but nine others were missing and likely captured.[30] Later that evening, Company C was released from its assignment with the 3rd Armored Division in Stolberg, by which time it "looked like a section of Pittsburgh planked down with slag heaps."[31] These men took over positions held by Company L, commanded by Capt. William F. Chaplin, a twenty-seven-year-old native of Altoona, Pennsylvania, permitting his soldiers to join up with the rest of the 3rd Battalion that night.

While this move was taking place, Lieutenant Colonel Daniel was assembled with all of his company commanders and their platoon leaders. The time had arrived for a last-minute review of the 2nd Battalion's plan of attack for the next morning; they still needed to work out the details. Exchanges to determine friend from foe were given; the password would be "Texas," with the proper reply, if friendly, "Star." Jeeps and aid trucks had been getting flat tires faster than they could be fixed, so to facilitate medical evacuations Daniel had obtained some fully tracked Studebaker-built M29 cargo carriers; the soldiers called them "weasels." But the biggest concern everyone shared was just how the tanks and TDs would fare when they tried to get over the railroad embankment. "We didn't want to be without these weapons any longer than necessary," Daniel explained that night.[32]

This concern was justified. The railway tracks were at different elevations around Aachen, but on Daniel's immediate front they were 30 feet high to his left, and about 15 feet on his right. The armored vehicles needed a spot where they could get over the tracks, otherwise the only means of ingress would be through the debris-filled underpass at the Rothe Erde railway station; even here, any breakthrough would be delayed while engineers cleared the obstructions. All agreed this was not an acceptable risk, so Daniel made a decision. He sent the tank platoon leader out with a strong patrol, and they returned around midnight with word that they had found a spot where the three tanks would not get bogged down in the mud, and still be able to get up enough speed to climb over the embankment and down the other side. The far side of the bank was indeed steep; the tank platoon leader even wisecracked about expecting to reach enough speed while climbing up the embankment so the 35-ton tanks could somersault and land upright if they had to. This undoubtedly lightened the mood in the CP, but Daniel decided two tanks would be plenty under the circumstances; others would go in when the underpass was cleared out. They continued going over last-minute details well into the night.

Outside of Aachen, the Germans again focused on the Ravelsberg during 12 October. At about 0800, twelve of their tanks came down the Aachen-Würselen road and turned into the woods on the southeast corner of the hill. More armored vehicles arrived during the day. Company B's Captain Miller made frequent calls for artillery fire, but results could

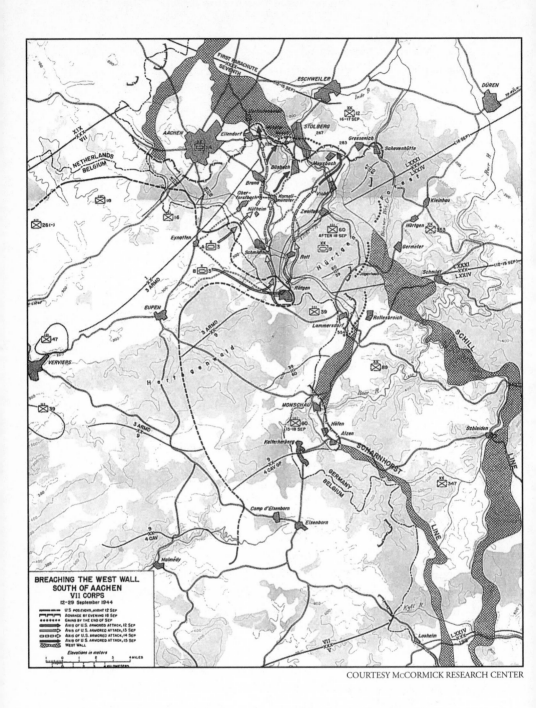

BREACHING THE WEST WALL
SOUTH OF AACHEN
VII CORPS
12–29 September 1944

	U.S. POSITIONS, NIGHT 12 SEP
	ADVANCE BY EVENING 16 SEP
	GAINS BY THE END OF SEP
	AXIS OF U.S. ARMORED ATTACK, 12 SEP
	AXIS OF U.S. ARMORED ATTACK, 13 SEP
	AXIS OF U.S. ARMORED ATTACK, 14 SEP
	AXIS OF U.S. ARMORED ATTACK, 15 SEP
	WEST WALL

Elevations in meters

0   1   2   3   4 MILES
0   1   2   3   4 KILOMETERS

not be observed because more and more tanks were able to find cover under the trees; air support requests were answered, but the planes arrived too late to spot any of the enemy tanks. By afternoon, hostile artillery fire was adding to the growing tension, and just before dark about a hundred Germans were observed advancing from the woods, well extended in columns of twos. This time the Americans unleashed their more mobile "goon guns," 4.2-inch chemical mortars with 25-pound heavy explosive shells and a payload-on-target rate far faster than the 105mm artillery shells had been providing; they quickly broke up the attack. The rest of the night was quiet, interrupted by only occasional enemy mortar fire and a call Captain Miller received from Lieutenant Colonel Learnard. He wanted Miller to know that division had reported there was now a possibility he was going to be hit by the 116th Panzer Division.

This was good intelligence, but on the night of 12–13 October the 116th Panzer Division was ordered to release only Combat Group Rink for the Aachen fight; the division itself was entangled in bitter fighting near Birk. Battalion Rink was named for its commander, high-spirited *Obersturmführer* Herbert Rink; he would not get into Aachen with his men for another two nights. "The presence of the division and Combat Group Rink created some worry in the heads of the American leaders," noted the 116th Panzer Division's postwar historian, to which he added quite correctly, "Nevertheless, the commanders insisted on continuing the attack on Aachen."[33]

H-hour for Colonel Seitz's 26th Infantry on 13 October was delayed one hour to 0930 to accommodate final coordination for artillery support and to wait out yet another air strike. The weather had improved; it was clear but much colder than it had been for the past several days. Flight groups appeared in the brilliant sunshine just ahead of 0900 and began dropping what would become 11.5 tons of bombs on Aachen, this time avoiding the 500 yards of frontage by the railroad embankment that Daniel's forces would use as their avenue of advance into the city. When it became the artillery's turn, three battalions of light, medium, and heavy guns bracketed on the 400 yards closer to the 2nd Battalion's line of departure. Captain Fuller's 81mm mortar sections launched their explosives into the nearest 100 yards at the same time. Then at exactly 0930 the men of Companies E and F heaved about 1,000 hand grenades over the bank, removing any doubt in the minds of German soldiers in the 6th, 8th and 14th Companies of the 352nd Regiment that American infantry would be next.[34]

Indeed they were. The men of Captain Weeks's Company F scrambled over the top of the embankment down into the city where they quickly spread out along Stolbergerstrasse, and headed for a section of block houses where fifteen stunned Germans of the 6th Company were taken prisoner. Avoiding exposure on the open street, Weeks's platoons then started moving through an orchard off to the right side of the roadway. They experienced little return fire, but when the 3rd Platoon emerged from this cover, the men started receiving heavy machine-gun fire from the direction of Hohenzollern Platz. It was fortunate the two tanks that had concerned the commanders the previous night had by this time been able to negotiate the steep descent into the city; the 3rd Platoon scout on point was killed by the enemy fire, but a tank was now close enough to open up on the German machine-gun location, killing its gunner and ammo bearers. By 1115 hours Company F was close to the old limestone mausoleum at the Karhol Friedhof cemetery, the site of Catholic graves dating back to the early 1800s.[35] The cemetery was located at a bend where Stolbergerstrasse came into Adalbertstein Weg at St. Josefs Platz, where the great gothic church here would be casting shadows over bullet-pocked grave markers bruised by German and American gunfire in the fighting ahead.

Captain Smoot's Company E had cleared the buildings east of Adalbertstein Weg by this time; the process had been painfully slow, but methodical. The combined tank/infantry tactics anticipated during the planning for the attack paid off; the accompanying tank used delayed-fuse heavy explosive shells, allowing time for their entry through windows, doors, and even lighter outside walls before exploding. The armored vehicle's personnel then joined with Smoot's heavy machine-gun crews and riddled snipers in windows, Germans on rooftops—anything in the way of the infantry. Concussion grenades often convinced their opposite numbers to give up. But they had expended a tremendous amount of ammunition through the morning, and Captain Smoot had to temporarily suspend his attack while more ammo was sent up; Lt. Ladimer F. Jelnick's A&P platoon, consistent with Daniel's planning, delivered the necessary loads shortly after noon.

Still, not all had gone according to plan. A disturbing announcement was made by the BBC before Lieutenant Colonel Corley's 3rd Battalion jumped off from the factory district; it was first overheard on a radio station at the division CP a little after 0900. It stated: "Strong U.S. patrols were in the factory area and were meeting stiff resistance."[36] The BBC report should not have revealed U.S. troop locations, even though the local Germans opposing the Americans certainly knew they were there. An intelligence officer on General Huebner's staff also knew he had the basis for a "serious accusation," but he wanted "something to back it up first." This concern had merit. The possible entry of enemy reinforcements through the factory district weighed heavily on the minds of the commanders, both in the CP and on the ground. Plans to protect the area were quickly put in place, but it would be hours before a composite unit from Colonel Smith's 18th Infantry could be put together and rushed down from Haaren to fill the gap.

By this time Lieutenant Colonel Corley's forces were already pushing west into an area of congested apartment buildings. Captain Botts's Company I, first advancing along the railroad tracks out of the factory district, was soon clearing the structures to the north. One of his platoons split off at a bend in the line and headed toward Gruner Weg; the rest of the company veered south onto Lombardenstrasse. Stiff resistance started interfering soon afterward and shell fire began raining in from what appeared to be an artillery piece on Observatory Hill, but the German aim was off; five to six of their own were wounded by what was supposed to be friendly fire. Thirty others from the 6th Company of the 352nd Regiment were taken prisoner.[37]

Captain Corwell's Company K at the time was going down Julicherstrasse intent upon making a turn onto Thomashofstrasse, but a 20mm antiaircraft gun firing down Josef von Gorres Strasse slowed the men. Then a German using his *Panzerfaust* managed to hit both of the tanks accompanying Corwell's lead squad; one immediately erupted in flames. The shocked tankers in the other were evacuated by Texas native Alvin R. Wise, the sergeant leading the squad.[38] Wise returned to the tank while under hostile enemy fire, mounted it again, and made his way to the machine gun; now he fired through the holes that had been blasted into the nearby houses before the tank was set on fire. While Sergeant Wise was emptying this gun, Privates Brown and Gafford used its noisy and lethal cover to rush up and join him; they emptied the tank of its burning equipment. Soon Wise was out of ammunition, so he dismounted, grabbed a light machine gun and this time remained in an open position while continuing to neutralize the enemy fire. Incredibly, Brown and Stafford were able to grind the tank back to the relative safety of Julicherstrasse while Sergeant Wise again covered them. Neither had ever been in a tank before; they had no way of knowing how to start it, or operate it, but somehow they did both.

Company L was moving down Julicherstrasse at the time with the mission to clear out the apartment buildings southward toward Talstrasse, and then along Peliserkerstrasse. This street overlooked the Karhol Friedhof cemetery and was the boundary between the 2nd and 3rd Battalions on 13 October. Chaplin had first moved all three of his platoons out abreast, but there was too much fire coming down Julicherstrasse so they had to split up. One platoon went after the pillboxes in their paths; another went around the back of the apartment buildings that all seemed to butt up against one another, and got over their walls to attack. The third platoon raced through holes that had been blasted by the armor in the front of the houses. By noon, three pillboxes near Blucher Platz had been reduced and seven prisoners, including the commanding officer of the 8th Company, 352nd Regiment, were taken.

During the noon hour, the Americans made several adjustments and tackled various problems. Calls from both battalions came in requesting more ammunition. The rail underpass at the Rothe Erde station still needed to be cleared and more armored vehicles were desperately required in the city. Prisoners had been flowing into the regiment's POW cage all morning, but the real problem was the numerous civilians seeking refuge from the attacks. Many had described conditions inside the shelters: They leaked badly and some were submerged in a foot of water; no windows or ventilation made for terrible problems; plumbing was essentially nonexistent; sanitary facilities were limited; the stench was sickening. German soldiers who had deserted their units were masquerading as civilians; many of obvious military age wore ill-fitting clothing that made them instantly suspicious. Lieutenant Colonel Corley's forces were running into enemy troops of higher caliber than they expected. The concealed artillery pieces on Observatory Hill needed to be silenced. The BBC was still reporting Corley's movements, prompting one intelligence officer upon learning from prisoners that their commanders had no way of communicating to quip, "The BBC was taking care of that for them."[39]

Then at 1250 hours a report came into Daniel's CP telling him that Captain Weeks's Company F had run into real trouble. His 2nd Platoon had come under heavy mortar and machine-gun fire from the vicinity of Josef von Gorres Strasse and Stolbergerstrasse; crossfire had taken a toll. Two Americans had been killed and eight wounded, including the platoon sergeant and one of his squad leaders. Their accompanying tank had been knocked out by a *Panzerfaust*. The 1st Platoon was in a fight on the edge of the cemetery, and in a clash here the platoon leader was killed. Then word came that Weeks had been mortally wounded while he was directing a firefight around some tombstones in the cemetery.[40] All hell had broken loose; prisoners revealed that the 7th and 8th Companies of the 352nd Regiment had bolstered their defenses just to the northeast of the cemetery. Adjustments were now mandatory; Company F had actually been stopped.

By this time a plan was evolving to bomb the artillery position behind Observatory Hill. Just before 1400 hours, Lieutenant Colonel Corley was contacted by Major Clisson, who asked if it was safe for planes to come in from the northeast and drop their loads. Corley responded favorably and urged it go off right away, but it took another forty-five minutes before the first plane hit the area and the results were uncertain. Another flight came in after artillery marked the target with red smoke, this time nearly an hour later. Then more flights soared in right behind the first fighters. Clisson, who had stayed in contact with Corley during this time, evinced both of their concerns about the danger of the bombs hitting their own men, so when the air liaison officer contacted regiment and said they could bring in more planes, the S-3 said, "Anything you want; just keep it west of the east edge of that green hill. It's OK to strafe if they come in and break out to the west. That last flight did a good job."[41]

Another round of red smoke, actually remembered by the men on the ground as "lots of smoke," was on its way within the hour. Twelve planes roared in low, making down-the-groove maneuvers so their pilots could get good bursts of machine-gun fire on the hostile artillery position. They pulled up to avoid any ground fire and zigzagged westward to become just distant dots in the sky outside of harm's way; the mission was over in less than fifteen minutes. Botts's Company I was also working its way westward at the time, and enemy mortar and artillery fire began to slacken; the last air mission had been very effective.

At this point Corley wanted to get his companies linked up for the night. Chaplin's Company L men were still on Perliserkerstrasse being held up by Germans who were using increasingly clever ways to survive; they had been working their way through the underground maze of sewage systems, often popping up behind the advancing Americans who had no choice but to double back and drop grenades into the smelly sewers before manhandling covers back over them. This had been very time consuming. Companies I and K finally met up at 1725 hours on Passstrasse next to Farwick Park. Corwell's men halted on the east side of the street, but had outposts on the other side closer to the park; Botts got his forces completely across Passstrasse. Chaplin's men had no choice but to stay on Perliserkerstrasse, protecting the rear of the other rifle companies while having to watch their own when they spotted any Germans moving about over their shoulders.

At 1900 hours, Lieutenant Colonel Corley ordered the battalion to button up for the night; he reported to regiment that he had a solid line in place, but that there was an enemy company in the park that appeared to be equipped with mostly automatic weapons. Lieutenant Nechey's 81mm mortars were set up in the road junction at Lombardenstrasse and Ungarnstrasse, behind Corwell's and Botts's men; Nechey's heavy machine guns were emplaced on the flanks of both companies, providing an all-around defense. Corley later reported that Chaplin's men had actually made contact with some of Lieutenant Colonel Daniel's Company F squads during the afternoon; they had been fighting Germans in the same buildings on Perliserkerstrasse.

But neither badly battered Company F nor Captain Smoot's Company E had reached the 2nd Battalion's phase line objective; this was Victoriastrasse, and it ran perpendicular to and due south of the Karhol Friedhof cemetery below where Adalbertstein Weg and Stolbergerstrasse came together. Lieutenant Colonel Daniel desperately needed to get more tank and TD support up to his men and to commit Lieutenant

Walker's Company G, but it wasn't until late afternoon that the engineers found a way to get the armor through the underpass; they had instead demolished walls and busted down doorways in the railway station itself. Now Daniel needed to consolidate his companies nearer to Victoriastrasse. He sent up Company G, and they got a block short of there after being slowed by scattered resistance and taking over fifty Germans prisoners. Smoot's men converged on Victoriastrasse at about the same time the two weakened platoons of Company F did; the other platoon would spend the night getting what sleep they could among the graves in the cemetery. At 1910 hours, Daniel reported to regiment that he had a solid front flanked by tanks and TDs on his first day's phase line objective. The 1st Battalion's Company C had his men's back; they had moved up to guard the underpass and to keep any enemy units from entering Aachen by way of Rothe Erde.

The open door through the factory district now behind Corley's 3rd Battalion was finally closed closer to 2100 hours. Colonel Smith had been able to cobble together a composite company within the 18th Infantry that was made up of men from his mine platoon, the regiment's Intelligence and Recon Platoon, and a squad from the 634th Tank Destroyer Battalion; these men were not expected to fight their way into Aachen. Their sole mission was to block to the west and northwest "to prevent any infiltration of stuff driven down by the 30th Division."[42]

By this time, 139 prisoners had been processed to the POW cage by Corley's men, and 30 more were inbound; all were from the 5th, 7th, 8th, and 14th Companies of the 352nd Regiment.[43] Daniel's 2nd Battalion had bagged 138 Germans from Companies 6, 8, and 14. The 689th Regiment Headquarters Company, their Training Company, and the Stoss Company were also represented in the prisoner ranks. One soldier taken from the 404th Regiment confessed during his interrogation that two companies of this regiment had snuck in from Würselen through the railroad station outside the factory district; this likely took place before Colonel Smith's composite unit arrived. Perhaps the most discouraged POWs were nine Aachen policemen still in their normal duty uniforms who had been forced to fight as German infantry.

Later that night Lieutenant Colonel Corley was questioned by an operations officer at division as to whether a SP-155 gun might work on the apartment buildings along Peliserkerstrasse that had proven to be a real problem for his Company L during the day. These tracked, self-propelled vehicles were normally used for long-range indirect support, so the idea was very intriguing. Corley offered, "I don't know; the tanks and TD's don't even bother the buildings, but I'll let you talk with Chaplin; he can give you an eyewitness view."[44] Chaplin was quickly patched in and he stated; "I watched the firing on the buildings and it didn't even bother the enemy troops; they just stay there and take it. 155's might work. They have a terrific blast."

The operation officer then promised to "take the matter up with the general," cautioning that he would ask for a couple of 155s, but Corley would have to commit to keeping them well protected since they had no armor plating. It did not take long to get an answer. At 2215 Corley got another call, this time saying the DIVARTY commander, Gen. Clifton Andrus, had bought in, but he was only committing one gun. The Ivy League–educated Andrus, a native of Fort Leavenworth, Kansas, and who was stationed at Pearl Harbor on December 7, 1941, added this when he spoke to Corley:

> I think it would be best if you fired it through the windows with a quick fuse. The blast should drive them out. I do not want it closer than 400 yards. If that doesn't work, we can adjust 8-inch on it and you can get an observer out there and we can creep back on it until we make a hit. The gun section has been alerted and an officer will be right over.[45]

The gun would come in through Haaren; Corley was told to have a protective force there at 0530 the next morning, and for its commander to let the guide with the SP-155 know what he wanted to do with it.

Total casualties for Colonel Seitz's 26th Infantry on 13 October were four killed and fifteen wounded in Corley's 3rd Battalion, with fourteen still missing and probably prisoners of the Germans.[46] Daniel's losses were fewer, but he had suffered painful numbers in killed, particularly in Company F's leadership. Much had been learned during this first day of urban combat that would minimize losses in the days ahead. Lieutenant Colonel Daniel certainly spoke for every man in his battalion when he said, "We quickly learned that in street fighting, strange to relate, one should stay out of the street."[47]

CHAPTER 11

The Northern Jaw

"Nobody will ever know what this has been like up here."

CAPT. JOSEPH DAWSON, 16TH INFANTRY

During the chilly night of 13 October, the well-camouflaged Tiger tanks and Panzergrenadiers of the 3rd Panzer Division, commanded by *Generalleutnant* Walter Denkert, reached their assembly locations in the Reichswald, a big wooded area east of Würselen. This fully motorized division was to fight its way into Aachen. The 8th and 29th Panzer Grenadier Regiments were to attack abreast, first moving out to either side of the Aachen-Duren railroad tracks, next advancing past the outpost line of the 12th Infantry Division, and then capturing the hills south and southwest of Verlautenheide. Once this was accomplished, the regiment on the right was to retake Crucifix Hill and the Ravelsberg. After overrunning Verlautenheide, the important ridge outside of the village, Quinx, and the northern part of Eilendorf, the left regiment was to push all the way down into Rothe Erde with the objective of establishing a line from the slaughterhouse in the northeast section of Aachen at Julicherstrasse to the southern edge of Haaren.

The 3rd Panzer Division, known to the Germans as the "Bear Division," had been activated near Berlin back in late 1935. Since that time it had participated in the Polish campaign of 1939 before distinguishing itself in France during the Battle of Dunkirk. In June of 1942 the division was part of the Russian offensive and under the command of future *Generalfeldmarschall* Walter Model; it took part in the fighting around Kiev and the later drive on Moscow before suffering heavy losses during the Kharkov battles in the fall of 1943. After bitter fighting around Cherkassy and Uman at the start of the winter, the division was surrounded at Kirovograd in early January, but escaped capture and managed to retreat over the frozen wintry roadways of Ukraine and east Poland.

Generalleutnant Denkert, a native of the seaside city of Kiel on the Baltic coast of Germany and a recipient of the Knight's Cross of the Iron Cross, had been in the Führer Reserve before taking command of the division in June of 1944. Its proud Prussian roots still influenced the Bears; despite being understrength at this time—meaning between seven thousand and nine thousand men according to 1st Division Intelligence estimates—"morale of the troops was elevated."[1] In addition to his fifteen to twenty Tiger tanks, Denkert now had elements of the 506th *Panzerjäger* Detachment (antitank), with about fifteen to twenty more vehicles, for the upcoming fight. The *Volksartillerie* Corps and a *Volkswerfer* Brigade, located in the middle sector of 7th Army, would provide additional support; the offensive would also be backed up by the artillery units of the 12th Infantry Division.

The attack was first slated for early morning on 15 October, when the clear and cool weather of the fourteenth would give way to forecasted rain under cloudy skies, thereby preventing American fighter groups from disturbing the planned assault.[2] Reconnoitering and familiarization with the terrain had been completed. With sloping grassland leading up toward Verlautenheide, early morning fog and smoke cover would assist the German tanks and their mounted Panzergrenadiers in reaching the village undetected; the heavily canopied edge of a forest to the east would initially provide cover and an assembly area for these efforts. The *Panzerjäger* Detachment would be committed with the regiment on the right, where American tanks were certain to challenge any German vehicular movement along the main road into Aachen.

But all did not go according to plan, at least from the perspective of *General der Infanterie* Köchling. He learned that he would not oversee the attack, an "astonishing interference with the command of LXXXI Corps," according to one account.[3] Instead, direction of the 3rd Panzer Division would be by 7th Army from its command post well to the rear in Inden. No "official explanation" was offered at the time, but one cannot help but wonder whether *Generalfeldmarschall* Model's former command of the division played some role in this decision. Or, was it simply Model's impatience with the deteriorating situation around Aachen and wavering confidence in the local commanders? Regardless, Model was now wielding the big stick; he refused to wait another day for the attack and insisted it be conducted later on 14 October when coming darkness in his estimation would provide adequate cover. Every one of his subordinate commanders argued against this, including Denkert, but Model of course prevailed. Accordingly, the strike was moved up to 1830 that evening.

Anticipating the attack but obviously unaware of its new timing, the 18th Infantry's Colonel Smith had ordered adjustments along the regiment's entire front earlier that morning.[4] Mine fields were planned and laid, barbed wire was strewn and installed, and many positions were sandbagged. Captain Russell's Company K was moved up from Haaren to relieve Captain Miller's Company B on the Ravelsberg; Miller's soldiers dug foxholes for the new arrivals on the hill's reverse slope before pulling back to the cellars in Haaren. Captain Folk's Company L was put on alert and told to anticipate moving up to Ravelsberg Hill at the first sign of trouble. A platoon from Capt. Charles A. Penick's Cannon Company was sent up; his self-propelled vehicles mounted 105mm short-barreled howitzers that had 7,000-yard range and would weigh in with extra firepower for the defense.

Comparative quiet then passed from morning into midafternoon on the common front of the soon-to-be-attacking Germans and the defense-fortifying Americans along the important northern jaw positions outside of Aachen.

In the city itself, both battalions of Colonel Seitz's 26th Infantry went on the attack shortly after 0600 on 14 October. Lieutenant Colonel Daniel first ordered Company G to push down Kaiser Allee to bring these men abreast of his other two rifle companies on Victoriastrasse; this consumed a good part of the morning.[5] Company F, now commanded by Lt. Chestnut W. Webb, a Gaylesville, Alabama, native and son of a state senator, had his 1st Platoon still fighting its way out of the cemetery. A two-story pillbox guarded its approaches, and it had to be taken before the company could join the drive westward into the core of the city. Webb, a veteran of North Africa, Sicily, and Normandy, wasted little time before electing to commit all three of his platoons for this effort.

Using rocket guns and rifle grenades against both level apertures, they silenced the larger enemy weapons poking out of the fortification. Both sides hurled hand grenades back and forth as Webb's 2nd Platoon charged the massive pillbox; German machine gunners and others bearing deadly Sturmgewehr machine pistols laid down heavy fire, but this failed to stop the Americans and the pillbox was theirs before noon. But when Webb's 1st Platoon tried to exit the cemetery by first jumping over its high walls, the exposed soldiers took numerous casualties from enemy rifle fire and even *Panzerfausts*; the men who landed safely returned fire and destroyed two of the German guns. By this time Captain Chaplin's Company L had made limited contact with one of Company F's squads, but Webb had to leave a small force behind to assure a firmer linkup before lining the rest of his men up with the other 2nd Battalion companies for the day's main effort westward.

At 1230 hours, Daniel finally ordered all three companies to begin this push from Victoria; Captain Smoot's Company E immediately started working over the buildings off Adalbertstein Weg, with remarkable success. As Daniel pointed out:

> We were attacking now to the west and since our artillery was placed south of town it was now firing parallel to our front. This permitted the artillery to fire very close to us without danger from short rounds. We found that shells could be dropped into the same block in which we were working. With delayed fuse, the shells would penetrate one or more floors before exploding and the Germans would simply not stay in the buildings with that coming in; we could, therefore, mow them down as they fled from the building.[6]

But Daniel's men also discovered that not everyone evacuating buildings could be cut down. As the afternoon wore on, Lieutenant Walker's Company G had the battalion's first experience with air raid shelter occupants in Aachen; the drab structure was three stories high and so strongly built that direct fire by his accompanying tank destroyers produced just slight damage to its walls. Machine-gun fire only forced most of the defenders back inside. Walker decided to head for one of its entrances with an interpreter. He demanded surrender; German officers and the police had the entrance blocked. When they refused, the American company commander called for a flamethrower. The interpreter explained what would happen if they did not give up, but again they refused. With this, Walker reached into his pocket for a box of matches, ignited the flamethrower, and squirted a jet of burning gas at the door. When the flame had burnt out, this time another German officer emerged from inside the shelter, and attempted to negotiate terms through the interpreter before surrendering. Walker told the interpreter to tell this German that there would be no negotiation of terms whatsoever; either surrender at once or be burned. Some seventy-five enemy soldiers and about three thousand civilians eventually emerged.

"The doors opened and out came the drabbest, filthiest inhabitants of the underworld I had ever seen," wrote war correspondent George Mucha. "People came stumbling out into the light, dazed, then catching a breath of fresh air, started to jabber, push, scream and curse. 'We have been praying every day for you to come,' said a woman with a pale, thin face. 'You can't imagine what we have had to suffer from them.'"[7] "All had been living like animals for several weeks," an American officer later noted. "The ventilation and lighting facilities were inadequate. If one of us entered without a torch, he found himself suffocating in the stench-filled corridors."[8]

Farther to the north, Captain Botts's Company I and Corwell's Company K were attacking Farwick Park. Enemy resistance at first proved to be strong around the austerely ornamented St. Elizabeth's Church, but both companies eventually attacked jointly and overran the Germans. One of Botts's platoons even started climbing up the forward slope toward the Hotel Quellenhof but eventually ended up on another hillside along Robensstrasse. Captain Chaplin's Company L, after finding the newly arrived SP 155 gun so effective that it literally blew holes through the houses back along Perliserkerstrasse, was still having trouble making contact with Lieutenant Webb's Company F squads outside of the cemetery. "This situation was reported to regiment," Lieutenant Colonel Daniel noted. "We were then told to hold where we were [and] be ready to defend to the east in case a breakthrough was made by the Germans."[9]

Detachments of SS Battalion Rink had again been prevented from reaching Aachen that day, but with American forces now within mere spitting distance of his command post in the Hotel Quellenhof, *Oberst* Wilck had been appealing over and again to LXXXI Corps for more reinforcements. The Army official historian even noted that Wilck had at one point radioed *General der Infanterie* Köchling "in what was apparently a gross exaggeration" and told him "American tanks had enveloped his command post."[10] But in light of Wilck's exhortations, Battalion Rink was actually strengthened with elements of Fortress Assault Gun Company 106, Assault Gun Brigade 341, as well as the 2nd (Antitank) Company of Artillery Regiment 246. Only six assault guns and two howitzers arrived in Aachen that night; it was later learned that Wilck and his staff abandoned the Quellenhof. It would be another day before the rest of Battalion Rink finally battled its way through Teuterhof and into Aachen.

On the hills outside of Aachen, the highly anticipated debut of the 3rd Panzer Division produced mixed results at best on 14 October; a German officer's account recorded the main events this way:

> Although surprised in the beginning, with striking rapidity the Americans concentrated their artillery fire on the attacking forces as soon as they were located. Murderous fire met the spearhead approaching Verlautenheide and Quinx. After the first local counterattack by tanks from Quinx was reported, it became evident that both surprise and the attack had failed.[11]

However, around 2200 hours that night a strong enemy patrol infiltrated between Captain Dawson's Company G of the 16th Infantry on the ridge outside of Eilendorf and Lieutenant Colonel Williamson's Company G positions in front of Verlautenheide.[12] After first cutting the communication wires to two of Dawson's platoons, about forty Germans came in through his left flank and headed for a house being used as shelter for his weapons men. It was soon surrounded and one American guarding the home was killed and another wounded. Then a German ran up with a pole charge and placed it into a doorway; even though the structure's walls were 2 feet thick, the charge still blew half the house down. Whooping enemy soldiers entered what was left of the house, striking matches so they could see their way around. Outside, two machine guns were set up, one next to a wall that had not crumbled in the earlier blast and the other about 50 yards behind it.

All the men in the weapons platoon were in the cellar by this time, but its shaken commander still had a wire to Dawson's command post; the company commander immediately ordered his boys to go up and fight, using their carbines and pistols. So the men raced upstairs and managed to force more than half of the German intruders out of the three rooms in which they had holed up, killing many in the process. Quick thinking by Dawson had also resulted in three friendly squads outside of the house attacking at the same time; after yells were made for their own men not to shoot, these soldiers rushed in, drove the rest of the Germans away, and destroyed their machine-gun emplacements.

After Captain Dawson sent a patrol out to reestablish communications with his two platoons that were cut off earlier, he learned that these men had also been attacked around midnight; the Germans here were driven off by the mortar and murderous artillery fire that had caused 7th Army to order the general withdrawal of the 3rd Panzer Division's 29th Panzer Grenadier Regiment that night. But prisoners revealed that there would be another strike by two of their battalions the next day; the Bears would be back.

Cold, pouring rain and thick clouds covered Aachen and the surrounding area at first light on 15 October. It was destined to be a day of hard-fought gains and losses for Lieutenant Colonel Corley's 3rd Battalion in muddy Farwick Park. Captain Chaplin's Company L had finally linked up with Daniel's forces in the cemetery, so his men were able to leave the Perliserkerstrasse area in the early going and work their way north to Passstrasse to join in the fight. With chemical mortar strikes assisting, Corley's men took the garden buildings and the Kurhaus, but the German defenders in the sturdy Hotel Quellenhof would not budge. Adjustments became necessary; Company I's Captain Botts split up his men. One of his platoons moved from the east side of the park to clean out the defenders along Krefelderstrasse between Passstrasse and Margratenstrasse; another improved their positions on Rolandstrasse. Corwell's Company K held in front of the hotel.

The Germans were arrayed in preparation for their second attack on the ridge outside of Eilendorf before any light filtered through the rain and fog that morning. A company of grenadiers with at least two tanks and one SP gun had been hiding in front of Captain Richmond's

Company I platoons since 0400. Five more tanks with their accompanying personnel had been able to advance under the deafening downpours
up into Captain Dawson's left front; his platoon here was also being
stalked by three more tanks to its right. Another three were rumbling
ghosts in the fog, ready to throw their weight between Dawson's right
flank and Lt. Stanley A. Karas's Company E. Four were captured American Shermans; one still had the insignia of the 5th Armored Division on
it. The rest were thickly plated 60-ton Mark VI Tiger tanks mounting
long-barreled 88mm guns.

Richmond had divided his company into two platoons for their
defense; he had few supporting weapons. Captain Dawson had a section
of light tanks and just one tank destroyer with its 3-inch gun. Both companies were undermanned. It was the 29th Panzer Grenadier Regiment's
intention to spearhead its effort by first breaching both companies' lines
while blocking Karas's Company E from getting into the fight. Then
more forces and tanks would pour in, work the remainder of the American line along the high ridge, then glance off and drive right into the
positions of Lieutenant Colonel Williamson's 2nd Battalion of the 18th
Infantry in Verlautenheide.

At 0500 the Germans started through a stand of trees to Dawson's left
and attacked; some walked through ankle-deep mud. Others crawled
because unobserved, but preplotted, American artillery and mortar shells
had somehow found them. Many were stopped within 15 feet of the foxholes Dawson's men had dug; a few died at even closer range and often
their bodies fell right into the rain-filled holes beside the U.S. soldiers who
had killed them. In one case, a soldier somehow waited for the German
who mortally wounded him to reach his foxhole; he then emptied his M1
into him. The shots echoed the din of death as the grenadier fell on the
American and groaned his last words. More rifle fire got others; hand
grenades were thrown at the Germans who were moving more slowly and
still crawling on their bellies toward Dawson's lines. The grenadiers fared
no better when they tried to penetrate Company I's front; the smashing
effect of grenades, small arms, and bayonets exacted revenge on the Germans who dared to attack. As Captain Richmond told everyone later,
"The men were draping [them] right over their foxholes."[13]

Why their tanks did not accompany the grenadiers was uncertain;
the battalion's S-3 thought that the slippery, wet conditions on the slope

leading up to the ridge might have been a factor in this decision, but mud-slicked roadways had not deterred the Germans from assembling their armored vehicles behind a row of houses near a railroad junction just north of Verlautenheide for another attack. At about 0800 forward observers with the 18th Infantry's 634th Tank Battalion finally saw two other enemy tanks leave an area just northeast of Waumbach and head for the woods closer to the ridge outside of Eilendorf. But with the visibility being so poor, Lieutenant Duffy's nearest TD did not have sufficient time to go after them before these two armored vehicles faded through the mist into the tree cover.

Then two more tanks were spotted, both hulking Mark VIs; they were also trying to reach this assembly area. This time, Duffy's TDs were able to get at them; cleverly they waited until the tanks showed their tails where their armored plating was comparatively thin. But the TDs' 76mm fire merely harassed their targets, as neither German tank even bothered to return fire while they continued their run to the woods. "They were damn poor shots [on the occasions] they did fire back," Duffy recounted later.[14]

At 0900 hostile artillery fire suddenly poured across Verlautenheide, followed by the appearance of the tanks and several SP guns that had been behind the railroad junction; three tanks closed to within 100 yards of Captain Koenig's Company F perimeter. Two of the guns and one armored vehicle overran Company E's outpost, but mines, bazooka fire, and the Antitank Company's 57mm guns stopped any further progress, and the Germans withdrew.

Then, yet another attack came around noon, this time hitting Captain Dawson's and Captain Richmond's platoons again; Captain Wozenski, the 16th Infantry's 2nd Battalion executive officer, first reported this. At 1227 he escalated the situation to serious, then critical at 1240 after a runner came up from Richmond's command post and reported that both Companies G and I were being overrun. Minutes later, an alarmed Lieutenant Colonel Hicks relayed word to regiment that three to four tanks were closing in on Karas's Company E; he also confirmed that eight tanks and an unknown number of dismounted grenadiers were now on top of Dawson's and Richmond's men.

At 1258 the 16th Infantry's commander, Colonel Gibb, weighed in; he wanted more details. Hicks, by now evincing severe signs of battle stress, told him that he was out of communication with the besieged companies, but that a messenger had just come in from Dawson's CP with requests for fire support; based on this Gibb decided the situation needed to be upgraded to very critical. Accordingly, artillery fire was delivered by every available FA battalion; requests were made for one battery to place constant rounds on and in front of the railroad draw behind Verlautenheide to cut off any further 29th Panzer Grenadier Regiment attempts to use this avenue of approach. Even 81mm mortar fire delivered by Company H of the 18th Infantry landed on the Germans off Dawson's left flank.

In the minds of the American commanders, they needed even more adjustments. At 1336 Captain Miller's Company B of the 18th Infantry was ordered up to Eilendorf; one of his platoons was soon inserted between Dawson's soldiers and Captain Jeffrey's Company G on the edge on Verlautenheide. Miller's other platoons took up positions behind these men, in case of a breakthrough. Major Adams's 1st Battalion of the 26th Infantry was put on alert. General Huebner even appealed to General Collins, requesting that he "alert anything the 3rd Armored Division might spare."[15] Then, just ahead of 1400, the Germans pushed toward the 18th Infantry's lines again.

By now air support was doing its best to thwart the attacks; friendly planes came out of the lead-gray sky just after 1340, first strafing the triangle coordinates of the German assembly area in the nearby woods to prevent more of their tanks from entering the fight. Ten minutes later, a squadron which had already dropped most of its bombs in the 30th Infantry zone appeared over the 16th Infantry lines; two 500-pounders were released on top of the German tanks.

One flight of P-47s led by Capt. George W. Hurling Jr. dove very low into red smoke that had been laid down by the artillery and delivered machine-gun fire quite close to Dawson's and Richmond's positions; urgency dictated this risk. "They came in about 25 feet from our front lines and strafed the hell out of the enemy and came down so low they could tell the difference between the uniforms," the G-3 of the 1st Division reported. "It was a beautiful job."[16] Captain Dawson explained later, "I also had to call for the artillery right on us, only ten yards in front of us, and they saved lives because the Germans were literally overwhelming us in numbers."

Raising the alert level to very critical and the resulting collective actions of the air, artillery, and mortar units had actually caused the attack to wind down. The battalion's S-3, Capt. Fred W. Hall, a 1941 ROTC graduate of the University of New Hampshire, first reported this to regiment at 1345 hours; he had received word that a forward observer in Verlautenheide saw tanks withdrawing from their front. More good news followed; at 1417 the 1st Division's G-3 also heard from a forward observer of the 7th Field Artillery that their shells had devastating effects and the attack was being beaten off. Just after 1500 hours the enemy tanks were seen disappearing into the woods from which they came; American artillery was still pounding away at them. At 1614, the penetration was completely sealed off; all that could be seen were the dead bodies of Germans sprawled along the front, vibrant red blood covering their tattered field gray uniforms where they lay in the mud.

Generalmajor Denkert later commented on the attacks of 15 October by first offering that "the artillery fire was so strong that a continuation of the attack, even if the fire ceased, was not possible." He added:

> Our armored vehicles had difficulties on the bad terrain, and the artillery fire separated the infantry from the tanks. [I personally observed] that the infantrymen who accompanied the tanks were soon without crews. As the tanks alone could not continue the attacks, they withdrew to good cover, part of them to the border [Waumbach] where they could wait for nightfall. [I] ordered the forces to dig in, to hold their reached positions and to make reconnaissance.[17]

The 12th Infantry Division's *Oberst* Engel reflected the same sentiments, although skewed by a mercurial attitude because his division had not been engaged in the fight:

> The factors of incorrect timing of the attack, the superiority of the enemy artillery and last, but not least, the use of a unit unacquainted with the terrain features and the peculiarities of local combat conditions in an attack under the most trying circumstances, brought dire results. It should also be mentioned that Army and Corps had proposed to Heeresgruppe that the 12th

Infantry Division, which was well acquainted with the local fighting conditions and the terrain features, should have taken part in the attack.[18]

LXXXI Corps' *General der Infanterie* Köchling speculated after the war as to why his command decisions regarding use of the 12th Infantry Division had been interfered with at the time, offering, "I suppose that [*Heeresgruppe*] estimated the Corps as being troubled too much with the defensive battle in and around Aachen."[19] Facts on the ground in the city itself during the afternoon of 15 October proved there was indeed much trouble afoot.

At 1550 hours the German garrison began the heaviest attack Lieutenant Colonel Corley's 3rd Battalion experienced since entering the city. After an intense 120mm mortar barrage, six tanks and a battalion of Rink's newly arrived infantry first hit between the flanks of Captain Botts's Company I and Captain Corwell's Company K; the strike actually came from three separate directions. From the northwest, two Mark IVs and one company closed in on Botts's men. Discharging heavy machine-gun fire, supported by deadly 120mm mortars, the attackers rapidly closed into small-arms range and minutes later the charging Germans were engaged in close hand-to-hand fighting with the Americans.

The 120mm mortar fire was then elevated toward the observatory atop Farwick Park where Botts's weapons squad and Lieutenant Nechey's heavy 81mm mortars had their outposts; this position took an amazing thirty-six direct hits. Tank fire added to the mayhem as their 7.5cm main guns blasted at the Americans huddled under the tower. As Captain Botts would later say, "It was then touch and go for more than an hour."[20]

A pair of Mark VI Tigers loaded with grenadiers, plus another full company of infantry on foot, also closed in on the Kurhaus and attacked across the left flank of Corwell's line. It was touch and go here too. The company's bazookas fired at the tanks, but only slowed them. One tank roamed past one of the greenhouses and drove to within 200 yards of Lieutenant Colonel Corley's command post. The overwhelmed U.S. soldiers did the best they could with their small-arms and automatic-rifle fire; one BAR man, Pfc. Short, fired fifty-nine magazines of ammunition alone. Mortar and artillery fire were laid in; Lieutenant Nechey's heavy mortars fired 300 rounds, trying to locate and knock out their opposite numbers' 120mm mortar position; the effort failed. Company K held, but Botts's men were forced from their positions beneath the observatory.

Battalion Rink then struck Botts's right flank and drove a dangerous 300-yard gap between the two companies. Corley answered by ordering up a platoon of Captain Chaplin's Company L to fill this opening and reclaim the Kurhaus. Other orders followed; three tank destroyers under the command of Sgt. Leo F. Samek were moved closer to Corley's CP. Two more were directed to support the efforts of Chaplin's men. The TDs engaged the two German tanks creatively; they could not be directly observed, so the Americans fired at their muzzle blasts. Cpl. Wenzlo Simmons of Hendrix, Oklahoma, an assistant gunner in one of the tank destroyers, fired thirteen rounds at one enemy tank and was credited with knocking it out of action. The other retired from the fight. The TDs then shifted and fired fifteen rounds at the tanks lurking over Botts's platoon near the Kurhaus. Results at the time were not clear, but one American could clearly see what was happening from atop the observatory. Incessant hostile mortar fire rained on his position, yet he still called down friendly artillery fire to help the Americans trapped beneath the tower.

Back down on street level, Roland Platz was now swarming with Germans. Corley would later claim it was the loss of this area that stopped the day's fighting; efforts to retake the Kurhaus had also been abandoned. By 1700 the momentum from Battalion Rinks's attacks had exhausted the Americans and Corley suspended offensive operations.[21] Twenty-six of his men had been wounded; two had been killed.

The rain also made the stubborn house-to-house fighting more difficult than it had been during previous days for Lieutenant Colonel Daniel's 2nd Battalion men. Their attack did not go off until late afternoon; Walker's Company G worked both sides of Kaiserstrasse before a German counterattack came down Hinderburgstrasse and penetrated a couple of blocks into Zollernstrasse, but this deep left flank breech was sealed off after two hours of brisk fighting. Enemy *Panzerfausts* took a toll as the afternoon lengthened. After more guns fired down Adalbertstein Weg, one tank destroyer, an American antitank gun, and a heavy machine gun were lost. Lieutenant Webb's Company F took numerous German prisoners after an officer bearing a white flag surrendered a bunker. Daniel also suspended further attacks at 1800; by now word had come down from division indicting General Huebner had again called off any further offensive moves in Aachen until the situation outside of the city was stabilized.

There was just cause. As darkness was consuming the ridge outside of Eilendorf, a forward observer in Captain Dawson's Company G managed to spot at least a company of grenadiers and two tanks moving out of the woods to his left; these vehicles turned out to be captured American Shermans again. Flares suddenly lit up the area, but the Germans still succeeded in overwhelming two squads on the right flank and took over their foxholes. The tanks closed to within a very dangerous 10 yards of another platoon's area to the left, putting direct fire on Dawson's CP, but these Americans held fast while more Germans exploited the gap between the two forces; hand grenades soon paralyzed the only TD defending the area. Then a *Panzerfaust* tore into one of Dawson's light tanks, crippling its suspension system. Another was mounted and quickly booby trapped. "Suddenly, there was chaos all over the Company G area," Company I's Captain Richmond recalled later. "Nobody knew what the situation was because the enemy was in front of and on both sides of them."[22]

Toward midnight, Richmond's men became the target of the continuing attack. Approximately twenty Germans raced toward a pillbox between his two platoons and hit a friendly tank with a *Panzerfaust*, killing its crew. Some of the enemy broke off and placed a pole charge against the side of a tank destroyer; it was not occupied but it was still put out of service. Then all hell broke loose when another two companies of grenadiers struck Richmond's left platoon; wounded on both sides were soon strewn everywhere. Many of the friendly casualties were from artillery strikes again called down on their own positions. At least forty Germans were later discovered dead. The situation remained critical; Richmond sent his executive officer, Lt. Eugene A. Day, running to battalion to ask for urgent help as things continued to deteriorate. Company B of the 26th Infantry was rushed up with its men, tanks, and TDs.

Yet another German attack came in at first light, aimed squarely at Richmond's front. The attack was repulsed, but it took two hours before any signs of a withdrawal began to appear. The Germans were driven out of the foxholes they had taken from the Americans; one angry U.S. soldier rushed them by himself and was credited with killing eight, wounding three, and capturing five. A sergeant and four of his men cleaned out the rest. One prisoner reported that 4.2-inch mortar fire caused about forty casualties in his company. Captain Hall, the battalion's S-3, also reported this at the time:

> I just returned from Companies I and G. Things are a little rough—in fact, very rough. Here is the story. In front of Company I, Jerries are in the woods. They are down a little trail, lined up there. The pillbox lost by Company I is occupied by eight officers and their bodyguards, according to a PW. Company I had eight men in that pillbox that had fought them out, and then tanks returned and fired right at the box. Richmond's men had to abandon it again and they went into position on the right side. He is not in contact with them, but figures they are OK. No casualties reported. The grouping up indicates another attack. Dawson doesn't know if he can hold another attack; the men are worn out.[23]

Hall was right about another strike. By 0955 the remaining enemy tanks had pulled back, but a number of stubborn grenadiers attacked and again attempted to harass Richmond's 3rd Platoon; they charged these men in groups of ten to fifteen with bayonets fixed every half hour, one determined group after another. Three attempts were made and all were beaten off. "There was much moaning and groaning out in front of Company I," one account noted after the melee ended. "A 20-man stretcher team worked for nearly two hours, evacuating German wounded; 60mm and 4.2-inch mortars continued to fall the entire time. Later, someone came out with a large Red Cross flag, and then the American fire ceased."[24]

Back in Captain Dawson's CP, several war correspondents had remained with him during the fighting; some had talked to the soldiers and a few had even managed to visit some of the men in their foxholes. Gordon Fraser of the NBC Blue Network described the command post:

> Scattered around Dawson's basement CP was a table with maps and magazines. On another table against the far wall, dance music was emanating from a small shiny radio. Next to the radio

were two field phones—black phones resting on tan leather cases. They connected the captain to his platoons out in mud less than a hundred yards away, and the 16th Regimental CP in the rear. Beside the phones, radio and maps were one candle and a small kerosene lamp for illumination; it was enough so we could see each other's faces.[25]

Dawson, "so thin, his uniform hung loosely on him" because he had lost twenty-five pounds in the preceding five weeks, told the gathered correspondents:

Do you know why we have this cellar here? You know why this candle burns here? It's because of those guys out there, and I don't have to tell you what they've got. It's mud. It's deep in the ground, and water seeps in. It's horrible. It stinks. It's got lice in it. It's cold and it's exposed. Out there is this ridge, starting fifty yards from here, there are kids who have nothing, except wet and cold and shelling and misery and the Germans coming at them, and they're dying.[26]

Trying to imagine describing these conditions to their readers, Dawson told the gathering, "Nobody will ever know what this has been like up here. You aren't big enough to tell them, and I'm not big enough to tell them, and nobody can tell them." Bill Heinz of the *New York Sun* still promised to do his best. Before the interview ended, Dawson broke down. There was not a sound in the room, nor did anybody move while with his head in his hand, he wept.

Colonel Smith's 18th Infantry in Verlautenheide did not escape the Germans' attention on the morning of 16 October. Just before dawn the commander of Company F's 2nd Platoon, Lt. Freddie T. Towles, contacted Captain Koenig and told him that three German tanks were right outside his window and one was actually up against the house that the captain was using for his CP. As it turned out, there was a full platoon of enemy infantry with four *Panzerfausts* and one tank in front of Towles's position. They had approached under German artillery fire, but three of their accompanying tanks were knocked out by minefields in the railroad junction; unsupported, many of the grenadiers elected to surrender after their comrades had been wounded or killed. One prisoner, the commander of the platoon, stated that he had been given orders to meet his CO in the square beyond the first row of houses that Lieutenant Towles's men occupied.

Captain Jeffrey's Company G was also attacked at first light, this time by twenty-nine grenadiers and two tanks that came crunching down the Quinx road. Little time was wasted before artillery was called for and well-placed rounds did an excellent job in dispersing the German foot soldiers. But the tanks drove past four houses and some of their accompanying personnel actually got inside the company's final protective line. Friendly tanks and TDs disposed of the enemy tanks; the German armored vehicles withdrew. Most of the grenadiers elected to retreat; others became casualties or were taken prisoner.

Capt. P. K. Smith, the 32nd Field Artillery's liaison with Lieutenant Colonel Williamson's 2nd Battalion, remembered what came next:

> I was on the third floor of a big building, and our front line ran behind the building. I looked out from here and saw what looked like the whole German army coming right at me. They were coming over the brow of a hill—tanks coming straight at me. There were lines of infantry with them. Their discipline was absolutely amazing.[27]

The first attack hit Koenig's Company F again; six tanks rolled in from the direction of Wambach and were soon firing at Lieutenant Towles's forward command post. Then another column of five German tanks approached along the Quinx road. American tank destroyers answered with long lances of fire from a distance, running and still firing away, finally closing near enough to scare off three of the enemy tanks. But the six larger tanks were still coming in from Wambach, turrets traversing and firing stout 88mm high-muzzle velocity shells from left to right while their machine guns sprayed sweeping fire into both Company F's and G's front lines. But friendly artillery fire found the enemy tanks, slowing them down, eventually bringing a lull in the action.

This ended when three tanks came back later in the morning and moved to defiladed positions in a ground depression in front of the companies' lines; three others came in from behind Wambach and joined in the attack. Captain Coffman's Company E took the brunt of this strike. Adding to the mayhem, five more tanks suddenly appeared; these approached from the direction of Weiden, accompanied by rigid grenadiers in formation. Some of these tanks got very close to Verlauten-heide, but a TD in an orchard got the drop on one of them and let go with eight rounds. The shots just bounced off the Mark VI Tiger's thick armor, but it stopped this vehicle and others nearby also came to a halt. Infantry quickly dismounted and started charging into Company F's positions; Koenig's men responded with tremendous rifle and machine-gun fire, hitting at least thirty of the German soldiers. Then friendly mortar and artillery fire joined in, and the remainder of the Germans ran. At noon, another TD commander bravely brought his vehicle to within 100 yards of another Tiger tank and fired five rounds at point blank range; the German tank turned and fired back. This time one of its 88mm shells penetrated the TD, killing the gun sergeant and seriously wounding two other crew members.

By now more Americans had fallen, many recent replacements. Another artilleryman of the 32nd FA remembered seeing Company G's Captain Jeffrey in his command post at the time; he later recalled:

> It was a bitter, fruitless damn series of attacks. No one was going anywhere. Gordon was absolutely disconsolate. He showed me the payroll. Fifty percent of his company was redlined. He said, "You know, some of these kids that are dead, they'd come in and I'd never even seen them."[28]

More attacks started up outside of Eilendorf that afternoon, but the weary U.S. soldiers were ready for them. At about 1800 Captain Dawson's Company G light weapons men fired their 60mm mortars on the Germans that were still occupying positions to their front. They kept up this barrage for thirty minutes, after which fourteen men from Dawson's 1st Platoon and eleven from the 2nd Platoon attacked with bayonets fixed; they also hurled hand grenades as they charged. These men, all who were left in their respective platoons, closed in and killed every German but one who was taken prisoner. They also overran an antitank gun, but more of the enemy soldiers were still holed up in a nearby house.

Captain Hall again reported on the situation to his regimental S-3:

I just talked to Dawson and he says that he has his position restored where the gun was; it was definitely knocked out. He was not able to take the house. Said he would get it tomorrow if necessary. Now Dawson is trying to effect relief. He has one squad relieved. He is consolidating his men on the right of this group. Dawson's men killed 17 Jerries, including five from a tank crew which was in the back of the house. The attack to capture the positions killed eight here and one was captured. Total enemy killed—25. Richmond is trying to get the pillbox back. He is not pulling his men back for relief, but putting extra men in the gap. Both companies will try and put wires and mines out later when things quiet down. The men have had no food for 24 hours. Their last hot meal was the night before last. Possibly we can get them a meal tomorrow. I feel that Jerry will be back. Time will tell.[29]

The Germans did return. There was some shelling and limited attempts to infiltrate both companies' lines, but every attack failed. Captain Richmond's Company I and Dawson's Company G were later awarded a Distinguished Unit Citation for their actions during 15–17 October; part of the citation read:

In this 72-hour battle, the defenders faced at different times three battalions of enemy troops and approximately 25 tanks, sustaining 37 major casualties against an estimated 300 for the enemy. The magnificent heroism, combat efficiency, and brilliant achievement of [the companies] helped pave the way for the eventual capture of Aachen.[30]

"The highest honor and privilege that I had was to command the finest group of men God ever put on this earth," Joe Dawson remembered nearly fifty years later.[31] But thirty-seven "major casualties" meant thirty-seven dead or seriously wounded American soldiers during that mid-October's chill and rain. They fell on an 840-foot-high, 400-yard-wide ridge with panoramic views into three European countries on a clear day—nothing but a bucolic farm divided into pastures in the years before the war that became a brutal field of death during the battle for the first major city in Germany.

Six Americans were killed and thirty-nine suffered various wounds around Farwick Park in Aachen on 16 October; Company L's commander, Captain Chaplin, was a casualty.[32] An 80mm enemy mortar landed near him while he was in an open position directing defenses, and when its main charge ignited, shards of sharp steel burst, killing him; Lt. Vincent I. Shepard assumed command. It was supposed to be a day of limited offensive action and consolidating positions for all of Corley's 3rd Battalion companies, but probing attacks by Battalion Rink infantry and hailstorms of hostile artillery fire halted any movement at all. Direct self-propelled enemy gunfire from a tube near the Hotel Quellenhof even destroyed a building near the observatory atop the park.

Lieutenant Colonel Daniel's 2nd Battalion companies made limited attacks during the day. Captain Smoot's Company E moved westward to Kaiserplatz where these men and the Germans sniped at each other from damaged but richly ornamented art nouveau houses on opposite sides of the broad square. Webb's Company F moved a short distance along Adalbertstein Weg; enemy mortar fire that was believed to have come in from the Lousberg slowed the company's advance.

Even with Aachen now choked off, General Huebner still planned to hold the 26th Infantry forces in the city back for another day. The Germans, however, would have little opportunity to catch their breath. The final blow by the Americans would bring two new battalions of tanks and armored infantry of the 3rd Armored Division into the city; Task Force Hogan was already rolling out of Stolberg on its way to Brand, staging for a deadly right hook into what remained of Battalion Rink and *Oberst* Wilck's forces in Farwick Park and around Lousberg Hill.

Moving northward from Camp d'Elsenborn in the V Corps sector, a battalion of the 28th Division was on its way to augment Lieutenant Colonel Daniel's drive through the core of old Aachen right to the railroad embankment at the city's western limits. The 110th Infantry would fill the growing gap between his battalion and the 1106th Engineers while Daniel delivered this punch.

The Germans now recognized that unless the 3rd Panzer Grenadier and 116th Panzer Divisions could break the encirclement by retaking Ravelsberg Hill, Aachen was lost. "On 16 October the beginning of the fall of Aachen became apparent," LXXXI Corps confessed in its war diary.[33] *General der Infanterie* Köchling nevertheless held out what hope he could; "The garrison was repeatedly instructed to fight further on unconditionally because strong liberating forces would break the ring."

CHAPTER 12

The Gap Closes

"I'm going to give you an order to attack all along the line and close the gap." According to witnesses, the words "close the gap" were repeated four times.

GENERAL CORLETT TO GENERAL HOBBS
1920 HOURS, 15 OCTOBER

While the Big Red One was fending off attacks both in the city and on the hills to the east of Aachen, the Germans were making it clear to the commanders of the 30th Division that their linkup with the Americans on Ravelsberg Hill could not be taken for granted. Würselen had been the objective for General Hobbs's regiments since 9 October. With positions stretching from Alsdorf southwestward through Ottenfeld to Herzogenrath on that morning, Würselen indeed appeared to be within grasp, once a dominating hill 300 yards south of the nearby tiny crossroads village of Birk was taken. From here U.S. troops would be able to see with their naked eyes out over the surrounding sugar and beet fields and make out the tall church steeple in North Würselen, even the St. Sebastian Catholic Church in Würselen proper. Past the oak tree-dominated wooded area before the rise onto Hill 194 southeast of Wurselen, a man on this hill could focus his binoculars beyond the "big road" and see a fellow soldier atop the Ravelsberg.

But it would not be easy. The German soldiers had advantages befitting to those now defending their cherished homeland; between their villages they maintained excellent defensive positions in pillboxes, hedgerows, and deep zigzag trenches that overlooked the open country over which the Americans would have to advance. The street layouts of the towns themselves provided excellent defense: muddy, sometimes winding roadways and intersections connected the villagers to their small shops, taverns, even farmhouses and barns that had become strongholds. The fortunes of war also found the U.S. soldiers burdened with unexpected opposition, for late on 8 October Model had released Panzer Brigade 108, to include the 506th Tank Battalion, from Regiment von Fritzschen near their positions outside of Alsdorf and reinforced these forces with the 404th Infantry Regiment. Their mission now was to thrust southwest toward Bardenberg to help prevent the linkup.[1] Destiny would have the Germans unwittingly crisscrossing the American advance toward Würselen the very next day.

It was very foggy that Monday morning when Maj. Harold S. Griffith's 1st Battalion of the 120th Infantry started their drive toward Birk; minimal enemy artillery and small-arms fire interfered with the advance as two of his companies made their way through Esel.[2] The Germans here were literally caught off guard, and the Americans took fifty prisoners along with an 88mm gun and several wheeled *Panzerfausts*. But at 1100 hours the American thrust was stopped at the railroad embankment fronting Birk; other enemy soldiers held the adjacent high ground to either flank and had the area covered with machine-gun fire and accurate mortars. The embankment suddenly became a no man's land; movement was impossible. The battalion was pinned down.

Just after noon, ten Panzer Brigade 108 tanks made another thrust toward Euchen without any artillery preparation and struck at the 120th's 2nd Battalion companies as they were digging into positions along the railroad tracks on the western edge of this hamlet. Enemy machine-gun fire raged while their armored vehicles fired round after round into the Americans; mortar fire added to their misery as the men jumped into foxholes that the Germans had dug earlier when they were defending the area. Capt. Ralph A. Kerley, commanding Company E, realized that he would have to call down friendly artillery fire very close to his men's positions if they were to escape from the onslaught; he did just this, and it invoked enough confusion and smoke cover for both his company and Company F's men to extricate themselves and fall back to safer defensive ground around nearby Schleibach.

The Germans wasted little time before they again regrouped and directed another effort at Griffith's 1st Battalion men still clinging to the embankment in front of Birk. The attack, made by elements of the 404th

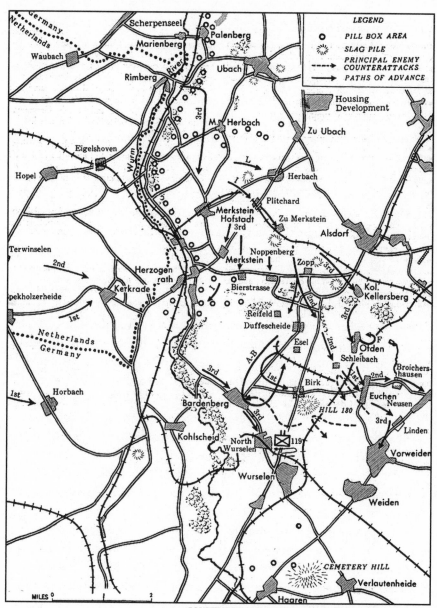

Infantry Regiment and Panzer Brigade 108, came in midafternoon, and this time the Americans were ready for them; artillery knocked out seven tanks, and the surviving grenadiers retreated back to safer ground near Euchen. But with their positions on the embankment still zeroed in by hostile artillery, the two American companies also had to leave the area and head down the Duffescheide-Bardenberg road southward, this time to pivot and come back at Birk from the west. This almost worked. Company A ran into five enemy half-tracks that started spraying 20mm gunfire toward them; it cost the company twenty casualties and cut it in two. It was bazooka fire on the enemy half-tracks that saved the rest of the men, allowing them to withdraw back to Esel under the protective canopy of early nightfall. But the day was far from over. Major Griffith required evacuation[3]; he was suffering from battle fatigue and command passed to Capt. Chris McCullough of Fayetteville, North Carolina, the battalion's executive officer who had just returned from the hospital himself. The Germans pounded Birk with artillery fire until 0430 the next morning. Then their batteries went silent and they finally rested.

When other forces of Panzer Brigade 108 pushed on toward Bardenberg in their half-tracks on 9 October, they collided with an understrength American company left behind at a roadblock after two of Colonel Sutherland's 119th Infantry battalions had "crushed the halfhearted resistance from demoralized remnants of the 49th Division"[4] and "in a last burst of energy before night set in, charged southeastward more than a mile into North Würselen." Ravelsberg Hill was suddenly a mere 3,000 yards away, and "closing the gap looked like little more than a matter of mop up and patrols." Events at the roadblock proved this was not to be the case.

Captain Simmons's Company A men had put in the roadblock on the far side of a cemetery edge during the late afternoon to prevent the Germans from getting back into Bardenberg. With just forty fighting men, the roadblock was simply not strong enough to withstand the arrival of the Panzer Brigade 108 detachments. A prisoner taken later estimated that "about 300 infantry, plenty of half-tracks and some tanks constituted the force that had overrun Company A's roadblock."[5] The single tank destroyer Simmons had at his disposal never even got a shot off. The men in one platoon sought refuge in North Bardenberg; others were wounded or captured. Just eight Americans made it back to the new

CP Simmons had found in the church tucked into the northwest edge of the village. "We built up all around," Simmons remembered. "But we were still forced back about a block."[6] It was a bad night for what was left of the company. The regiment's 2nd Battalion was inbound, but these forces were stopped short; to avoid being surrounded, Simmons snuck the men with him out a window of the house in which they were hiding and into another in the center of town. "They expected to wake up and find Jerries all around them," a later report noted. Simmons revealed that "it was the closest I came to being captured. They coulda took me."

Only Company E of the 2nd Battalion got into North Bardenberg that night; these men were stopped by 20mm antitank fire when they reached the same church to which Simmons's few soldiers had first escaped. This company was also split up; Sgt. Neal M. Bertelsen, after heading for the basement, remembered that "he could see enemy infantry and tanks going up and down the street."[7] Sgt. George Petcoff was stuck with ten other men in a beer garden cellar and surrounded. Sergeant Holycross and his 2nd Platoon were cut off in another part of the village. But they were all lucky. Sergeant Bertelsen was able to keep battalion informed by whispering their positions over his 300 radio. And even though "the Jerries were not more than 15 yards away," they never made any house-to-house searches.

During the afternoon, Lieutenant Colonel Brown's 3rd Battalion had experienced "beautiful success in its drive aimed at North Würselen," but now his companies were cut off. As Lieutenant Knox of Company L recalled, "Everything was falling in North Würselen. We moved on through, however, behind Company K, into the northern part of the village [to a place] we called 'The Mine.'"[8]

> I went down a shaft here to see what was going on and to deter-
> mine if I could find a suitable CP. People were packed in it for
> safety. We finally set up in part of the main office of the mine.
> Battalion was in a different part. Just after dark we received news
> that there was pretty much of a concerted counterattack being
> tried by the Germans. We were kept on alert all that night.

Panzer Brigade 108 forces had indeed poured through onto more streets in North Würselen; it was later noted that "although the Germans had not known it when they planned their thrust, the chance timing of the attack made them appear Argus-eyed and omniscient. By striking when they did, they made it hurt."[9]

It hurt everywhere along the division front on 9 October. At noon, General Hobbs had approved Colonel Johnson's request to have his 117th Infantry companies defend the division's east flank from Alsdorf, Scaufen-berg, and Kol-Kellersberg rather than what had been their original objective that day—Mariadorf. Remnants of Regiment von Fritzschen here had stopped the Americans from advancing over the open ground into their positions. "Evidence existed to indicate that the 117th's long period of attack without rest—a total of more than a week—had begun to tell," a later report confessed.[10] But by being where they were now, the Americans would prove to be as omniscient as the Germans in the days to come.

At 0530 the next morning, Captain McCullough's 1st Battalion of the 120th Infantry started out down the Duffesheide-Bardenberg road in eight columns. Four columns headed for the roadblock outside of North Bardenberg where Captain Simmons's men had been caught off guard the previous night; it was taken back and a hasty defense was set up. The other four columns made a sharp turn eastward and surprised the German security detachment at their posts in Birk. There had been no artillery preparation to wake them, nor did the single errant friendly rifle shot during the stealth attack rouse "the sleepy, groggy enemy."[11] Fifty prisoners were taken. The important 180-meter-high elevation just south of the village was open, bald ground and under enemy observation. It could not be occupied, but the Americans also had it under their watchful eyes.

The Germans then tried to retake Birk throughout the morning. Captain McCullough's men first experienced small strikes, but at 1100 the enemy struck furiously from the south end of Birk. Their tanks also came through draws around the reverse slopes of Hill 180 and at one time closed within 50 yards of McCullogh's Company A positions. The men here answered by turning the wheel-mounted *Panzerfausts* captured the day before on the incoming German armor; one was hit at 200 yards out. Another, in defilade, suddenly withdrew. Friendly artillery fire, a single tank destroyer, and American machine-gun crews added to their opposite number's misery. Before it was over, thirteen enemy panzers were disabled or destroyed; from his command post in a farmhouse near the front line in Birk, Captain McCullough later tallied counts showing more than thirty Germans killed or wounded.

When Lieutenant Colonel Cox's 2nd Battalion of the 119th Infantry renewed their attack to clear out North Bardenberg earlier that morning, there was no indication that the commanders of Panzer Brigade 108 in town knew that their supply line through Birk had been severed. Entering through Pley, the fighting was bitter as Cox's men tried to reach the center of the village. Here, the Germans had their five tanks out of view in gardens and behind houses on side streets. Their many half-tracks mounted frightening multibarreled 20mm antiaircraft guns—frightening because there were ten to twenty at a time roaming the roadways, and this was the first time the Germans had used these weapons on 30th Division forces. Consequently, efforts to extricate them from the center of North Bardenberg failed as the morning wore on, despite instances of selfless heroism on the part of one tank commander:

> The lead tank, commanded by Lieutenant Lambert V. Wieser, tried to cross an intersection and was fired upon by an assault gun set up in the street to his left. Lieutenant Wieser turned his tank into the face of this fire and traded shot for shot with the assault gun as he bore down on it. Although his fire had no effect on the assault gun, he continued firing until he was 50 yards away, even though his tank was burning. He evacuated his crew, took command of another tank and went after the gun again. The second tank was destroyed by a captured German bazooka, but Lieutenant Wieser sustained burns which caused his death.[12]

Lieutenant Colonel Brown's 3rd Battalion reports for this same day—10 October—indicated that for his men it was "the stiffest fighting of the entire Siegfried Line operation."[13] Grenadier Regiment 404 launched five powerful counterattacks against the battalion, "sending in the first wave of approximately 30 men and then a second wave of battalion strength, which covered the advance of the first wave." The attacks, however, were judged to be unsuccessful because Brown's forces were able to stop the first wave with their machine-gun and small-arms fire, then the second wave suffered a similar fate when mortars rained down on them. Again, an individual initiative punctuated the action that day:

> Lieutenant Donald J. Conway had pushed an observation post forward to a high water tower in the coal mine 50 yards from the enemy. This OP was maintained through four direct hits by enemy artillery, but the fifth made it untenable.[14]

"The artillery continued to be mighty rough," Company L's Lieutenant Knox remembered later. "It wasn't safe. Two of our men were killed going up a road. Communication wires were always out. As soon as we could get them fixed, out they would go again. The situation kept the runners and myself busy."[15]

It was around this time that the surrender ultimatum was delivered to the Aachen battle commander down in the city. Pressure to draw the noose with the linkup was foremost in the minds of both XIX Corps' General Corlett and the 30th Division commander General Hobbs. Hobbs, for his part, maintained that he needed more troop strength in order to affect the juncture; this was understandable given nearly ten days of sustained combat operations and the resulting casualties that his forces had experienced.[16] But there was only one reserve unit available to Hobbs—his own 3rd Battalion of the 120th Infantry—and Corps had no reserves it was ready to commit.

By midafternoon it was clear that Brown's 3rd Battalion troops would remain cut off at the mine in North Würselen. Even though the rest of Colonel Sutherland's forces were ringed around the village, probing attacks by the Germans necessitated defensive strategies that were sapping the necessary fighting stamina it would take to get through Würselen proper to make the linkup. Thus XIX Corps granted Hobbs's request that afternoon to "pummel the town with artillery, to pave the way for a more secure junction."[17] As General Hobbs would say in a call to Sutherland early the following morning, "This thing has to drive through."[18]

When Supreme Command West received word that same night indicating that the situation near Bardenberg and Würselen had become critical, permission was granted to move a hastily organized and reinforced regimental group of the 116th Panzer Division into the area for its defense on 11 October.[19] XIX Corps' intelligence unit had been anticipating the division's arrival at the front, and the commanders of the 116th Panzer Division had hoped that they would attack as a native fighting force, rather than being doled out piecemeal. But at 2030 hours on the night of 10 October, the chief of staff to 7th Army ended such thoughts when he informed LXXXI Corps that they would receive the reinforced Panzer Grenadier Regiment 60 and Combat Group Diefenthal for the next day's fight; the latter unit was "a hybrid collection of survivors of two defunct divisions in strength of about two battalions."[20]

Other units were also committed. Three hours later, *Oberst* Johannes Bayer, commander of Panzer Regiment 16, arrived with his forces in an assembly area southwest of Jurlich.[21] His regiment was attached to the 246th Division and out of this came the formation of Attack Group North, presumably to distinguish itself as not part of the Aachen inner-city defenses; this new group would be under Bayer's command. In turn, Bayer had two battalions of 650 men each from Panzer Grenadier Regiment 60 assigned to him, as well as nine "battle worthy" Panthers and four Hummels from Armored Artillery Regiment 146. Battalion Rink was also assigned to *Oberst* Bayer; at the time its strength was three Panzergrenadier companies and an antiaircraft platoon. Bayer also received eighteen additional guns when Assault Brigade 902 arrived. Attack Group North's mission was to relieve Panzer Brigade 108 in Bardenberg that very night; reports indicated that five Panthers and three Tigers of Panzer Battalion 506 were still in service here.

It was foggy again in the early hours of 11 October. The Germans in Bardenberg, after suffering from artillery strikes through the night, were pummeled once more with a terrific artillery preparation ahead of the new American offensive. Major Greer's 3rd Battalion of the 120th Infantry had moved from their reserve positions in Noppenberg and was assembled on the fringes of Bardenberg, ready to attack. Greer, in preparation for the fight, had used his photomap overlay to create quadrants in the village, and he had assigned sectors for each of his companies. At 0900, his men jumped off.

They encountered "virtually no opposition" when they stepped into town.[22] Instead the men went from house to house, making careful searches, still finding no opponents. But when they reached the southern half of Bardenberg in early afternoon the battalion met the grenadiers of Panzer Brigade 108, their tanks, and half-tracks. Here, and in the woods on the edge of the village, the Germans had arranged well-coordinated positions that were providing mutual cover for their companies. An account of the subsequent action said, "Major Greer personally did much to get the attack rolling. Grabbing a bazooka, he worked his way up to within range of one tank and knocked it out with one shot. Almost at once another tank fired, hitting the building he was in and knocking his helmet off. But a few minutes later, he reloaded and moved to a vantage point for a shot at the second tank. It worked."[23]

Staff Sgt. Anthony A. Tempesta of Company A, 743rd Tank Battalion, was one of the first to spot an assault gun covering an intersection as he led his platoon southward along the main street near the building Greer was in. Another report provided this account of what he did next.

> Tempesta boldly knocked it out with three shots, first swinging his tank cannon around toward the assault gun, then moving fast into an open firing position in the center of the intersection the assault gun was covering while a bazooka team also fired. Enemy snipers dropped grenades from upstairs windows but his tank moved ahead, knocking out another assault gun as he had the first, and eventually disabling six half-tracks. Tempesta assumed command of his company at 1400 after all of the officers had been wounded.[24]

Spurred on by actions of Greer and Tempesta, "similar crowbar tactics, here against a half-track sprouting 20mm shells, there against a machinegun or a tank, finally disassembled the matrix of German defenses."[25] By the end of the day, the battalion had destroyed 6 tanks and 16 half-tracks, killed at least 30 Germans, and taken 100 prisoners.

Captain McCullough's 1st Battalion men at the Birk crossroads had again kept the Germans from sending any help or supplies to their worn-down comrades in Bardenberg; four squadrons of XIX Tactical Air Command fighters had also aided in this effort during the late afternoon. Nevertheless, McCullough's forces were fired on for most of the day; between shell bursts and mortar fire the battalion took more than eight casualties. There were also enemy tank and infantry thrusts, but these attacks proved to be just a small reconnaissance in force with approximately fifty men. Every attack was driven off, and the battalion after-action report stated that fourteen enemy tanks were disabled and nineteen prisoners of war were taken. By this time the 2nd Battalion had moved over to Schleibach to take up positions on the railroad line between this tiny hamlet and Euchen in order to also help protect the regiment's left from intruders.

After Major Greer's companies cleared out Bardenberg, he sent Capt. Charles R. Shaw's Company I down to make contact with Brown's 3rd Battalion of the 119th Infantry in Würselen. Shaw's men destroyed ten half-tracks while capturing over forty Germans, including three officers, from Panzer Brigade 108's Armored Engineering Company 2108. A diary entry by its commanding officer, *Hauptmann* Heinz Albert, evidenced that elements of *Oberst* Bayer's Attack Group North had arrived as planned that afternoon.

> As of 1300 hours, sporadic infantry fire left rearward; mortar fire; the hits are almost in my positions. Towards 1700 hours, grenadiers arrive at our position; immense astonishment to find us here. Target of their attack: Pass west of the Würselen church and advance to Bardenberg.[26]

Panzer Grenadier Regiment 60's 1st Battalion, supported by tanks of Panzer Regiment 24, had reached the railroad station in North Würselen an hour earlier, and had engaged with some of Lieutenant Colonel Brown's men in houses just to the northwest of the station. Unknown to Brown, Battalion Rink had also occupied Kohlscheid just to the west of the mine he was using for his command post; the village was across the Wurm River. While the attack past the St. Sebastian Church into Bardenberg did not happen on 11 October, there was ample reason for concern.

General Hobbs had already received an updated report that day that confirmed the rest of the 116th Panzer Division was expected in the area; other reports verified the German buildup, "with the likelihood of a large scale thrust from the east or southeast."[27] This presented the 30th Division commander with a dilemma. Should he push his left flank outside of Alsdorf eastward, or even southward, into what appeared to be certain peril, or should he have Colonel Johnson's 117th Infantry and the two battalions of the 120th Infantry hold in place? Ultimately Hobbs decided to wait it out on this flank and see what developed when German intentions became more evident; instead his focus would be on the fight in Würselen, which was in line with his very firm orders from XIX Corps' General Corlett to finally draw the noose around Aachen by closing the gap.

General Hobbs did not have to wait long to see what the enemy's intentions were. At 0645 the next morning the S-3 of Lieutenant Colonel Franklin's 1st Battalion reported to division that tanks could be heard moving about in the fog out in front of their positions near Mariadorf. The 2nd Battalion of the 120th also sent word that their forward observers could see the ghostly outlines of enemy tanks to the south outside of Euchen. Then heavy artillery shelling began and did not let up for another half hour. Preparing to strike the American positions were a battalion of the 246th Division, a company of Panzer Brigade 108 with fourteen Mark VI Tiger tanks, two other companies with a mix of Mark IVs and Vs, as well as approximately four hundred men and ten more tanks attached to Panzer Grenadier Battalion 506. To their left, newly arrived Panzer Grenadier Regiment 156, accompanied by a half dozen more tanks under the command of *Oberleutnant* Willi Erdmann and belonging to the 2nd Battalion of Panzer Regiment 16, stood before Birk. At 0700 the Germans started attacking.

First hit were the 2nd Battalion positions near Schleibach, but the main assault quickly swung westward into Captain McCullough's companies after two battalions of grenadiers poured out of pillboxes around Euchen into well-deployed formation with sixteen armored vehicles and closed across the open fields toward Birk. *Oberleutnant* Erdmann's six tanks approached from the direction of Würselen. Two American 57mm gun crews near pillboxes in Company A's positions were among the first to see the enemy tanks, and they quickly reported that they were Tigers and Mark Vs. Draws made it difficult to spot the tanks lurking in front of Company B's location; at least three tanks were also spotted in front of Company C's defensive lines.

The 57mm antitank gun crews opened fire when the German tanks got inside 500 yards of Company A's positions; one crew fired three rounds and detracked a Tiger that was "silhouetted on the skyline,"[28] and another American tank put a shell through its turret. A Mark V immediately returned fire, destroyed the gun, and killed the American gunner and his assistant. The second 57mm gun emplacement was also hit, but the unwounded men of this crew stayed at their positions. A section of friendly heavy machine guns fired directly at the Germans who had their tank hatches open; the panzer crews quickly slammed them shut before their tanks burst into flames. One crew was not as fortunate; American machine gunners killed the men running from the burning wreckage. But another Mark V took aim at both Company A machine-gun positions, destroyed their guns, killed one, and wounded six others. Minutes later two TDs were found; the Germans took quick aim and also knocked them both out.

An artillery observation post on the exposed slope in front of Company A's positions now faced peril. An observer here was wounded after horrific enemy shelling found him; another who was rushing forward to take over the outpost was hit before he got there. Then, the tides of battle shifted. Capt. Michael S. Bouchlas, McCullough's liaison officer from the 230th Field Artillery, started up the hill to the OP alone. "We knew that he had made it when our own artillery, which up to this point was sporadic and was even throwing stuff at us, stopped and then began adjusting its fire," nearby Company A rifleman shared later. "We all felt good about it."[29] Although Company A had sustained forty-eight casualties, including its captain, another account noted that "massed artillery was soon pounding the attackers and within a half hour the threat was over."

Company B, at the crossroads in Birk, caught the wrath of ten other tanks attached to Tank Battalion 506 before it was all over, however. Later reports singled out Sgt. Melvin H. Bieber, a tank commander who forced the Germans to abandon a Tiger and knocked out a Mark V after twelve hits. Together with the friendly artillery fire that was saving Company A's men, the Shermans with Bieber's unit accounted for five more tank kills; others were still smoldering in front of the company's lines farther out, abandoned by their crews. *Oberleutnant* Erdmann later revealed that "under violent tank fire, since our infantry [was] not here but the enemy continually increases his fire, [2nd Battalion Panzer Regiment 16] finally pulled back to Weiden."[30] By 1030 Col. Branner P. Purdue, the 120th Infantry's commander for just six days, was finally able to report to a concerned General Hobbs that the situation was under control. "I have no complaints," Purdue added when Hobbs asked him how he was doing. "These are the bravest men you ever saw. That 1st Battalion fought them off with the outposts. I never did see men going like they have been going. We are as strong as strong can be."[31]

General Hobbs could only hope now that closing the gap was more likely because his forces in and around Würselen and Bardenberg had also held their own during the morning. Early reports from Colonel Sutherland had "about 100 enemy infantry spotted grouping for an attack across the bridge near Kohlscheid."[32] These forces were likely the newly arrived elements of Battalion Rink that had been sent to the Würselen area to relieve Grenadier Regiment 404; they were finally being freed up to rejoin the 246th Division and the fight to retake the Ravelsberg. Other forces of Panzer Grenadier Regiment 60 had already seized a group of bunkers 800 meters west of the Gouley mine. But, as the 116th Panzer Division's historian later wrote, "By 1020 hours the attacks came to a standstill because enemy artillery fire and attacks by fighter bombers became too intense."[33]

"Our artillery broke it up," a 119th Infantry account agreed. "From Bardenberg south toward North Würselen, the flank was held for periods by elements of Company D and even by the kitchen train of the 1st Battalion."[34] In the area being defended in Bardenberg by Captain Shaw's Company I of the 120th Infantry, one gallant action by Staff Sgt. Jack J. Pendleton stood out. A German machine gunner had placed his weapon at an intersection that allowed him to control any movement through the streets toward his position; there was no cover or concealment to be found for Sergeant Pendleton's squad. Prior attempts to get at the gun had failed; artillery could not be called for because his men and the Germans were too close. Pendleton decided the only way to knock the gun out was to lead his men in doing it. They advanced over 100 yards toward the gun while under withering fire; he was seriously wounded in the leg as he got closer to the enemy position. Here Sergeant Pendleton decided to go it alone and signaled for his men to stay back. He moved slowly and painfully, with just grenades in his hands. As was noted later, "With no hope of surviving the veritable hail of machinegun fire which he deliberately drew onto himself, he succeeded in advancing to within ten yards of the enemy position."[35]

Sergeant Pendleton was killed by a burst of the enemy gun moments later, but in doing so he had diverted the attention of the gunners solely onto himself; his sacrifice enabled his squad with the help of another to advance on the machine-gun nest and destroy it. Another of Captain Shaw's platoons neutralized a second gun emplacement providing covering fire for the first, permitting the company to continue its advance through Bardenberg. For his intrepidity above and beyond the call of duty, at the cost of his life, Staff Sergeant Pendleton was posthumously awarded the Medal of Honor.

Two more threats had shown up elsewhere around Bardenberg after 1100 hours, but artillery was able to thwart the attackers in these locations. By noon, reports indicated "every German thrust had been contained. The infantrymen were quick to transfer much of the credit to their supporting artillery and to fourteen squadrons of fighter bombers that droned about the front all day like reckless but disciplined wasps."[36] In the woods outside of Bardenberg, additional credit was given to the 30th Division Reconnaissance Troop and the 119th Infantry Regimental I&R Platoon for keeping enemy patrols out of the village. Even units stationed in the rear were praised. The division's Signal Company improvised a way to replace otherwise unobtainable special batteries for the bazookas; by "working out an ingenious way of mounting ordinary flashlight batteries, still plentiful, on a bazooka, almost all of the rocket launchers in the division—507 in all—were thus modified and kept in service."[37]

But no appreciable ground had been gained; on 12 October the Germans' primary goal was to defend the "big road," Highway 57, which led into Aachen through Würselen. In this they had succeeded; they were preventing the linkup. "We were pecked at in some places, strong at others," Hobbs reported to General Corlett about the morning's actions.[38] At midafternoon, the Germans still "were nibbling and pushing, but no general attack" was the report General Hobbs gave then. "Everything is under control; the men have their tails over the dashboard." But totally aware now of the German buildup of their defenses, with more forces to come, Corlett offered his own assessment. "If the 116th Panzer Division and Adolf Hitler, the I SS Panzers, are in there, this is one of the decisive battles of the war." General Corlett later reported to his Army commander, General Hodges, about the situation, and when he got back to the 30th Infantry Division commander after this a highly pressured Corlett told him that despite the new German opposition, "We have to close the gap some way."

Their options were limited. Corlett first suggested crossing back over the Wurm again, then driving south along the river through Pley; uncertainty about the 116th Panzer Division's intentions nullified this plan. There were even suggestions that troops of the 1st Infantry might attack northward to make the junction, but General Hodges ruled this out when he made it clear that the 30th Division owned the plan to make the linkup. One thing was repeated over and over: General Hobbs wanted more troops. Later he would say, "You should not have to drive men as they were being driven; men should be led, not driven."[39] He was clearly being supportive of his division. Finally they hatched a plan, with General Corlett's approval. Hobbs would get more troops. Two battalions of the 116th Infantry Regiment, under the command of Col. Philip R. Dwyer, would move into North Würselen from their positions west of the Wurm where they had been containing pillboxes near Kerkade; Lt. Col. Hugh W. Colton's 1104 Engineer Group would take over here. To add armored strength to the mission, three companies of the "Iron Knights," the 3rd Battalion of the 66th Armored Regiment under Lt. Col Hugh R. O'Farrell, would also be attached to the 116th Infantry.

The attack would continue from North Würselen, even after other options were offered. General Corlett thought a "wide end run southeast from the vicinity of Alsdorf" might work[40]; Hobbs and his regimental commanders "demurred, reluctant to abandon good defensive positions on the east and southeast lest the indicated German strength materialize." Perhaps this decision was influenced by a prisoner taken later in the day by the 117th Infantry who stated during his interrogation that "four panzer divisions were on the way to Mariadorf to engage in what he termed 'the Battle of the West Wall.'"[41] There were other reasons to believe the Germans were building up forces in the area. At 1830, enemy planes were spotted in the skies overhead; they were marking their front lines with yellow star clusters. Later, green flares were fired into the air by German troops. At 2215 Company F reported "armor was moving around in Mariadorf."[42] A little over a half hour later the 3rd Battalion S-3 reported the same thing. It had been happening for the past two hours. Then, at the stroke of midnight, Captain Culp's Company K reported that his men "could see light flashing in the vicinity of Bettendorf."[43]

The 116th Panzer Division orders for 13 October included continuation of the attack along the line from Euchen to Birk and offensives "from the vicinity west of Würselen toward Bardenberg."[44] At 2240 hours, while tanks were roaming around Mariadorf, Battalion Rink was informed that it would be relieved by *Hauptmann* Hans Appel's Armored Engineer Battalion 675. Armored Reconnaissance Battalion 116 would be positioned between Würselen and Teuterhof and link up with the 246th Division in order to prevent entry into Aachen; the only passable way into the city, other than on Highway 57, ran from the center of Würselen westward to Teuterhof, then after crossing the Wurm it curved southward toward Kolscheid and Soers before stretching down into Aachen; this route also had to be sealed off. Panzer Grenadier Regiment 156 would move to the north edge of Würselen. Like Roman soldiers before them, for both the Germans and the Americans everything would now depend on their success or failure fighting on a narrow front in the buildings and streets of Würselen.

Friday the 13th began with American intermediaries at the Robert Ley settlement west of Würselen demanding the surrender of a newly arrived company of *Hauptmann* Appel's Armored Engineering Battalion 675; the Germans declined. According to Combat Group Rink battle reports, the demand had come about because "the enemy had become aware of [its] relief."[45] But the relief had not happened because of some confusion with the orders Rink received and the probability that the Germans got wind of General Hobbs's plans to bring reinforcements into the area. Following the refusal to surrender, unidentified American units right after 0800 "broke into the right and left of the armored engineer battalion position with tanks and infantry and dispersed it, developing a dangerous threat to the flank of the 2d Battalion, Panzer Grenadier Regiment 60, which was adjacent to the left."[46]

Captain McBride's Company B of the 119th Infantry was in all probability the unidentified American unit; his men and their accompanying tanks had been trying to clear this area and had come upon "some five tanks to their left and three to their right front" that morning.[47] The always aggressive McBride had gone forward to a building just 75 yards short of the first tank he saw and directed artillery fire on it; the tank was knocked out. After calling in more adjustments, he scored two additional hits on a second. *Hauptmann* Appel "found a hero's death" when he personally "threw himself toward the enemy breach." Paymaster Richard Wolff-Boenisch wrote in his diary later that day:

> It was a black day for the engineer battalion. Oberleutnant Heinrich Dieckmann, Leutnant Matthias Leufen, and Leutnant Gunther Muller wounded; our commander Hauptmann Appel killed. This is how they leave us, one by one. I felt really bad about the commander; I believe there was no man more decent, unselfish and humble than he.[48]

The drumbeat of artillery fire nullified further offensive operations for both sides as the morning wore on. Attacks "were to no avail," wrote the Army official historian. "Because the attack was on such a narrow front, the Germans were able to concentrate [on us] the fire of an estimated six to seven battalions of light artillery, one or two medium battalions and at least two batteries of heavy artillery."[49]

"Artillery and mortar fire on the 116th Panzer Division advances were bitterly heavy and succeeded in neutralizing many approaches to the network of [their] positions, thus cutting down maneuverability," another account noted.[50] Wire lines for both sides were constantly split by artillery shelling, cutting off communications between units and hamstringing command and control at many levels. Tanks of both sides, whether offensive or defensive in their efforts, could not move into any open areas. "Finally, the action called for willingness to take losses in gaining ground, one of the most difficult things to communicate along the chain of command."

Most units simply held their positions, assisted with firing plans, marked friendly mines to their front, and maintained guards at gaps until further orders came down. Intense artillery even interfered with the insertion of Colonel Dwyer's 116th Infantry forces; after making contact with Brown's 3rd Battalion of the 119th Infantry at the Gouley mine, the new arrivals took up positions next to the 1st Battalion west of Würselen. Both Companies G and B of Lieutenant Colonel O'Farrell's 66th Armored Regiment battalion were also brought to a halt by *Panzerfaust* and artillery fire along the main road on the northern outskirts of the village.

Company B's commander, Capt. James M. Burt, a 1939 Norwich University graduate who interrupted his civilian career as a chemist in western Massachusetts to join the army two years later, "did more than his share to alleviate the situation."[51] Two of his leading tanks had been "shot out from underneath him." Burt, still nimble from his days as a high school football player, dismounted his tank and worked through his armored infantrymen to a forward position where he could direct artillery fire. Despite exposing himself, he even managed to rescue several of his men who had been wounded before he returned to his command tank; here he continued to direct the company from its rear deck. This time he was wounded in his face and neck, but by "dominating and controlling the critical situation through the sheer force of his heroic example" he held his forces together that day.[52]

Dawn on 14 October brought clear skies and another good day for artillery forward observers to see their targets. Almost every attack on the American side saw any momentum stall as "the old pattern of enemy fire was resumed across the brief spaces separating the two forces."[53] Armored Engineer Battalion 675, now being commanded by *Leutnant* Otto Varnholt, maintained contact with Colonel Sutherland's 119th Infantry forces between Würselen and Kohlscheid; Varnholt mostly dispatched reconnaissance patrols. Panzer Grenadier Regiment 60 "carried the burden of the fighting,"[54] but again the main forces of the 116th Panzer Division did not attack in the area because of continued uncertainty about the use of the Greyhounds among the German command; the division's services had been contemplated for the attack on Verlautenheide and Eilendorf with the 3rd Panzer Division the next day, but this only "created amazement" in the view of the 116th's historian in light of the conditions around Würselen, and use with the 3rd Panzers never materialized.

The 116th Infantry's 2nd Battalion had a particularly bad day: an exploding shell fragment wounded its CO, Major Cawthorn, in the left leg and forced his evacuation. The battalion executive officer, Capt. Eccles H. Scott, took command. The commander of Company E, Capt. Robert E. Garcia of San Jose, California, was wounded when he "unwisely peeked around the corner of a house and was the recipient of a shell blast."[55] Historian Joseph Balkoski wrote:

The men of the 116th were not used to this kind of combat. The Germans were close, often within range of a hand grenade, but were so effectively dug in that they only rarely showed themselves. When they did, even for a few seconds, the impact on the Americans was usually deadly. The 29ers [a general reference to 29th Infantry Division soldiers] learned that movement of any kind in the open, even at a dead run, was likely to attract the attention of an invisible German sniper, who was surprisingly skilled at his job. If the 116th were to push the Germans out of Wuerselen, obviously the only way to do it was to reduce strong points by direct assault, one after the other, a process that might eventually succeed but would take time and inflict a number of casualties that could cripple the regiment's spirit for a long time.[56]

The Iron Knights fared a bit better during the day. Company G's tankers got about a thousand yards closer to Würselen, but these men were stopped when their infantry had to withdraw to cover because of the combined hell of enemy artillery, mortar, and *Panzerfaust* fires; Mark Vs also struck, but this attack was repulsed without losing any ground. In late afternoon, Captain Burt's Company B attacked to cut off the roadway that the Germans had used for their approach into Company G's positions and took this crossroad.

Progress was being made, but at an excruciatingly slow pace. That night, an increasingly perturbed General Hodges bypassed Corlett and called General Hobbs directly, "expressing great dissatisfaction" that the gap was not being closed.[57]

Nor was anyone happy with the outcomes the following day. "Wuerselen was defended fanatically by excellent troops," noted Major Greer's 3rd Battalion of the 120th Infantry's after-action report.[58] His men pushed deep into the western part of town, "up to 600 meters south of the settlement," according to the 116th Panzer Division historian.[59] But a counterattack by Armored Reconnaissance Battalion 116 and the division reserve, the 1st Battalion of Regiment 156, "threw the enemy back to the settlement." This counterattack was supported by six *Jagdpanthers*, heavily armored, turretless, 88mm gun-equipped versions of the

Panther. Major Greer lost five of his tanks and twelve of his men; all were killed, including two officers. During the fighting, heavy German artillery fire blasted two stories away from an observation tower and "constantly shook [Greer's] command post."[60] CPs were under attack all day; the 116th Panzer Division reported:

> In these battles, the commander of 1CO, Panzer Grenadier Regiment 156, Oberleutnant Kurt Heiberger, and Oberfeldwebel Helfried Orb of 3CO, Armored Reconnaissance Battalion 116, distinguished themselves. Orb and his platoon rescued the command post of 2CO; it had been surrounded at the Scherberg schoolhouse. They brought four comrades back to freedom and captured 15 Americans.[61]

German forces at the crossroads just north of Würselen also stopped the 66th Armored Regiment companies. Capt. Joseph S. Roberts's Company G was repulsed by blistering *Panzerfaust* fire, and he lost three tanks. Company H, commanded by Capt. Cameron J. Warren, barely reached the roadway before being stopped. Captain Burt's Company B was the only unit that gained yardage; his tanks ground forward about 300 yards, but two were knocked out. During this time, Burt again displayed outstanding courage; he dismounted his own tank several times to direct friendly artillery fire and remained in the open for nearly an hour, calling in adjustments. Captain Roberts also dismounted his tank while under fire and went forward to regroup his infantrymen and reorganize his tanks. Sgt. Dozier K. Smith was later recognized for his gallantry when he risked his life by racing 150 yards toward the German line so he could give first aid to a wounded tanker. Sgt. Arden W. Gatzke of Company H remembered:

> We went about a hundred yards past [a] group of houses and pulled up behind a brick house and a brick fence. The road in front of the house was the dividing line between us and the Germans. One tank of ours got hit and the tank commander got a broken arm. As he jumped off the tank he broke both ankles. Rest of the crew unhurt. We were under heavy artillery fire all night. Raining.[62]

It was just as grim elsewhere around Würselen. The 116th Infantry made little progress during the day; advances were measured in yards with no meaningful ground or objectives gained by the regiment in the past seventy-two hours. Eight days had now passed since closing the gap looked inevitable, but there were still thousands more yards to go. General Corlett, under increasing pressure from Army's clearly impatient General Hodges, phoned General Hobbs at 1920 and told him, "I'm going to give you an order to attack all along the line and close the gap."[63] According to witnesses, the words "close the gap" were repeated four times.

Hobbs's G-3, Lt. Col. Harold E. Hassenfelt, later modestly admitted "that he was the one responsible for the division's plan to close the gap on 16 October."[64] This plan featured an attack all along the line as General Corlett had called for; the main effort fell onto the shoulders of Colonel Sutherland's 119th Infantry. Lieutenant Colonel Cox's 2nd Battalion would relieve the 1st Battalion in North Würselen before first light, then attack southward by way of the western fringes of the village. "Our plan was not to push directly through Wuerselen to cut the highway," Cox noted.[65] In doing so his men would actually be closer to the eastern banks of the Wurm River than they would to be to Würselen proper, thereby avoiding any fighting through the village; going down the east side of the river would also leave the pillboxes along this route on Cox's right flank with their aperture openings conveniently facing westward. The battalion's objective was to seize Hill 194 just across the Aachen-Würselen highway, northwest of Ravelsberg Hill.

In the new scheme of operations Lieutenant Colonel Herlong's 1st Battalion and Brown's 3rd Battalion would cross the Wurm and move into Kohlscheid; Herlong's men would mop up here while Lieutenant Colonel Brown's forces pivoted off the southern edge of the village and continued to fight their way to their objective, a hilltop near Soers. By taking this route, Brown's companies would draw the attention of the Germans manning the pillboxes on the other side of the Wurm, but in doing so it would divert their focus from Cox's main effort to link up with the Americans on the Ravelsberg.

Another diversionary effort in Hassenfelt's bold plan would be undertaken by the 116th Infantry forces still holding out in Würselen. Major Greer's 3rd Battalion of the 120th Infantry would assist in the frontal attack here. Their main mission was to draw fire; if any ground was gained two companies of the 743rd Tank Battalion and a new arrival—the 99th Infantry Battalion that General Corlett had provided from Corps' reserve—would hold it. Colonel Johnson's 117th Infantry forces southeast of Alsdorf in Kol-Kellersberg, as well as the other 120th battalions near Birk and Euchen, were to put on shows along the far eastern flank of the division in order to divert attention away from Würselen altogether; Hassenfelt also envisioned feints of company strength toward Mariadorf in his plan, to convince the Germans that the main attack on 16 October would actually be here.

Rain fell all night and was expected to continue through the day. Still, it was noted that "there would be no tolerance for halfway measures. This was it."[66]

Thus, the plan went off. Lieutenant Colonel Brown sent a squad across the Wurm shortly after midnight; the men's mission was to feel out the enemy in Kohlscheid. It did not go well. They were spotted and a mortar barrage was directed at them, wounding three of the men. Others in the reconnaissance force started back after probing the enemy defenses, and they ran into a strong patrol. The men had to take refuge in a nearby house, where close fighting broke out after grenades and rifle fire escorted the German attackers through its doors and windows. The American patrol was captured; Pfc. Paul Howard, a medic, had moved the three wounded men to a safer location in an abandoned enemy bunker by this time. They waited in hope that others would rescue them when the 3rd Battalion commenced its move toward Soers.

Nearly a thousand U.S. soldiers began fording the Wurm at 0500. Right behind them, the industrious engineers of the 105th Engineer Battalion went to work and completed their first treadway bridge a half hour later, well before first light and despite being under strong and accurate mortar fire. Tanks quickly rushed across to catch up with the infantry, now well on their way to Kohlscheid. Herlong's 1st Battalion men met scattered but stubborn resistance as they double-timed it to the northern edge of the village; the leading platoon of Captain Simmons's Company A was pinned down by machine-gun fire until Sgt. John Overman courageously charged the Germans manning the gun and killed three of them with his own submachine gun, allowing the battalion columns to move again.

When the leading platoon of Lieutenant Colonel Brown's 3rd Battalion came down the road toward the southern outskirts of the village, these men had to scatter into ditches; machine-gun fire also came in at them, causing several casualties. Company I's Lt. Vincent S. Scurria was ordered to swing this platoon to the left so they could cover the route the tanks were using to come up in support. They did not get far. Scurria's men were quickly pinned down by crossfire from two other machine-gun emplacements, but not for long. Lieutenant Scurria "stood up into the machinegun fire and maneuvered his platoon into positions where they were at least able to knock out the machinegun nests," a later account noted.[67] Dawn was fast approaching, and both battalions were closing in as quickly onto the muddy streets of Kohlscheid. Back across the Wurm, Cox's 2nd Battalion had jumped off at 0600, moved quickly past the west side of Würselen and advanced nearly a thousand yards toward a slag pile closer to Teuterhof. Here the lead company was clobbered by both artillery and tank fire; the starring 119th Infantry effort to close the gap was suddenly stalled.

But, along the front of the 117th and 120th Infantries from Birk to Alsdorf, Colonel Hassenfelt's planned diversionary efforts to get Cox moving again were going off. It was noted "the Germans bit."[68]

Two things made this happen. By this time, Lieutenant Stanley of the 117th Infantry's Company C had led a small combat patrol right up to the sunken rail line on the edge of Mariadorf. His men's mission had been to draw fire and, if possible, capture some prisoners. They did both. Mortar fire hit the patrol as it was moving along the edge of the thick woods between Kol-Kellersberg and the rail line, and when the men closed in on the track itself members of the squad spotted Germans moving about in the draw to their right. Stanley was the first to open fire, followed by others. Most of the Germans were killed, but six were taken prisoner. Now there was just cause on the enemy's part to believe Stanley's men were the tip of the spear in front of a general attack into Mariadorf.

At 0700 there was more reason to believe this. DIVARTY joined with the 81mm and 60mm mortar fires of 117th Infantry's line companies, smoked the ground to their front for a half hour, and then hammered away at the town buildings, shops, taverns, and brick houses along the main street in Mariadorf in what would hopefully be received as a preparatory barrage ahead of an even larger attack. German artillery quickly confirmed their local commanders believed it was so.

To the Americans in their foxholes who were suddenly pummeled by "the thunder of these German fires," it felt and looked like the heaviest concentration of explosions in their combined European campaign experiences to date.[69] Every caliber of enemy weapon "awed the most seasoned fighters." But the intended results were now happening; German attention was quickly focused on protecting Mariadorf "to break up the attack that appeared imminent," and not on Lieutenant Colonel Cox's forces west of Würselen who were clinging to a hilltop halfway toward Hill 194.

And the Americans had even more tricks up their sleeves; the main diversionary attack toward Mariadorf was not even scheduled until early afternoon. Fighting raged elsewhere throughout the morning. Against Panzer Grenadier Regiment 156, supported by the 2nd Battalion of Panzer Regiment 16, Colonel Dwyer's 116th Infantry attack in North Würselen "was still a study in frustration in terms of ground gained," but his men were nevertheless tying down the Germans here.[70] Across the Wurm in Kohlscheid, both battalions of Colonel Sutherland's 119th Infantry were making progress in their fight against elements of the 246th Division. Lieutenant Colonel Herlong's 1st Battalion cleared out the northern half of the village by noon and his men were now heading southwest toward a slag pile in front of Ursfeld.

Companies K and L of Brown's 3rd Battalion met some initial resistance when these men reached the southern outskirts of Kohlscheid, but as one officer remembered, "We were soon walking through the village, checking houses, and keeping our eyes open."[71] Brown's forces were now preparing to fight their way to a little hilltop next to Soers, offering flank protection to Lieutenant Colonel Cox's 2nd Battalion forces across the Wurm on their way there.

It was now time for the main diversionary attack. At 1300 hours Capt. George H. Sibbald's Company E of the 117th Infantry was detailed to seize the railroad station in Mariadorf; two squads of Company A, under the command of Sgt. Robert Q. Fortune, would protect his left flank. Company K of the 120th was slated to be on Sibbald's right. Their mission was to be shot at during this final feint to keep the

Germans' attention off Cox's men. The attack was preceded by friendly smoke, mortar, and artillery fire; Panzer Grenadier Regiment 156 responded almost immediately with battery and battalion concentrations in calibers from 75mm to 210mm, or larger.

Things went wrong quickly. In the woods closest to the railroad line the Germans were dug in on an elongated slag pile and on a high embankment that overlooked the tracks. They opened up with machine-gun fire while several grenadiers raced down to the thick underbrush that covered their final protective lines and started shooting. This devastating fire drove back one of Captain Sibbald's platoons, but the other struggled forward and got almost to the railway embankment. Here, more Germans emerged from tunnels and a mine shaft. The platoon was surrounded. Six Americans eventually made it back; the others were either killed, wounded, or captured.

Sergeant Fortune's squads had done everything possible to avert this disaster. His men had moved forward "on the double" through the woods to the left of Company E, proceeding quickly enough for most of his soldiers to get ahead of the German mortar and artillery fire. Fortune had ordered them to dig in on a little knoll about 30 yards from the edge of the woods where they could observe the enemy. As he later explained:

> Each squad dug in standing foxholes and we placed BAR's cov-
> ering both flanks. We got a good deal of small arms fire across
> the open fields to our front and left. After we had been at it
> about an hour, the Jerries started throwing artillery at the edge
> of the trees to our immediate rear. Suddenly Company E started
> withdrawing through my lines. I could hear, just barely, the
> voice of the company commander, but for a long time couldn't
> understand what he was saying over the 536. Finally, I got the
> information that we should withdraw if we could. I tried to send
> out men between barrages, but it was rough going. My platoon
> guide, Staff Sergeant Robert Schwartz was killed by a tree burst.
> Thinking he was alive, I dragged his body back to my foxhole.[72]

Tall, mustached Captain Sibbald had been using his 536 radio to request permission to use his reserve platoon in an attempt to rescue his surrounded men. For more than an hour they "fought doggedly through a hail of small arms and shellfire."[73] But his regimental commander, Colonel Johnson, eventually ordered him to withdraw. Sibbald obeyed, but "he refused to report to the Regimental CP or leave the woods until he personally saw that all wounded that it was possible to reach had been evacuated to safety."[74] Johnson later "characterized this action as the finest example of leadership by a company commander in [his] regiment."[75] Company E's morning reports eventually showed that twenty-one men were missing, all likely captured; Lt. John F. Doyle, one of the platoon leaders, was among them.

Sergeant Fortune was no less earnest in his efforts to evacuate the men of his squads. After locating what he thought was most of them, he "looked around and hollered twice; nobody answered," so he went back and reported to Captain Sibbald. "Then I began to think," he recalled later.

> Where were Masters and Evans? Are they still out there wounded? Did I leave them there to be killed? I don't remember anything else until I woke up two days later in a hospital in Holland. They had me down for "Combat Fatigue–Serious." The major said I had hollered all night like I was crazy; "I killed my own men, I let them die, it's all my fault."[76]

Sergeant Fortune was eventually released and sent back to his company. But he spoke for many when he later said, "It's funny how you can be cool as a cucumber when there's all hell breaking loose, and then go to pieces when the danger is over."

Lieutenant Colonel Cox's 2nd Battalion forces had still been clinging to the downward slope of the hill just 500 yards from the highway that led into Aachen during the 117th Infantry's feint. The Germans were arrayed to either of their flanks; SS Battalion Bucher of *Kampfgruppe* Diefenthal attached to the 246th Division was to Cox's right. To his left was the 6Co of Militia Training Battalion II from the 116th Panzer Division. Theses combined forces had created a critical situation; the Americans were being clobbered with hostile artillery fire and the pillboxes

with German machine gunners in their trenches were proving to be difficult to overrun. Rain was coming down; the hillside was full of mud; the
American tanks were stuck in it, and Cox's infantry dared not move to
either flank without them.

The German Mark VIs had more maneuverability because their
tracks were much wider than the American armor; their commanders
took full advantage of this and sent six of their Tigers, accompanied by
about forty grenadiers, onto the hill. But Sergeant Holycross, who had so
aptly demonstrated how pillboxes should be taken a week earlier, again
rallied his men. He "pinned the defenders next to their shelters with fire
and worked his men in, successfully reducing seven pillboxes and capturing 50 of his opposite numbers."[77] And as the Mark VI Tigers and
grenadiers got closer, they were driven off by the combined fires of American bazookas, artillery, and small arms. Then, as the 116th Panzer Division historian later noted:

> When the German artillery had to move its fire over toward the
> American attacks [northeast of Würselen] the 2nd Battalion
> 119th Infantry broke through the boundary between the 116th
> Panzer Division and the 246th Volks-Grenadier Division, which
> had detoured from Kohlscheid to Richterich . . . the road to Hill
> 194 was therefore open to the enemy. Only the bunkers south-
> west of the Kaisersruh station now formed a barrier.[78]

At 1544 hours, General Huebner's 1st Infantry Division chief of staff
phoned General Hobbs's command post and told them "his observers
reported friendly troops [in sight] and that a patrol was being sent out."[79]

Lieutenant Arn of Company F received immediate orders to send his
forces across the now darkening and rain-swept valley; a ten-man patrol
under the command of Staff Sgt. Frank A. Karwell was hastily assembled
with two scouts—Pvt. Evan F. Whitis and Pfc. Edward Krauss. It did not
start well; when the patrol jumped off they were greeted by strong
machine-gun fire from both of their flanks and even frontally. Karwell
got hit before the patrol could cross the Aachen-Würselen roadway.
His last words to Krauss and Whitis were to "keep going and make the
contact."[80]

Through continued interlocking German machine-gun fire they did, and according to their own narratives they "eventually stumbled into the 1st Division's positions." "We're from Company K," shouted Staff Sergeant Chastin from Ravelsberg Hill. "Come on up!"[81] Together, Krauss and Whitis yelled back, "We're from Company F; come on down." Chastin proved more persuasive; the two scouts came up, they all shook hands, and closing of the Aachen Gap was finally accomplished.

CHAPTER 13

Surrender

*Night found the American flag waving over the first
captured German city in World War II.*

26TH INFANTRY AAR, 21 OCTOBER 1944

At 0530 on 17 October, German planes started dropping both heavy and antipersonnel bombs into Aachen, but amazingly few landed in the 26th Infantry Regiment battalion areas. Three of these bombers continued flying back and forth over the city; then at 0630 the first friendly American aircraft screamed into the German airspace and their planes peeled away and disappeared. Little activity had initially been planned after more daylight enveloped Aachen; Lieutenant Colonel Corley's 3rd Battalion companies were to sit in place, rest, receive replacements, and prepare for their new offensive in Farwick Park the following morning. But with the situation on the hills northeast of the city now under control, General Huebner permitted Lieutenant Colonel Daniel's 2nd Battalion to go back on the attack. "Our zone widened considerably to both the north and the south as soon as Wilhelm Strasse was crossed," Daniel later recalled while also adding, "Enemy resistance became more fanatical."[1]

It was Captain Smoot's Company E and Walker's Company G that first ran into this renewed German vigor. Wilhelmstrasse was one of the city's main streets; the buildings on nearby streets were in such ruin from shelling and bombing by this time that the Germans were using their fragile façades as offensive targets for their *Panzerfausts*. Inauspiciously, Americans started receiving injuries from falling brickwork as soon as they started making their way to Wilhelmstrasse where it intersects with Hinderburgstrasse.

The enemy forces had even better fields of fire here; according to Lieutenant Bays, leader of the TD platoon operating with the companies, this was where they really "caught hell."[2] A panzer-supported attack by enemy infantry quickly developed. Direct antitank fire roared in from the rubble around the once-proud Aachen state theater, where famed maestro Herbert von Karajan had conducted Beethoven symphonies before the war came to the city. Now a pillbox in front of the theater was being used to lull the Americans into a trap; direct antitank fire was set up around it, and Bays's only operational TD could not get into an effective location to return fire due to the claustrophobic layout of the streets. "The Germans were running tanks back and forth across Hindenburg right in front of our eyes," Lieutenant Colonel Daniel explained later. "All we could do was chase them with artillery and mortar fire and this was not a satisfying procedure."[3]

Daniel quickly thought through a plan to rectify the problem and he wasted little time putting it in place. Like Corley's 3rd Battalion, General Andrus had also entrusted Daniel's forces with a 155 SP gun. It had been kept out of harm's way up to this point. Now, in preparation for its opening performance, Daniel first had Lieutenant Bays move his TD into a courtyard behind one of the houses on Hinderburgstrasse and then he directed him to blast a hole straight through one of its brick walls. The battalion's attached tanks then worked their way into positions on the other side of the street; they were accompanied by a platoon of Walker's Company G men whose job was to prevent any *Panzerfaust* teams from firing on the American armor.

After blowing the hole through the house, Bays repositioned the TD so its crew could join the Shermans and start firing down the cross streets along Hinderburgstrasse. The purpose was to discourage German tanks from emerging and being able to shoot any rounds toward the house with the clearly visible hole now in it. About a half hour later, satisfied that the enemy forces were occupied and well distracted by his armor feint, Daniel played his hand and ordered the SP gun into position. It was moved up to the brick house and its muzzle was soon seen poking through the blown opening. A dozen rounds of 1,400-feet-per-second velocity shells were fired directly into the pillbox, at the *Panzerfaust* positions around the state theater, and toward the cross streets between them. The pillbox turned out to be a camouflaged tank; it was completely destroyed. One of the SP gun's shells hit another German tank just as it was nosing around a building and starting to aim its gun at the Americans. "The firing of our gun was spectacular and satisfying," a contented Lieutenant Colonel Daniel told everyone later.[4]

By the time all offensive operations were suspended at 1700 hours, both Companies E and G had closed into positions near the central rail-road station. But Lieutenant Webb's Company F was stuck back on Adalbertstein Weg; an enemy antitank gun firing from the corner of Lutherstrasse and Kaiser Platz denied any advancement. It had also been a rough afternoon for Walker's men; one platoon faced intense enemy machine-gun fire while crossing one of the open areas leveled by the ear-lier bombing. The enemy gunner teams were well hidden among the rubble and ruins around other houses. Still, the Americans attacked; two German tanks joined the fight, laying 88mm fire into Company G's advancing skirmish lines. Heavy casualties resulted, but the rifle platoon pressed on; a friendly machine-gun section carried the fight directly toward the enemy tanks while the remaining U.S. soldiers charged the hostile machine-gun nests. More walls crumpled; bricks flew. Then the German tankers buttoned up their vehicles and withdrew. The rest of the enemy forces withered; their positions were finally cleared out. Survivors surrendered.

While the 3rd Battalion companies saw no combat during the day, Lieutenant Colonel Corley and his staff kept very busy. Visitors first arrived at 1000 hours; General Rose was in company with Lieutenant Colonel Hogan. Along with Colonel Seitz, the command group was there to review plans and coordinate their forces for the attack the next day.

Corley's mission was broadly defined as taking back every enemy position in Farwick Park, but his primary objectives were the Kurhaus and the Hotel Quellenhof. Once these were back in Corley's possession, a portion of his forces were to move on to Salvatorberg in order to pro-tect the flank of Task Force Hogan as his armored forces drove toward Lousberg; Hogan was to then wheel north up to Laurensberg about 2 miles north of Aachen, an ancient Roman sanctuary site before it was occupied by Napoleon during the French Revolution. Remnants of the

49th Infantry Division still held Laurensberg. The briefing ended before noon, but Lieutenant Colonel Corley's staff was only getting started; typewriters were now being dusted off because Seitz had warned everyone that another important visitor would be by to review the plan later in the day. "This was the only time in 13 months of combat in which a written order was put out while engaged in battle," a startling, later memo to the 26th Infantry Regiment's S-3, Major Clisson, revealed.[5]

Somewhat derisively entitled Field Order Number 1, Corley nevertheless presented it to General Huebner when he arrived with Colonel Seitz in the CP at 1500 hours; the order detailed attachments and objectives for each company.[6] Captain Botts's Company I would have five tanks and three TDs for his men's attack; it would be preceded by fires from the 155 SP gun before they moved along Rowlandstrasse and came into Farwick Park from the north. Corwell's Company K would attack along Manheim Allee, which fronted his objective—the Hotel Quellenhof; a squad of engineers would perform necessary demolition work and two bazooka teams would provide added firepower. Lieutenant Shepard's Company L was tasked with retaking the Kurhaus; he was expected to then send a platoon over to hold the hotel. Two tanks, two TDs, and a section of heavy machine guns would support this platoon; Shepard's other two platoons would stay back as the battalion reserve, to be used as needed.

Corley then turned General Huebner's attention to the planned support for Task Force Hogan's thrust up to Laurensberg. First, the Antitank Company would be used to defend the north flank of his battalion by going into positions on Krefelderstrasse and Passstrasse; this would also afford flank protection for Hogan's armored vehicles as they passed by the area. Lieutenant Nechey's Company M, less the section of heavy machine gunners that would be with Shepard's men, would also help protect Hogan's forces; the 81mm mortar platoon, with 4.2-inch chemical mortars joining, would escort Task Force Hogan as they continued their drive by pouring blinding concentrations of smoke and fire on the Lousberg. To satisfy Huebner's penchant for timing, Corley told him he expected to have the objectives in Farwick Park taken by noon, allowing for mopping up through the afternoon. General Huebner was undoubtedly even more pleased to hear that the 81mm and 4.2-inch mortar teams had warmed up for their assignment by thoroughly working over the area south of the tennis courts that very afternoon just before his arrival in the CP.

Lieutenant Colonel Corley's opponents were also planning their defensive strategies, undoubtedly spurred on by messages of encouragement from their higher ups.[7] *Oberst* Wilck exclaimed in a written memo to his forces that "All of Germany is watching our battle with pride and admiration." Himmler reinforced this sentiment by radio, announcing to Wilck's men, "The eyes of all Germany are on the defense of the ancient city by Battle Group Aachen." Brandenberg of 7th Army added to the pitch by writing, "Your fight for the imperial city is being followed with admiration and breathless expectancy; you are fighting for the honor of the National Socialist German Army." *General der Infanterie* Köchling even joined in with his own inspirational message, stating "The 81 Corps renders the highest tribute to the Aachen defender's valor in the fight to the end for Führer and Nation." These words of encouragement were later found neatly folded in the pockets of captured Germans.

About 150 men from the 1st SS Panzer (Hitler) Division found their way into Aachen during the night of 17–18 October. Lieutenant Lafley, the 26th Infantry's S-2 noted, "The gap was thought closed, but this group got through."[8]

They brought in an anti-tank platoon of 75's; one infantry howitzer platoon of two 75's, another AT platoon of three 20mm [antiaircraft guns], and the rest infantry. They were probably sent in to bolster morale. An estimated 125 Aachen police were also given rifles and put in the line in their police uniforms. They were broken down into squads of eight, with each squad being given a machinegun. The chief of police, Major [Paul] Zimmermann, was in charge. The previous night, about 80 police also arrived from the Cologne area.

Total enemy strength remaining in Aachen was uncertain. Lafley estimated that there were 3,350 men still under *Oberst* Wilck's command in the city on the night of 15–16 October. The U.S. Army historian claimed Wilck had a total of 4,392 "combat effectives," plus eleven surgeons and thirty-four medics on 17 October. The difference in their estimates may have been rooted in the actual disposition of the 246th Division's forces; Wilck still had units outside of the city under his direction.

The mission of Denkert's 3rd Panzer Division on 18 October was again to reestablish contact with *Oberst* Wilck's forces inside of Aachen; plans included assistance from the 116th Panzer Division.[9] The first task was the seizure of the Ravelsberg and a group of bunkers south of the hill mass in a surprise attack. Then all available forces were to push farther west and reopen access to the city. But judging by the sentiments of the 116th Panzer Division's commander, *Oberst* Siegfried von Waldenberg, despite his Prussian sense of duty, he confessed this in his pocket calendar on the night before the attack:

> It is very, very tough fighting and casualties are high accordingly. Contrary to expectations, the American fights very well. The Americans succeeded in the encirclement of Aachen; they broke the 246th Division. My front held its own . . . but nothing helps anymore; enemy fire is too strong.[10]

For Colonel Smith's 18th Infantry, this same day was confidently devoted to making adjustments in expectation of their opposite numbers' last attempts to take back their hard-fought-for positions outside of Aachen; they were prepared for any so-called surprise attacks. Captain Folk's Company L men were even engaged in bitter fighting for the pill-boxes fronting the Ravelsberg; two TDs had been ordered up from Haaren to provide assistance. They cruised through the area west to northwest of the hill all morning, blasting the pillboxes from 300 to 500 yards out; Folk's soldiers eventually took one hundred prisoners attached to *Oberst* Wilck's 246th Division. Later, at about 1700, the TD crews set up a roadblock on the northern slope of the hill, but upon spotting three German tanks approaching from Würselen, their commander, Lt. Ira W. Blackwell, ordered them back to Haaren[11]; two squads of Captain Russell's Company K 3rd Platoon assumed responsibility for guarding the roadblock.

The weather was suddenly a big factor; the skies became pitch black that night, the wind started blowing harder, and rain began falling in sheets. It was a cold, wet night at the roadblock. Then, at 0530 on 18

October, the two American squads were leaving this position and returning to Ravelsberg Hill where the roadblock could be observed from an outpost; Germans suddenly came in behind them and overran the roadblock before they could make it back up the hill. In a very short time, Russell's opposite numbers grew in strength and captured all of the pillboxes that belonged to the 3rd Platoon—numbers 2, 3, 4, and 6 on the north slope of the hill. Two Mark Vs eventually started firing directly into Company K's positions farther back, knocking out Lieutenant Heinrich's machine-gun emplacements. Approximately twenty-two more German tanks were forming up; enemy SP guns were now starting to throw fire into the hill mass. The Americans had been surprised; from one German who was taken prisoner, Captain Russell learned that the attackers were the vanguard of the 3rd Battalion, 8th Panzer Grenadier Regiment of the 3rd Panzer Grenadier Division.

Russell had seen this kind of attack before when he was a lieutenant with the company in North Africa; then it was the entire 10th Panzer Division at El Guettar in Tunisia. His men may have been initially shocked by the sheer size of the force attacking the company now, but their adrenaline-fueled spirit soon had them using their BARs, machine guns, small arms, and hand grenades to repulse their attackers. Eleven Germans who were close to one another fell quickly in front of pillbox 6; their bodies were piled up in a ditch. Farther out, fifteen to twenty more grenadiers were killed or severely wounded; they were strewn over each other in some places. But their superior numbers prevailed. Despite their casualties, the enemy forces retained possession of pillboxes 6, 3, and 4. To prevent more grenadiers from getting to the crest of the hill, Captain Russell had his other two undermanned platoons take up defensive positions on a line southwest to northeast. As he looked out from the hill, however, he could still see that even more grenadiers and their panzers were regrouping for another frontal attack.

It came at approximately 1000 hours. An estimated two of their platoons attacked Russell's 1st platoon on the left; they were greeted by withering fire and the Germans again suffered heavy casualties. Then another wave came, first covered by their tank and mortar fire. This time they went after pillboxes 5, 7, and 8. But Russell's men stopped them cold; the grenadiers were forced to withdraw, leaving most of their killed and wounded behind.

Lieutenant Colonel Peckham, commanding the 3rd Battalion, later recalled the difficult circumstances he was now confronted with:

> Plowed fields, rain and open country made the hill an impassable mass for our tanks, TD's or anti-tank guns. We could not get anything on the hill that could live for anti-tank protection. Therefore, the hill had to be held by the infantry alone.[12]

Just before noon, Captain Miller's Company B was ordered out of Verlautenheide and over to the Ravelsberg to help out. By now Company K had suffered numerous casualties. But before Miller could get his men in position, the Germans again tried to gain entrance into Russell's lines on the hill; more high-volume rounds of American fire stopped them, but the grenadiers managed to retain possession of the three pillboxes on the forward north slope of the Ravelsberg as the afternoon wore on.

The fight for Farwick Park was well under way by this time. The area south of the tennis courts had again been worked over by the 81mm and 4.2-inch mortars; interdictory fire had also been laid along Ludwigs Allee and Kupferstrasse to deter movement of any enemy reserves into the park. Lieutenant Colonel Corley took advantage of the poor dawn light that morning and moved a platoon of Lieutenant Shepard's Company L opposite the main line of the German forces south of the tennis courts right after the mortars had performed their work. Corley had even held off artillery fire until Shepard's attack started in order to keep the enemy forces off balance. These maneuvers indeed caught Battalion Rink by surprise and completely demoralized its men who were occupying fixed positions in the center of their defensive line.

The SP 155 had also thrown its weight in. From the gun's position on the corner of Rolandsstrasse and Margratenstrasse, it fired fifteen rounds into the buildings suspected of housing German forces south of Roland Platz. Then Captain Botts's Company I moved out; their attack first went off smoothly, but slowed down as they approached Pippinstrasse. It was now nearing 0800, and by this time the 155 SP gun had been moved over to support Company L; it was emplaced south of the tennis courts, drawing some enemy fire, but as soon as the gun got off its initial shots there was no more trouble. A total of thirty menacing rounds were fired into the Kurhaus and the Hotel Quellenhof, further demoralizing the Germans defending these positions. Combined with fire from the TDs and tanks, both objectives were neutralized. Lt. William D. Rachford's 2nd Platoon moved up at 0900 and entered the hotel's once ornate lobby; these men immediately started looking through the rubble for entrances to the basement where Battalion Rink's forces were suspected to be holding out in order to escape the tenacious American shelling of the upper levels.

By now the Kurhaus had been taken back; it turned out to be a command post. Captain Corwell's Company K platoons were also clearing out the elegant but heavily damaged homes on both sides of Monheims Allee by this time; snapped trees covered the strip of park between the two lanes of the boulevard and the Americans disposed of the Germans hiding there. The 155 SP gun had been moved again, to Rolandstrasse and Passstrasse. Here, the powerful tube was employed to neutralize a Battalion Rink outpost in the Church of St. Salvador on Salvatorberg hill; it was being used to spot American troop movements and to adjust artillery fire. All open enemy resistance ceased by 1030 hours, well ahead of the time Corley promised to General Huebner. Only the Hotel Quellenhof, its main lobby "a maelstrom of discarded clothing, weapons, food and broken furniture," still held Germans.[13] Rachford's men had by this time been through the main reading room where "not one of the oil paintings of hunting scenes had fewer than a half dozen bullet holes in them," and found the three entrances that went into the basement; they quickly set up defenses to keep these Germans holed up where they were.

Company M's Lieutenant Nechey had accompanied Rachford's platoon when they came into the hotel; he was making a reconnaissance since his machine guns would be used for the continued defense of the area. By this time, some scattered fighting had broken out in the west wing of the lobby, where the 155 SP gun had blown a gaping hole in its outside wall; a few of Lieutenant Rachford's men had already started searching the upper floors of the hotel. Nechey decided he would see what he could do about clearing the Germans out of the basement.

He hastily organized a squad, and together they started down one of the stairwells into the basement; Nechey led. He was greeted by enemy fire, but avoided getting hit. One of the quick-thinking squad members threw a "potato masher" grenade that had been taken from a captured

German; the grenade looked like a stick and had a pull cord that ran down its hollow handle and detonated the explosives. A five-second delayed fuse first ignited its charge, and when it went off its blast effect scattered steel fragments everywhere. The Germans reciprocated by throwing several grenades toward the stairway, but by this time the Americans were safely back up in the lobby. Nechey had decided to go to another one of the entrances, bringing just two men with him this time; he left the others to guard the doorway they had just left. The trio quickly went through a second doorway at the other end of the lobby, with Nechey again the first to take the stairs down into the vast cellar. This time he threw several hand grenades as he descended, and when he hit the bottom stair he started firing his automatic carbine at the Germans. The men at the other entrance also raced down those stairs again while emptying their weapons, and this proved to be too much for their opposite numbers. All who were not wounded or killed in this creative double envelopment immediately surrendered; Nechey took fifteen prisoners, including two lieutenants.[14]

Lieutenant Rachford had by this time cleared out the upper floors of the hotel with his men. Some of the Germans had succeeded in setting their ammunition on fire before surrendering; a few others threw empty champagne bottles at the Americans. They found an abandoned 20mm antiaircraft gun installed in a second-floor window that must have been hand-carried up the stairways piece by piece. The hotel had become a "wasteland of torn walls, shattered glass, bodies and bloodstains," an account noted. "The coppery stench of blood, along with the sulphuric odor of spent gunpowder and the dusty pall of fallen timbers and plaster, all permeated the hallways and rooms."[15]

By nightfall all mopping up had been completed; the hotel and the rest of Farwick Park belonged to the Americans. Two TDs had advanced with Captain Botts's Company I through Roland Platz then down Rolandstrasse to Monheims Allee; every house on those streets had been emptied of Germans. The whole area between Monheims Allee and Krefelderstrasse, plus the circle west of Krefelderstrasse, was also firmly in American hands. Enemy losses were later tallied at 30 killed, 45 wounded, with 135 taken prisoner.[16] Corley lost 2 men who were killed; another 19 had been wounded.

It had been an equally busy day for Lieutenant Colonel Daniel's 2nd Battalion. The area around the state theater had redeveloped into a strongpoint; the Germans set up machine-gun positions and moved *Panzerfaust* teams into places among the rubble and burned-out structures hit the day before. Daniel wasted little time over this; his 155 SP gun poured seven rounds in "to considerable effect" and this opened the way for a deeper drive into the cathedral area.[17] But they confronted more trouble. This time Lieutenant Walker's Company G was held up by sniping rifle fire from a church that his men had already passed; believing that it had been emptied of enemy soldiers, a platoon circled back and conducted a more detailed search, this time discovering that they had overlooked the steeple. Walker ordered his tanks and TDs to take aim at it, which they did but to little effect because the steeple tower was heavy concrete. So the 155mm gun was brought up again, and it blasted the tower apart with a single shot.

Shortly afterward, Walker's men captured another air raid shelter in the area. "Civilians trudged through the wreckage to the safety of a little colony which had been established for refugees," Don Whitehead wrote in a dispatch back to the States. "They came from the dank shelter like a procession of lost souls, pushing little carts filled with a few belongings. Here is a defeated Germany on parade."[18] Nearby, machine-gun fire coming from a convent slowed the Americans down; it took a combination of bazooka fire, rifle grenades, and tank fire to finally subdue this strongpoint. Lieutenant Webb's Company F encountered little resistance as his men worked their way westward on Adalbertstein Weg after finally breaking out from where they had been held up the day before along Lutherstrasse and Kaiser Platz.

But Daniel was confronted with two bigger problems as the day wore on; both of his flanks were dangerously exposed. "By night Company G had become so overextended that something had to be done," he remembered.[19] The quick but imperfect solution was to first have Walker's men bend their defensive line back to an area just west of the underpass on Wilhelmstrasse. Then good fortune came Daniel's way; the 2nd Battalion of the 110th Infantry, 28th Division, arrived and was placed on his south flank, covering most of the ground cleared that day by Company G, thus permitting these men to concentrate on driving farther westward.

Circumstances had also become challenging on his right flank. Smoot's Company E was assisting Captain Botts's Company I in clearing the area northeast of Monheims Allee and Krefelderstrasse for most of the afternoon, forcing Daniel to end operations by curving the battalion's line to the corner of Heinrichs Allee and Julicherstrasse in order to maintain contact with the 3rd Battalion. This line was now getting close to the foot of the Lousberg, but relief came later that night when Daniel received Company C of his own regiment's 1st Battalion to cover this flank.

It was near dark by the time Captain Miller's Company B finally reached Ravelsberg Hill. Nevertheless, Lieutenant Colonel Peckham already had a plan in place to retake the forward pillboxes lost earlier in the day. Accordingly, Miller moved his 2nd Platoon up to reinforce Company K's line near pillboxes 11 and 14; Company K's 1st Platoon took up the defense of Pillboxes 15, 16, and 17, but two of Miller's squads would assist Russell's 1st Platoon in retaking Pillbox 3. During the afternoon the Germans had managed to occupy a fourth pillbox on the hill's northern slope—Number 5. Company K men would wrestle with this one.

After Miller checked to be sure that his men were ready with their pole charges, bazookas, and grenades, the attack jumped off. Eleven prisoners were quickly taken from Pillbox 3; the pole charge alone had intimidated the Germans. No other shots were even necessary. But chaos suddenly enveloped Ravelsberg Hill. The grenadiers had been alerted by the attack on the box, and this made taking Pillbox 5 back more difficult. Worse, the Germans were now firing American machine guns they had captured from the outlying pits of Pillbox 6 into both companies' lines.

Darkness was also enveloping the hill, but the fighting raged on; Pillbox 4 surrendered. Then, an individual action by one of Company K's noncoms exemplified courage above and beyond what could be expected from a single man during this kind of intense fighting. Earlier that afternoon, while he was removing one of his wounded men from the blood- and rain-soaked Ravelsberg, Sgt. Max Thompson of Haywood County, North Carolina, saw Germans moving in on the company's 3rd Platoon to his right. According to an eyewitness, "One of his guys mentioned surrender; Max said 'When you're the last man up here, then you can do what you want, but until then we'll keep fighting.'"[20]

Thompson then moved quickly, ran to a nearby abandoned machine gun, and started firing on the swiftly closing grenadiers; he unloaded round after round until enemy return fire knocked the gun right out of his hands. Dazed and shaken, Thompson somehow regained his sense of purpose and picked up an automatic rifle lying in the grass; he then emptied several bursts into the remaining grenadiers now closing with their bayonets fixed.

But then the rifle jammed. Somehow Sergeant Thompson still managed to find an antitank gun, readied it, and took aim at the Germans and a light panzer that was supporting them. "I don't know how one guy could do it," Staff Sgt. James E. Osborne, a nearby noncom later recalled, "But I can verify that he personally knocked out two of the tanks with rifle grenades and a bazooka."[21]

This action lit up the area as one of the tanks erupted in flames. "There were so many dead Germans in front of his gun at this time, members of Sergeant Thompson's squad told me they could walk to the tank without putting their feet on the ground," the 3rd Battalion's Executive Officer, Maj. Sam Carter, told everyone later. But at the time, Thompson was exhausted and now wounded badly. He noticed that some of his squad members were still having trouble taking back Pillbox 6. Somehow, despite his wounds, he managed to crawl toward it, and as Sergeant Osborne later regaled:

> Less than 100 yards from the box, Nazi fire opened up. We hit the dirt, but not Max. He fingered his grenade bag and took off. Throwing grenades as he ran, he was wounded by shrapnel, but he never quit. He got up to that pillbox and threw two more hand grenades. The Krauts inside waved the white flag and hollered, "Kamerad!"

"It took three of Sergeant Thompson's men to get him out of the bunker the next morning," Carter went on to explain. "When they got him back to an aid station where our battalion surgeon, Captain Lawrence Caruso, could work on him, he was completely out of his head. He was apparently stunned from the time he took the light tank out, and had no idea what he was doing after this. So many times the tide of battle is determined by the actions of one soldier, and Max

Thompson was the one soldier who did on Ravelsberg Hill that day."[22] Personally drafting the Medal of Honor citation later awarded to Sergeant Thompson, Carter finished with, "His courageous leadership inspired his men and materially contributed to clearing the enemy from the last remaining hold on the hill."

In Aachen, *Oberst* Wilck was now very worried about his own ability to hold out. After Farwick Park fell, he sent the following message to LXXXI Corps:

> Strong enemy breaches in Aachen at the Quellenhof, city center and Laurensberg. Last defense takes place at Lousberg. Direct counterattack only possible way to break out. Decision requested. Battle strength now about 1,200 men. Battle value insufficient because of continuous demands. Wilck.[23]

That night an impatient Wilck evinced more anxiety, this time warning: "situation in Aachen such that last resistance probably coming to an end 19 October. Breakout via Soers still possible. Request decision soon. Wilck."

He got what he asked for; Bradenberg responded later that night, admonishing "the main task of the 246th Division remains the defense of Aachen to the last man." Wilck was also told his forces had to be combined as the situation called for. "Further, the division has to maintain a mobile force in the area north of Aachen prepared to link up with the SS-Panzer Corps as its attack progresses in the general direction of Soers."[24] The order did reflect some consideration for Wilck's men; preparations were allowed to evacuate his wounded.

Later that same night, the edict to fight to the last man was strengthened by *Generalfeldmarschall* Model, with strong words to *Oberst* Wilck emphasizing the need to persevere, closing with, "You shall hold the venerable German city to the last man and will, if necessary, allow yourself to be buried under its rubble."[25]

It was another cold and rainy morning on 19 October. Task Force Hogan, comprised of the 33rd Armored Regiment with troops of the 2nd Battalion 36th Armored Infantry, plus a platoon of engineers, departed from the factory district at 0730. The 30th Infantry Division had taken

Hogan's original objective, Laurensberg, so his orders were modified by General Huebner; after clearing the northern half of the Lousberg, the task force was to wheel north to secure the railroad junction on the Aachen-Laurensberg highway near the Rahe Chateau just south of the village.

As the task force rolled down Soerser Weg it came under some artillery fire from a 150mm howitzer that was called down by German observers on the forward slope of Lousberg Hill. But as Lieutenant Colonel Hogan later noted, "This fire was inaccurate and caused no damage."[26] That was because the plan the Americans had so carefully put in place was working. Corley's forces had moved out before dawn and Botts's Company I had reached the southern end of Salvatorberg by the time Task Force Hogan was approaching the Lousberg. This had permitted Shepard's Company L to attack the eastern edge of the hill mass before Task Force Hogan turned onto Pourweider Weg. Shepard's men confronted the last stubborn German defenders holding out in their pillboxes and in the complex tunnel and cave defensive positions that had been carved into the hill with shovels and jackhammers; the enemy used these advantageous locations to emplace their machine guns.

In a desperate effort to hold, *Oberst* Wilck had inserted three hundred SS troops of Combat Team Rink to counterattack. Shepard's men responded to this challenge by crawling under the trajectory of their guns and moving in close enough to seal off the mouth of the caves with their own fire, enabling other riflemen to trap the German reinforcements in the tunnels themselves. Lieutenant Nechey's mortar crews worked at top speed, turning their searing 81mm tubes a reddish blue while they poured in round after round on more of the SS troops. Combined with the 155 SP gun, which was fired at the observation outpost atop the Lousberg, the effectiveness of the fire on Task Force Hogan was consequently, as Hogan pointed out, initially minimal.

When the task force reached Struver Weg, it split; Companies E and F of the 36th Armored Infantry dismounted and swung south toward the Lousberg's north slope as planned, while the remainder of Hogan's armored vehicles pushed up Struver Weg to Ziegeleiweg and over toward the railroad junction just south of Laurensberg. A platoon of Company F commanded by Lt. Norman C. Streit eventually found a trail that led his men to the base of the Lousberg; here the Germans, other remnants of Battalion Rink's SS troops, were staked out in more emplacements and pillboxes.[27] After an hour of small-arms exchanges Streit decided to move his men away from their fields of fire. Searching the adjacent area on Buchen Allee westward, they found a new trail; the platoon's men saw an opportunity to get at the Germans from the rear.

Lieutenant Streit used this trail to reach a spot on the Lousberg's majestic northernmost slope. Here the soldiers were able to exact the revenge they sought on the gun that had been disturbing the task force's armored vehicles as they were wheeling northward over the sticky clay roadways toward Laurensberg. Streit's men would deal with the Germans in the pillboxes below them later; darkness was settling in by this time. Hogan had moved his armored vehicles close to the Rahe Chateau, but 200 yards short of the railroad junction. His armored vehicles stopped here for the night. Back in Aachen, Lieutenant Colonel Daniel's 2nd Battalion had worked steadily toward the railway station leading from the city up to Laurensberg, destroying *Panzerfaust* positions one by one while clearing out cellars and backyards and battering down walls that blocked their passage. Company F's Lieutenant Webb noted, "This was found more profitable than advancing down the open streets; the cellars were connected and this expedited our advance."[28]

Late in the afternoon, a now nearly defeated *Oberst* Wilck issued this final order to his men:

> The defenders of Aachen will prepare for their last battle. Constricted to the smallest space, we shall fight to the last man, the last shell, the last bullet, in accordance with the Führer's orders. In the face of the contemptible, despicable treason committed by certain individuals, I expect each and every defender of the venerable Imperial City of Aachen to do his duty to the end, in fulfillment of our Oath to the Flag. I expect courage and determination to hold out. Long live the Führer and our beloved Fatherland.[29]

German field kitchens also issued the men's last hot rations, a sparse serving of sausage, hard bread, and bitter black coffee.

The 3rd Panzer Grenadier Division commander, *Generalleutnant* Denkert, had already seen many of his men fight to the last bullet on the Ravelsberg this same day; the 116th Panzer Division forces were too busy around Würselen and had not come to their assistance. The struggle began at daybreak when Captain Russell's 1st Platoon assaulted the only pillbox still occupied by the grenadiers. Fierce fighting broke out inside the box itself; twenty-three POWs, including one officer, were eventually taken. But heavy casualties from the previous day had crippled Russell's chances to continue to defend the hill; tremendously undermanned, the task of holding the forward pillboxes would now have to be shouldered by one of Captain Miller's platoons. Reorganization and bracing for the next attack consumed the rest of the morning, and then at 1400 hours it came.

The Germans suddenly shelled the Ravelsberg unmercifully from three sides—frontally, on Miller's and Russell's left flank, and from the rear by the few artillery pieces still available in Aachen. A later account described just how intense these barrages were:

> The enemy fired all calibers of assault guns, mortars and artillery. It was believed that they used 75mm and 88mm tank fire, 80mm and 120mm mortars, and 105mm, 150mm, 170mm and possibly 210mm artillery. It was estimated that 100 or more rounds per minute fell onto Ravelsberg Hill; 3,000 to 4,000 shells fell in an area 300 by 300 yards in just thirty minutes. This was the heaviest barrage and the most concentrated artillery and mortar barrage laid down [on us] by the Germans in this war.[30]

Nearly every American in a foxhole and not in the more protective cover of a pillbox was either killed or wounded by this incredible volume of fire. Then, adding to the soldiers' misery, smoke was laid in front of the hill to screen the advance of what was later estimated to be three companies of grenadiers, supported by at least five tanks. At 1430 hours, they began their attack. Pillbox 3 fell back into German hands; all of Miller's men in or around the box were killed. Pillbox 6 was overrun again, but the Company K men would not give up; they continued to fight. One squad from Captain Miller's platoon came over to assist, killing many of the Germans who were molesting this box.

A later Distinguished Unit Citation given to the defenders of the Ravelsberg most adequately describes the continuing action:

> Realizing the importance of the terrain they occupied, new men left the shelter and protection of the pillboxes to go forward and

occupy the same exposed and unprotected foxholes which their dead and wounded comrades were in to prevent the enemy from penetrating their positions. These men persistently refused to yield ground and held on with a tenacity gifted to only the most courageous.[31]

There was a stand of trees that ringed several of the pillboxes and the grenadiers were also trying to take the ground here from the Americans. Without hesitation, Lieutenant Colonel Peckham called for artillery fire on this position; despite the risk to his own men, this strategic ground could not be surrendered to the Germans. It was imperative that they knock down the trees so friendly mortar and artillery fire could be better observed, adjusted, and therefore effective. Company K men were in the eye of this storm, but the artillery barrages proved to be very effective, as observers saw rounds also knock out three panzers that had ventured into the company's fragile lines; however, friendly casualties still resulted from shells that exploded too close to the men.

Others bravely fought on. One squad retook Pillbox 3, killing many and capturing eighteen extremely fatigued grenadiers. Then falling darkness became a friend to both sides; the remaining Germans started withdrawing, leaving two hundred of their dead behind. But the withdrawal did not mean the end to hostilities. Mortars and enemy artillery continued to rain down in a last desperate attempt by the Germans to leave their mark on the Ravelsberg. Rather than "allowing Company K, reduced to a pittance of their original number, to relive Custer's Last Stand and be annihilated," Peckham ordered the soaked and exhausted survivors off the hill.[32] Captain Hess's Company I arrived to relieve them, but the Germans were never to attack again. "Only a few of the brave assault group came back," the 3rd Panzer Division's *Generalleutnant* Denkert later remembered.[33]

When Task Force Hogan reached the Rahe Chateau that same night, the men found a great deal of ammunition for a 150mm howitzer, as well as mortars and bazookas that the Germans had left behind; there were also empty liquor bottles and discarded flasks scattered over the grounds. Unlike their comrades on the Ravelsberg, it was later noted somewhat wryly in an interview with Lieutenant Colonel Hogan that on that same day "instead of fighting to the last man here, they fought to the last bottle."[34]

At daylight on 20 October, Hogan's Company H captured a *Panzer-faust* gun crew and the observers for the 150mm howitzer who had left their ammunition back on the Rahe Chateau grounds. A barrage of fire was then laid both into the underpass and the surrounding embankment at the railroad junction. This proved to be too much for the remaining Germans here, and they gave up. Then at about 0830 a column of seven half-tracks came forward to surrender; most were loaded with wounded. Hogan placed all of them under the guard of two Company H light tanks. Not long afterward a column of horse-drawn vehicles approached and also surrendered; 145 additional prisoners were taken from this group.

Later that morning Hogan's infantry came off the Lousberg to assist the remainder of the task force at the railroad junction. These men approached the lower pillboxes they had bypassed the night before from the rear as planned and found them all to be abandoned. Lieutenant Colonel Corley's men had evacuated hundreds more civilians and wounded from a nearby hospital; by noon over 400 prisoners were taken in the 3rd Battalion zone of operations around the Lousberg. Daniel's 2nd Battalion forces also had a good day; just after noon a German officer and two of his men came into Captain Smoot's Company E area carrying a white flag; they had started out from a building on the heavily damaged Technical High School's grounds. The officer told Smoot that if an American commander would go back with them, he would surrender his men. This was agreed upon, and as the party approached the building, anxious enemy soldiers started pouring out through windows and doorways; 125 more prisoners marched off to the POW cage. The only active enemy combatants were now corralled in the westernmost fringes of the city. As one American officer aptly noted, "The end was in sight."[35]

Lieutenant Botsford of the 1st Division G-2 Section, a prewar journalist who after the war became a celebrated editor at *The New Yorker* magazine, went through four-fifths of the city that afternoon; he surveyed the damage, later remembering that "not one building was untouched by the blasts of the saturation bombings or artillery strikes over the last ten days."[36] He saw burst sewers, broken gas mains, streets covered with shattered glass, downed electric power lines, wrecked cars, trucks, abandoned German armored vehicles, and guns littering the streets. Many were impassable, except on foot; the stench of dead animals "raised an overpowering smell in parts of the city," prompting Botsford to further write, "The city is dead as a Roman ruin, but unlike a ruin it has none of the grace of gradual decay. It is now of no historic interest, except as an object lesson in the power and application of modern warfare."

> The buildings that stood up the best were those built during the Victorian period like the Deutches Bank on Ursuliner Street and the newer state buildings like the town library and the local courthouse. However, nearly all the rest of the older part of the city had ceased to exist. The town hall had been hit repeatedly and the steel framework of its spire had collapsed and was hanging over the edge of the roof. There remained only a spire and two walls of St. Foillan's church. Destruction of the historic monuments was evident; only one church—St. Joseph's—suffered lighter damage. All of the stained glass windows of the great Munster Cathedral on Munsterplatz were shattered, but the vault over the main altar appeared to be firm, even though it had taken a direct artillery hit that pierced the groining. The entire interior of the church was covered with dust and plaster from the ceiling, which was still in relatively good shape.[37]

The power and application of modern warfare did not extend to the Aachen citizenry who had been evacuated from the air raid shelters around the city. "These people had been led to expect harsh treatment," Maj. J. J. Kohout, the 26th Infantry's Military Government Officer, noted. "They expected to be put in barbed wire enclosures with no shelter of any kind. They expected to have their families broken up."[38]

Instead, a barracks area outside of Brand was used to house the approximate 3,700 civilians. Most had "marched" here on foot, carrying what personal belongings they could; when empty trucks were headed out of the city, they were given transport. There were seven individual barracks; a civilian leader was appointed to each one. Billeting was left entirely up to this leader, or the committees that he appointed. Any troubles were taken up with them, and not the American soldier. Families were kept together as often as possible. Any Germans who were either in military uniform, or suspected to be soldiers, had already been interrogated and processed through military channels.

"The women worked in the kitchens and kept the place clean, while men worked on the surrounding farms," Major Kohout revealed later. He also pointed out:

> Thirty tons of captured enemy food supplies were sent from Liege. They were fed entirely from food supplies captured in France, Belgium and Germany. Not a single American ration was furnished them. In addition, they were fed the by-products of the land.
>
> The food was prepared in two messes, one serving 2,000 and the other the balance. The people brought their own containers, received their food, had their cards punched and generally took their food back to their rooms to eat it. When they needed meat, they requisitioned it. An IOU (or bill) was tendered and accepted as payment. This bill will be paid by the city of Aachen when it begins to function as such again.
>
> When the time comes to release them, it [will] be done on a priority basis. Doctors, nurses and farmers will be among the first.[39]

The end came on Saturday morning, 21 October, when Captain Botts's Company I and Corwell's Company K closed in on a bullet-riddled three-story air raid bunker south of Lousbergstrasse. They set up the 155 SP gun; Lieutenant Colonel Corley had no desire to risk the casualties that would result by fighting it out with the remaining Germans holed up inside.

Inside were *Oberst* Wilck, his staff officers and their men, as well as a cadre of prisoners. Wilck purportedly said, "When Americans start using 155's as sniper weapons, it's time to give up."[40] Then he ordered this dramatic, but strange message be sent to LXXXI Corps:

> All forces are committed in the final struggle! Confined to the smallest area, the last defenders of Aachen are embroiled in their final battle! The last defenders of Aachen, mindful of their

beloved German homeland, with firm confidence in our final victory, donate Reichsmark 10,468 to the Winterhilfswerk [Winter Relief] Project. We shall fight on. Long live the Führer![41]

Sometime later, the radio operator sent out a final message: "We now sign off, with regards to our comrades and the folks back home." After this, the radio set was destroyed.

Among the thirty American prisoners were Staff Sgt. Ewart M. Padgett of Jacksonville, Florida, and Pfc. James B. Haswell from Houston, Texas; they were with Company B of the 238th Combat Engineer Battalion and had been captured while on a patrol four days earlier. During their brief time in captivity, they had been treated well and fed properly. They had not divulged any information of military value to their captors; instead they had actually befriended their interrogators. One was *Obersturmführer* (SS Lieutenant) George Schwabb. He spoke fluent English and had told Padgett and Haswell that he had a cousin in New York City who was on the police force; in a candid moment Schwabb had even told the Americans that he hated Hitler, and that the war would be over soon.

At mid-morning on this fateful day, Schwabb came into the dingy room where the POWs were and started talking to a small group of men; Sergeant Padgett was not among them at that time, but Pfc. Haswell was. Later, Padgett described what happened:

> Haswell came over to me and asked to borrow my cartridge belt. When I asked him why he wanted to borrow it, he said that the Germans had two men killed trying to get out of the bunker with a white flag to surrender the fort, and Lieutenant Schwabb wanted a volunteer from one of the PW's [*sic*] to now carry the flag out. So Haswell volunteered. Lieutenant Shipley, another PW, told him to wear a cartridge belt to look more like an American soldier.[42]

Instead, Sergeant Padgett put on the cartridge belt and told Haswell that he was going to go with him. Next, the two were led to the bunker's doorway by Schwabb and *Oberst* Wilck's executive officer. Another German soldier was rolling out a white flag for them. He handed the flagstaff to Padgett and together with Pfc. Haswell they exited the bunker and ran into the middle of Lousbergstrasse, waving the white flag of surrender back and forth. As had happened in the earlier confusion, friendly small-arms fire was aimed at Wilck's saviors. Padgett waved the flag more vigorously until the firing ceased. Stillness filled the air for moments that seemed like minutes, and then an American officer leaned out of a window in a house about 100 yards away; he motioned for the two to come to him. Padgett yelled back toward the bunker for the two German officers there to come out and follow them. They did; then a mortar shell landed right where the Germans had been standing in front of the bunker.

This pair, who had been trying to catch up to the Americans, dove into a ditch; Padgett now waved the white flag as hard as he could. Still, more mortars crashed, closer, just about 20 yards away. Then the area fell completely silent; word had finally reached the mortar crew to stop firing. The German officers rejoined Padgett and Haswell, and moments later the foursome was standing in front of a Company I rifleman. He led them to his platoon leader; this officer told them they had forty-five minutes to march the entire garrison out in columns of fours with their hands over their heads. The surrender party returned to the bunker.

By 1100 the order was being carried out; the first of approximately two hundred of Wilck's men started coming out of the bunker, but the Aachen commandant was not among them. Instead, he had directed *Obersturmführer* Schwabb to fetch Padgett and Haswell again. This time *Oberst* Wilck asked the two Americans to personally lead him and his eight staff officers, as well as the remaining prisoners, out of the bunker. Sergeant Padgett detailed what followed:

> We were led to the colonel's room where he and his entire staff had assembled their equipment. We asked the colonel for his pistol, so he removed it, threw the clip under the bed, laid the pistol on the table, smiled and left the room. Lieutenant Schwabb said that was his way of giving us the pistol, because he could not hand it to us.[43]

Everyone left the bunker together a few minutes later; the white flag of surrender was waved again. A few shots rang out, this time from somewhere in the German ranks. Through Schwabb, Padgett told Wilck to make it stop; it quickly ceased. Then the group started marching up the street to meet Lieutenant Boehme, the same interpreter who had accompanied another party when the surrender ultimatum was first given to the former Aachen commander eleven days earlier. Now Boehme directed Wilck in formally surrendering the garrison. They were driven to Lieutenant Colonel Corley's command post in a jeep. Wilck sat next to the driver with his head down, staring at his spit-shined boots, while his immediate staff officers sat in the rear seat; among them was Lieutenant Keller, the adjutant officer Boehme had encountered during that first attempt at surrender. Padgett recalled:

> Upon our arrival at the CP, Colonel Wilck ordered his entire staff to come by and shake our hands. He then came up, snapped to attention and saluted; we returned the salute and he then saluted us again and said something in German, which Lieutenant Schwabb quoted to us. "He said he and his staff wish to thank you for your display of gallant bravery in carrying the white flag."[44]

Wilck even said that he was recommending the two Americans for "a high award." Terms of surrender were then discussed with Lieutenant Colonel Corley while they awaited the arrival of Colonel Seitz and the 1st Division Assistant Commander, Brig. Gen. George Taylor. Final negotiations were concluded in their presence. The surrender statement was prepared; effective 1205 hours, 21 October 1944. It read:

> I, Colonel Gerhard Wilck, commander of the German garrison of Aachen Germany hereby surrender as of this hour, all troops, arms, material, and fortifications under my command to the United States Army, it being agreed that all said troops will be treated as prisoners of war. Likewise, the medical personnel, sick and wounded are turned over for disposal in accordance with the provisions of the Geneva Convention of 1929. All these troops have been disarmed.[45]

"Then the colonel asked for and was granted permission to speak to his troops outside the building," wrote correspondent Don Whitehead. "His eight staff officers were with him, all as immaculate as their commander. One of them had been a student at Heidelberg and there were scars of dueling foils on his face."[46]

Moments later, *Oberst* Wilck climbed up into the jeep he had ridden in to Corley's CP and stiffened while his men drew to attention. Then, with heavy emotion he said:

> This is a painful occasion on which I must speak to you. I have been forced to surrender, as ammunition, food and water are exhausted. I have seen that further fighting would be useless. I have acted against my orders which directed that I would fight to the last man. At this time I wish to remind you that you are German soldiers and to ask that you will always behave as such. I wish you all the best of health and a quick return to our Fatherland when hostilities have ceased so that you may help in the rebuilding of Germany. The American commander has told me that I cannot give you the "Seig Heil," or "Heil Hitler," but we can still do it in our hearts.[47]

Wilck and his men were then evacuated to the 26th Infantry Regiment POW cage. But with the German communication systems completely broken down, he had no way to relay the terms of surrendering to his troops. Captain Botts was chosen to join with one of Wilck's staff officers in an armored vehicle so they could go out and lead in the collection of the remaining enemy forces. Approximately 1,600 were eventually rounded up to join *Oberst* Wilck and the other 1,830 already held captive. "Among the PW's [*sic*] taken on 21 October was a former member of the 1st Division, now in the wrong army," a later report stated. "This soldier, named Karl Young, served in E Company 18th Infantry during the late 1920's. In 1939 he returned to Germany to straighten out some domestic affairs, was snatched up by the Wehrmacht, and has since been in Poland and Russia. He was somewhat depressed by the fact that he had not been captured by his old outfit, but had been picked up by comparative strangers in the 26th Infantry."[48] But absent were two prominent commanders; it was later learned that *Obersturmführer* Rink and nineteen of his SS men had made a daring escape back to the German lines when Aachen's surrender became inevitable. *Oberstleutnant* Erich Stach, one of Wilck's 246th Division battalion commanders, and a lieutenant disguised themselves as Franciscan monks; they somehow escaped despite being detained for a short time.

At 1615 hours Colonel Seitz reported the end of hostilities to General Huebner: "Mission out here complete as of now and we are through with Task Force Hogan."[49] That night found the American flag waving over the first captured German city in World War II. In fact it was the first time a major German city had fallen into enemy hands since the Napoleonic Wars of the early 1800s, some 130 years earlier.

Gerhard Wilck was subsequently interrogated by 1st Division intelligence teams; some of the findings and observations were later documented thusly:

> He was an inadvertent spokesman for the confused loyalties which motivate many of the German officers now passing through our POW cages. As a soldier of 28 years' experience and discipline, he obeyed orders from higher echelons without question of default. On the other hand he was aware of the military futility of many of these orders and appreciated the dismal situation of the German army today as a product of the rattle-brained strategy of his Commander-in-chief, Hitler. The climax of this conflict came when the Colonel, after two hours of interrogation at the prisoner of war cage, broke into tears while discussing the present position of Germany in the war.[50]

In spite of his weakened emotional state, Wilck refused to reveal the location, nor the identification or composition of other German units outside of Aachen. But he was perfectly willing to discuss his own defense of the city. The American's use of the 155 SP guns provoked "considerable consternation." Wilck told his captors "a shell from one of them pierced three houses completely before exploding and wrecking a fourth." He then revealed that he had taken command right after the ultimatum to surrender was delivered back on 10 October. When he was asked why he had not surrendered the city at the time, Wilck sternly replied that his "conscience, plus the prospect of a generalship, forbade it." This begged another question. Asked why he had declined to inform his superiors of Aachen's surrender, he explained that with no word from him, Corps would presume he was killed in action, and therefore not responsible for the defection. "I wish I had been killed," Wilck said. "It is difficult for a German officer of 28 years' service to end up in a prisoner cage."

It was while discussing the dissimilar situations of the American and German armies that the emotional catharsis overtook the Colonel. The fabric of the German army, he said, is disintegrating at an ever-increasing rate. The most critical shortage exists in officer material. Not only do present organizations suffer from this lack of troops, but there is no prospect of improvement. As for the quality of troops, the Colonel pointed out that one only had to consider the 689th Regiment of his division, all of which was physically unfit for combat.[51]

Asked if the overall German soldier's tolerance for fighting was at a low, Wilck gave a surprising answer. "Even if you surround them in pockets, the German soldier will fight to the end to carry out the Führer's orders." Silenced followed, for Wilck had certainly not done this himself; moments later he added, "The only cement which holds many German officers in place is fear, not only for their own lives, but of reprisals against their families at Himmler's hands."

Then, perhaps thinking of his own wife and children, *Oberst* Wilck's final gesture was to look directly at his captors and say softly, "Only America can save us now, as I don't believe in miracles anymore."[52]

AFTERWORD

asualties during the battle for Aachen were about equal. German divisions suffered approximately 5,000 killed or wounded. An estimated 5,600 others were taken prisoner in and around Aachen; 3,500 either surrendered or were captured in the city. U.S. losses exceeded 3,000 in the 30th Infantry Division alone. The 1st Infantry placed their casualties at 1,350; 150 were confirmed as killed. The total number of Americans who lost their lives during the five-week period approached 1,000, including those reported by the 2nd and 3rd Armored Divisions.

In "The Battle of Aachen in Memory of the City: From Capitulation to the Liberation (1944–2014)," Dr. Peter M. Quadflieg, a current-day Aachen historian, traces the way the people of Germany have interpreted the end of World War II. He points out that over the past seventy years a "reinterpretation" has evolved of the problems Germans have had with the historical date and the public discourse that has since led to seeing the cessation of hostilities in early May 1945 "as a day of liberation from war and Nazi dictatorship. In parallel with these patterns a regionally shaped culture of remembrance developed in Aachen. The surrender of the city on October 21st, 1944 has been reframed as an act of liberation."

Americans always saw it as such. The solemn words of President Franklin D. Roosevelt, sent to the mothers and fathers of U.S. soldiers who lost their lives during the Aachen fight, framed their losses some seventy years ago:

He stands in an unbroken line of patriots who have dared to die
That freedom might live, and grow, and increase its blessings.
Freedom lives, and through it, he lives—
In a way that humbles the undertakings of most men.

NOTES

As in my previous book, I have relied heavily on primary source material that was recorded immediately following the Aachen fight. Other reliable sources included monographs written by U.S. officer participants when they conducted Advanced Infantry courses at Fort Benning, Georgia, right after the war. Unit histories written during the same period, often necessarily sentimental, were culled for quotes that materially contributed to a better understanding of the content about the actions described in this work.

Identification of German units came from several primary sources: reliable translations of Corps and division-level after-action reports; interrogations conducted with prisoners of war at the time they were captured and their American translators; and interrogations of German generals who participated in the Aachen battles, conducted when they were taken into captivity near or at the end of the war. Most reliable were accounts written by Hans Gunther Guderian, 1st General Staff Officer of the 116th Panzer Division, after May 1944 in his later book *From Normandy to the Ruhr*. Any errors in German unit identification found in this book were either misstated in U.S. reports or mine.

In describing topography in the city of Aachen and surrounding towns, I used what was found in primary source material. Some of this may seem difficult to follow, as the Aachen area today is much different than it was in 1944. I made every attempt to remain faithful to how it was seen through the eyes of the combatants at the time. Such was the case in identifying street names, particularly in Aachen proper. Some do not exist today, but I used the same map relied upon by American commanders in 1944 to identify their unit locations and the streets they attacked through. Again, any errors are solely mine.

Finally—names. Wherever possible, I provided the full name of combatants, both American and German, when they are introduced in the book. Much effort was made to confirm spellings, often in error or inconsistent in after-action and other reports written in 1944. Here again, if a name is misstated, it was my error.

Abbreviations

Following is a list of abbreviations used to identify the archival repositories from which records were retrieved, as well as military units, words, and other phrases.

AAR	After-Action Report
AD	Armored Division
CMH	Center for Military History, Washington, D.C.
DIVARTY	Division Artillery
FA	Field Artillery
ID	Infantry Division
INF	Infantry
NA	The National Archives, College Park, Maryland
MRC	McCormick Research Center, Cantigny First Division Museum, Wheaton, Illinois
OH	Research Pages, www.oldhickory30th.com
RCA	Rifle Company in Attack
RCT	Regimental Combat Team
TB	Tank Battalion
TDB	Tank Destroyer Battalion
TISFBG	The Infantry School, Fort Benning, Georgia
USAMHI	Military History Institute, Carlisle, Pennsylvania
WHWF	Work Horse Western Front

CHAPTER 1

1. 3rd Armored Division History, Roetgen, Germany and the Siegfried Line; www.3ad.com/memoirs.pages (accessed November 2007).

2. 3rd Armored Division History, Chapter III Rhineland; www.3ad.com/history (accessed November 2007).

3. Situation Report for Reserve Grenadier Battalion 328 to LXXXI *ArmeeKorps*, 12 September 1944, Feldgrau postings March 2006 from feldgrau.net, provided to author 27 March 2006 by Mark J. Reardon, CMH.

4. William A. Castille, *Siegfried Line—Task Force 1 (Lovelady) 12–25 September 1944*, Documents on CCB, 3rd Armored Division 1943–45, including manuscripts compiled by Capt. William Long entitled: *War Diary, Combat Command B, 3rd Armored Division*; USAMI, July 1980, 2–4.

5. Lt. Fred L. Hadsel, *Engineers in the Siegfried Line Penetration, Combat Command B 3rd Armored Division, 12–22 September 1944*, 2nd Information and Historical Service, 1st U.S. Army, C-1-264-407-427 Box 24089, NA, 4. In describing engineering operations author also relied on *Engineer Operations by the VII Corps in the European Theater, Volume IV, Pursuit into Germany*, Office of the Chief Military History General Reference Branch, provided to author by Mark J. Reardon, CMH.

6. Hadsel, 5–7.

7. *Generalmajor* Paul Wilhelm Mueller, *Account of the Deployment of the 9 PZ Division for 11–19 September 1944*, Historical Division, Foreign Military Studies B-345, USAMHI, 1945, 1–2.

8. Ibid., 6.

9. *First United States Army Report of Operations*, 1 August 1944–22 February 1945, The Battle of Germany 10 July 1946, CMH, 51–52

10. Samuel W. Mitcham, *The Siegfried Line, The German Defense of the Westwall, September–December 1944* (Stackpole Military History Series; Mechanicsburg, PA: Stackpole Books, 2009), 48.

11. *General der Infantrie* a.D. Friedrich August Schack, *LXXXI Corps 4–21 September 1944*, Historical Division, Foreign Military Studies B-816, USAMHI, 1946, 19–20.

12. Mueller, 5.

13. *Generalleutnant* Paul Mahlmann, *353 Infantry Division, 9–18 September 1944*, Historical Division, Foreign Military Studies B-232, USAMHI, 46–47.

14. Major Murray H. Fowler, *Spearhead in the West*, Supplement, G-3 Official Record of Combat, History of the 3rd Armored Division in World War II, 1946, www.3ad.com/history/wwII/spearhead.west (accessed November 2007).

15. Mueller, 7–9.

16. Lt. Fred L. Hadsel, *Siegfried Line, 3rd Armored Division, Combat Command B, Task Force 1 (Lovelady), 12–25 September 1944*, Interviews with: Lt. Col. William B. Lovelady; Capt. George Stalling; Lt. V. L. McCord, CO Company E 36th Armored Infantry Regiment; Lt. J. L. Haldeman, CO Recon Company, 33rd Armored Regiment; Lt. J. W. Wilson, 1st Platoon, Recon Company, 33rd Armored Regiment, NA, 4–6.

17. Interview with Lieutenant Robert M. Ells, *Engineers in the Siegfried Line Penetration, Combat Command B, 3rd Armored Division, 12–22 September 1944*, NA, 9.

18. Ibid.

19. Interview with Lt. G. W. Burkett and Lt. Heril L. Brown, *Siegfried Line 12–25 September, B Company, 703rd Tank Destroyer Battalion*, Dorsey, T/4 R.C., Breinig, Germany, NA, 1.

20. Schack, 17.

21. Warren C. Giles, Company B, 117th Infantry, 30th Infantry Division—Tennessee National Guard, www.30thinfantry.org/unit_history_117 (accessed November 2007).

22. Elements of the German Seventh and Fifteenth Armies suffered approximately two thousand killed and thirty thousand captured around Mons Belgium in early September of 1944 when the 3rd Armored and 1st Infantry Divisions came through the area. Gen. Omar Bradley maintained that "this collision at Mons cost the enemy his last reserves . . . it was this little-known victory at Mons that enabled First Army to break through the Siegfried Line and within six weeks take the city of Aachen." Omar N. Bradley, *A Soldier's Story* (New York: Henry Holt and Company, 1951), 408.

23. *Generalleutnant* Hans Schmidt, *275th Infantry Division (5–14 September 1944)*, Historical Division, Foreign Military History Studies B-372, USAMHI, 1945–1954, 1–2.

24. Ibid., 4.

25. Ibid., 7–9.

26. *After Action Reports, Headquarters 119th Infantry, 1 October 1944*, 330-INF, NA, 2–3.

27. Schmidt, 9.

28. Lieutenant David F. Knox, *Journal of David F. Knox, Company L—119th Infantry Regiment, 20 August 1944 to 08 May 1945*, 9–10.

29. Schack, 18.

30. *Generalleutnant* Gerhard Engel, *12th Infantry Division, First Battle of Aachen, 16–22 September 1944*, Historical Division, Foreign Military Studies A-971, Translated from German by F. Lederer, 27 March 1946, USAMHI, 21.

31. Ibid., 18–19.

32. Ibid., 1–4.

33. Heinz Gunther Guderian, *From Normandy to the Ruhr with the 116th Panzer Division in World War II* (Bedford, PA: The Aberjona Press, 2001), 141.

34. Ibid., 142.

35. H. R. Knickerbocker, et al, *Danger Forward: The Story of the First Division in World War II* (Atlanta: Albert Love Enterprises, 1947), 257. According to a Company D account, "Charlie Company men were the first foot troops to cross the German-Belgian border on 12 September 1944 at 1515 hours," letter, Eric Gillespie to Harley Reynolds, 3 February 1998, MRC.

36. H. D. Condron, *Penetration of the Siegfried Line by the 16th Infantry Regiment 8–22 October 1944*, 2nd Information and Historical Service, 407-427-Box 24012, WWII Operations Reports, Combat Interviews, NA, 2.

37. Guderian, 130–31. Lt. Col. Edmund F. Driscoll received the Silver Star for gallantry in action 12–23 September 1944.

CHAPTER 2

1. Guderian, 142.
2. Translation of Evacuation Order—District KOLN Aachen—*Instructions for Evacuation of Residential Sections*, ANNEX to Periodic Report #122, Headquarters First Army, Office of AG of S, G-2, APO 230, 10 October 1944, 1.
3. Guderian, 142–43.
4. Ibid., 143.
5. Ibid., 132.
6. Hadsel, based on interview with V. L. McCord, 7.
7. Interview with Lt. George E. Conley, *Engineers in the Siegfried Line Penetration, Combat Command B, 3rd Armored division, 12–22 September 1944*, C1 264-407-427-24089, NA, 1.
8. Ibid., 5
9. Lt. Fred L. Hadsel, *Siegfried Line, 3rd Armored division, Combat Command B, Task Force 1 (Lovelady), 12–25 September 1944*, 7–9.
10. Castille, Siegfried Line—*Task Force 2 (King) to 14 September*, 2–4.
11. Interview with Lt. Robert M. Eells, Company B 23rd Armored Engineers, and Sergeant E. C. Henagan, Engineers in the Siegfried Line Penetration, CCB 3rd Armored Division, NA, 10.
12. Ibid., 11.
13. Lt. Fred L. Hadsel, *Siegfried Line, Combat Command B, Task Force 2*, Commander: Lt. Col. R. H. King to 14 September, NA, 6.
14. Hadsel, *Task Force Lovelady*, 9–11.
15. AAR, *67th Group, Armored Field Artillery, 3rd Armored Division*, September 1944, C1-264-467-427-24089, NA, 9.
16. Lt. Fred L. Hadsel, *Notes on Enemy Order of Battle*, Siegfried Line 12–25 September 1944, Combat Command A 3rd Armored Division, C1-264-407-427-24089, NA, 1.
17. Mueller, 10.
18. *Cracking the Siegfried Line*, Task Force Doan, Combat Command A, Third Armored Division, 13–19 September 1944, Interviews with Col. L. L. Doan and Lt. Col. William R. Orr, NA, 2–3.
19. T/4 R. C. Dorsey, *Interview with Lt. Ralph L. Henderson*, 1st Platoon, A Company 703rd TD Battalion, Task Force X, CCA, 3rd Armored Division, 2nd Information and Historical Service, VII Corps Team, First US Army, C1-264-407-427-24089, NA, 2.
20. *Cracking the Siegfried Line*, 2.
21. LTC Andrew Barr, *Spearhead in the West*, Breaching the Siegfried Line, www.3ad.com/history/wwII/spearhead.west (accessed November 2007).
22. Doan Interview, *Cracking the Siegfried Line*, 3.
23. Vic Damon and Dan Fong, Clarence Smoyer, E Co., 32nd A.R., 3rd Armored Division, *My Combat Story*, www.3ad.com/history/wwII/memoirs.pages/smoyer.pages (accessed November 2007).
24. Doan Interview, *Cracking the Siegfried Line*, 3.
25. Ibid., 4.
26. Capt. Armand R. Levasseur, *The Operations of the 1st Battalion 26th Infantry 1st Infantry Division during the Initial Penetration of the Siegfried Line in the Vicinity of Nutheim, Germany, 13–20 September 1944*, Advanced Infantry Officers Course 1947–1948, TISFBG, 13.

27. *Stolberg—Penetrating the Westwall,* 1st Battalion 26th Infantry Regiment 13–22 September 1944, 26th Infantry Regimental Association, 1999, MRC, 12.

28. Henderson Interview, 4.

29. *Stolberg—Penetrating the Westwall,* 12.

30. *Spearhead in the West, Breaching the Siegfried Line,* www.3ad.com/history/wwII/spearhead.west (accessed November 2007).

31. Schack, 26.

32. Mahlmann, 48–49.

33. Mueller, 10.

34. Ibid., 12.

35. Lt. H. D. Condron, *Penetration of the Siegfried Line by the 16th Infantry Regiment 8–22 October 1944,* WWII Operations Reports, 2nd Historical Division, 407-42-24012, NA, 3.

36. *Journal, 3rd Battalion 18th Infantry Regiment,* 13 September 1944 entry, MRC.

37. Guderian, 134.

38. Lt. John Baumgartner, 1st Sgt. Al De Poto, Sgt. William Fraccio, Cpl. Sammy Fuller, *16th Infantry Regiment 1861–1946* (Millennium Edition; Du Quoin, IL: Cricket Press, 1999, MRC), 116.

39. *Generalleutnant* Hans Schmidt, *275th Infantry Division 5–14 September 1944,* Historical Division, Headquarters US Army, Europe, Foreign Military Studies Branch, MS B-372, USAMHI, 10.

40. Guderian, 134–35.

CHAPTER 3

1. Capt. Franklin Ferriss, *Operation of Task Force Stokes September 1944,* based on Interviews with Lt. Col. William M. Stokes, Maj. Hugh R. O'Farrell, Maj. Henry Zeien, Lt. Henry W. Johnson, Lt. Joseph S. Roberts, Maj. Harold D. Hansen, Capt. Donald E. Svarstad, Capt. Herbert Melin, Lt. Murton Swenson, NA, 1–2.

2. Capt. Lester D. Royalty, *The Operations of the 117th Infantry Regiment (30th Infantry Division) in the Breaching of the Siegfried Line in the Vicinity of Alsdorf, Germany, 2–8 October 1944,* Advanced Infantry Officers Course 1948–1949, Academic Department, TISFBG, 6.

3. William J. Lyman Jr., *Curlew History: The Story of the First Battalion 117th Infantry, 30th Division in Europe during World War II* (Chapel Hill, NC: The Orange Printshop, 1948), Office of the Chief Military History, General Reference Branch, CMH, 43.

4. Warren C. Giles, Company B, 117th Infantry Regiment, 30th Infantry Division, Tennessee National Guard, 2.

5. Maj. Edward E. McBride, *The Operations of the 1st Battalion and Task Force Quinn, 119th Infantry (30th Infantry Division) in Breaching the Siegfried Line in the vicinity of Rimburg, Holland, 2–6 October 1944,* Advanced Infantry Officers Course 1948–1949, TISFBG, 8–10.

6. *Generalleutnant* Wolfgang Lange, *183rd Volksgrenadier Division September 1944 to 25 January 1945,* MS# B-753, Historical Division, Headquarters United States Army Europe, Foreign Military Studies Branch, USAMHI, 1.

7. Schack, 22.

8. Lange, 3.

9. First Army Report of Operations, 48.

10. McBride, 11.

11. Engel, 4.
12. Lt. Fred L. Hadsel, *VII Corps, 3rd Armored Division, Penetration of the Siegfried Line, 12–25 September 1944*, 2nd Information and Historical Service, NA, 3.
13. Castille, Task Force 2, 6.
14. Ibid., 8.
15. Ibid.
16. Ibid.
17. AAR, *67th Group, Armored Field Artillery, 3rd Armored Division*, September 1944, NA, 10.
18. Lt. Fred L. Hadsel, Task Force 1—Lovelady, 12.
19. Task Force 1—Lovelady, 13.
20. Lt. Fred L. Hadsel, *Penetration of the Second Line of Dragon's Teeth—Siegfried Line*, Interview with Col. L. L. Doan, CCA 3rd Armored Division, Busbach, Germany, 10 October 1944, NA, 1.
21. *Stolberg—Penetrating the* Westwall, 13.
22. Lt. Fred L. Hadsel, *1st Battalion 26th Infantry Regiment, Siegfried Line 12–25 September 1944*, Interviews with Maj. Francis W. Adams, Capt. Thomas Anderson, Capt. Armand Levasseur, Capt. Edgar Simons, Capt. Thomas Gendron (S-1), Lt. E. P. Jones, Lt. C. M. Robertson, NA, 5.
23. *Stolberg—Penetrating the* Westwall, 13.
24. Lt. H. D. Condron, *Penetration of the Siegfried Line by the 16th Infantry Regiment—September–October 1944*, WWII Operations Reports, Combat Interviews, NA, 11.
25. Mueller, 13–14.
26. Guderian, 137.
27. Schack, 30–31.
28. Guderian, 136–37.
29. Ibid., 10.
30. Ibid., 159.
31. Ibid.
32. Ibid., 164–65. In 1957 the city of Aachen honored Count von Schwerin with a ceremony, and in 1975 they named a street after him.
33. Schack, 30.
34. Combat Command B—Task Force 2, 11.
35. Task Force 1 (Lovelady), 12 September to 25 September 1944, 15–16.
36. Penetration of the Second Line of Dragon's Teeth, Doan Interview, 2.
37. Guderian, 167.
38. Lt. Fred L. Hadsel, *1st Battalion 16th Infantry Regiment, Action at Muensterbusch 15–22 September, 1944*, Interview with Lt. Col. E. F. Driscoll, 2nd Information and Historical Services, VII Corps, NA, 2.
39. *The Attack on Stolberg—15–18 September 1944, Company A 16th Infantry*, The Rifle Company in Attack, MRC, 5.
40. Ibid., 6.
41. *Penetration of the Siegfried Line by the 16th Infantry Regiment*, 14.
42. *Attack to Gain High Ground North of Eilendorf—15–16 September 1944, Company G 16th Infantry*, MRC, 1–2.
43. Guderian, 168.
44. *Attack to Gain High Ground North of Eilendorf—15–16 September 1944, Company G 16th Infantry*, MRC, 4.

45. Guderian, 169.
46. Engel, 3.
47. Ibid., 4–5.
48. Mueller, 14.
49. *Siegfried Line 12–25 September, 1st Battalion 26th Infantry*, 6.
50. Ibid., 7.
51. *Rifle Company in Attack, The Attack on Stolberg, 16–18 September, Company A 16th Infantry Regiment*, 7–8. Units of enemy captured were identified in Driscoll interview, 4.
52. *Penetration of the Second Line of Dragon's Teeth, Siegfried Line, 12–25 September 1944*, Interview with Doan, 2.
53. William S. White, "Germans Stage Death Attacks against Yanks," *The Palm Beach Post*, 18 September 1944.
54. *Combat Command B—Task Force 2—Mills*, 13.
55. *Siegfried Line, Mission of Colonel Edgar A. Gans, 16–17 September at Diepenlinchen*. Interview with Capt. J. F. Kuhns, S-3, Armored Infantry Regiment, 33rd Armored Regiment, 1. Kuhns kept a journal for this period and was at the command post during the action.
56. *Siegfried Line, 3rd Armored Division, CCB, H Company, 36th Armored Infantry Regiment*, Interviews with Lt. H. M. Bundrick, Executive Officer, Lt. M. E. Hulstedt, Leader 3rd Platoon, and Sgt. Francis X. Bell, Acting Platoon Leader, NA, 2.
57. *3rd Platoon, B Company, 703rd TD Battalion with Task Force Lovelady, CCB*, Interview with Lt. Ernest P. Silva, C1-264-407-427-24089, NA, 7–8.
58. Engel, 6.
59. Mueller, 15.
60. Mahlmann, 6.
61. Guderian, 171.
62. Schack, 34.
63. Lt. Fred L. Hadsel, *Penetration of the Siegfried Line 12–25 September 1944, CCB 3rd Armored Division*, Interview with Brig. Gen. T. E. Boudinot, 2nd Information and Historical Services, VII Corps Team, First US Army, NA, 1.

CHAPTER 4

1. *Penetration of the Siegfried Line by the 16th Infantry Regiment*, 16.
2. *16th Infantry Regiment 1861–1946*, 160.
3. *Penetration of the Siegfried Line by the 16th Infantry Regiment*, 17.
4. Ibid.
5. *Cracking the Siegfried Line, Task Force Doan, CCA 3rd Armored Division, 13–19 September 1944*, Interviews with Col. L. L. Doan, Commanding Officer Task Force X, and Lt. Col. William R. Orr, Commanding Officer, 36th Armored Infantry Regiment, NA, 7.
6. *67th Groupment FA*, AAR, 12.
7. *Cracking the Siegfried Line, Task Force Doan, CCA 3rd Armored Division, 13–19 September 1944*, 7.
8. Major Samuel Adams (S-2), *Siegfried Line, 12–25 September 1944, CCA 3rd Armored Division, Notes on Enemy Order of Battle*, NA, 2.
9. *Siegfried Line, Combat Command B, Task Force 2*, 13–14.
10. Ibid., 15–16.

11.   *Siegfried Line, 3rd Armored Division, CCB, Company D, 36th Armored Infantry Regiment, 16 September to 4 October 1944,* Interview with Captain Alfred J. Amborst. Later on 17 September Robinette was relieved of his command and Major Tousey took over the 2nd Battalion, NA, 7.

12.   Interview with Maj. C. H. Carter, *3rd Armored Division, CCB, Mission of Colonel Edgar Gans, 16–17 September 1944 and the Capture of Company E, 36th Armored Infantry,* NA, 1.

13.   *Siegfried Line, 12–25 September 1944, 2nd Battalion 36th Armored Infantry Regiment, Notes from the Notebook of the Operations Sergeant, Technical Sergeant R. M. Torgersen.* Sergeant Torgersen was with the rear CP and had no direct contact; the notes he made were received by radio. Casualty figures are from the regiment report, NA, 1.

14.   Amborst Interview, 2–6.

15.   Ibid., 4–5

16.   Engel, 10–11.

17.   *Siegfried Line 12–25 September, 1st Battalion 26th Infantry Regiment,* NA, 8.

18.   1st Lt. Hans Zeplien, Company Commander of 14th Coy/89 (Tank Destroyers), *Report on Action of 89th Grenadier Regiment, an Element of the 12th Volksgrenadier Division, in the Stolberg-Eschweiler Area, Autumn 1944,* trans. Heino Brandt (Stolberg, Germany: 1987), 7; copy provided to author by Mark J. Reardon, 2006.

19.   *Siegfried Line, 1st Battalion 26th Infantry Regiment,* 9.

20.   Ibid., 9–10.

21.   Ibid.

22.   *67th Groupment FA,* 13.

23.   *Stolberg—Penetrating the Westwall, 1st Battalion 26th Infantry, 13–22 September 1944,* 25.

24.   Zeplien, 14.

25.   Ibid., 8–9.

26.   *Siegfried Line, Combat Command B, Task Force 2,* 16–17.

27.   Engel, 11–12.

28.   *Penetration of the Siegfried Line by the 16th Infantry Regiment,* 18.

29.   Interview with Lt. Col. E. F. Driscoll, *Siegfried Line, 1st Battalion 16th Infantry Regiment (1st Infantry Division), Action at Munsterbusch, 15–22 September 1944,* NA, 6–7.

30.   Maj. Heinrich Volker, *Short Report on the State of the Troops to the 9th Panzer Division, Panzer Brigade 105, 22 September 1944,* Mark J. Reardon to author 2006, 1–3.

31.   Engel, 7, 13.

32.   Volker, 3.

33.   Interview with Gen. Doyle Hickey, Commanding General, CCA, *Siegfried Line 12–25 September, 3rd Armored Division CCA,* NA, 1.

34.   Doan, 4.

35.   *16th Infantry Regiment 1861–1946,* 162.

36.   Orr, 2–3.

37.   Doan, 4.

38.   Interview with Capt. R. W. Russell, S-1, 36th Armored Infantry Regiment, *Siegfried Line, 12–25 September 1944, 3rd Armored Division Reserve,* conducted at Brenig on 20 October 1944, NA, 1–2.

39. *Siegfried Line, 12–25 September 1944, Task Force Blanchard, CCA 3rd Armored Division*, Interview with Lt. Elton K. McDonald, CO Company D, 1st Battalion 32nd Armored Regiment, NA, 2.

40. *Siegfried Line, Combat Command B, Task Force 2*, 18–19.

41. *Report on Action of 89th Grenadier Regiment, an Element of the 12th Volksgrenadier Division, in the Stolberg-Eschweiler Area, Autumn 1944*, report by Sgt. Hans Martens, 15.

42. *Stolberg—Penetrating the* Westwall, 82–83.

43. Interview with Lt. Sam W. Hogan and Maj. William B. Walker, Executive Officer, *Siegfried Line, 12–15 September 1944, Task Force Hogan (CCR), 3rd Armored Division*, NA, 2–3.

44. Zeplien, 9–10.

45. *Siegfried Line 12–25 September, 1st Battalion 26th Infantry Regiment*, 12.

46. *Siegfried Line, 3rd Armored Division CCB, Company I, 36th Armored Infantry Regiment*, 4.

47. Interviews with Lt. H. M. Bundrick, Executive Officer, Lt. H. E. Hulstedt, Leader 3rd Platoon, and Sgt F. X. Bell, Platoon Sergeant and Acting Platoon Leader, *Siegfried Line, 3rd Armored Division CCB, Company H 36th Armored Infantry Regiment*, NA, 4.

48. CCB, Task Force 2, 20.

49. CCB, Task Force 1, 18–19.

50. *Stolberg—Penetrating the Westwall*, 30.

51. Engel, 13–14.

52. *Company I, 36th Armored Infantry*, 4–5.

53. Task Force Mills, 22.

54. Interview with Lt. G. W. Burkett, Company Commander, and Lt. Heril L. Brown, 1st Platoon Leader, *Siegfried Line 12–25 September 1944, Company B 703d Tank Destroyer Battalion*, NA, 3.

55. Zeplien, 11–12.

56. Driscoll Interview, 9.

57. Orr Interview, 4.

58. Interview with Lt. Col. E. W. Blanchard, TFY Commander, *Siegfried Line 12–25 September 1944, 3rd Armored Division (TFY), Stolberg Germany*, 25 October 1944, NA, 3.

59. Russell Interview, 3.

60. Ibid., 4.

61. *16th Infantry Regiment 1861–1946*, 163.

62. Engel, 16–17.

63. Lt. Col. E. C. Orth, S-4, *Evaluation of the factors stopping the 3rd Armored Division, September 1944*, NA, p. 1. NOTE: Statistics are from 12th Army Group reports attached to Orth's statements.

64. Orth, 1–2.

65. Company H, 36th Armored Infantry, 6–7.

66. Task Force Mills, 23.

67. Ibid., 24.

68. *16th Infantry Regiment 1861–1946*, 164.

69. Charles B. McDonald, *United States Army in WWII: The Siegfried Line Campaign, The Battle for Aachen*, 1993, CMH, 90.

70. Interview with Gen. Doyle Hickey, Commanding General, CCA, *Siegfried Line 12–25 September, 3rd Armored Division CCA*, NA, 3.

71. *After Action Against Enemy, September 1944,* Headquarters, 26th Infantry Regiment, APO #1, US ARMY, NA, 7.

72. War Department General Order Number 42, 1945, Presidential Unit Citation (Army), 12 February 1945, MRC, 1.

73. Schack, 43–49.

74. Ibid., 23–24.

75. *General der Infanterie* Friedrich Köchling, *Battles in the Aachen Sector September to November 1944*, Historical Division Headquarters, United States Army Europe, Foreign Military Studies Branch, A-977, USAMHI, 3.

76. Engel, 17.

77. *Annex 2 to Periodic Report 130 entitled Life Begins in the Fourth Reich*, G-2 Periodic Report, Headquarters First United States Army, Office of AC of S, G-2, APO230, 18 October 1944, NA.

78. Robert W. Baumer with Mark J. Reardon, *American Iliad: The History of the 18th Infantry Regiment in World War II* (Bedford, PA: The Aberjona Press, 2004), 269–70. Author was also fortunate to have numerous conversations in 2003 with Lt. Col. Sam Carter (U.S. Army-Retired). Carter, then in his early nineties and possessed of remarkable recall of the war, drafted the Medal of Honor citation for Staff Sergeant Schafer; he confirmed the pertinent facts to author without the benefit of referring to the actual Citation he wrote nearly sixty years earlier in 1944.

79. *First United States Army, Report of Operations, 1 August 1944 to 22 February 1945*, Office of the Chief Military History, CMH, Washington, DC, 54.

80. Guderian, 188.

81. *LXXXI A.K. AAR September 1944*, 3–4. Translated copy provided to author by Mark J. Reardon in 2006.

82. First Army Report of Operations, 54.

CHAPTER 5

1. Capt. Kenneth W. Hechler, 2nd Information and Historical Services, Interview with Pvt. Brent Youenes, 1st Platoon, B Company, 117th Infantry Regiment, (31 October 1944), *Breaching the Siegfried Line, The First Patrol to Cross the Wurm River, 22 September 1944*, NA, 2.

2. Youenes Interview, 3.

3. Ibid., 4.

4. Ibid., 4–5.

5. Hechler, Interview with Lt. William J. O'Neil, *Breaching the Siegfried Line, 1st Battalion 117th Infantry Regiment 30th Infantry Division*, 17 October 1944, World War II Operations Reports, Combat Interviews, NA, 2.

6. Charles B. McDonald, *United States Army in World War II: The Siegfried Line Campaign, The Battle for Aachen*, 253.

7. *Breaching the Siegfried Line, XIX Corps, United States Army, 2 October 1944*, Office of the Chief Military History General Reference Branch, 1946, CMH, 4–12.

8. Drew Middleton, *Bombs, Shells Shake Earth as Yanks Pierce Westwall*, by wireless to the *New York Times*, 2 October 1944.

9. Capt. Lester D. Royalty, *The Operations of the 117th Infantry Regiment (30th Infantry Division) in the Breaching of the Siegfried Line in the Vicinity of Alsdorf, Germany, 2–8 October 1944*, Advanced Infantry Officers Course, 1949, Academic Department, TISFBG, 5–8.

10. Capt. William H. Cox, *Operations of the 30th Division in the Battle for Aachen Germany, 2–17 October 1944*, Advanced Infantry Officers Course, TISFBG, 9.

11. McDonald, 257.

12. Excerpts from 1st Battalion Grenadier Regiment 330, BATTALION ORDER OF THE DAY, Order of Battle Notes for Period ending 6200 8 October 1944, Headquarters 30th Infantry Division G-2 Periodic Report, Siegfried Line Reports, OH, 4 (accessed February 2014).

13. *Generalleutnant* a.D. Wolfgang Lange, *183rd Volksgrenadier Division (September 1944–January 1945)*, Historical Division, Headquarters United States Army, Europe, USAMHI, 5.

14. This culvert was developed jointly by Capt. Edward Miller, Assistant S-3 of the 743rd Tank Battalion; Capt. James F. Rice, Company Commander of Company A, 105th Engineer Combat Battalion; and Capt. Frederick L. Hensler, Company C Commander. Source: Interview with Lt. Col. William D. Duncan, 5 October 1944, World War II Operations Reports, Combat Interviews, NA, 1.

15. McBride, 11.

16. Headquarters 119th Infantry APO 50, US Army, *Action Against Enemy/After Action Reports*, NA, 4 November 1944, 2.

17. McBride, 15.

18. *Breaching the Siegfried Line, Account of Lieutenant Colonel Courtney Brown*, CO of 3rd Battalion 119th Infantry, NA, 1.

19. Interview with Lt. Col. Robert E. Frankland, CO 1st Battalion; Maj. Henry R. Kaczowka, Battalion Executive Officer; Capt. David K. Easlik, S-3; Lt. Stanley W. Cooper, Company Commander, D (Heavy Weapons) Company; Lt. William J. O'Neil, platoon leader of the Pioneer Platoon, *Breaching the Siegfried Line, 30th Infantry Division 117th Infantry Regiment*, 18 October 1944, NA, 2.

20. O'Neil Interview, 3.

21. *Breaching the Siegfried Line, 30th Infantry Division 117th Infantry Regiment*, Officer Interviews, 6.

22. Ibid., 1, 4–5.

23. Hechler, Terrain Walks with Capt. John E. Kent, Lt. John M. Maloney and Others, 21 October 1944, *Breaching the Siegfried Line, Company A 117th Infantry Regiment 30th Infantry Division*, NA, 1.

24. Ibid., 3

25. Ibid., 4.

26. *Breaching the Siegfried Line*, XIX Corps United States Army, 2 October 1944, Chief Military History General Reference Branch, Washington, DC, 23.

27. Ibid.

28. Hechler, *Interview with Captain Robert Sinclair, C Company, 803rd Tank Destroyer Battalion, 21 October 1944*, NA, 1.

29. Hechler, *Breaching the Siegfried Line, 30th Infantry Division, 117th Infantry Regiment, Company B, 1st Battalion*, Interviews and terrain walks 17, 29, 29–31 October 1944, NA, 6.

30. XIX Corps, 63–64.

31. Headquarters Forty-First Armored Regiment, *Monthly Operational Report 1–31 October 1944*, Entry for 1 October 1944, Report dated 1 November 1944, 1.

32. O'Neil Interview, 3.

33. Ferriss, *Breaching the Siegfried Line*, Account of Capt. Ross Y. Simmons, Company A 119th Infantry, 30 October 1944, NA, 1.

34. Letter by Mrs. Wade J. Verweire Jr. of Fort Wayne, Indiana, 2 May 1945, AG 704 Dead (20 January 1950), *Review of Circumstances Surrounding the Disappearance of Personnel Presumed Dead*, IDPF Reports on Anthony T. Drabecki, OH, 5 (accessed May 2014).

35. Middleton, *New York Times*, 2 October 1944.

36. Hechler, Interviews with Lt. Col. D. V. Bennett, Maj. D. W. Way, Capt. D. J. Hasseltine, *Breaching the Siegfried Line, 62nd Armored Field Artillery*, 10 October 1944, NA, 2.

37. Hechler, Interview with Maj. Raymond Millican, S-3, *Breaching the Siegfried Line, 118th Field Artillery Battalion 30th Infantry Division*, 5 October 1944, NA, 1.

38. Hechler, Interview with Lt. Col. Bradford Butler Jr., *155mm (SP) M-12s and Breaching the Siegfried Line, 258th Field Artillery Battalion*, 10 October 1944, NA, 1.

39. 803rd TDB, 1.

40. XIX Corps, 15.

41. Ibid., 12.

42. Hechler, *Breaching the Siegfried Line, Report Number 25, 4 October 1944*, comments by Lt. Col. H. E. Hassenfeldt, G-3 30th Infantry Division, NA, 1.

43. Hechler, *Notes on Activities at the 117th Infantry Regiment CP*, 2–3 October 1944, NA, 1.

44. Hechler, *Breaching the Siegfried Line, Company C 117th Infantry Regiment*, Interviews with Lt. Thomas E. Stanley, 3rd Platoon leader and Lt. Clarence Johnson, 1st Platoon, NA, 1.

45. Cox, 13–14.

46. Hechler, *Breaching the Siegfried Line, Comments of Lieutenant John Lehnerd, Commanding Officer of Company D 117th Infantry Regiment*, 6 November 1944, NA, 1.

47. *Breaching the Siegfried Line, 92nd Chemical Battalion*, Interviews with Maj. Carl Wissinger, Battalion Executive Officer; Capt. A. A. Athanas, Company A Commander; Lt. Raymond C. Filipino, Forward Observer with the 119th Infantry Regiment; Capt. Robert Cole, Forward Observer with the 117th Infantry Regiment, 21 October 1944, NA, 1.

48. Ferriss, *Breaching the Siegfried Line, Company C 119th Infantry Regiment*, Account of Lt. Ferdinand Bons, Commanding Officer, 6 November 1944, NA, 1–2.

49. Simmons Company A Account, 2.

50. McBride, 17–18.

51. Ferriss, *Breaching the Siegfried Line, Company B 119th Infantry Regiment*, Account of Lieutenant Warne R. Parker, 22 October 1944, NA, 1–2.

52. Parker Interview, 2.

53. *Breaching the Siegfried Line, 117th Infantry Regiment (2nd Battalion)*, Interviews with Maj. Ben T. Ammons, Commanding Officer 2nd Battalion, 10 and 15 October 1944; Capt. Harold T. Hoppe, Commanding Officer Company E, 15 October 1944; Capt. Richard J. Wood, S-3 2nd Battalion, 15 October 1944, NA, 2–3.

54. Hoppe Interview, 3.
55. Ibid., 5.
56. *117th Infantry Regiment (2nd Battalion)*, 5–6.
57. *Breaching the Siegfried Line, Company C 117th Infantry Regiment*, Interviews with Lt. Thomas E. Stanley, 3rd Platoon Leader, and Lt. Clarence Johnson, 1st Platoon Leader, 29 October 1944, NA, 1.
58. Ibid., 2–3.
59. Ibid., 3.
60. Millican Interview, 1.
61. Company B 117 INF, O'Neil Interview, 12.
62. Ibid., 14–15.
63. Ibid., 7.
64. Royalty, 14.
65. 117 INF CP, 1.

CHAPTER 6

1. *Breaching the Siegfried Line, 743rd Tank Battalion*, Interview with Lt. Col. William D. Duncan on the activities of Company A in conjunction with the 117th Infantry Regiment, 2–4 October 1944, 5 October 1944, NA, 1–2.
2. 117 INF CP, 1–6.
3. Company B 117 INF, 5.
4. Ibid., 17.
5. Ibid., 18–19.
6. Account of Pfc. Richard L. Ballou in letter to parents in Providence, Rhode Island, 4 November 1944 OH, 4 (accessed March 2014).
7. Company B 117 INF Interviews.
8. Ibid., 21.
9. Ibid., 22.
10. Ibid., 23.
11. Ibid., 24.
12. Hechler, *Breaching the Siegfried Line, Company A 117th Infantry Regiment 30th Infantry Division*, Account of Activities based on Interviews with Company Personnel, NA, 4.
13. Company A 117 INF, 4.
14. Ibid., 7.
15. Lyman, 50–51.
16. Hechler, *Breaching the Siegfried Line*, Interviews with Maj. Ben T. Ammons, Commanding Officer 2nd Battalion 117th Infantry Regiment; Capt. Harold F. Hoppe, Commanding Officer Company E; and Capt. Richard J. Wood, S-3 of 2nd Battalion, 15 October 1944, 6.
17. 2nd Battalion 117 INF Interviews, 6–7.
18. Ibid., 7.
19. Ibid., 8.
20. Notes on activities at the 117th Infantry Regimental Command Post taken by Captain Ferriss and Captain Hechler, 2–3 October 1944, 6.
21. Hechler, *Breaching the Siegfried Line, Company Interviews, Company I 3rd Battalion 117th Infantry Regiment*, 24 October 1944, NA, 1.
22. 743rd Tank Battalion, 2.
23. 803rd TDB, 2.

24. Hechler, *Breaching the Siegfried Line, Comments of Lieutenant John Lehnerd, CO of Company D, 119th Infantry*, 6 November 1944, NA, 1.

25. Company C 119 INF, 2.

26. McBride, 19–20.

27. Ferriss, *Breaching the Siegfried Line*, Transcript of Notes Taken at the Command Post of the 119th Infantry on 2 October 1944, 2.

28. 119 INF CP 2 October, 4.

29. Knox Journal, 14.

30. 119 INF CP 2 October, 5.

31. Ferriss, *Breaching the Siegfried Line, Company F 119th Infantry*, Joint Interviews with Participants, 23 October 1944 at Company CP in Kohlscheid, NA, 2.

32. Middleton, *New York Times*, 2 October 1944.

33. XIX Corps, 15.

34. 119th Infantry History Book, The Rimburg Castle Attack, 59, OH, 4 (accessed May 2014).

35. Drew Middleton, "Exploiting of New Breach Watched Now as the Test," *New York Times*, 3 October 1944.

36. 119 INF CP, 2 October, 4.

37. Ibid., 5.

38. Company A 117 INF, 9.

39. Lyman, 52.

40. *30th Infantry Division, Findings of IPW Team #42* (117th Infantry Regiment), 1–2 October 1944, NA, 1.

41. *IPW Team #42*, 1.

42. Lyman, 52.

43. 117 INF 2nd Battalion Interviews, 9.

44. McBride, 21.

45. Köchling MS, 4–5.

46. Lange MS, 7.

47. McDonald, 258–59.

48. Col. James H. Cash, *The Operations of the 1st Infantry Division and the 30th Infantry Division in the Aachen Offensive 2–21 October 1944*, 1948–1949, TISFBG, 12.

CHAPTER 7

1. McDonald, 266.

2. XIX Corps, 68.

3. Millican Interview, 2.

4. *The Battle for Aachen, Development of the Enemy Position in Front of [LXXXI] Corps Line during the End of September to the Beginning of October 1944*, German translation to English provided to author by Mark J. Reardon, March 2006, 5.

5. Lt. W. D. Hart, *Breaching the Siegfried Line, Operations of the 1stt Battalion 41st Armored Infantry Regiment Combat Team, Task Force 2, CCB 2nd Armored Division, 3–6 October 1944*, NA, 2.

6. Company C 119 INF, 2.

7. McBride, 22.

8. Ibid., 23–24.

9. Hechler, Comments of Captain Smithers, Assistant S-3, regarding the operations of Task Force Quinn, *Breaching the Siegfried Line, 119th Infantry Regiment, 30th Infantry Division*, 14 November 1944, NA, 1.

10. 119 INF CP, 3 October 1944, 1.

11. Company C 119 INF, 3.

12. McBride, 24–25.

13. 119 INF History Book, 60–61, OH, 4.

14. McBride, 25.

15. 119 INF CP, 3 October, 1.

16. Knox Journal, 15–16.

17. Ibid., 16.

18. Ferriss, Comments of Major Laney, Executive Officer and Captain Hardaway, Battalion S-1, *Breaching the Siegfried Line, 2nd Battalion 119th Infantry 30th Infantry Division*, 17 October 1944, NA, 1.

19. McBride, 43.

20. Wayne Interview, 1.

21. Company C 119 INF, 3.

22. McBride, 27–28.

23. Company E 119 INF, 4.

24. Edward C. Arn and Jerome Mushkat, *Arn's War: Memoirs of a World War II Infantryman 1940–1946* (Akron, OH: University of Akron Press, 2006), 103–5.

25. 119 INF CP, 3 October, 2–3.

26. Knox Journal, 15.

27. Ferriss, *Account of Lieutenant Colonel Robert Herlong, CO of 1st Battalion 119th Infantry Regiment, and Captain Clayborn Wayne, Battalion S-3*, 15 October 1944, NA, 1.

28. Summary of telephone conversation between General Hobbs and Colonel Sutherland, 031802A October 1944, *Siegfried Line Reports 3 October*, OH, 4.

29. Summary of telephone conversation between General Corlett and General Hobbs, 031538A October 1944, *Siegfried Line Reports 3 October*, OH, 4.

30. McDowell and Lieutenant Robert Peters Interview, 17 October 1944, NA, 1–2.

31. 117 INF CP, 3 October, 8.

32. McDowell and Lieutenant Robert Peters Interview, 17 October 1944, 2.

33. 117 INF CP, 3 October, 8.

34. McDonald, 169–70.

35. 41st Armored INF, 2–3.

36. 117th INF CP, 3 October, 9.

37. Royalty, 21.

38. 41st Armored INF, 3–4.

39. McDowell Interview, 17 October 1944, 2.

40. Company L 117 INF Interviews, 1.

41. Company I 117 INF Interviews, 3.

42. Company A 117 INF Interviews, 10.

43. Operations of the 2nd Battalion 117th Infantry Regiment, 2–6 October 1944, NA, 1–2.

44. Company L 117 INF Interviews, 2.

45. Company K 117 INF Interviews, 2.

46. Company L 117 INF Interviews, 2–3.
47. Millican Interview, 5 October 1944, 3.
48. McDowell Interview, 2–3.
49. 119 INF History Book, 61.
50. Ibid.
51. Knox Journal, 16.
52. 119 INF History Book, 61.
53. McBride, 28–29.
54. Company C 119 INF Interviews, 3.
55. 1st Battalion 119th Infantry Regiment Journal, Wednesday 4 October 1944, NA.
56. Lange, 6–7.
57. McDonald, 271.
58. Operations 1st Battalion 41st Armored INF, 6–7.
59. Simmons Interview, 3.
60. Ibid.
61. Company E 119 INF, 4–5.
62. *Generalleutnant* a.D. Siegfried Macholz, the 49th Infantry Division, MS # B-792, Historical Division, Headquarters United States Army Europe, 1953, USAMHI, 25.

CHAPTER 8

1. Frankland Interview, 3–8 October 1944, 22 October 1944, 1.
2. Company I 117 INF, 3.
3. Company L, 117 INF, 3.
4. *Breaching the Siegfried Line, 30th Infantry Division 743rd Tank Battalion*, Interview with Lt. Col. William C. Duncan, CO, on the activities of Company A 5–10 October 1944, 1.
5. *Breaching the Siegfried Line, 30th Infantry Division 803rd Tank Destroyer Battalion*, Interview with Capt. Robert Sinclair, Company Commander Company C, 21 October 1944, NA, 3.
6. Company I 117 INF, 3.
7. Company E 119 INF, 5.
8. Ibid., 6.
9. Ibid.
10. Ibid., 7.
11. Ibid.
12. Company F 119 INF, 3–4.
13. Cox, 17.
14. McBride, 31.
15. Ibid.
16. Ibid., 34.
17. 1st Battalion 119th Infantry Regiment Journal, 6 October 1944.
18. LXXXI Corps, Reardon Translation, 6.
19. 41st Armored INF, 13.
20. 1st Battalion 67th Armored Regiment Journal 05/2230, 2.
21. *Report on Conversations between Different Pillboxes of the Siegfried Line on 4 and 5 October 1944*, Annex to G-2 Periodic Report, Headquarters 30th Infantry Division, 4 October 1944, Siegfried Line Reports 4 October, OH, 4 (accessed March 2014).

22. Report of Operations 1–31 October 1944, Headquarters 66th Armored Regiment, 2 November 1944, NA, 3.
23. LXXXI Corps, Reardon Translation, 6.
24. McDonald, 277.
25. 1st Battalion 119 INF, Herlong Interview, 3.
26. Journal 1st Battalion 119th INF, 6 October 1944.
27. McBride, 39.
28. Company E 119th INF, 8–9.
29. Company F 119 INF, 4.
30. Ibid., 6.
31. Ibid.
32. Ibid., 5.
33. Ibid., 9–10.
34. Knox Journal, 16.
35. Report of Operations for October 1944, Headquarters 66th Armored Regiment, 2 November 1944, NA, 4.
36. Company L 117 INF, 3.
37. McDowell Interview, 6.
38. G-2 Estimate of enemy Situation Annex, Headquarters 30th Infantry Division, Office of AC of S, G-2, Siegfried Line Reports 5–6 October 1944, OH, 4.
39. *The 67th Armored Regiment 1944*, WWII Operations Reports 2nd Armored Division, 407-427-15030, NA, 58.
40. 41st Armored INF, 14.
41. 67th Armored Regiment, 58–59.
42. Macholz, 26.
43. LXXXI Corps, Reardon Translation, 7.
44. Ibid., 8.
45. Herlong Interview, 3.
46. Brown Interview, 2.
47. Knox Journal, 16.
48. Ibid., 16–17.
49. Cox, 19.
50. Company I 117 INF, 4.
51. Curlew History, 53.
52. Company I 117 INF, 4.
53. Ibid., 4.
54. Company A 117 INF, 11.
55. Royalty, 26.
56. LXXXI Corps, Reardon Translation, 7.
57. Report of Operations, 66th Armored Regiment, 7 October 1944, 7.
58. McDonald, 279.
59. Frankland Interview, 22 October 1944, 3.
60. Company I 117 INF, 5.
61. *Cracking the Siegfried Line*, 3rd Battalion 117th Infantry Journal 3–8 October 1944, 1.
62. Narrative of OP defense based on *Recommendation for the Silver Star* to Lt. Col. Samuel T. McDowell (and all personnel named herein), Capt. William F. Butler, Adjutant, NA.
63. Duncan Interview, 3.

64. Robert L. Hewitt, "Workhorse of the Western Front: The Story of the 30th Infantry Division," *Washington Journal Press* (August 1946): 127.

65. Company I 117 INF, 6.

66. Ibid.

67. Ibid.

68. Knox Journal, 17.

69. Cox, 20.

70. Malcholz, 27.

CHAPTER 9

1. Annex No. 2 to G-2 Periodic Report No. 141, Headquarters 1st U.S. Infantry Division APO 1 US Army, 7 November 1944, MRC.

2. Maj. Edward W. McGregor, *The Operations of the 1st Battalion 18th Infantry in the Vicinity of Crucifix Hill Northeast of Aachen Germany, 8–10 October 1944 (Rhineland Campaign)*, Personal Experiences of a Battalion Operations Officer, Advanced Officers Infantry Course, TISFBG, 8.

3. McGregor, 8–9.

4. The Rifle Company in Attack, *The Attack on Crucifix Hill, 7–9 October 1944*, Company C, 18th Infantry, MRC, 3.

5. Lt. Gen. Robert H. York, "Bobbie Brown, Winner of Medal of Honor, Is Dead," *The New York Times*, 11 November 1971.

6. *16th Infantry Regiment 1861–1946*, 165.

7. The Infantry Battalion in Offensive Action, Aachen 8–20 October 1944, 2nd Battalion 26th Infantry Regiment, MRC, 2–3.

8. Capt. Alfred E. Koenig, *Aggressive, Hard-Hitting Leadership Is the One Major Factor in Overcoming the Loss of the Element of Surprise in Battle*, Advanced Infantry Officers Course 1949-1950, TISFBG, 5–6.

9. T/4 Ridgely C. Dorsey, *745th Tank Battalion Company B, 8–19 October 1944*, 2nd Information and Historical Service 1st US Army, MRC, 2.

10. Malcolm Marshall, comp. and ed., *Proud Americans: Men of the 32nd Field Artillery Battalion in Action, World War II, as Part of the 18th Regimental Combat Team, 1st U.S. Infantry Division* (M. Marshall, 1994), 218.

11. RCA, Company C, 5.

12. Capt. Bobbie E., Brown, *The Operations of Company C 18th Infantry in the Attack on Crucifix Hill*, 8 October 1944, Personal experiences of a Company Commander, TISFBG, 8.

13. Ibid., 5.

14. Ibid., 9–10.

15. RCA Company C, 3.

16. RCA, 6.

17. Clement Van Wagoner, Oral History. During the writing of *American Iliad* by author, conflicting accounts about the Attack on Crucifix Hill were sorted out with Van Wagoner. "Good luck, Bobbie" was retold by him to author at 2002 Combat Officers Dinner Reunion of the Society of the First Infantry Division in Washington, DC.

18. Brown, 17.

19. Phil Kruger, *Sgt. Bobbie Brown, '62 Notch' Sharpshooter Who Captured Crucifix Hill*, Article reprint from MRC.

20. Brown, 11.

21. Ibid., 12. Lt. Joseph W. Cambron was later awarded the DSC (posthumous) for his courage and bravery that day.

22. Ibid.

23. The exact time the cross fell was uncertain, but one eyewitness, Sgt. Richard Lobin of the 1st Platoon 634th TDB whose TD had observation on Crucifix Hill stated that "the cross was still up at 1500, but went down before 1700." Group Interview, *634th Tank Destroyer Battalion Company B 1st Platoon*, NA, 1.

24. Proud Americans, 220.

25. Phil Kruger article.

26. McGregor, 35–36.

27. 2nd Battalion 26th Infantry Regiment After Action Report, October 1944, 4.

28. Interviews with Officers, *1106th Engineer Group South of Aachen*, NA, 6.

29. Entry for 8 October 1944, Headquarters 26th Infantry APO 1 US Army, Report of Regimental Activities for the Month of October 1944, 1 November 1944, NA.

30. McGregor, 38.

31. Ibid.

32. Brown, 14.

33. Company C RCA, 10.

34. The Battle for Aachen, Annex No. 2 to G-2 Periodic Report, Headquarters 1st Infantry division, 7 November 1944, NA, 4.

35. Brown, 16.

36. McGregor, 32.

37. *This Soldier Equals 1 Infantry Regiment*, from copy of unnamed periodical, MRC, 54.

38. T/4 Ridgely C. Dorsey, Interview with Lt. Emmett R. Duffy, Leader 3rd Platoon, 634rd Tank Destroyer Battalion, Company B, 3rd Platoon (Attached to the 2nd Battalion 18th Infantry Regiment), 8–16 October 1944, 2nd Information and Historical Service, NA, 2.

39. *Battalion in Attack*, Verlautenheide, Germany, 8 October 1944, 2nd Battalion 18th Infantry Regiment, MRC, 6.

40. Annex No. 2 to G-2, 7 November 1944, 4.

41. McGregor, 49.

42. The [18th] Regimental Combat Team in Offensive Action, 8–9.

43. McGregor, 51.

44. Ibid., 52.

CHAPTER 10

1. Don Whitehead, "First Surrender at Aachen—Ultimatum to Aachen Is Grim One," *San Jose Evening News*, 10 October 1944.

2. Reprint of Ultimatum of Surrender titled People of Aachen!, CMH.

3. Selected Intelligence Reports, Volume 1, June 1944–November 1944, Office of the AC of S, First United States Infantry Division, Germany, 6 December 1944, 77–79.

4. Whitehead, *San Jose Evening News*, 10 October 1944.

5. Office of the Chief Military History, Original Surrender Demand Documents of the City of Aachen Germany, Geog M Germany 384.1, CMH.

6. Reprint To the German Troops and People of Aachen, CMH.

7. Whitehead, 10 October 1944.

8. Headquarters 26th Infantry, *Report of Regimental Activities for the Month of Octo-ber 1944*, 5.

9. Drew Middleton, "Aachen as Test for Germany: Defiance Necessary for Morale," *New York Times*, 10 October 1944.

10. The Battle for the Aachen Sector, September to November 1944, Interviews with *General der Infantrie* Köchling, Historical Division, Headquarters United States Army, Europe, MS#A-991, USAMHI, 3.

11. Battle for Aachen, Development of the enemy Positions in Front of the Corps Line, Reardon Translation, 12.

12. Samuel W. Mitcham, *The Siegfried Line: The German Defense of the Westwall, September–December 1944* (Mechanicsburg, PA: Stackpole Books, 2009), 107.

13. Select Intelligence Reports, Volume 1, 68.

14. Engel, 24.

15. Guderian, 209–10.

16. Battle for Aachen, Reardon Translation, 11.

17. Battle of Aachen, 18th Infantry Regiment, C-L-117, NA, p. 11.

18. Headquarters 2nd Battalion 18th Infantry Regiment, Battalion in Attack, Ver-lautenheide Germany, October 1944, 5–6.

19. Engel, 77.

20. Annex to Select Intelligence Reports, *Aachen Air and Artillery Strikes Overlay*, 11–12 October 1944, Targets by Number and Flight Path, 367th 1st Group, 404th 2nd Group, 368th 3rd Group, 370th 4th Group, NA.

21. Lieutenant Colonel Derrill M. Daniel, "The Capture of Aachen," A Lecture Pre-sented by [Daniel], Guest Instructor, Combined Arms Section, Marine Corps School, Quantico Virginia, Undated, NA, 5.

22. Daniel Lecture, 6.

23. Don Whitehead, *Beachhead Don: Reporting the War from the European Theater: 1941–1945* (New York: Fordham University Press, 2004), 263.

24. Ibid.

25. 26th Infantry Regiment AAR, 11 October 1944, 5–6.

26. Engel, 25–27.

27. RCT in Offensive Action, *The Attack on Verlautenheide, Crucifix Hill and Ravels-berg Hill*, 18th Infantry Regiment, 17.

28. 1st ID Select Intelligence, Annex No. 4 to G-2 Periodic Report No. 125, 22 October 1944.

29. 26th Infantry Regiment, *Clearing the Area South of the Railroad Tracks*, Battle of Aachen, 8–21 October 1944, NA, 6–7.

30. 26th Infantry Regiment, 3rd Battalion Journal, 12 October 1944.

31. Kenneth T. Downs, "Nothing Stopped the Timberwolves," *Saturday Evening Post*, 17 August 1946.

32. Daniel Lecture, 9.

33. Guderian, 215.

34. S-3 Unit Report for the Month of October 1944, Headquarters 26th Infantry Regiment, Prisoner interrogations revealing companies in the line 13 October 1944, NA.

35. S-3, 26 INF, Entry for 1113 Hours 13 October 1944.

36. S-3, 26 INF, Entry for 1430 Hours 13 October 1944.

37. S-3, 26 INF, Entry for 1500 Hours 13 October 1944.

38. 26 INF, Clearing the Area South of the Railroad Tracks, Battle of Aachen 8–21 October 1944, 12.

39. S-3, 26 INF, Entry for 1251 Hours 13 October 1944.

40. Report of Burial, Weeks, Rowland A. Company F 26 INF, Date of Death 13 October 1944, MRC.

41. S-3, 26 INF, Entry for 1626 Hours 13 October 1944.

42. S-3, 26 INF, Entry for 1656 and 2125 Hours 13 October 1944.

43. S-3, 26 INF, Entries from 1500 to 1840 Hours 13 October 1944.

44. S-3, 26 INF, Entry for 2030 Hours 13 October 1944.

45. S-3, 26 INF, Entry for 2120 Hours 13 October 1944.

46. 3rd Battalion 26 INF Journal, 13 October 1944, 63.

47. Daniel Lecture, 11.

CHAPTER 11

1. Select Intelligence Reports, 1st ID, Volume 1, 80.

2. *Generalmajor* Walter Denkert, 3rd Panzer Division in the Battle of Aachen, October 1944, Historical division United States Army in Europe, Foreign Military Studies Branch, MS # A-979, USAMHI, 3–5.

3. Guderian, 217.

4. 18th RCT, 12.

5. Daniel Lecture, 11.

6. Ibid.

7. Charles Whiting, *Bloody Aachen, Westwall* Series (Conshohocken, PA: Combined Books, 2000), 116.

8. The Infantry Battalion in Offensive Action, Second Battalion 26th Infantry Regiment, Aachen 8–20 October 1944, 9.

9. Daniel Lecture, 11–12.

10. McDonald, 312.

11. Engel, 33–34.

12. Attack on G and I Companies 16th Infantry Regiment During the Battle for Aachen. MRC, 1–2.

13. G and I Companies 16 INF, 3.

14. Interview with Lt. Emmet R. Duffy, *634th Tank Destroyer Battalion, Battle for Aachen*, NA., 3.

15. McDonald, 292.

16. Ibid.

17. Denkert MS, 6.

18. Engel, 35.

19. Köchling MS # A-991, 13.

20. 26 INF 3rd Battalion Journal, 15 October 1944.

21. Ibid.

22. G and I Companies, 16th INF, 4.

23. 16th INF, 1861–1946, 171.

24. G and I Companies, 16th INF, 4.

25. Cole C. Kingseed, *From Omaha Beach to Dawson's Ridge: The Combat Journal of Captain Joe Dawson* (Washington, DC: Naval Institute Press, 2005), 216.

26. Ibid.

27.   *Proud Americans*, 235.

28.   Ibid., 225.

29.   16th INF Regiment 1861–1946, 171.

30.   Presidential Unit Citation, Companies G and I 16th Infantry Regiment, Eilendorf Germany, 15–17 October 1944, War Department General Order No. 14, 1945.

31.   Dawson Interview with John Votaw, MRC, 16 April 1991, MRC.

32.   26th INF 3rd Battalion Journal, 16 October 1944.

33.   Köchling, MS# A-991, 4.

CHAPTER 12

1.   McDonald, 295.

2.   120th Infantry Regiment, Draft of Unit Citation, 2–3, OH, 11 (accessed March 2014).

3.   1st Battalion 120 INF, 3.

4.   McDonald, 297.

5.   Robert L. Hewitt, *Work Horse of the Western Front: The Story of the 30th Infantry Division* (Washington, DC: Washington Infantry Journal Press, 1946), 130.

6.   Simmons Interview, *Breaching the Siegfried Line, Company A's Road Block at Bardenberg*, NA, 4–5.

7.   Ferriss, Comments of Major Laney, Executive Officer of 2nd Battalion 119th Infantry, and Captain Hardway, Battalion S-1, 17 October 1944, NA, 2.

8.   Knox Journal, 18–19.

9.   McDonald, 297–98.

10.   Ibid., 297.

11.   120 INF Unit Citation, 4.

12.   119 INF History Book, 69.

13.   Brown Interview, 3.

14.   119 INF History Book, 69.

15.   Knox Journal, 20.

16.   Hechler, Interview with Maj. Gen. Leland S. Hobbs, CG 30th Infantry Division, Highlights of 30th Division Activities, 2–10 October 1944, NA, 1.

17.   McDonald, 299.

18.   WHWF, 135.

19.   Guderian, 210.

20.   McDonald, 300.

21.   Guderian, 211.

22.   3rd Battalion 120th Infantry Regiment, 1–21 October 1944, 4. OH, 11 (accessed March 2014).

23.   WHWF, 133.

24.   Ibid.

25.   Ibid.

26.   Guderian, 212.

27.   McDonald, 299.

28.   WHWF, 135.

29.   Ibid.

30.   Guderian, 214.

31.   WHWF, 136.

32.   119 INF History Book, 70.

33. Guderian, 214.

34. 119 INF History Book, 70.

35. Medal of Honor Citation (posthumously) Staff Sgt. Jack J. Pendleton, Company I, 120th Infantry Regiment, 30th Infantry Division, Bardenberg, Germany, 12 October 1944.

36. McDonald, 302.

37. WHWF, 136.

38. 30th ID S-3 Journal, 12 October 1944.

39. Hobbs Interview with Hechler, 1.

40. McDonald, 302.

41. 117th Infantry Unit Journal 12 October 1944, OH, 3 (accessed March 2014).

42. 117 INF Journal, 12 October 1944.

43. Ibid.

44. Guderian, 215.

45. Ibid., 215–16.

46. Ibid., 216.

47. 119 INF History Book, 70.

48. Guderian, 216.

49. McDonald, 303.

50. WHWF, 138.

51. Gordon A. Blaker, *Iron Knights: The United States 66th Armored Regiment* (Shippensburg, PA: Burd Street Press, 1999), 280.

52. Blaker, Medal of Honor Citation for Captain James M. Burt, 280.

53. WHWF, 138.

54. Guderian, 218.

55. Joseph Balkoski, *From Brittany to the Reich: The 29th Infantry Division in Germany, September–November 1944* (Mechanicsburg, PA: Stackpole Books, 2012), 229.

56. Ibid., 233–34.

57. WHWF, 138.

58. 3rd Battalion 120th INF, 1–21 October 1944, 5.

59. Guderian, 218.

60. 3rd Battalion 120th INF, 2–21 October 1944, 5.

61. Guderian, 218.

62. Blaker, 276.

63. WHWF, 139.

64. Ferriss, *Closing the Aachen Gap 16 October 1944*, Comments of Lieutenant Colonel Hassenfelt, G-3 of 30th Infantry Division, 17 October 1944, NA, 1.

65. 119th INF History Book, 71.

66. McDonald, 305.

67. 119 INF History Book, 71.

68. McDonald, 305.

69. Ibid.

70. Ibid., 306.

71. Knox Journal, 21.

72. 117th Infantry Regiment, *The Diversionary Attack of 16 October*, Interviews with Col. Walter Johnson, T/Sgt. Robert Q. Fortune, Citation Text of Recommendation for Silver Star for Capt. George H. Sibbald, NA, 2–3.

73. McDonald, 306.

74. Sibbald Citation Text, 2.

75. Johnson Interview, 2.

76. Fortune Interview, 3.

77. McDonald, 305.

78. Guderian, 220.

79. WHWF, 141.

80. Ferriss, 2nd Battalion 119th Infantry, 30th Infantry Division, *The Closing of the Aachen Gap*, Composite Account of Lt. Edward C. Arn and Lt. Warne R. Parker, 15 November 1944, NA, 3.

81. WHWF, 141.

CHAPTER 13

1. Daniel Lecture, 15.

2. 26th INF, Battle of Aachen, *Clearing Area South of the Railroad Tracks*, 18.

3. Daniel Lecture, 14.

4. Ibid., 14–15.

5. Memo to S-3, *Most Successful Attack—Reduction of Farwick Park*, 3rd Battalion 26th Infantry Regiment, 23 June 1945, NA, 1.

6. Headquarters 3rd Battalion 26th Infantry Regiment, *Field Order Number 1*, 18 October 1944, NA, 1.

7. Translation of Documents Taken From Prisoners of War Captured in Aachen, Annex No 3 to G-2 Periodic Report No 124, Headquarters 1st Infantry Division, 21 October 1944, NA.

8. Lt. Harry D. Condron, The Fall of Aachen, 2nd Information and Historical Service, 1st US Army, NA, 4.

9. Guderian, 223.

10. Ibid., 222.

11. Battle of Aachen, *634th Tank Destroyer Battalion Company B 1st Platoon Attached to 3rd Battalion 18th Infantry Regiment*, 8–17 October 1944, NA, 6–7.

12. Headquarters 3rd Battalion 18th Infantry Regiment Journal, 18 October 1944, MRC, 1.

13. Aachen, Military Operations in Urban Terrain, 26th Infantry Regimental Combat Team 8–20 October 1944, 26th Infantry Regimental Association, 4th Edition, November 1999, MRC, 46.

14. 26th Infantry Regiment 3rd Battalion Journal, October 1944, 64.

15. John C. McManus, *Grunts: Inside the American Infantry Combat Experience, Killing for the Ruins, World War II Through Iraq* (New York: Penguin, 2011), 124.

16. 26th INF, Battle of Aachen, *Clearing Area South of the Railroad Tracks*, 20.

17. The Infantry Battalion in Offensive action, 2nd Battalion 26th Infantry Regiment, 8–20 October 1944, 11.

18. Whitehead, 272.

19. Daniel Lecture, 16.

20. The Decoy Doughboy, *Sgt. Thompson Latest Medal of Honor Man*, Souvenir Edition "By and for the Men of the 18th Combat Team," Printed in Czechoslovakia 23 May 1945.

21. Ibid..

22. LTC (Retired) Sam Carter, "Max Thompson and the Medal of Honor," *Bridgehead Sentinel* (Spring 1997): 7.

23. Guderian, 225.
24. Ibid.
25. Ibid., 225–26.
26. T/Sgt. Frederick P. Cooper, Interviews with Lt. Col. S. M. Hogan and Maj. William S. Walker, Battle of Aachen, 3rd Battalion 33rd Armored Regiment 3rd Armored Division, 1 December 1944, NA, 2.
27. T/Sgt. Frederick P. Cooper, Interview with Lt. Norman C. Streit, Company F 2nd Battalion 36th Armored Infantry Regiment, NA, 1.
28. Lawrence Manley, *F Company's Actions in the Battle of Aachen*, MRC, 3.
29. *15 TWX, OB West to OKW/WFSt, 1740, 20 October 1944, OB West KTB*, Befehle und Meldungen, McDonald, 315.
30. Headquarters 3rd Battalion 18th INF, 24 October 1944, 2.
31. Ibid., 1.
32. Ibid.
33. Denkert, MS # A-979, 10.
34. Hogan Interview, 2.
35. 26th INF, Report of Regimental Activities for the Month of October 1944, 10.
36. 1st ID Select Intelligence Reports, 80.
37. Ibid., 81.
38. *Evacuation of Citizens from Aachen*, Interview with Maj. J. J. Kohout, Military Government Officer 26th Infantry Regiment, NA, 4.
39. Ibid., 1–3.
40. *Right of the Line, A History of the American Field Artillery*, World War II, US Army Field Artillery School, Fort Sill, Oklahoma.
41. McDonald, 316.
42. First US Army G-2 Periodic Report No. 154, *Experiences of Two American Prisoners of War Held in Aachen Germany*, 11 November 1944, NA, 5.
43. Ibid., 5.
44. Ibid., 5–6.
45. Commanding Officer Battle Group Aachen, Select Intelligence Reports, 1st Infantry Division, Annex No.4 to G-2 Periodic Report No. 125, 22 October 1944, NA, 1.
46. Whitehead, 274.
47. Surrender of the City of Aachen, Select Intelligence Reports, 1st Infantry Division, Annex No. 4 to G-2 Report No. 125, 22 October 1944, NA, 1–2.
48. Annex to G-2 Periodic Report No. 134, Auld Lang Syne, NA.
49. Report of Regimental Activities for the Month of October 1944, 26th INF, 11.
50. Annex No. 4 to G-2 Report No. 125, 22 October 1944, 1.
51. Ibid., 3.
52. Ibid.

BIBLIOGRAPHY

Arn, Edward C. and Jerome Mushkat. *Arn's War: Memoirs of a World War II Infantryman, 1940–1946*. Akron, OH: University of Akron Press, 2006.

Balkoski, Joseph. *From Brittany to the Reich: The 29th Division in Germany, September–November 1944*. Mechanicsburg, PA: Stackpole Books, 2012.

Baumer, Robert W. with Mark J. Reardon. *American Iliad. The 18th Infantry Regiment in World War II*. Bedford, PA: Aberjona Press, 2004.

Baumgartner, Lt. John W., 1st Sgt. Al DePoto, Sgt. William Fraccio, and Cpl. Sammy Fuller. *The 16th Infantry, 1861–1946*. DuQuoin, IL: Cricket Press Millennium Edition, 1999.

Blaker, Gordon A. *Iron Knights: The United States 66th Armored Regiment*. Shippensburg, PA: Burd Street Press, 1999.

Combat History of the 119th Infantry Regiment. Bangor, ME: Bangor Community: Digital Commons, 1946.

Guderian, Heinz Gunther. *From Normandy to the Ruhr with the 116th Panzer Division in World War II*. Bedford, PA: Aberjona Press, 2001.

Hewitt, Robert L. *Workhorse on the Western Front: The Story of the 30th Infantry Division*. Washington, D.C.: Infantry Journal Press, 1946.

Kingseed, Cole C. *From Omaha Beach to Dawson's Ridge: The Combat Journal of Captain Joe Dawson*. Annapolis: Naval Institute Press, 2005.

Knickerbocker, H. R., et. al. *Danger Forward: The Story of the First Division in World War II*. Atlanta: Albert Love Enterprises, 1947.

Lewis, Jon E. *The Mammoth Book of How it Happened: World War II, The Fall of Aachen by George Mucha*. London: Constable & Robinson, 2006.

Lyman, William J. Curlew History, *The Story of the First Battalion 117th Infantry 30th Division in Europe During World War II*. Chapel Hill: The Orange Printshop, 1948.

Marshall, Malcom, et. al. *Proud Americans: Men of the 32nd Field Artillery Battalion in Action, World War II, as part of the 18th Regimental Combat Team, 1st U.S. Infantry Division*. New London, NH: self-published, 1994.

McDonald, Charles B. *The Siegfried Line Campaign: United States Army in World War II*. Washington, D.C.: Center of Military History, 1993.

McManus, John C. *Grunts: Inside the American Infantry Combat Experience, Killing for the Ruins, World War II through Iraq*. New York: Penguin Group USA, 2010.

Mitcham, Samuel W. *The Siegfried Line: The German Defense of the Westwall, September–December 1944*. Mechanicsburg, PA: Stackpole Books, 2009.

Votaw, John F. and Steven Weingartner. *Blue Spaders: The 26th Infantry Regiment 1917–1967*. Wheaton, IL: Cantigny First Division Foundation, 1996.

Whitehead, Don. *Beachhead Don: Reporting the War from the European Theater: 1941–1945*. New York: Fordham University Press, 2004.

Whitlock, Flint. *The Fighting First: The Untold Story of the Big Red One on D-Day*. Boulder: Westview Press, 2004.

Woolner, Frank. *Spearhead in the West: The Third Armored Division, 1941–1945*. Frankfurt am Main-Schwanheim: F. J. Henrich, 1980. Reprint of 1945 edition.

ACKNOWLEDGMENTS

This book took nearly ten years to research and write. During this time there were those who took interest in its development, revisions, and final iterations. Others provided support and encouragement. Here they are, in no particular order of importance.

The late Roger Hilsman, President John F. Kennedy's assistant secretary of state for Far Eastern Affairs in the early 1960s and author of many books, graciously provided valuable assistance in getting my efforts at writing about military history topics to publishers back in the 1990s. While he was too ill to review drafts of this book, to this day I remain exceedingly grateful to Roger for his earlier help in jump-starting my writing career.

It was also my good fortune to have befriended Lt. Col. Mark J. Reardon (Ret.) as the years progressed. Mark, then a senior historian at the U.S. Army Center of Military History in Washington, D.C., coached me to write in a way that put emphasis on unit historical records and personal accounts written during World War II, thus preserving it like it was and allowing the actions of individual officers and soldiers to speak for themselves. He also contributed to this book by providing primary source material, mostly narratives and histories from the German side.

As it was for the first book that I wrote with Mark's help, *American Iliad: The 18th Infantry Regiment in World War II*, Andrew Woods's and Eric Gillespie's support at the Cantigny First Infantry Division Museum and McCormick Research Center in Wheaton, Illinois, during the development of this book deserves special mention. I am also sincerely grateful to Mr. Warren Watson for his vast help in allowing me to become more knowledgeable about 30th Infantry Division participants during the battle for Aachen; his website www.oldhickory30th.com contains numerous oral histories, primary source material, maps, and pictures that helped birth chapters of this book. And I also want to thank two very special people at the National Archives Still Picture Reference Center in College Park, Maryland: Holly Reed and Theresa M. Roy assisted me with genuine kindness and immeasurable patience in retrieving and copying pictures that I hope are helpful for visualizing the Aachen fight.

It is not an exaggeration to say that this book may have never found its way to you were it not for my lifelong friend and cousin Cyrus Clark III and his wife, Judy, of Somers, New York. They provided both encouragement and nudging to knuckle down and write when I needed it most. Judy's late father, Jack Mates, was extremely kind over the years to me. A World War II B-17 pilot, he was instrumental in forming the Distinguished Flying Cross Society after retiring from a successful business career. Words he wrote to me in 2013 when he sent a copy of *On Heroic Wings: Stories of the Distinguished Flying Cross* provided a touching inspiration for me to keep writing about his selfless generation.

Charles Perini and his wife, Nancy, in Mystic, Connecticut, dear friends for many years, were always there when it counted. Charles pushed me as only a true friend can and encouraged me to focus on visualizing and writing this book. How can I ever really thank you, Carlo?

The same for Arnie and Deb Wheaton of Rochester, New York, two people I've been fortunate to know since the 1970s. Arnie took the time to read some excerpts before this book was published, and his genuine eagerness and encouragement deserve special mention. Thank you, Weedo, for your unflagging support.

Others also made a difference with their help during the time this book was being written. Barry Konet of Madison, Connecticut, deserves special mention, as does Paul Braschi of Norwalk, Connecticut. A college fraternity brother, a friend during all the years since, and an immensely successful business and family man, John C. White of Scottsdale, Arizona, was particularly instrumental in making this book possible.

At Stackpole Books, Dave Reisch cast a professional eye in guiding the book from manuscript form to publication. Brittany Stoner was very efficient in overseeing the book's actual production. Wendy Reynolds's work in doing the pagination and final layout of the book is most appreciated. I want to especially thank Ryan Masteller for his work as copyeditor; his task was not easy, but he conducted it with patience and a mind for clarity.

In the midst of the fight to establish a firm bridgehead across the Wurm River north of Aachen on 3 October 1944, Col. Walter M. Johnson of the 117th Infantry was overheard breaking up the tension by needling a writer. "Get that regimental historian up here to the CP," he shouted loud enough for everyone to let loose with a laugh. "He is supposed to be writing combat history and how can he write it when he is sitting back in the rear?"

Thank you, colonel. Without the narratives written at the time by that Army historian and the many others who chronicled the Aachen fight, it would not have been possible to write this book seventy years later. Nor could American fighting prowess at its best have been read today by those of you who turn the pages of this book.

My most heartfelt thanks to you as well.

Robert W. Baumer
Ormond Beach, Florida

INDEX

Page numbers in italics indicate maps.